Organizational Models for Global Architecture

The Generic Sublime

Ciro Najle

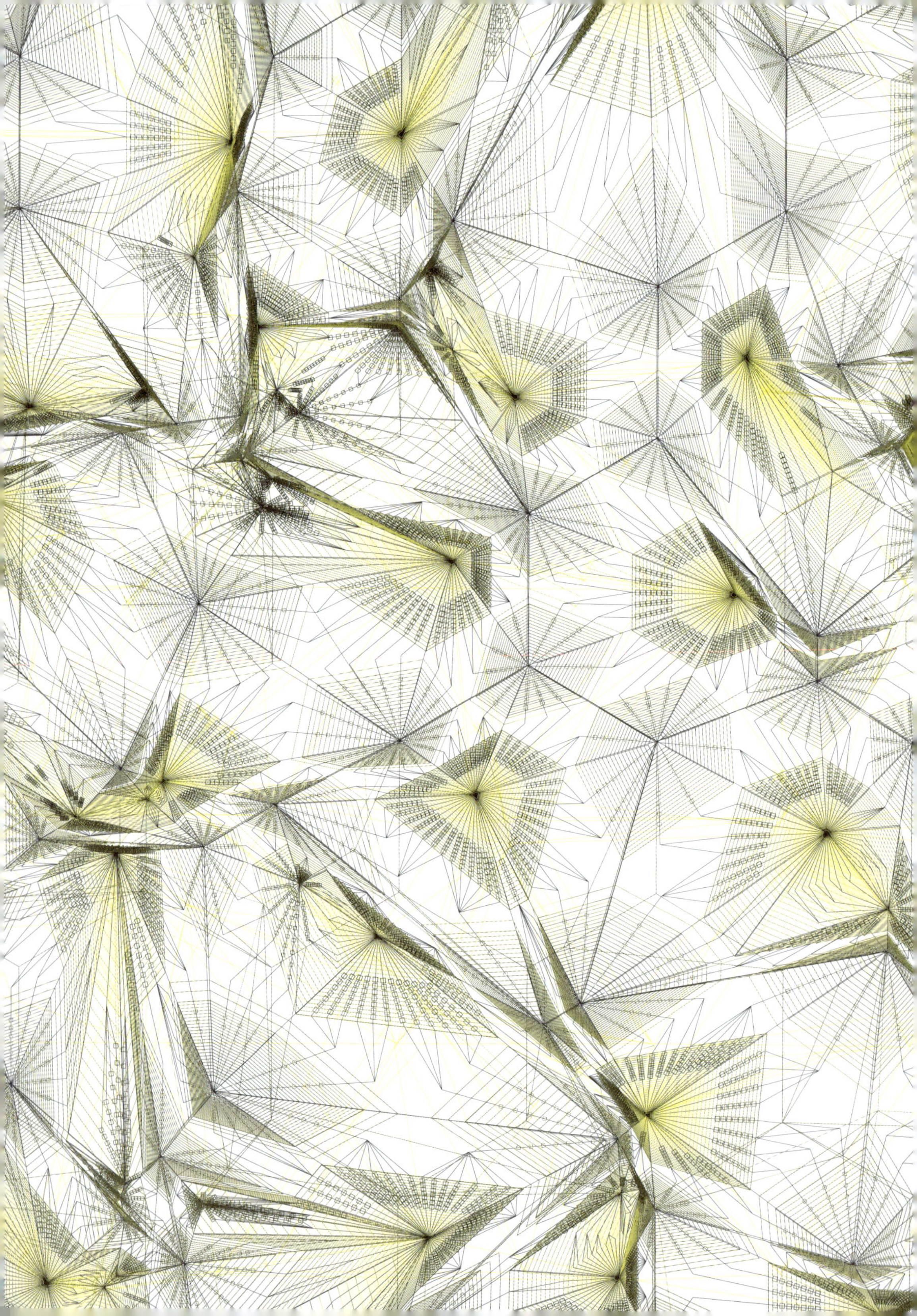

This book features design research and projects developed under the direction of Ciro Najle by graduate students at the Harvard University Graduate School of Design between 2010 and 2013, as part of the Generic Sublime studio series.

Contents

Foreword

Ciro Najle draws us into his ambitious project with a provocative pairing of terms. Why the *generic*, when the act of design inherently suggests the specific and the particular? Don't architects design buildings with the aim of making something different from what has come before? You study a site to find its characteristics, its special features, and then you try to give shape to the most fitting unison of program with form, of architecture with site. So why this focus on the generic, when the demand is more typically for the unique?

Yet, in our contemporary architectural culture, that which is considered unique tends to disappear in a sea of what might ultimately be minor stylistic differences. Like a generic drug, generic architecture is comparable to an unidentifiable brand, lacking any of its own distinguishing marks. Similar to the pharmaceutical industry, the architectural "industry" is awash with generic products whose existence depends on replicating the characteristics of some original reference. However, whereas by law a generic drug has to perform the same function as the original brand, it is not clear that the generic in architecture always fulfills its duties so diligently. The generic in architecture is always an indicator of a certain loss of identity or unmet promise, yet the urban landscape keeps getting filled with generic buildings.

And why the *sublime*, when we have traded the complexities and complications of aesthetic and sensory judgment for the security of the predictable? From our food to our buildings, we revel in the pleasures and comfort of the familiar—the things that don't surprise us, like the standard-issue hotel room, the ubiquitous burger chain. What is crucial here is the erasure of any possible disjuncture between anticipation and fulfillment. By contrast, the sublime calls forth a different kind of aesthetic experience—one rooted in the act of discovery and therefore uniqueness. The sublime is often associated with a form of awe-inspiring and at times almost overpowering sensory encounter. At least that is how the term was used when it first became a specific category of aesthetic engagement, relating in particular to the viewing of untamed nature—wild mountain landscapes, stormy seas.

The Generic Sublime is therefore an oxymoron whose realization—*becoming*—requires a radical rethinking of the site of architectural production. Terms such as Najle's Overurbanism and Neonatures have been used to construct a dense and deep spatial investigation of architecture and its site in order, perhaps, to create architecture as site, a form of systemic inseparability between the figure and the ground. In these operations, Rem Koolhaas's *Delirious New York* acts as an alibi, the starting point for a different narrative—one that begins with the idea of the generic but that through a series of architectural procedures is transformed, visibly disconnected from its original reference. It is only when this transformation, akin to an alchemical process, produces a feeling of exceptional sensory pleasure—of uniqueness—that a given project achieves its goal of becoming an exemplar of the Generic Sublime.

The challenging exploration of ideas presented in this book was furthered through a series of studios conducted at the Harvard University Graduate School of Design. It is through such rigorous investigations that the school's commitment to advancing discourse is realized.

Mohsen Mostafavi Cambridge, January 2016

Preface

The Generic Sublime is the outcome of an extended investigation of extra-extra-large developmental typologies carried out by graduate students under my direction at the Harvard University Graduate School of Design in the departments of Architecture, Urban Planning and Design, and Landscape Architecture. Conducted between 2010 and 2013, the investigation was framed as a design research series. This book presents the production of this series, integrated into a synthetic and technically explicit architectural model.

The work was developed along four autonomous lines. Following an introductory studio named the Overskyscraper–which identified the methods, typologies, and spectrum of interests for the subsequent investigation–the initial line of research, termed Neonatures, focused on the formal and systemic convergence of geomorphological models with extra-extra-large building typologies. The second studio, Overurbanism, challenged students to construct processes of differentiation out of the organizational protocols embedded in contemporary generic developments. Neokoolhisms, the third studio in the series, revisited and updated the paradoxical conceptual body advanced by Rem Koolhaas in the 1970s around Manhattan's "culture of congestion," as a sieve to redefine the status of anti-urbanism in global developmental culture. The fourth and final studio, Utopioids, examined and reframed canonical utopian projects and manifestos of the past century to provide an implausible yet surprisingly adequate ground for a new form of architectural practice.

This volume integrates and organizes the materials, methods, and outcomes of this series into three discrete sections, creating operative taxonomies that can be understood as the consecutive steps in a continuous procedure that moves from the actual to the prospective by means of a process of abstraction, differentiation, integration, and singularization. "Generic Sublime Forms" presents case studies exemplifying the developmental phenomena already at work around the globe. "Generic Sublime Models" describes a set of organizational models and presents an open manual of processes and techniques for breeding the sublime from the ordinary. "Generic Sublime Organizations" presents a series of propositions that synthesize the investigation developed across the previously mentioned thematic lines. Together, these forms, models, and organizations embody the double agenda of unpacking and escalating architectural-territorial models out of current developmental forms.

Around this central core of research and construction of architectural models, two sets of writings by noted theoreticians and practitioners contextualize the work and contribute to expand its conceptual and operative spectrum. Preceded by my own introduction to the project, the initial set of essays substantiates, debates, and challenges the theory of the Generic Sublime. The concluding set of writings presents a series of open-ended discussions in which I participated directly or indirectly–a public conversation on the sublime, a personal interview on methods, a glossary of concepts created in dialogue, and a technical-theoretical report–attempting to further elucidate the ideas and the potentials of the Generic Sublime.

Ciro Najle Cambridge, February 2016

Acknowledgments

While teaching the Generic Sublime studio series at the Harvard University Graduate School of Design, I was pleased to have the support and encouragement of the departments of Architecture, Urban Planning and Design, and Landscape Architecture. I taught the Neonatures studio with the teaching assistance of Anna Font and the participation of graduate students Youngju Cho, Yao Dong, Ana María Flor Ortiz, Song He, Jung Hyuck Im, Laura Janka, Víctor Muñoz Sanz, Seong Seok Ko, Rodia Valladares Sánchez, Di Xia, Kaz Yoneda, and Jing Zhang; the Overurbanism studio with the teaching assistance of Kaz Yoneda and the participation of graduate students Steven Yingnien Chen, Dongjae Cho, Fred Chung, Lucas Correa-Sevilla, Day Jiménez, Mireille Kameni, Mariusz Klemens, Ostap Rudakevych, Elena Tudela Rivadeneyra, Zhou Wu, Mo Zhou, and Danxi Zou; the Neokoolhisms studio with the teaching assistance of Lucas Correa-Sevilla and the participation of graduate students Pablo Barría Urenda, Jeffrey Butcher, Mariano Gomez Luque, Lisl Kotheimer, Quardean Lewis-Allen, Nicholas Potts, and Peter Zuroweste; and the Utopioids studio with the teaching assistance of Pablo Barría Urenda and the participation of graduate students Georgios-Spyridon Athanasopoulos, Alessandro Boccacci, Elle Gerdeman, Parsa Kamali, Jielu Lu, Héctor Tarrido Picart, Emmanuel Torres, Simon Willet, and Max Wong.

A number of architectural theoreticians, academicians, and practitioners contributed to the discussions of the different studios through their regular participation in reviews, juries, seminars, and presentations, including Iñaki Ábalos, Paul Andersen, Leire Asensio Villoria, Katy Barkan, Pierre Bélanger, Sergio Forster, Preston Scott Cohen, K. Michael Hays, Eric Howeler, Timothy Hyde, John Hong, Mariana Ibáñez, Hanif Kara, Simon Kim, Sanford Kwinter, George L. Legendre, Christopher C. M. Lee, Jorge Francisco Liernur, Pablo Lorenzo-Eiroa, David Mah, Rahul Mehrotra, Michael Meredith, Mohsen Mostafavi, Farshid Moussavi, Erika Naginski, Lluís Ortega, Chris Perry, Chris Reed, Eduardo Rico Carranza, Florencia Rodríguez, Rafi Segal, Jorge Silvetti, Charles Waldheim, Enrique Walker, and Cameron Wu, among others.

I would sincerely like to thank all the students, without whose significant commitment and singular contributions this research would not have acquired the necessary intensity and consistency. Similarly, I would like to thank the teaching assistants and studio guests, whose constructive comments and critical judgments valuably contributed to the sedimentation of the ideas initially proposed. Among these, I would especially like to thank Dean Mohsen Mostafavi, not only for his comments throughout the process but also for his strong belief in and constant support of my academic and professional work since the late 1990s. Finally I would like to thank the chairs of the various departments of the Harvard University Graduate School of Design, who generously lent their confidence to the work throughout its development: Preston Scott Cohen, Charles Waldheim, and Rahul Mehrotra.

From the various periods of teaching and research that preceded my pursuit of this particular studio series, and from my formative years as an architect and as an educator, I want to mention the invaluable influence of the following colleagues and friends: Marcia Krygier, Sergio Forster, Martín Ibarlucía, and Roberto Lombardi; Lluís Ortega, Sebastián Khourian, Julián Varas, and Francisco Cadau; George L. Legendre, Michael Hensel, Michael Weinstock, and Mark Hemel; Hanif Kara, Charles Tashima, Nikolaus Hirsch, and Yusuke Obuchi; Brett Steele, Patrik Schumacher, Tom Verebes, and Chris Hight; Chris Perry, Marcelo Spina, David Ruy, and Pablo Lorenzo-Eiroa; Paul Andersen, David Salomon, Michael Meredith, and Enrique Walker; Mohsen Mostafavi, Iñaki Ábalos, Stan Allen, and Sanford Kwinter; Farshid Moussavi, Alejandro Zaera-Polo, Nanako Umemoto, and Jesse Reiser; and Tony Díaz, Luis Ibarlucía, Hugo Salama, and Justo Solsona. All have more or less directly influenced the work presented here: from learning and enthusiastically experimenting together to opening up new territories and encountering unusual forms of sensitivity and sense in the thinking and doing of architecture; from diverting my interest toward other fields of knowledge to supporting my confidence through the process and helping me clarify what was at stake in my investigations; from seeding the spectrum of the work with new questions to mercilessly challenging the work's very premises; from generously offering ideas and sources to projecting their outcomes for better or more mature purposes. Without their physical or imaginary presence throughout these years, the ideas behind this book would not have consolidated. I also extend my appreciation to the graduate and undergraduate architecture students who participated in studios I taught before and after the Generic Sublime. With their intense and often extraordinary work, they were crucial in the maturing of the scope and the clarification of the focus of this research.

I would also like to mention the resolute support of Senior Editor Melissa Vaughn, Editor-in-Chief Jennifer Sigler, and Assistant Dean for Communications Benjamin Prosky of the Harvard University Graduate School of Design; Project Manager Nancy Eklund Later; and Designer and Publisher Ramon Prat of Actar. I extend my gratitude to Kaz Yoneda, Pablo Barría Urenda, Mariano Gómez Luque, and Mariusz Klemens for their earlier contributions in the preliminary editing of material from each studio, and to Andrew Pringle for his invaluable collaboration in the generation of drawings and models for this book. Lastly, I want to thank Anna Font, who meticulously worked with me throughout the production process, preliminary design, and editing of the book, unconditionally standing by me in the difficult times of the project and intellectually inspiring me in the fertile ones.

I dedicate this book to my parents, Clide Brianni and Osvaldo Najle.

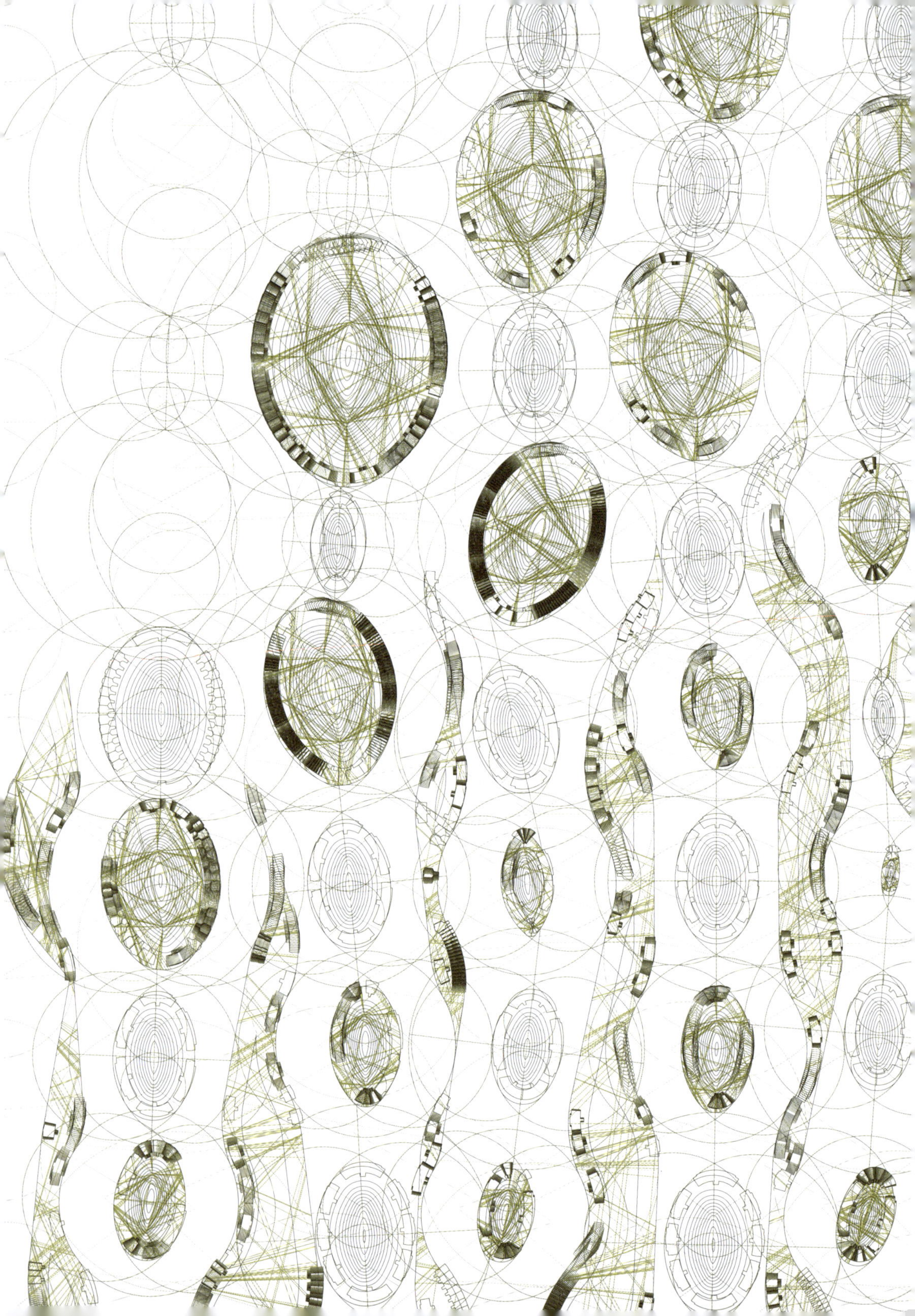

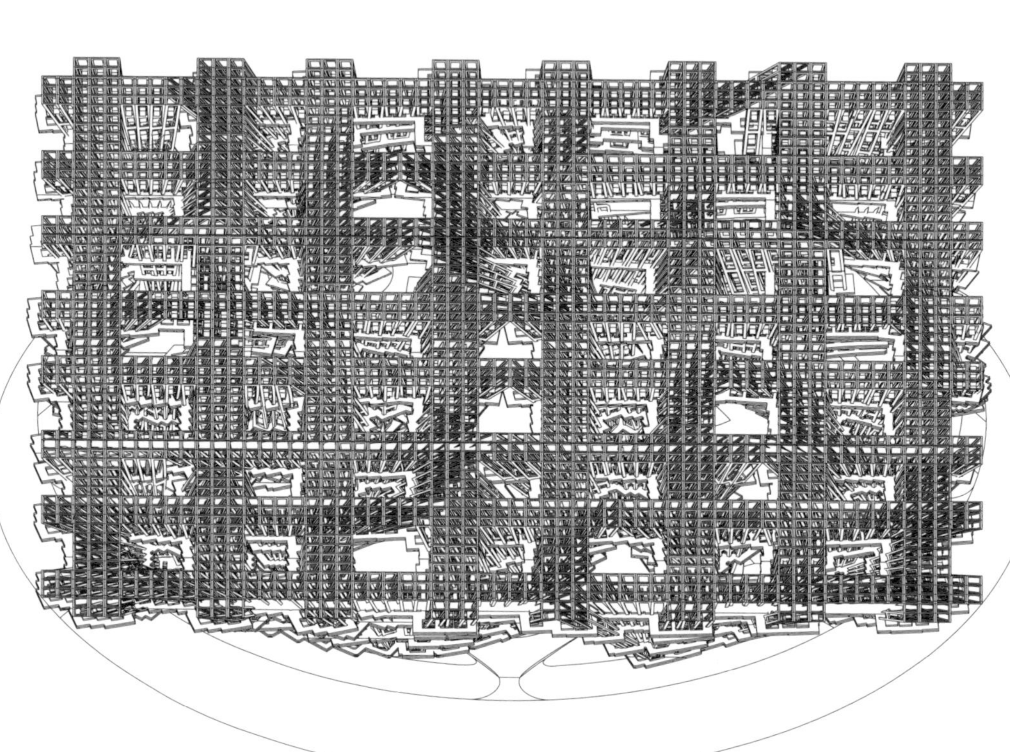

The Generic Sublime

Ciro Najle

Beyond a certain scale, architecture acquires the properties of Bigness. The best reason to broach Bigness is the one given by climbers of Mount Everest: 'because it is there.' Bigness is ultimate architecture.
Rem Koolhaas

[T]he destiny of humanity [architecture] depends upon the attainment of its highest type.
Friedrich Nietzsche

Approximately 40 years ago, a set of wild images and poignant narratives borrowed from and simultaneously projected back onto the undeniably congested reality of Manhattan were condensed into a retroactive manifesto for contemporary architecture by the young architect Rem Koolhaas. With its "unconscious" theory of Manhattanism and its antiurban concepts of programmatic instability, auto-monumentality, vertical schism, the irresistible synthetic, and the technology of the fantastic, *Delirious New York* insolently challenged all remaining forms of public life and brought into question the alleged self-evidence of an urbanism of good intentions.

Koolhaas documented his revolutionary model with "a mountain range of evidence without manifesto"—a series of developmental forms of early 20th-century Manhattan, distributed across the island as an amoral pile of defiant architectural debris. Processed and presented retroactively, Koolhaas's matter-of-fact yet custom-made theory became the definitive expression of the so-called culture of congestion: an archipelago of skyscraper islands made of extreme solitudes, plotted on a matrix that radically segregated one from the other, and floating imperceptibly on the vast sea of capitalism.

What may be regarded as the definitive expression of this model, Rockefeller Center, perfectly embodied the formulations of Manhattanism by paradoxically taking them beyond their limits of performance and scope of imagination. Through the relentless amalgamation and integration of technologies and motifs, this unique, complex artifact both incarnated and defeated the conditions that nurtured it, introducing a radical challenge to the ubiquitous grid that hosted it and gently anticipating a second leap, still to come, that would not only exceed the domesticated logic of the urban through the antiurban but engulf the territory itself, promising a new threshold for architecture.

Since then, two major phenomena have fundamentally transformed the volatile scene of contemporary architecture culture: the assimilation of complexity theory and the advent of digital culture. Both have been incorporated and vastly naturalized by the discipline, empowering its capabilities as a medium of integration of diverse domains of practice, irreducible forms of expertise, and disparate organizational scales. Concurrently, the wild rationales of extra-extra-large developments have begun to technically converge and fulfill this promised territorial threshold in the real. The Generic Sublime takes, by means of these radical disciplinary transformations, the open possibilities of Manhattanism beyond

Manhattan, by synthesizing—this time in real time and without cynicism—the process of becoming territory of architecture, at the age of global developmental culture.

Skyscraper collectives, tower agglomerations, high-rise housing, mixed-use developments, luxury condominiums, airport hubs, suburban office enclaves, industrial and technology parks, hotel complexes and resorts, conference and financial centers, entertainment venues, gated communities, theme parks, branded cities, new central districts, and satellite cities: what is the latent potential of extra-extra-large typologies if freed from the typological traditions of urbanism and the segregation of disciplinary domains? What is the reach of this potential in rethinking the contemporary urban condition and reimagining future architectural models?

The Generic Sublime explores the sublime condition that generic organizations attain when operating in multiples. It investigates how the modernist concept of the generic—once assumed to achieve universality by means of organizational homogeneity, formal neutrality, programmatic blankness, lack of identity, and insipidness of character—holds the potential to turn into its very opposite: the singular, the irreducible, and the extraordinary. This book investigates the principles embedded in extra-extra-large developments to construct models of the ubiquitous and self-contradictory phenomenon by which urbanization constructs the territory in which it is grounded.

The Generic Sublime embraces the project of its predecessor, the American skyscraper, to radically integrate the urban in a single, antiurban, cybernetic universe: a large-scale architectural machine that breeds unpredictable organizations through organizational complexity, systemic inclusiveness, paradoxical coexistence, and reciprocal intensification. But it initiates a second, simpler and vaster, megalomaniacal leap: the envelopment, in an all-embracing, multiplicitous architectural interiority, of pure territorial exteriority, where infrastructures, ecologies, and urban conditions interact in the synthetic spatial field of a single building.

Like the skyscraper, the Generic Sublime constitutes a tightly contained system of systems, where the discrepancy between the convoluted complexity of the interior and the compact uniqueness of the envelope engenders the unprecedented power of liberating the artificiality of the antiurban. However, the potentials of its anthropomorphic ancestor of the past century are here upgraded by the self-superseding form that the antiurban takes when assembled in a collective: the configuration of instantaneous archetypes made of a multiplicity of "cities within the city," now cohesively unified into the ultimate form of primeval architecture.

If the American skyscraper brought into architecture culture the opportunity of a real-time, open-air laboratory in which to explore a whole new set of forms of collective life that, as Koolhaas writes, "explode the texture of normal life to offer an aggressive alternative reality that discredits all naturalistic urban realities" and incarnate the metropolitan unconscious in a medium for the "thoughtless constitution of theories," then the Generic Sublime aims to consciously develop model-manifestos of the global architectural unconscious, crafting contemporary forms of the sublime out of the multiplication, assemblage, and magnification of the generic. Ultimate expressions of a future anterior, these upcoming archaic configurations escalate ordinary versions of the present to extraordinary versions of the future, here among us. Implausibly banal, astonishingly vulgar, and, more often than not, plain tacky, these versions both embody and betray their initial premises—based on the ruthless logic of maximum commercial benefit in global development—by radically following and alienating them as a result of sheer organizational excess and endless territorial extensiveness. The Generic Sublime appeals to the highest level of non-linear emergence in architecture and engenders a prosaic form of the grandiose.

Radically domesticated, the territory breeds the artificial wildness of the boldest architectural artifacts, shifting the intellectually comfortable condition of estrangement through shock into that of self-alienation through differentiation, where architecture takes on the blunt force of an artistic invention through a self-propelling condition, which can be concurrently regarded as neo-natural, over-urban, or utopioid. Restricted, austere, simple in its premises, plentiful, expansive, extreme in its expressions, and fundamentally unbound by any dependence on reason, the Generic Sublime employs rationality as the ultimate means for the propagation of its canon: brutal indifference.

Note: The epigraphs above are taken from Rem Koolhaas, "Bigness (or the Problem of Large)," in *Small, Medium, Large, Extra-Large* (New York: Monacelli Press, 1995), 495; and Friedrich Nietzsche, "The Highest Man as Legislator of the Future," in *The Will to Power,* ed. Walter Kaufmann, trans. Walter Kaufmann and R. J. Hollingdale (New York: Vintage Books, 1968), ch. 6, sect. 987, 516. Originally published in German in 1901. Quotations and references in the body of the essay are taken from Rem Koolhaas, *Delirious New York: A Retroactive Manifesto for Manhattan* (New York: Oxford University Press, 1978).

The Laboratory of Ciro Najle

Iñaki Ábalos

Recent attempts to address the urgencies of the great contemporary metropolis frequently dissolve into the domains of urban geography, urban sociology, or urban ecology: so much so, that one begins to wonder if the discipline that Ildefonso Cerdá opened up—urbanism—exists beyond the limitations of the ethical or social contingencies specific to each urban formation. In Ciro Najle's investigations, in contrast, we find no trace of this type of approach: instead, we find a resolute pursuit of a revision of the technical instrumentality and methodologies of modernity. Najle's work is notable for its surprising and rigorous formalism. The architecture, the landscape, and the urbanism of modernity are sieved through the formal logics of process-driven informational and mathematical protocols, providing a response to the most decisive problem that the city presents to us today: that of providing consistent forms to contemporary urbanization as it unfolds before us on a brutal scale and at an explosive velocity.

We are generally accustomed to experiencing two types of approximations within schools of architecture: those concerned with the self-centeredness of the embellished architectural building, regarded as a recognizable and measurable object of scale, and those attempting the nostalgic and improbable exercise of controlling the urban by means of disciplinary resources of the most diverse affiliation. The laboratory that Najle has been directing for many years positions itself, with a particularly unusual stubbornness, beyond the limitations of both of these groups, largely as a result of what at first appears to be an impulsive conviction: that a projective methodology of the metropolis should be constructed with neither moral commentaries nor disciplinary debts but rather through the systematicity of the lab.

In the laboratory, the first step is to completely isolate the body under study and analyze its laws of proliferation. As Bruno Latour describes it, a laboratory is not a place disconnected from reality, where people are imbued with supernatural powers, but a place with a precise topology and a specific work mechanics.[1] Displacing the laboratory from the world—from the "out there"—allows the scientist to isolate a phenomenon from its customary context and examine it within the new setting. This is where true knowledge can be produced. Treated as new material, free of external competences, this isolated phenomenon shows its vital laws and crucial forces or weaknesses under ultimate conditions. From this new knowledge of its behavior, and through a process of trial and error, eventually an antidote emerges or a new field of experimentation opens up. These actions disrupt the traditional knowledge about the phenomenon and take it to a completely new domain, where the scale of analysis constantly varies from the micro to the macro. These languages of inscription involve procedures to write, teach, and register in the context of a prospective drive.[2] Surprisingly, often the solution to the recognized problem comes from inoculating the problematic body—or the body perceived as problematic—with higher doses of what, under different circumstances, would be, by itself, able to generate its own antibodies to combat. Such is the case of the anthrax vaccine, the discovery of which made Louis Pasteur a national hero in France.

Latour also draws attention to the point at which the experiment does not end inside the ascetic rooms of the laboratory but rather continues outside, requiring other work to be done. This work is not added on but implicit within the same experiment. It involves the construction of a rhetoric that endows the experiment with a social meaning: a movement from the laboratory to the society, a broadcasting and divulging movement, where the laboratory shows itself as the only repository of the specialized knowledge needed for social wellbeing. This again is the case with Pasteur, who could isolate the bacterium causing anthrax and find the laws that enable the discovery of its antidote, a knowledge that was unobtainable by other specialists (such as veterinarians and hygienists) who were working at the scale of natural reality. Presenting himself as a savior of French cattle, after the spectacular rehearsal of his vaccine, Pasteur became an unquestionable social force. If one understands politics as the speaking voice that represents the forces through which a society is molded, then Pasteur is a completely political man.

Recently, in his own laboratory, Najle has been working obsessively on the isolation of two phenomena that have had enormous impacts on the modern city: the topological, programmatic, and scalar transformations implicit in the idea of the skyscraper; and the expansive and self-sufficient explosion of grand real estate operations—residential, commercial, and infrastructural. His hypothesis is that both phenomena, ostensibly antiurban and regarded as marginal to any disciplinary discourse, are not only irreversible but also contain the key for a new approximation of a contemporary metropolitan project. Genetically hyper-productive, they launch and make incarnate not only the scalar but also the temporal leaps of the metropolis—temporal, because the city must now be produced as an instantaneous whole, without any historical sedimentation.

The formalism of this methodology is double: on the one hand, it is inspired by a scientific—or more concretely, mathematical—formalism based on the idea that formal systems are artifices, sets of rules and symbols that get joined to each other by logical chains that can be manipulated to configure new logical chains by means of protocols of iteration and proliferation. But this methodology is also intensely impregnated with the aesthetics of Kantian formalism, reborn in the 1960s as a movement against the emotional, romantic approximations of the successful informalism taking place back then. The critical fortune of this aesthetic formalism has been countered by its detractors to the point where it has been accused of being endogamic or onanistic, only to make more evident how antipathetic it can be to vindicate abstraction and disciplinary autonomy.

Within the architectural domain we find that, on various occasions, Najle suggests a precise and fertile genetic family that is highly revealing of the ultimate interest of his work. We could synthetically circumscribe this genealogy by making reference to three authors: Ludwig Hilberseimer, Robert Le Ricolais, and Andrea Branzi, whose influence, unlike that of many of their contemporaries who were more celebrated in their own time, has grown and expanded as time has passed. I will refer only to the most important aspects of their work to have received new life in Najle's laboratory.

The abstraction of the metropolitan problems developed by Hilberseimer, both in Europe and America, is evidently one. The German planner's aseptic exploration of the scalar and spatial logics of the new modern metropolis provide both a model for high density and a map for suburban sprawl. Also present—and why not—is the influence of the extremely beautiful calligraphies developed throughout Hilberseimer's work, which now unfolds across Najle's own. A similar absence of moral explanation is present throughout; the same acceptance and hypertrophy of technical and formal mechanisms. Even an analog concentration on the most intensive and extensive typologies speaks to us about a reference that is simultaneously procedural and formal.

In the work that Le Ricolais developed at the University of Pennsylvania we recognize another set of important characteristics, such as the definition of a field of research operating in the margins but still based on the historical disciplines. In the French architect and engineer's case, experimentation concerns the forms that tension takes when considered in the context of microscopic biological structures. But we can also recognize the inspiration of Najle's work in the aims of Le Ricolais's investigation, radically different from those of his pragmatic contemporary, Buckminster Fuller, and obsessively anchored by a distinct lack of scalar properties, by the absolute absence of an immediate practical finality, and by the construction of precise families of objects, embedded and charged with an open logic—this being, from my point of view, one of the most notable values in the work of both.

In the work of Branzi—especially in No-Stop City (1969)—we finally find an entire set of features in common with Najle's, but I would prefer to highlight only two of them. First, the format of the Italian architect's work and its graphic technique: the pages of a book that succeed one another without comment, configuring a machinic world through the use of different pre-digital variants of the typewriter. And second, and more intensely, the great intuition of Branzi: the emergence of a new form of the sublime, no longer inspired by the scale and brutality of certain natural phenomena (as with Edmund Burke) as much as by the scale and brutality of human technical capabilities, and by the reduction of all historical complexity in the city to a minimum cycle with a wholly unknown, proliferating capability—the production/consumption cycle understood as a metropolitan desideratum.

I insist on these references (although here offered in the form of a mere blueprint) because they may enable an understanding of the reach, limits, fundaments, and aesthetics of a work, produced at the margins of almost all contemporary debates, that has been constructing, silently and patiently, not only an operative methodology whose fertility we will see materializing in the near future but also, and perhaps more importantly, a work that contains a precise aesthetic proposition, an idea of beauty—the Generic Sublime, in Najle's own words—which I do not hesitate in presenting as both visionary and necessary: an aesthetics, it has to be noted, unreachable if not through the devices and methodological rigor self-imposed by its author. These provide some evidence not only of the academic value of this laboratory but, more broadly, of the urgent necessity with which architecture is confronted at present: to abandon the agitation to which we have comfortably accustomed ourselves and concentrate instead on what is possibly the only warranty of architecture's survival—the identification of completely new models of formal and aesthetic consistency.

1. Bruno Latour, "Give Me a Laboratory and I Will Raise the World," in *Science Observed: Perspectives on the Social Study of Science*, ed. K. Knorr-Cetina and M. Mulkay (London: Sage, 1983), 141–70.

2. "Languages of inscription" involve the idea of acting formulations, which are not merely inclusive but are predisposed to and induce action. J. L. Austin, *How to Do Things with Words*, ed. J. O. Urmson and Marina Sbisà, 2nd ed. (Cambridge, MA: Harvard University Press, 1975).

Urbanism after Geology

Charles Waldheim

The Generic Sublime, as described in this publication, is the intellectual and practical endeavor of Ciro Najle, as he articulated a program of design research over several years at the Harvard University Graduate School of Design. The research agenda of the project might be described as, among other things, explorations in alternative urban form. Beginning with rigorous investigations into the generic conditions for urbanization internationally, the projects published here might be described as alternatives to the dominant paradigms of urban order that they seek to diagram and, in so doing, decenter.

This work productively perturbs two of the most canonical antecedents to urban form in the Western tradition. First, it reflects a distinct ambivalence toward the inherited wisdom of the Law of the Indies and its ur-urbanism in the parcelization of land and traditional street structure. Second, it ultimately undermines the equally hegemonic tradition of geological determinism evident in the Anglo-urbanism of the past century. In so doing, these experiments examine alternative, and often counterfactual, histories for the origins of urban form.

Najle's trajectory departs from the indexing and analysis of the ubiquitous, large-scale urban programs that tend to characterize contemporary urban form globally: high-rise housing, waterfront developments, airports, conference centers, theme parks, gated communities, and the like. His work represents a return of the urban disciplines to questions of typology, albeit in this instance through the radical autonomy of the architectural project. The Generic Sublime deploys digital environments and computational capacities as analogs to ecological and urban formations. The work thereby constructs computational environments sufficiently distanced from the authorship of the architect to claim a putative criticality while being informed by parameters from across the cognate subdisciplines attendant to urbanism and ecology. This is often accomplished through the aggregation of practices and positions adhered to a range of disparate disciplines, from biology and landscape ecology to civil engineering and real estate development. These complex computational environments provide a range of affordances. They allow for the simultaneous presence of multiple, irreducible parameters across disciplines. They privilege the temporal and phenomenal dimensions of urban morphology. They expand the field of potential iterative relations between types and their antecedents. Each productively decenters the default assumptions of ongoing urbanization globally.

In this context, Ciro Najle's design research provocatively proclaims a critical distancing of authorship while proffering alternative urban morphologies. These tendencies are evident in several student projects, such as Alluvial Ecospheres: Braided Research Field (Kaz Yoneda); Andinarchitecture: The Legend of the Shopping Rock and the Lagoonar Crust (Víctor Muñoz Sanz); and Karst Palace: The Fantasy Interior-Exterior Continuum (Ana María Flor Ortiz and Rodia Valladares Sánchez). To take but one example, Alluvial Ecospheres conflates fluvial and geomorphological structures with the potential for an alternative urban morphology of ovoid amphitheatrical megablocks. These postgeological megastructures remain sufficiently generalized so as to allow for a reading of the larger morphology of the new district on the grounds of the former Ecological Reserve, located on the eastern face of Buenos Aires fronting the Río de la Plata. These and other experiments excavate the deep structures of knowledge informing the shape of the city. By these means, the Generic Sublime unearths alternatives to the geological determinism of contemporary planning practice and its moralist corollary in ecological planning, thus shedding new light on the emancipatory potential for alternative forms of ordering large urban agglomerations as informed by deep ecological structures. In so doing, it productively illuminates the potentials for urbanism after geology.

Critical Mass: The Double Life of the Generic Sublime

George L. Legendre

The Generic Sublime is the working concept behind four strands of research—Neonatures, Overurbanism, Neokoolhisms, and Utopioids—spun by Ciro Najle and his graduate students at the Harvard University Graduate School of Design. As descriptive concepts go, the Generic Sublime is polysemic. First and foremost, it refers to a nondescript urban or environmental condition, recorded in proximate or distant places from Latin America to Japan—which the moniker simultaneously names and crystallizes. In addition, the term variously applies to a highly formalized design approach, an immersive group-minded pedagogy, a conceptual and literary heuristic device, or a deeply personal state of mind.

The Generic Sublime does many things. From the perspective of this critic, however, it is most profitable to explore it simultaneously from the vantage point of what it does and the vantage point of its opposite. The unique character of the Generic Sublime is best understood through the prism of the following oppositions: it is minimal as well as redundant, strict as well as hedonistic, material as well as disembodied, site specific as well as utopian, authorial and individual as well as authorless and collective, singular as well as iterative, and—like its proponent's writing style—very expressive as well as completely expression free. The scope of each opposition is nowhere near as clear-cut as this list suggests, but each says something essential about the nature of this unique research, while bringing it within closer range of (or drawing it further afield from) the disciplinary boundaries of architecture. Let us examine these oppositions one by one.

The Generic Sublime is minimal as well as redundant.
Comparing any two consecutive diagrams in this book suggests that the Generic Sublime satisfies the formal definition of a Markov chain:[1] the transition from one diagram to the next depends solely on the latest move itself (not the one before last, or even the first one in the series) and hence, each step—an extended line, a split circle—is necessarily minimal and axiomatic. Since the iterative character of the method will not yield anything useful unless allowed to expand indefinitely (thereby producing, step by step, a critical mass), it will leave in its wake much evidence of redundant accumulation. From the hexagonal series of Alluvial Ecospheres[2] (Neonatures) to the modular aggregations of Culture of Liberated Congestion[3] (Neokoolhisms), minimalism and redundancy are in this sense the twin pillars of the work.

The Generic Sublime is strict as well as hedonistic.
Taken one at a time, the axiomatic step of the Generic Sublime seems both blank and mechanical. In practice the accumulation of many such steps will be voluptuously full, and its use of color and texture frequently unbridled. As it builds its way toward the desired critical mass, the iterative proliferation of self-similar motifs reaches an intoxicating climax, where the redundant concentration of figures will make itself felt, erotic and delightful.

The Generic Sublime is material as well as disembodied.
Broadly posited as a material discipline, the Generic Sublime lays claim to an empirical materialism variously rooted in natural formations, landscape tectonics, hydrological processes, tensile structures, and architecture without architects, from Patagonia to Manhattan.[4] In parallel, this physical (as in "physics") emphasis on process is systematically counteracted by the occurrence of the site-less, the a-material, and the gravity-free, delivered with statistical inevitability by the random walks of the Markov chain-like procedure on which the Generic Sublime depends (see first opposition).

The Generic Sublime is site specific as well as utopian.
From the alluvial plains of the Rio de la Plata tidal regime (Neonatures) to the canyons of western Manhattan (Neokoolhisms), and further back to the entire Latin American continent (Minor Civilizations), the Generic Sublime is first and foremost site specific.[5] Its take on site, however, is as temporal as it is geographic, including for instance the art-historical space-time of visionary luminaries (Buckminster Fuller, Kenzo Tange, Ludwig Hilberseimer), whose most significant work may be said to be site specific only in a historical sense. Sometimes, at its ultimate best, this temporal site specificity will delve into a future-anterior tense, where its haunting reinventions of what might have been recall simultaneously a fictional modernist past and a dystopian, science-fictional future.[6]

The Generic Sublime is authorial and individual, as well as authorless and collective.
As a rule the Generic Sublime eschews all references to the common, the traditional, the standardized, the fashionable, or the déjà vu. Discrete projects such as Neonatures or Overurbanism do not reference anything other than themselves, their immediate predecessors, or the premises of the Generic Sublime itself. When genuinely successful (the rate of success here is about as high as it is elsewhere), the Generic Sublime does produce work of unparalleled power and originality. This strategic obsession with exclusive originality requires the supreme authority of the method over the whims of the individual (or the fashion of the day). This in turn requires a surrender of individuality to the collective via an absolute standardization of means. In practice, every move will follow a given template. There are templates for planimetric diagrams, templates for images, templates for three-dimensional models, templates for generative scripts, templates for word processing, and even templates for internal emails. The official justification for such constraint is the need to produce work in publishable format, but the true reason probably lies elsewhere: the originality of the project as a whole requires an authorless and collaborative approach, which only a template guarantees.

The Generic Sublime is both very expressive and completely expression free.
The operative monikers Neonatures, Overurbanism, Neokoolhisms, and Utopioids owe as much to the physical context in which they are situated as they do to the written word. Read carefully and you will see that the Generic Sublime is deeply embedded in the form

of Najle's numerous critical essays, project briefs, and introductory statements.[7] "Tropo-structures," "Protocology," "Ottoist," "Fulleristic," "Ricolaisiac," "Nervian," "Borrominated," "Auratic," and of course, "Generic Sublime": the expressiveness of the written word yields a series of astonishing neologisms, which do much more than their fair share of introducing and framing the work.[8] Everywhere else, however, from type to paragraph and from paragraph to page, the expressiveness of the written word is snuffed out by the deployment of blank fonts, the uniformity of capitalization, the recurring trope of the list, the liberal use of clause delimitation and the minimal use of the verb, all of which make Najle's prose gradually descend into a semantic continuum of blankness. Here too, regardless of what it purports to say, each statement serves an axiomatic purpose at the service of the whole. Hierarchies, factual or semantic, do not apply. Yet, as Roland Barthes said of the work of Roman Jakobson—and this writer will restate about Ciro Najle's own work—every word, sentence, or paragraph that emphasizes the *form* of the message is automatically poetic, and that simple fact sums up quite nicely the double life of the Generic Sublime.

1. The term, used in statistics, refers to a mathematical system that undergoes transitions from state to state. In this chain, the next state depends only on the current state and is said to be memory-less.

2. Kaz Yoneda, Alluvial Ecospheres: Braided Research Field, from Neonatures, studio, Harvard University GSD, 2010.

3. Nicholas Potts and Peter Zuroweste, The Culture of Liberated Congestion: A Manual for the Proliferation of Land Value, from Neokoolhisms, studio, Harvard University GSD, 2012.

4. Material Discipline, studio, Cornell University, 2005–2006.

5. Minor Civilizations, studio, AA School, London, 2002–2003.

6. Mariusz Klemens and Steven Yingnien Chen, Territorial Schism: Toward a Regional Metropolitanism, from Overurbanism, studio, Harvard University GSD, 2011, the finest research piece according to this writer.

7. It is curiously absent, however, from his emails, which are typically monosyllabic, direct, and subject-line free.

8. In this regard, one cannot help wondering what goes on in Spanish.

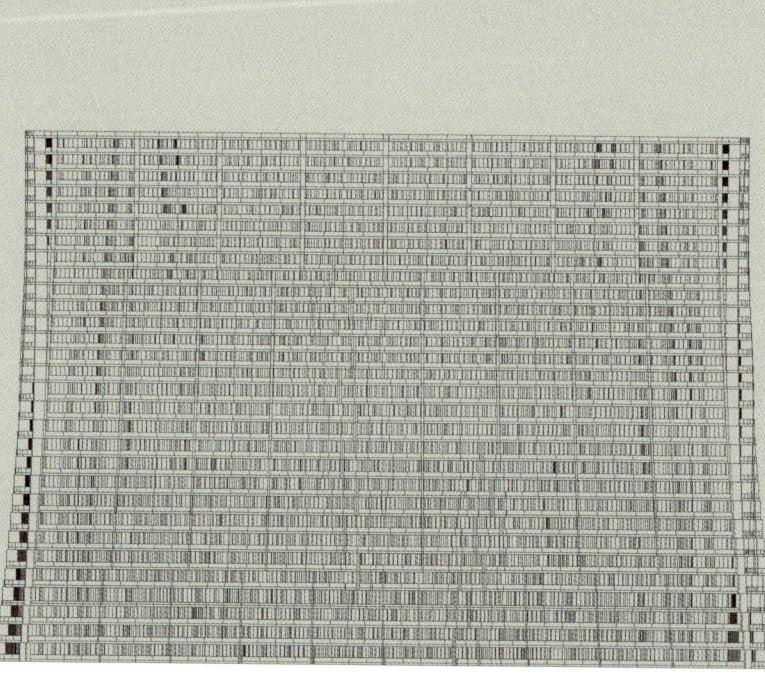

Some Things Don't Go Away

David Salomon

It would seem that things which elsewhere are taken for granted are not taken for granted in architecture. Hence the superfluous question as regards symmetry.
O. M. Ungers

Some things don't go away. You think they do, but they don't. Like when you hear something that you know immediately is true, even though you don't want it to be. You try to ignore it, especially when it contradicts a long-held belief you've had. When the source is someone you respect and trust, it's even more unsettling. It nags at you. It surfaces from time to time. You look away. But it is real, so it returns.

For example, when I encountered the phrase "no model, no theory" a number of years ago during a lecture by Ciro Najle, I felt a pang. He didn't explain it. He didn't even mention it. It was a barely legible caption that I could only see because I was sitting up front. Was it so fundamental to him that he didn't need to define it? Was it a throwaway line that he didn't want to discuss? Did I ask him about it afterward? Did he tell me what he meant by it? I don't remember. I just know that it wouldn't go away.

It returned to me from time to time because it challenged my understanding that an architectural model was a specific manifestation of a type. A model, I thought, is something that illustrates a theory. Therefore, it comes after a theory is established, not before. But I was wrong. Or I was thinking about a different kind of model. I couldn't shake it because "no model, no theory" rightly suggests that in order to generate a new theory, both concrete examples and a structure for making sense of them need to be in place. Models are not objects minus ideas; they are ideas plus objects.

Plans, sections, and elevations can function as this kind of architectural model. Vitruvius's *utilitas*, *firmitas*, and *venustas* do as well. Symmetry too. None of these have ever truly gone away, though some have been in hiding. They are the tools and tropes that the discipline comes back to time and again, tools and tropes that are sometimes are taken for granted and sometimes are directly reexamined. Such phenomena should not be mistaken for essences. Rather, they are the disciplinary constants, or models, from which architectural objects and architectural theory are generated.

"No model, no theory" came rushing back to me when I was reading Bas C. van Fraassen's book on the relationship between symmetry, math, and science. The philosopher positions symmetry not as a universal law or all-encompassing theory of the universe but as a highly efficient model for understanding it.[1] Model: that's the term he uses. I knew immediately that there was some connection between his idea, Najle's aphorism, and the work he and his students do—work that often relies on symmetry. Could symmetry perform the same function in architecture as it does in math and science? Namely, could it be used as an elastic model for understanding something larger? If so, what kind of theory would this model generate? And if not, what was symmetry's role in the work? In short, why so much symmetry, Ciro?

Symmetry, within the history of architecture, is, surprisingly, a moving target. It is not just the mirror image of something. It is not limited to the Greek's taut organizational strategy. It is not confined to Vitruvius's notion of "good proportions," or to Perrault's equal distribution of identical parts. It is not just Durand's efficient organizational technique. It is not ornamental tessellations. It is all of these, and more.[2] Today, any of these examples can and are being used to inform design. If none have been accepted as dominant or embraced as up-to-date, neither have they been abandoned. They linger.

The coexistence of multiple definitions of symmetry echoes the modern understanding of what symmetry is. The mathematician and physicist Hermann Weyl is credited with coining the modern definition of "symmetry" as an "invariance of a configuration of elements under a group of automorphic transformations."[3] Picture a cube made of uniform construction. Pick it up, rotate it 90 or 180 or 270 degrees, or any combination thereof. Put it down. It looks the same but the location of all the vertices and planes is different. There are 24 different but equivalent solutions (and 48 ways to achieve them) that make up this group. In this definition, symmetry is not a static, isolated, or idealized phenomenon. It is plural. It simultaneously embodies stasis and change.

Although this definition is more accepted today in math and science than it is in architecture, the automorphic operations Weyl refers to are the same reflections, rotations, and translations in space used by traditional designers of ornament and architecture. Weyl himself emphasized the concept's importance to (1) artist artifacts, (2) natural phenomena, and (3) physical theories. For him, the connection between the three fields—art, natural sciences, and physics—is not the weak one provided by metaphor or metaphysics. The important link among them is provided by the common presence of the hard, mathematical facts of group theory. While traditional makers of ornaments, and later, 19th-century crystallographers, understood how to use these rules, it was group theory that examined, systematized, and codified these relationships. What began as the description of concrete objects became, in the 20th century, a system for describing complex formal and abstract relationships.

Although the mathematical understanding of symmetry and groups grew out of work done in geometry, algebra, and crystallography, its precision and complexity have proven to be especially useful in modern physics, especially quantum mechanics. In particular, this understanding has greatly aided the codification of the knowable-yet-unpredictable nature of quantum movement.[4] It does so by providing a surprisingly useful constraint that made solving complex equations easier—a constraint that also enabled researchers to predict behaviors and to develop and test sophisticated theories. It can do this because symmetry, and especially symmetry groups, provide a population of unique yet equivalent solutions to a problem rather than one (and only one) answer.

The ability to replace one thing with another without a change of form or performance has implications for understanding how symmetry could be used in architecture. As Katherine Brading and Elena Castellani note in *The Stanford Encyclopedia of Philosophy*:

On the one hand, we might say that symmetries are associated with unavoidable redundancy in our descriptions of the world, while on the other hand we might maintain that symmetries indicate a limitation of our epistemic access—there are certain properties of objects, such as their absolute positions, that are not observable.[5]

The presence of redundancy suggests that there is always more than one correct way to describe any given state of the world. That we may never be able to know what position is current, which will be next, and which is optimal suggests that the physical world, like the designed world, is inherently open-ended, iterative, and stochastic. Limited as it is, however, by the constraints of symmetries (of space, time, and energy), there is not an infinite number of forms it can take, either. The range of possibilities is circumscribed by the size of the invariance group. More symmetry means fewer, but always multiple, options. Each symmetry group contains a range of correct but non-hierarchical solutions.

A set of equally valid solutions to a specific problem; an open-ended, iterative, stochastic, yet circumscribed process: these qualities have also been used to describe the (wicked nature of the) design process. As a design technique, however, symmetry is historically associated with its previous manifestation. From Vitruvius to Perrault to Durand to New Urbanism, symmetry has increasingly been used to reinforce and reproduce that which is already known. In contrast, the current scientific understanding of symmetry—combining consistency with redundancy—has enabled it to function as an agent for generating new knowledge.

Could this newer understanding of symmetry serve as a model from which a new theory of architecture could be built? Would tapping into its current non-architectural definition provide more than a metaphor? Or could its status as an endemic architectural issue, combined with a reconceived understanding of it as inherently multiple, enable it to create a new architectural theory? Is that what Najle's use of symmetry does?

Even a cursory glance at his work reveals that multiple symmetries are at play. Sometimes symmetry can be found in the case studies he and his students analyze—in the architecture, the structure, and the landscape. Sometimes it's in the patterns underlying the natural phenomenon they study. Sometimes it's in the diagrams they generate out of their investigation of these phenomena. Sometimes the symmetries are local. Sometimes they are global. Sometimes they are fractal. Sometimes they are subdivided. Sometimes they are aggregated. Sometimes they are reflective, sometimes rotational, and other times translational. Often they are incomplete or broken.

A closer look at these varied examples uncovers a complex interaction between symmetrical and asymmetrical zones. Symmetry is not seen as autonomous and formal, whereas asymmetry is responsive and functional: instead, they are understood and deployed as two points along a highly elastic continuum. Yet symmetry is always recognizably present as a limiting condition. Seeing the work as the many versions made during a highly recursive process reveals how these two states are not juxtaposed as much as they are blended with one another. The various options proposed illustrate how equivalent solutions are not identical ones. Symmetry enables one to see them as a family without restricting their specificity.

This is how physicists (and chemists and biologists and geologists) understand symmetry's presence.[6] As a model of the physical world, perfect symmetry is pervasive and highly effective. As a physical entity, it is rarely found. But this analogy should not be mistaken as another case of science envy or mimicry. There is no indication that Najle relies on group theory, or physical or biological notions of symmetry and symmetry breaking, to achieve these results. If fact, there is every indication that symmetry is used primarily as an architectural technique.

If there is something to be taken from how science has used symmetry, it is its insistence on perpetually examining, refining, and updating its own disciplinary tools and models rather than prematurely abandoning them.[7] Today's scientific definition of symmetry is related to, but very different from, its past definitions. This is not yet the case in architecture. The understanding and use of symmetry espoused by Vitruvius, Perrault, Durand, and others may have exhausted themselves, but that does not render the concept itself obsolete. In fact, the adjustments made to symmetry by Perrault and Durand are examples of how updating and enlivening disciplinary constants (invariants) can reinvigorate the discipline in the context of changing (transformed) historical conditions. As O. M. Ungers recognized, symmetry is a real and inevitable disciplinary issue[8]: it returns again and again, whether you want it to or not.

The question remains: What, if anything, is different this time? Is symmetry once again a law one must conform to, or is it a disciplinary device that enables one to learn and grow? A difference one finds in Najle's use of symmetry is that it is not so much broken as it is aggregated. One symmetrical operation is combined with another; an asymmetrical element is fused with a symmetrical one. The presence of asymmetry never negates or erases the presence of symmetry: sometimes it augments it, sometimes it camouflages it, and sometimes it highlights it. By adding (and multiplying and dividing) the many modes of symmetry with one another, he avoids the trap of it becoming autonomous or isolating. It is not an ideal to which one aspires or a template to which one conforms. Symmetry is a sophisticated device with which one experiments. In Najle's hands it is combinatory and multiple, never essential or reductive. Call it "schizo-symmetry."

Here symmetry is not code for a return to order, nor is it a call for formal autonomy; it exists not in opposition to these but instead in dialogue with them. And despite the many iterations and meticulous documentation it produces, symmetry in Ciro's work does not serve as an example of parametric variation either. Rather, it is a robust, multipronged architectural device deployed to produce numerous, specific, and equivalent proposals. Whenever it is used, it does act as a constraint: to the inherently varying conditions of site, program, client, budget, climate, history, and the like. But as a constraint it is neither pure nor rigid. It provides a limited but broad range of options. Regardless of whether the symmetry is perfect or only approximate, it supplies the legible formal framework to accommodate and sometimes exaggerate spatial, programmatic, and climactic differences.

The validity and source of this kind of architecture (one could even call it a theory of architecture) does not rest on anything external to architecture. It comes straight out of a number of architectural invariants. It can be related to mathematic and scientific uses of symmetry—and it benefits from that comparison—but it does not rely on or come from them. After all, as the historians of symmetry can tell you, symmetry was an architectural issue well before it was a scientific and mathematical one. Does this make symmetry *the* model for architectural theory? It would be premature to answer "yes" or "no." Other disciplinary devices—plans, section, structure, space—must also be considered. Not surprisingly, these elements are also central to Najle's work and research.

This multiplicity of possible sources suggests that architecture can never be as precise or foundational as math or physics. And, because it can't be reduced to a limited set of laws, it may remain marginal in a world that only values absolutes. But does such a world really exist? The definition of symmetry as simultaneously invariant and transformed suggests that the physical world is, like architecture, specific and imprecise, multiple and mutable. Perhaps architecture would be more central if it took itself and its own ideas more seriously. Ciro Najle certainly does.

We end by returning to an updated version of the uncanny phrase we began with. Now it reads: "no architectural model, no architectural theory." While architecture must pay attention to historical changes, Najle's approach is one that understands architecture and its attendant methods and models as being robust enough to generate their own theory. But this capacity is dependent on it perpetually adjusting, augmenting, and updating those methods and models. It can neither accept them as eternal nor dismiss them as obsolete.

As others in this volume have suggested, Najle's work and research understand architecture not as "the knowledge of form, but as a form of knowledge."[9] That knowledge is connected to other fields but ultimately is grounded in its own examples and operations. Symmetry is one such example and operation; others have been mentioned. All of them are used by him to test architecture's capacity to learn from and inform the unique yet repeatable relationship it has with the cultures and environments within which it exists. It is a symmetrical relationship. It is real. It won't go away.

1. Bas C. van Fraassen, *Laws and Symmetry* (Oxford: Clarendon, 1989).

2. Bernard R. Goldstein and Giora Hon, *From* Summetria *to Symmetry: The Making of a Revolutionary Scientific Concept* (Dordrecht: Springer, 2008).

3. Hermann Weyl, *Symmetry* (Princeton, NJ: Princeton University Press, 1952).

4. Bernard R. Goldstein, "Unpacking 'For Reasons of Symmetry': Two Categories of Symmetry Arguments," *Philosophy of Science* 73, no. 4 (October 2006): 419–39.

5. Katherine Brading and Elena Castellani, "Symmetry and Symmetry Breaking," *Stanford Encyclopedia of Philosophy*, ed. Edward N. Zalta, Spring 2013, http://plato.stanford.edu/archives/spr2013/entries/symmetry-breaking/.

6. Giora Hon and Bernard R. Goldstein, "From Proportion to Balance: The Background to Symmetry in Science," *Studies in History & Philosophy of Science,* part A36, no. 1 (March 2005): 1–21.

7. Alan Colquhoun, "Composition Versus the Project" (1986), repr. in *Modernity and the Classical Tradition: Architectural Essays, 1980–1989* (Cambridge, MA: MIT Press, 1989), 33–55.

8. O. M. Ungers, "Operations of Equalibration: A Response to a *Daidalos* Inquiry," *Daidalos* 15 (March 1985): 26, part of an entire issue addressing the art of symmetry.

9. Bernard Tschumi, "Spaces and Events," in *Architecture and Disjunction* (Cambridge, MA: MIT Press, 1994), 140.

Cue The Sun!

Paul Andersen

There is a moment in the 1998 film *The Truman Show* when we see the constructed, self-contained world of Seahaven from the control center concealed in its artificial moon. In this, the ultimate reality show, there are thousands of hidden cameras, radio communications systems linked to every actor on the ground, even software for monitoring and altering the weather. Everything, from traffic patterns and product placement to Truman Burbank's personal relationships and emotional responses, is directed from above.

For the film's audience, the extent of the television producers' control over Truman's life is simultaneously distressing and intriguing. The discomfort of predetermination is balanced against the attraction of creating an enclosed, artificial environment the size of a city, a tension that conjures up the distant legacy of Futurist proposals, modernist universal urbanism, and megastructures. But if analogs to *The Truman Show* are common in architecture's past, today they are few and far between. The Generic Sublime pushes a new agenda for the megaproject, one that provides a much-needed contemporary view of nature and a new swerve in architecture's history of experimenting with different forms of control.

Ciro Najle's studios are known for their rules. There are rules for how diagrams are set up, how geometry is modified, how variations are made, how prints are laid out, and how project presentations are organized. In some cases, there are even rules for how jurors are to respond in reviews. There are advantages to the structure that rules provide: they establish high levels of control in the design process and intricacy in the projects' forms. Discussions at reviews inevitably zero in on the particulars of how a given feature or effect was generated, which is only possible because of the highly regulated geometry that permeates the project. And then, occasionally, it becomes clear how an individual work violates the rules on which it was initially based. In fact, most projects are defined more by rule violations than by the rules themselves.

It would be easy to conclude, based on this apparent commitment to rigor, that Najle's studios venerate a rules-based approach to design. Far subtler are the ways in which the work challenges deeply entrenched predilections for how architects influence the environments that they design. During the past two decades, the image of the architect as a heroic figure has been all but totally dismantled. The audacity that characterized the 20th century's most polemical urban design has been discouraged on two fronts. First, an obsession with establishing secondary and partial means of control over the built environment has developed. The combined forces of indirect control and unpredictable feedback are assumed to be capable of creating a richer palette of material and social behaviors than is autonomous authorship. Second, the complex web of people involved in a project—particularly a large one—makes overarching command of the design process impossible. A top-down approach is assumed to be as impractical as it is hubristic.

In the Generic Sublime, the megaproject makes a comeback, but along different lines than its modernist predecessors. Each project is unique. Specificity and, more importantly, richness are the products of an elaborate series of geometric operations, the logic of which is endemic to the project itself. A project's colossal size is more practical than initially may be assumed. The designs for massive real estate developments taking form throughout the world are often controlled by a single architect (or a small number of architects). New Urbanist developments in the United States, urban plans and skyscrapers in Central Asia, and gated communities in South America provide but a few examples. Ironically, the domed "set" in which *The Truman Show*'s fiction takes place is in reality an actual town: the New Urbanist development of Seaside, Florida. When it comes to design influence, many built projects allow extraordinary levels of control. The Generic Sublime drives the banal regulations of contemporary development to extremes—far beyond conventional thresholds—to reach a point where new formal, organizational, social, and economic features begin to appear. Form paradoxically becomes more relevant as size increases. The projects' extruded blocks meet the demands of large-scale commercial construction and, coupled with sophisticated aggregation techniques, acquire more intricacy the larger they become. Running counter to the prevailing theory that form doesn't matter once something gets big enough, the projects of the Generic Sublime invert the dominant form-size relationship. This requires the introduction of noise—that is, a set of rule-countering strategies—at both low and high levels. Despite their detailed and rigorous series of geometric operations, the projects embrace nonlinear shifts in the design process. Scripts are drawn step by step rather than automated. Intuitive shifts establish ever-new patterns of formal evolution to create a blend of top-down and bottom-up control.

The noise of human control is an integral component of these new worlds. A long-standing regard for purity that isolates urban design from nature gives way, in these projects, to a cosmopolitan mixing of the two. Geologic formations of apartments, offices, stores, and nightclubs are designed for the systematic and mutual development of human activity and buildings. It is easy to imagine new forms of collective life—new cultural institutions, new shopping experiences, new municipalities, new recreational activities, new kinds of wars—materializing in these agglomerates. The reliance of this expanded city life on the developments' form, size, and character suggests a coevolution between outward appearance and internal organization. They look like rock formations and function as complete ecosystems, with distortions in one realm having consequences for the other. On both fronts, there is no distinction between artificial and natural, not because they are given equal standing but because they are integrated. Man and man-made can be as generic-sublime as anything else.

When a gardener plants an apple tree, the apple is controlling the gardener as much as the gardener is controlling the apple. We tend to think that we are in command, that our decisions about which variety to plant, where to plant it, and how aggressively to cultivate it give us a position of authority. But the apple is also tempting us into advancing its evolutionary cause. In Generic Sublime worlds, control and attraction go hand in hand.

Permanent Mobilization

Lluís Ortega

When addressing the production of the working teams that Ciro Najle has been recently directing in academic environments, one is confronted with a crystallization of previous architectural investigations that, on the one hand, produce the typical anxiety of the ungraspable and of the forces that the unintelligible displaces—the potence of the sublime—and on the other hand, instantaneously install a challenge that violates the known and mobilizes all of the resources of the discipline—the politization of the subject. At first glance, these two registers are not symmetrical. The sublime is argued, unfolded, and deployed as the visible public face of the investigation, but there is no apparent declaration of its political dimension. Yet this nondeclaration is itself the format of the political plan of this project. By constantly evading the rhetorical, it intentionally centers its focus on the performative. If enough attention is given to the details of this work, it becomes progressively evident that its political dimension is not developed through the form of a proclamation but rather via the direct deployment of actions. There are imperceptible traces of this background politics, as in the depiction of the generic as sublime and the sublime as generic. The Generic Sublime turns architectural poetry into a political weapon and constructs the framework for a politics without a horizon of emancipation: a politics of permanent mobilization.

Whereas traditional emancipating politics work from the perspective of modernistic innocence, based on a blind belief in progress, the politics of permanent mobilization have no idealized framework of stability. Instead, these politics turn transformation itself into a territory of development. Thus the relationship between the political and the sublime is reconstructed as a result of a structural assembly, neither opportunistic nor merely reactive, that systematically actualizes itself in the need to constantly confront the unknown as a means to expand the discipline. This experience of constant displacement can be engaged from two extreme perspectives: that of the stranger-intruder who remains with his/her mouth open and enjoys the impact produced by the artificially constructed landscapes of the work, and that of the technician who introduces himself/herself to an extreme, radical terrain. More often than not, these two perspectives get fused, either in the form of the "astonished technician" or of the "technified enthusiast." Both illuminations equally demand an act of opening on the side of the actor-spectator, who surreptitiously becomes an instant investigator and a highly politicized explorer. When this vertiginous breach does not take place in the receiver who has insufficiently exposed himself/herself to the work, then, inevitably, as in any tense political scenario, there appears some form of violence in the effect. Indifference, in any case, is not possible.

Unfolding the precise and relevant categories within this double register is a difficult task, and often of little use. Each project in the research assembles several categories and claims a complexity of reading that evades univocal taxonomies. However, the insistence on a recurrent terminology enables an approximation of the overall significance of the work. Its jargon configures a language that mediates and makes bearable the radical attack on the modernistic rationality of the material under transformation. On the one hand, projects are consistent, precise, and expansive, and explore the production of beauty from the point of view of semi-figurative fields. To the challenges and demands of architects such as Stan Allen or Peter Eisenman, who regard the figure as a means to overcome the purely abstract field of the 1990s, Ciro Najle presents the development of consistently beautiful fields. Figuration here does not refer to a natural form but rather to a natural system-formation process. Form is replaced by performance. This recourse to the systemic is what, without a doubt, opens the proposals to a form of dialogue that is simultaneously ecological and disciplinary.

On a different terminological order, projects are bare, obsessive, and violent. Their provocative condition explores cultural limits through the despoliation of the unnecessary and the contingent in architecture. The obsession with systematicity charges architectural documents with aesthetic depth, as it forces the creation of an innovative argument and disqualifies as inadequate any preconceived form of critique. Such systematic dismantling of any form of prefabricated argumentation and such frontal exposure to architectural bareness intensifies any honest debate over the work and gives it an innovative force, which follows naturally out of a non-predetermined approximation of the notion of "value" in architecture.

Najle's academic work is one step further in the displacement of the tradition of the politics of desire of Spinoza and Deleuze into another mode of practice. This is especially relevant today, as the present seems to require a model of interrupted politics: that of the Nietzschean *Übermensch*, as Najle consistently claims in his programmatic statements. From the techniques and ethics of continuity based on the idea of a pure, endless process, one can now intuit in the work a new turn toward a more abrupt procedure. Naturally, this is nothing but a bet, disguised in the form of a conclusion. But it has become increasingly evident that further attention must be paid to what the next concept will be that takes the place of the current "generic" of the equation.

Over-research

Leire Asensio Villoria and David Mah

The Generic Sublime, the studio conducted by Ciro Najle at the Harvard University Graduate School of Design, is candidly presented as an exercise in employing the academic studio environment as a generator of research. Within a larger body of work that spans Najle's pedagogical career, the Generic Sublime sits comfortably within a more general ambition to move design education away from its construction as a site for the transfer of professional knowledge or signature sensibilities. A more habitual emphasis on training and apprenticeship is exchanged for the opportunity to mobilize the collective intelligence of the design studio tradition toward the production of professional and disciplinary knowledge. Although it is apparent that the work is a form of research with clear intentions, what is perhaps less evident is the nature of the knowledge it produces. This lack of clarity may suggest a flawed relationship between hypotheses and adopted research techniques (techniques that typically imply the production of impoverished information). But while the production of the studio may not appear to respond to initial premises, the work offers a body of knowledge that is clearly loaded with professional and disciplinary value, which involves precisely the construction of premises.

It is quite probable that the undeniable value of the investigation lies in its ability to be read as a form of both applied and pure research. Upon closer study of the work, it becomes unclear as to what extent we are invited to see these projects solely as literal propositions for the metropolis. When asked, Najle (or his students) respond with emphatic declarations that these works are actual propositions for metropolitan models. Without a doubt, the work clearly describes and represents a series of organizations, forms, spaces, environments, and atmospheres that offer visions (or versions) of the metropolis. However, as with a lot of other valuable forms of inquiry, there is frequently a life for the work that goes far beyond its author's intentions. In the same way that conjectures frame or inform other, more specific and applied fields of study, the information generated within the Generic Sublime operates as speculation on the broader issue of the contemporary and/or modern metropolis. Understood in this light, it is the production of knowledge prior to its direct application that is at stake here—contemplation as a means to construct a theoretical frame that may be adopted for action on or within the metropolis.

The production of the Generic Sublime could thus be viewed as a number of different forms of inquiry operating simultaneously and spanning exploratory, explanatory, descriptive, constructive, and correlational modes. Equally propositions for and reflections on the contemporary metropolis, the projects eschew linear models of research that are necessarily circumscribed. Much of the work operates both as a legitimate proposition of potential metropolitan models, ready to be implemented within sites of current, rapid global urbanization, and as an illustration of the uncanny effects and consequences of the motivations and forces that underlie contemporary urbanizing processes. In other words, these propositional models work as didactic instruments for contemporary urbanization in general. This is revealed through a close reading of the techniques and processes deployed in the research development.

The studio research process is decisively systematic, rigorous, and controlled. Examining this process discloses numerous impulses and inclinations that drive the work. The grids and matrices widely employed within the studio borrow information formats typically used for correlational studies. Here they are used to graphically conflate and compare sample data from a number of metropolitan projects. These matrices and grids quickly transition, however, to become the literal organizers of the proposal: in other words, they become the proposal's plan or section. The significance of the research and the way in which the work may be read is encapsulated in this deft action. The enigmatic artifact produced by this operation acts simultaneously as a register and ordering device of metropolitan data sampling and as an associative model for different metropolitan configurations—that is, as both an analytical and an operative tool. The resonance with emblematic urban forms, organizations, and models affords the deployment of statistical diagrammatic instruments multiple associations—to performances as well as meanings.

In this context, the Generic Sublime clearly demonstrates the benefits generated by non-linear modes of research. The studio presents us with a model of over-research. Clear, linear research processes, characterized by direct links between stated objectives and the nature of the information produced, are often motivated by a myopic or overly focused ambition to search for knowledge. In the case of Najle's studios, a wider scope of ambitions—both stated and concealed—provides the space for the unfolding, out of the research process itself, of a potentially richer body of knowledge.

Drawing conclusions from certain graphic quotations that are legible within the production of the studio, its affiliation with Hugh Ferris's illustrations becomes evident. Like Ferris's work, the Generic Sublime makes graphically explicit the unrealized potential of existing metropolitan protocols, compelling us to recognize this work as providing very real models for the contemporary metropolis.

Type:Topo:Typo(logy)

Pablo Lorenzo-Eiroa

During the last 40 years, the field of architecture has relaxed its boundaries to explore several forms of disciplinary expansion. Site specificity has played an important role in this process, as these explorations have largely avoided making reference to any determinate spatial categorization. Lately, however, this disciplinary trajectory has reversed course, to target generic typologies and spatial containment. Within the last decade, architecture has been testing the previous experiences of disciplinary expansion by inverting them, as if in an enfolding movement, revisiting the relative stability of architectural typologies. Proposing the new now means to address generic types through topological displacements, questioning the late post-structuralist assumptions that quite simply ignored the architectural reference.

In this new setting, a large number of contemporary architectural practices have chosen to assume that their work still operates in the realm of post-structuralism, negating any referential structure, for instance through the nonfigural field condition of their projects. It is becoming evident, however, that this kind of work disregards the usual solutions that become structural to the field, or even the same conditions that prescribe the origin of a project (as is the case with computer interfaces). This architectural claim is based in an apparently emergent yet unresolved complexity that, in fact, does not target the determination of the departing structures but rather confirms them as they are. There is, however, an emerging structuralism growing from within, evidenced by a form of computation that can be regarded as a reaction to these omissions. The Generic Sublime proposes an alternative model to the way in which the relationship between typology and topology is considered in this context.

The work of Rem Koolhaas has consistently proposed an interesting tension between generic structures and typological displacements, both introducing innovative architectural typologies and critiquing structuralism. OMA's Agadir Convention Center (1990), for instance, displaces Le Corbusier's universal free plan by means of a diversified spatial topography. In the proposed variation of this formula for Inside-Out City (1993), the topographic undulation of the slab displaces the universal flat slabs of the free plan and creates topological continuity among the different levels. Stacked Freedoms (1989), which OMA applied in the Seattle Public Library (2004), similarly references Louis Kahn's tartan grid, which alternates service spaces with larger spaces, disrupting their repetition and alternating structural strategies. This move can be related to Le Corbusier's organizational spatial structure at the Villa Stein (1926) that references Palladio, as Colin Rowe has pointed out, albeit here in section rather than in elevation. Finally, Koolhaas's Bordeaux House (1998) proposes an elevated, suspended/ungrounded volume, and below, in tension, a partially topographic underground house. The postmodernism of Koolhaas can indeed be formulated as a mechanism of escaping simple oppositions, borrowing the critical-paranoid method of Surrealism and its double-negative dialectic, "not this, not that," as many of his buildings start by proposing the negation of a referential typology (not this), in tension with its negative dialectic, the displacement of that originally referenced type (not that). Koolhaas engages with a structural critique of history by continually attempting to resolve typological innovation at the generic level of the architectural container. This innovation affects the generic organization of the space, the program, and the standard construction systems. The target of this attitude may also be extended to his critique of capitalist systems, which may reside in simply making evident and thus accelerating emerging cultural problems.

The academic research of Ciro Najle, in this scenario, incorporates a concern with a critiqued parametric order. His work addresses the notion of "emerging logic" based on (but irreducible to) an attention to the parameterization of relative factors in a project. The work gives preference to a bottom-up tactic, resisting a generalizing reasoning that tends to homogenize typological differences. By resisting predetermination, his work proposes a clear position with regard to post-structuralism and does not tend to generalize typology as such; nor does it endorse generic, preconceived structures. As a consequence, it also does not get lost in the mere mapping of topographical differences. What his methodology preferences is, rather, a discovery of typological structural differences. It does so by focusing on the emergent organizing potential of relative factors, instead of getting trapped in the attention to the structuring aspects of the project. Therefore, even though the focus of the work lies in relative factors and intentionally leaves the project open, in a state of indeterminate suspension, it radically questions the origination of generic types through an accumulative process of relative variation.[1]

Structuralism as Continuity after and through Post-structuralism

In architecture, typology can be thought of as a generic category that results from a process of stabilization, conforming to a disciplinary reference both in terms of organization and containment. Structuralism has been criticized for constructing categories that reference generic conventions, as this can obscure real differences. In Gilles Deleuze's idea of difference without concept, differentials are understood as real differences.[2] He notes, for example, the value of the curvature in itself, independent from other assumed referential categories. Structures and their negation can be related to typology and topology. In principle, typology is the opposite of topology (*topos*[3] + *logos*). "Topo-logos" refers to the various definitions of space relative to topographical differentiation, which are manifest in the placement of antique Greek sanctuaries.[4] In this sense, topology is the inverse of the idea of categorical classification since, within a given continuity, each topographical moment is unique. For Friedrich Nietzsche, topology implies a genealogy, a displacement of "relative forces," and the typological, a variation in absolute values.[5] For the German philosopher, as well as for Deleuze and Jacques Derrida, Hegelian dialectics provide a false image of difference through the creation of categorical generic oppositions, which generate contradictions based on reactionary forces. Deleuze resolves this tension, as he considers the platonic inversion by stochastics between a state of becoming (in reference to ideal form) and substance. What one must resist is the tendency that appears in each discipline to known types, which, if not displaced, continue to wrongly prescribe order and establish a false idea of difference.
In biology, in turn, D'Arcy Thomson proposed the understanding of structure as an elastic, topological relational reference, mathematically measuring degrees of change within a species while leaving unresolved the differences among species. Henri Bergson resolved this problem by understanding form in relationship to time. Bergson developed a biological theory of form, where structural change can be understood in continuity with and as a consequence

of variations in degree, establishing that structural change results from the emergence of order out of an accumulative process: a creative evolution, but also a theory of topology.

To dislodge the tension between typology and topology from the set of artificial signifiers that constitute architecture as a discipline: this seems to be our aim at present. But rather than resisting one position for the other, it has become evident that, today, both the emerging structuralism, raised by the need of the discipline to displace consolidated types, and the motivations of late post-structuralism, which tends to ignore the consolidation of these structures, must be equally subjected to rigorous critique, suspending the cyclical, reactionary pendulum predestined, as if naturally, to be the only way to continuously renew the discipline and activate its critical process.[6]

Redefining the Relative: New Origins

Today, it is necessary to develop a critical understanding of the relationship between typology and topology to overcome predetermination in architecture. Peter Eisenman's formal methods attempted to develop an increasingly complex diagram from a series of basic, step-by-step displacements of specific, sedimented historical structures. Whereas Greg Lynn's animate form theorized relative topological variations, the architect claimed that any solution in the series was equally valuable and that the origin (or first organizational structure), while progressively left behind through the series, was not transcended through the process but was rather being avoided by means of a purer form of indeterminacy.[7] Alejandro Zaera-Polo, in turn, described Eisenman's process as a machinic diagram, where computed solutions opened up noncritical relationships, as for example at the Berlin Memorial (2004).[8] The machinic and the systemic are actually what are being critiqued in contemporary digital architecture, making it necessary to question not only the parameters of a system but the conditions themselves that constitute them. In his February 2014 *Artforum* article, Mario Carpo contrasted the way in which architects worked with manageable amounts of data in the 1990s (by designing through nonuniform rational basis spline curves, or NURBS) to the way in which contemporary architects work to process large amounts of data today.[9] While Carpo argued for a shift to a nondeterministic paradigm, one should rather question the deterministic structuralism that is present in the algorithmic calculation through which big data is processed, therefore not only adding signification back to the data that it is mapping but also implicitly prescribing the structure that defines the project.

Alain Badiou asserted the impossibility of arriving at solutions within a system outside of its own structure. For the philosopher, part of the problem is how to question the system and not simply come up with an interesting solution determined by the system itself from which it emerges. In architecture, this problem could be traced all the way back to how the project starts, since a project does not begin with a certain initial organization but instead with the systems of representation that structure the organization of a project in advance, as its very first sign. And although post-structuralist approaches attempted to resolve these problems by disregarding the departing structure altogether (finding alternative solutions instead within variations that place the problem in movement as a default condition), these strategies focused on the variation of parametric solutions that do not challenge their own parameters or the structure of the system itself. The prescriptive order that the systems of representation induce was, as a result, never really critiqued.

In the past few years, it has become clear that if architects do not acknowledge and displace the referential structures that index the project, their work will remain confined by the set of ideas, cultural projects, and aesthetic agendas accumulated within the structure of the discipline and the systems of representation used. This necessarily puts into question the notion of authorship within the design process—that is, the process of creating novel structures that are able to revolutionize reference.[10] In order for new models of space and organization to truly emerge, it is necessary to displace—and then transcend—both the sedimented structures that have stabilized the discipline and the emerging generic typological structures that put it in crisis.

Any process should overcome the arbitrariness of its point of departure. And progressive topological displacements must seek out that break in a conceptual differentiation, aiming for changes to be typologically significant. During the last decade, projects started dealing with computer coding as a reference in itself. In this scenario, reference is no longer related to a historic disciplinary precedent, nor to an existing site. Rather, what become self-referential are the digital signs that constitute the project. The implicit project here is to resolve, within the ductile capabilities of relative topological displacements, a structural, typological change that can both critique and transcend the initial organizational structures on which they stand, including the very systems of representation that, to start with, structure the work. Furthermore, architects must aim for a transformation that lets them exit the set of parameters that constitute the system within which they are working. By these means, architecture may be able to coordinate, at the same level of signification, the multiple cognitive structures that take part in a project, ranging from the deep structures that regulate the object to the superficial ones that affect its relationship with the subject. Ultimately, such a project will be able to reclaim its own origination, by arriving at the constitution of a fully integrated system that includes the interfaces that structure the work.

1. This notion echoes Henri Bergson's biological formal theory in relation to time, referenced below.
2. Gilles Deleuze, *Difference and Repetition*, trans. Paul Patton (New York: Columbia University Press, 1994). Originally published in French in 1968.
3. Aristotle, in *Physics*, book IV, defines "topos" as the "site-space."
4. Christian Norberg-Schulz, *Meaning in Western Architecture* (New York: Praeger, 1974).
5. Gilles Deleuze, *Nietzsche and Philosophy*, trans. Hugh Tomlinson (London: Atholone Press, 1983). Originally published in French in 1962.
6. Heinrich Wölfflin described the group of architects that reacted to the Renaissance as Baroque, and defined historical progress in the arts as resembling a pendulum swinging from one revolution to the other. Heinrich Wölfflin, *Renaissance and Baroque*, trans. Kathrin Simon (Ithaca, NY: Cornell University Press, 1961). Originally published in German in 1888.
7. Greg Lynn, *Animate Form* (New York: Princeton Architectural Press, 1999).
8. Alejandro Zaera-Polo, "Eisenman's Machine of Infinite Resistance," in *El Croquis*, special issue, *Peter Eisenman, 1990–1997* 83, no. 1 (1997): 50–63.
9. Mario Carpo, "Breaking the Curve: Big Data and Digital Design," *Artforum* 52, 6 (2014): 168–73.
10. Authorship relative to computation was one of the main issues I raised at the ACADIA 2010 conference. In *The Alphabet and the Algorithm* (Cambridge, MA: MIT Press, 2011), Mario Carpo refers to the dissolution of authorship through computation and collaborative environments.

Novelty

Alberto Delorenzini

I

The disaster that initiates the phantasmagorical trip of Edgar Allan Poe's "MS. Found in a Bottle" cannot be analyzed as a progression of events. When the ship emerges from the torrent of foam—after the wave abruptly hits the deck, sweeping it from bow to stern—it has been converted into a ruinous hull. Only two of the crew and passengers survive. With its first gust, from one moment to the next, the storm establishes the fullness of its power. In the judgment of the narrator and survivor, "The extreme fury of the blast proved, in a great measure, the salvation of the ship."[1] If the rigging or anchor cable had offered any resistance, he explains, the ship would have sunk, irreparably lost.

Paradoxically, the ultimate proof of the "extreme fury" of the onslaught is not the ruin of the ship, incapable of resisting, but rather the ship's permanence afloat. Inversely, the infinite destructive capacity of the crush ignores the destruction itself. Obviously, the ship *can* survive because it stays afloat by itself. But this power that still remains in the ship does not at all correspond with the other, to which it serves as a proof only negatively, through the impossibility of confronting it. In this sense the word "accident," used by the narrator, precisely defines both the character of the disaster and its consequences—the afterlife granted the shipwrecked survivors. The aim of the ship is not simply to stay afloat: that can be done just as easily by a bottle, used to transport a message, or a manuscript. Its aim is to navigate, to follow a certain course using the natural forces in its favor. The trip that starts here, then, can only consist of a posthumous wander.

Redefined in England during the 18th century from a reading of Pseudo-Longinus, the sublime in modern times has been understood as a trend antagonistic to the "serene grandeur" of the beautiful. "The sublime theorized by [Edmund] Burke," Rosario Assunto writes, "is, exactly, the contrary not only of *the beautiful* [...] but of *the sublime,* just as it appears in the classical treatises, which often ended up getting confused with *the beautiful.*"[2] And if "pain, terror, [and] horror are [...] the psychological fundaments on which the Burkean conception of *the sublime* stand,"[3] Immanuel Kant, critically extending it, defines the satisfaction that the sublime produces as a measure of a displeasure, explaining that "since the mind is not just attracted by the object but is alternately always repelled as well, the liking the sublime contains is not so much a positive pleasure as rather admiration and respect, and so should be called a negative pleasure."[4] In this way the objects of a nature that we judge to be sublime—"threatening rocks, thunderclouds piling up in the sky and moving about accompanied by lightning and thunderclaps, volcanoes with all their destructive power, hurricanes with all the devastation they leave behind, the boundless ocean heaved up, the high waterfall of a mighty river, and so on"—reduce our faculty to resist, as compared with their force, to an insignificant smallness. As long as we are in a safe place, however, these objects of sublime nature "raise the soul's fortitude above its usual middle range and allow us to discover in ourselves an ability to resist which is of a quite different kind."[5] Because as long as the sublime objects (a misnomer, as "sublimity is contained not in any thing of nature"[6]) expose the impossibility of exposing the sublime itself, their representation is judged as appropriate only to a suprasensitive contingent *use*—that is, to lead thought to the infinite.

Everything that the narrator says explicitly about the sublime refers not to a natural object but rather to one produced by man. It is the fall of the ghostly wraith of the ship that will produce a second catastrophic shock, before it directly swoops down on them. The mass, weighing ten times more than they do, pauses still for an instant at the edge of the liquid precipice that surrounds them, "as if in contemplation of its own sublimity."[7] The "feeling of a momentary inhibition of the vital forces," as opposed to the "feeling of life's being furthered," which the beautiful promotes, is, according to Kant, typical of the negative pleasure obtained through the sublime.[8] This displeasure, however, overcomes itself through the verification that no sensitive form can be adequate to expose the intelligible, as "the mind is induced to abandon sensibility and occupy itself with ideas containing a higher purposiveness."[9] Hence, the moment of suspension or stoppage has nothing to do, by itself, with contemplative stillness. On the contrary, it has to do with the impossibility of reaching it by means of a sensitive form. However, in the passage that we are focusing on, the external immobility of an object—the ship—is transferred precisely to that of an internal character, which is opposed to the previous one and therefore positive, and corresponds to the state of contemplation—immobile, *restful*—of the sublime. This is nothing other than the sublime itself held in a state of suspension, in which the force of the object (force that, considered by the subject as infinite and therefore insuperable, constitutes the negative moment of the "dynamic sublime," according to Kant) presents itself as stagnant or detained. In this state (which, as Kant intuits, is nothing other than that of self-exposure), the sublime not only paralyses but itself remains negative, irreducible within its own objectuality, which consists of a stillness: that of the living appearance of the beautiful. Contemplation cannot find repose in the form of the object, but it also cannot abandon it in pursuit of a higher finality. From the moment in which the denial of any interest for the existence of the thing is demanded here by the thing itself in a state of inert suspension, the contemplative attitude can only move between both extremes. By colliding every time with its own impossibility, it is returned from one to the other and involved in a circular movement that is incapable of transcending the limits of the object.

This contemplation, which turns into a vacuum, corresponds in the tale by Poe to an objectively determined disinterestedness. This is because the capability of resisting—that is, that which depends on the finality that is proper to men and things—can only be granted accidentally, within conditions where the rule is its most complete annulment. In this way, in the episode of the second catastrophe, the narrator suddenly and unknowingly recovers control of himself for an instant, and with this, the sense of his own sublimity in the Kantian sense: to confront death without fear. But the persistent scream of the Swedish sailor to the ear of the narrator ("See!"), instants before perishing, is something other than a wake-up call. Effectively cancelled in their capacity to resist, Poe's creatures become fascinated in front of the imminence of their own destruction. "The utter hopelessness of hope itself" is the consequence of a time barely scanned by the "imminent expectation" of the next hit.[10] Thus, the sublime is determined in this tale by the exposition of human beings as much as of things in their total insignificance, without there being the tiniest aesthetic correspondence between the one and the other as a result of this analogy.

In order to refer here to an aesthetic correspondence, we shall go back to the opposition between the beautiful and the sublime, so as to verify that, on the way, change in the structure of meaning has been produced. This structure only appears when we presuppose that "instinct [...] of beauty" that Baudelaire attributes to a maximum degree to Poe: an "instinct" by which we consider "the Earth and its spectacles as a [...] correspondence to Heaven."[11] That is, insofar as we conceive beauty under the concordance of the diverse with the one, which transfigures the natural and bestows art of its vivifying sense. But in the same way that the beauty of Berenice, for fear of Egaeus, only starts to have meaning when it is a *dying* beauty, the sublimity of the vessel—which stands on the pinnacle of the wave in order to precipitate itself right after into the abyss—*radiates* from a second life of sorts. This exchange of properties—this mutual determination—becomes readily noticeable in the fact that the disinterestedness of the contemplative attitude gets unified with the negativity of the sublime, in a sudden movement of elevation and descent. In the same way that it is elevated, the ship is sent back, by the circularity of the contemplative movement, to the most painful lack of expressivity of the thing: mere "descending mass," simple instrument, counterpart of the flight to regions "beyond the albatross." But this will provide the motivation, immediately, of a more detailed reflection.

II

It is again the violence of the "shock"—the word whose transformation in an aesthetic category, in the context of the theory of art not centered in reception, we owe to Walter Benjamin[12]—that saves the narrator of the manuscript from the second catastrophe. The enormous mass of the unknown ship, which has just entered the scene, succeeds in falling on the bow of the first ship, which, on the very brink of sinking "with her head," lies at the bottom of an abyss open in the middle of the flood. The hit generates a contrary impulse that throws, from the stern of one ship to the rigging of the other, he who will, this time, be the only survivor of the shipwreck. Such explanation seems to mark the tale's highest point of tension ("*comique*?" the translator of a French edition wonders[13]) between the normal course of the natural phenomenon and the miracle that suspends it. Even more, when, at the occasion of the first "accident" and in contrast to a similar interpretation of the facts, a reference to a miraculous salvation had been made, although in the most usual sense of the word. A passage of Hegel's *Aesthetics* will help clear up this question, returning to a decisive aspect of the experience of the sublime:

> Yet miracles in this sense are not a strictly specific expression of sublimity because the normal course of natural phenomena, as well as their interruption, is produced by the will of God and the obedience of nature. The sublime in the strict sense we must look for, on the contrary, when the whole created world appears entirely as finite, restricted, not bearing or carrying itself, and for this reason can only be regarded as a glorifying accessory for the praise of God.[14]

It is important to remember here the desacralized character of the finite world that Hegel determines, in contrast to the miracle that makes the sublime reside in the split between the sacred and the profane. It is about a world where natural laws assert their rights, populated by figures whose prosaic condition results close to us and is intelligible, only acquiring sense negatively. From this point of view, the tale by Poe seems oddly out of focus: on the one hand, the facts that the author describes are not only exceptional but they are produced, as in the episodes of the catastrophes, in total concord with the laws of physics, which grants them an ambiguous sense that, however, does not affect their immanence. On the other hand, the "meaningful" accident—the saving coincidence or the word inscribed by chance—is an extreme case of the accident, which does not connect anymore with the object of faith. As a consequence, the same function of the negative, "the praise," has to be modified.

Without a doubt, the exorbitant peculiarity of the "occurrences" destabilizes the experiences that the narrator had considered his most certain possession, if not his only one. Among these experiences are those that concern the tale itself (how would it be possible, in the face of such circumstances, to have access to their origin and postulate a development from it?), no less than the aesthetic ones (in what way formless objects could embrace, as their correspondent sensitive presence, the activity that dislocates them?). To suffer "shocks," in this context, is to experiment (if that were at all possible) with the nullity of "the lessons of by-gone times." In one stroke, followed by others, indefinitely juxtaposed to the first, the world of the physis is reduced to debris. For the subject, the attribution of these shocks to a superior will depends much less on the necessity of explaining them than on the possibility of recovering himself in the feeling of his own infinitude. But this is precisely what remains blocked as a consequence of the iterative character of the stimulus, as if Poe, by not letting, between blow and blow, any space whatsoever for meaning, had intended in advance to take to an extreme (according to what Baudelaire calls his "probabilism") the question that the poet of the *Flowers of Evil* would confront in his lyric poetry. This question, as specified by Benjamin (whose reading of Baudelaire we here reference), asks "how the lyric poetry could be founded in an experience for which the reception of shocks has become a norm?"[15]

Already in the new ship, the narrator, guided "perhaps" by the "indefinite sense of awe" inspired by the crew members, decides to hide. What makes the explanation of his behavior twice as enigmatic is not so much the conjectural mode as the fact that he, to whose "pyrrhonism" he dedicates a "premise" or introduction, must admit without a doubt the awakening to this new "sense," which, however, recognizes such diffuse sources. "I was not willing to confide in," he annotates, "a race of people, which, at the quick look that I had given, offered so many points of vague novelty."[16] The question about the relationship between the "awe" and the "non truth" imposes itself.

Awe, according to Kant, is a disposition of the spirit frequently associated with sublimity, which, however, has nothing to do with it. It is alien to it to such an extent that, depending on whether it is present or not, it is possible to distinguish religion from superstition: "The latter establishes in the mind not a reverence for the sublime, but fear and dread of that being of superior might to whose will the terrified person finds himself subjected but without holding him in esteem."[17] When represented by human beings, sublimity demands, in contrast, respect. "Respecting age"—given the case that we are dealing with—would be a practical prescription that obtains its validity from moral law. But the effect that this particular age produces in the spirits of the narrator of Poe's tale is, precisely, awe. This, when the rejection of superstition has been made explicit, for good or for bad, not only as a presupposition of the tale but as that of a whole epoch. Nobody is less prone then the survivor, the witness, the *superstes*, to let himself be dragged "by the *ignes fatui* of superstition." Even so, the traces seem to sprout everywhere around him, too new, too resistant to be referred to as the principles of the "philosophy of physics": the narrator hits the root of objectivity exactly when it slips through his fingers. The fact that this is not a simple return to a primitive animism is attested to, first, by the anonymity in which he remains, the fact that he attempts to omit all references to himself that are not oriented toward accounting for "the positive experience." No less conclusive is the fact that the ship that bursts onto the scene belongs to a secular and political world, a world governed by means of commissions and documents that hold the signature of the sovereign as a determining act of will. Objectivity and sovereign will are the complementary and convergent fundaments that are pulled out from under the feet of the narrator and his eventual companions. Because the nature of everything they are is submitted to the continuous decay of nature, until the next gust, the next wave, erases them from the face of the Earth, what the majestic solemnity lends to the ship and its crew members is that postponement of which their survival consists. It is thusly that they configure, as a whole, the strange entourage of the life already passed.

1. Edgar Allan Poe, "MS. Found in a Bottle," *The Complete Tales and Poems of Edgar Allan Poe* (New York: Vintage Books, 1975), 118–26. Originally published in 1833. A longer version of my essay was originally published under the title "Novelty: The Sublime in a Tale by Edgar Allan Poe" in *Pasajes: Revista de teoría y critica del arte y la arquitectura*, vol. 1 (Buenos Aires: Centro de Estudios Amancio Williams/Facultad de Arquitectura y Urbanismo, Universidad de Buenos Aires, 2000), 35–46.
2. Rosario Assunto, *Naturaleza y razón en la estética del setecientos* (Madrid: Visor, 1989), 27. Translated into English by Zósimo González.
3. Ibid.
4. Immanuel Kant, "Analytic of the Sublime," *Critique of Judgment*, bk. II, trans. Werner S. Pluhar (Indianapolis: Hackett Publishing Company, 1987), sec. 23. Originally published in German in 1790.
5. Ibid., sec. 28.
6. Ibid.
7. Poe, "MS. Found in a Bottle," 121. "She paused upon the giddy pinnacle, as if in contemplation of her own sublimity."
8. Kant, "Analytic of the Sublime," sec. 23.
9. Ibid.
10. Poe, "MS. Found in a Bottle," 121.
11. Charles Baudelaire, *El arte romántico*, trans. Carlos Wert (Madrid: Felmar, 1977), 147. Originally published in French in 1868.
12. See Walter Benjamin, "Sobre algunos temas en Baudelaire," *Ensayos escogidos*, trans. H. A. Murena (Buenos Aires: Sur, 1967). Originally published in German in 1939.
13. Edgar Allan Poe, "Le Chat noir," *Le Chat noir et autres contes*, trans. Henri Justin (Paris: Le Livre de Poche, 1991). Originally published in English in 1843.
14. Georg Wilhelm Friedrich Hegel, *Aesthetics: Lectures on Fine Art*, vol. 1, trans. T. M. Knox (Oxford: Clarendon Press, 1988), 375. Originally published in German in 1942–1943.
15. Benjamin, "Sobre algunos temas en Baudelaire," 13.
16. Poe, "MS. Found in a Bottle," 122.
17. Kant, "Analytic of the Sublime," sec. 28.

The Burger

Marcia Krygier

Last time, I promised that we would have a burger together. More precisely, I promised that I was going to cook hamburgers for you! Work, trips, and everything going on are hard to combine, so instead, I guide you through the process.
Brain first!

00 Materials

Flour, yeast, sugar, salt, water, milk, butter, egg, sesame seeds
Meat, garlic, onion, green apple, cumin, coriander, cayenne pepper, black pepper, thyme, bread crumbs
Oil, egg yolk, mustard, lemon juice, salt
Cucumbers, dill seeds, fennel seeds, white vinegar, sugar, salt

01 Buns

When making bread two parallel efforts guide me: one, to accomplish the fermentation process in which the microorganisms in the yeast eat the carbohydrates and excrete carbon dioxide, giving the bread its crumb structure and its characteristic flavor; and two, to produce, through the mechanical working of the dough, the organization of the gluten, providing a structure that will hold the gas produced in the first step. I combine the flour and salt and make a crown. I make a well in the middle. The yeast does not like the salt, as it inhibits fermentation. So part of the maneuver is to keep the salt far away from the yeast. The yeast, instead, loves the sugar, and when sugar and yeast combine, the sugar causes the yeast to liquefy. I (suddenly) end up with a liquid mixture. I put the yeast mix in the middle of the crown and add some milk and water. I start hydrating the flour granules, forming the dough from the center of the crown. The main proteins in flour—gliadin and glutenin—start to hydrate, and gluten is formed. Before finishing the dough, I add soft butter in little pieces, like projectiles. This allows the butter to stay apart from the main structure of the dough and become a luxury ingredient. Starting with a few ingredients, I end up with a whole new compound that two minutes ago did not exist. It is not a transformation process but a formation process. I am excited. Soon—very soon—I start kneading the dough. Compression and folding provoke gluten, formerly a messy thread, to become a strong, ordered structure. Kneading also aerates the mixture, creating air pockets and determining the texture of the bread to come. I leave the dough to rise, covered, in a warm place. The enzymes will begin deconstructing the starch into sugars, and the yeast will start feeding on those sugars, reproducing and producing, as an outcome, carbon dioxide and alcohol.

02 Pickles

A while ago I pickled a bunch of cucumbers. Pickling is one of the most ancient techniques used to keep goods fresh. Using preserving agents like vinegar, salt, and sugar to create a medium with very low pH in which bacteria does not develop, pickling changes the taste and texture of produce and stops the natural rotting processes. Pickling makes goods available out of season, because it allows us to store them at their peak, when we have a surplus. I start mixing the vinegar with water, salt, and sugar. I add fennel seeds and dill seeds that I have previously crushed in a mortar. Grinding seeds causes flavoring agents to be released at the very moment they are mixed. I heat the liquid. The heat dissolves the sugar and the salt crystals, and helps to release the essence of the seeds by infusion. I pour the liquid over the cucumbers. They partially cook and become salty, sweet, acidic, and aromatic.

03 Burgers

Next I start grinding the meat. It seems I am destroying one entity to build another, incorporating layers of sense and taste, manipulating flavor and texture. I mix it with salt, spices, garlic, onions, grated apple (for extra moisture), egg, and breadcrumbs. I start kneading the meat to activate the protein in it, which, once activated, causes the chains to become strong. A structure is created—a bond between the meat particles. The burger will not fall apart in the pan. Finally, I shape the burgers with both hands, thinking about size.

Back to the bread: the dough has risen, doubling in volume. I deflate the dough, getting rid of all the carbon dioxide, and I divide it. I roll it into portions, giving each bun its final shape. I let the dough proof again, covered.

04 Mayonnaise

Now I make the mayo. I put an egg yolk together with some lemon juice and mustard. I start pouring in oil, drop by drop. This is crucial to creating the emulsion, a colloidal system in which, by using motion, one element is atomized into another one to make an impossible mix possible. Energetic beating breaks the surface tension and suspends little drops of oil into the other continuous phase. Egg yolk contains stabilizing agents such as lecithin that act as a help to form the emulsion. Mustard also helps. Again, I start with a few elements and end up with something that I would not have predicted.

05 Oven

I brush the bread with egg, sprinkle it with sesame seeds, and then, put it in the oven. The process has three moments. At the beginning, the temperature in the oven will cause the yeast to accelerate the process of producing carbon dioxide, so the bread will rise dramatically. This is called "oven spring." After the first few minutes, at 60 degrees Celsius, the yeast will die. During the next stage, the starch and the gluten will be transformed almost at the same time, and the sponge-like dough will become solid. In the last part of the baking process, browning reactions will impart both color and flavor to the surface of the bread. The sugar in the egg will brown, creating a crust. I take the buns out of the oven when the crust is golden brown and the inner structure feels set. To check, I tap on the bottom of the bun. If ready, the bread will sound hollow.

06 Pan

In the hot pan, the burgers start their cooking process. Heat gives meat its characteristic flavor. It mixes the three elements in meat: protein, water, and fat. Fat has a decisive role in creating the final texture and acts as a carrier for other flavors. Cooking has a dramatic effect on meat fibers: they shrink and shorten as the temperature increases. The high heat, coupled with the fact that I do not move the burgers at all, makes the natural sugars in the meat reach caramelization point over 120 degrees Celsius, creating Maillard, or browning, reactions. Maillard reactions are a series of complex processes characteristic of high-temperature cooking that involve amino acids and reducing sugars. As a result, lots of different flavor compounds are produced.

07 Table

The bread comes out of the oven. As it cools, the alcohol (a by-product of fermentation) starts to evaporate. The different temperatures even out: the dry outside will even out with the moist inside. I put the buns on a metal grid so that the steam does not condensate.

08 Plate

I cut the bread, smear the mayo on both halves, put the burger on the lower half, and lay out some of the pickles. I cover the unstable pile with the top half of the bun. I put a napkin on a white, immaculate dish, and then place the burger. This is almost a mechanical routine, but somehow the burger never ends up with the exact same face. There is a charisma about each one: all the same, never equal. It is time for the body to start decoding the flavors.

You are in front of the burger, finally. I made this burger for you. It is singular, but somehow linked to every other burger: one among many in the world of burgers. The special features of my particular doing become minimal, and the idea of burger-ness overcomes. You smell it, even if you do not want to, and the smell takes you over. There is a direct fiber between the receptor cells in the nose and the brain, so you instantly start feeling. Smell is primitive and evoking, deeply connected to memories. Since there is an airway that the nose shares with the mouth, smelling is simultaneous to tasting, so flavor is a mixture of these two sensations.

You start eating. You grab the sandwich with both hands and feel the contact, something very basic arising simply from having nothing in between your food and you. You feel the bread, soft and tender to your fingertips. When you take your first bite, you experience the crunch of the sesame seeds. Then you feel the egg wash, which has made a thin, resistant coat, and finally, the moist crumb, disintegrating in your mouth. You feel the layer of mayo as a soft, luxurious, lubricating medium, continuous throughout and somehow within everything else, melting with the heat of the burger. As you start feeling the grainy texture of the meat, it crumbles. But, you can tell, it is still a whole. It is now juicy, and you start feeling that your whole body is ready to receive it. The muscles in you mouth, in your jaw, and in your whole body get ready together. There is an ancestral thing about eating meat that is connected to hunting. Animals have a similar biochemistry to man, so their fibers are the perfect source of the amino acids we need. The cucumber appears, and suddenly the acid-salty-sweet makes you feel a crisp sensation. And crunchy, fresh. It allows you to appreciate even more the richness of the mix of the meat and the mayo. You feel the completeness of having all the food groups in just one bite.

The combination within a single medium is key. The bread acts as a plain, sweet sponge, which, as you eat, gets full of juices and is no longer plain. The meat is full of flavors and nutrition. The cucumber, fresh, crisp, acid-salty-sweet. The mayo, rich and velvety. Your brain feels connected to your tongue. The tongue is full of specialized epithelial cells gathered into taste buds. Each taste bud is penetrated by nerve fibers that transmit electrical impulses to your brain. The tongue is designed to provide us with a tool to help decide whether something is nutritious or poisonous. Taste, along with smell, are the only two senses that rely on chemical reactions: through them we decode the chemical composition of everything around us. These senses direct us to go for the sweet and salty nutrition and avoid the dangerous alkaloids.

You feel the road between the different points on your tongue as they activate: salty, sweet, acid, bitter. You feel the muscles in your jaw, craving the next bite. Your subjective sensation of juiciness occurs in two discrete moments. The moisture content of the meat determines the first impression of juiciness, as you bite. Then, the salivary glands kick in. Salival stimulation provides the medium in which we digest our food. Luckily, the more we enjoy the food, the greater the flow of saliva.

You finally feel the meat and the bread: basic, ancient, nourishing, and fun.
You start feeling altogether.
As you do, you realize that you are thinking of your mother.
Food. Family.
This single melting bite in your mouth makes you feel like an animal.
And yet, certainly, a person,
One more in history,
You are alive.

Bibliography: Harold McGee, *On Food and Cooking: The Science and Lore of the Kitchen* (New York: Collier Books, 1984).

Gravity Zero

Julián Varas

Gravity Zero Architecture is the manifestation of an act of emancipation from the humanist tradition in architecture and the symbolic and pragmatic affirmation that the *gravitas* of the architectural body is potentially greater than that of its context. Gravity Zero Architecture does not merely ignore context, nor does it insult it. It enacts an elegant detachment, the earnest cultivation of internal coherence, and the total reconfiguration of the space of experience such that no trace of what has traditionally been thought of as setting or location remains. It does not negotiate context, it does not register context, it does not comment on context, and it does not refer to context. It *is* context. Gravity Zero Architecture is the encounter of pure exteriority and ubiquitous interiority.

Program

Result of the creation of a fully artificialized environment, Gravity Zero Architecture disrupts the conventional codes of orientation by which the human body perceives its own configuration reflected in the organization of its surrounding envelope. Without deliberately seeking to affect a transfiguration of its psyche, it distorts the subject's perception of itself by placing it in a forest of mischievous mirrors that return to it confounded reflections, coalesced in a self-standing image. Cartesian space—that modern fantasy of absolute control—had been sanctioned, and later critiqued, as the undifferentiated medium of modern architecture: neutral, universal, homogeneous, infinite. Cartesian space could then be striated, through grids, bands, and zones, as well as through the bodies existing in it—bases, plinths, shafts, heads, crowns—subsequently being reconfigured through various forms of movement (Cubism, Futurism), distortion (Surrealism), camouflage (late Corbusier), proliferation (structuralism), collage (Pop), fragmentation (postmodernism), and liquefaction (vectorization). Yet despite these efforts, the Cartesian paradigm proved its stubbornness. Its categorical oppositions (above-below, front-back, left-right, inside-outside, before-behind, mass-void, center-periphery) tenaciously managed to remain in place. The critical apparatuses of modernity were condemned from the outset to comment on, distort, and resist such a framework and so were unable to truly liberate architecture from its claws, a huge section of its formal universe being restricted and remaining in the dark. Gravity Zero Architecture denies a place for these dualisms in its ontology and substitutes them for regimes of topology, fractality, and iteration. It foreshadows a new Cambrian explosion of architectural heterogeneity.

Genealogy

Placed at the root of the Western cultural tradition, the effort of humanist architecture has been to serve the needs of its users/creators but, equally, to symbolize them. However, since the early 20th century, the emergence of Gravity Zero Architecture has mounted an insistent attack on the tropes of anthropocentrism. Its history would have to be threaded through the seemingly individual efforts of coconspirators who attempted to break the primal identification of body and building. Mies van der Rohe denied the subject access to its customary coordinate systems in his Barcelona Pavilion (1929), insinuating the neutrality between up and down and their potential interchangeability by placing the observer's eye at mid-height between ground and ceiling and by making all materials in space reversible, continuous, and pluridirectional. Gerrit Rietveld denatured the very idea of enclosure, dissolved the basic interior-exterior distinction, and tampered with scale in his Schroeder House (1924), disfiguring the boundaries between building and furniture to the extent that, if these had ever been conceived as prosthetic extensions of the human body, the possibility of such representation was voided thereafter. Buckminster Fuller's geodesic domes and tensegrity structures cut transversally through scales by means of repetitive geometric devices, channeling forces through nonoriented, homogeneous elements. Peter Eisenman's early houses mirrored staircases, stripped them of function and directionality, reduced columns and beams to mere markers without structural meaning, and repeated, varied, and syntactically distributed the resulting emptied-out elements. Rem Koolhaas's Bibliothèque National de France (1989) carved uncanny egg-shaped and loop-the-loop rooms from an undifferentiated mass of book stacks, rendering obsolete previously known codes of use and inhabitation. His Agadir Hotel and Convention Center (1990) allowed the surrounding dune landscape to interject into the building and to be reflected to become the oppressive ceiling of its gigantic lobby. FOA's Virtual House (1997) developed a nonoriented topological diagram, the subtle inflection of its sectional geometry registering the effect of its own weight—a wink, directed at the venerable discipline of architecture. The unconscious collaboration of these agents of the inhuman has sustained the struggle of Gravity Zero Architecture, which is always in the making.

Setback

Despite what this lineage of strategies suggests, Gravity Zero Architecture is not just in pursuit of new effects. Nor is its goal to alienate for the sake of making itself felt. What passes for a set of resourceful tricks of architectural wizardry is in fact the result of organizational logics that draw their inputs from sources that exceed or viciously twist human body and site as their contexts of operation. The distortion, removal, and alienation of the context were historically the origin of Gravity Zero's phenomenology. The potency unleashed by recent developments in computation and complexity science, however, has had a stunning effect on Gravity Zero, which suddenly found itself empowered to expand its formal repertoire by recourse to the seductive concept of inflection. Exuberant new phyla of architectural artifacts (culturally speaking, canons) were bred through hyperindexical reference, often reintroducing the phenomenology of context through the back door. Complexity and continuous variation yielded formations with an ability to accept the influx of heteronomous forces: from moderation to decadence, from topography to topology, from smoothness to ruggedness, this variegated ecology of forms was concerned with the rhetorical incorporation of environmental forces. In this soft synchronization of universal forms and contingent conditions, globalization had found its trope. Having overcome the linguistic modes through which deconstruction had been assimilated—an attempt to destabilize the institutional forms of the received tradition of humanism by positing seemingly absurd, contradictory, or counterfactual organizations—parametricism became its eminent stylistic manifestation, and setback.

Singularity

In this context, the Generic Sublime runs along the Gravity Zero Architecture lineage, while accelerating it and recuperating its thrust toward the production of nonspecific singularities. No longer content with the capacity of the parametric to negotiate context and sow the seed for a universe of formal possibilities, its effort is now geared toward the refinement and orientation of the search process, so as to overcome the dualistic opposition between universality and contingency. The Generic Sublime forces previous architectural protocols into regimes of extreme abstraction that leave no room for any anthropomorphic representation of man or human institutions. It adheres to the condition of humanity's radical eccentricity and aims not to discard, or enter into, a dialectical negation of its inherited genetic material. It constructs historical continuities, avoiding the twin temptations of denial and retrogression that condemn culture to stagnation while distracting us with its pendular movements. For, otherwise, how difficult could it be to lead us to believe that the last two decades have been just a bad dream? The possibility to behave as if the threshold of complexity had never been crossed in contemporary culture is unsurprisingly alluring given the apparent difficulty of catching up and reprocessing history. Now we use software to design, but has anything else changed? It seems as if that splendid array of intellectual constructions that blossomed during the frenzied techno-cultural evolution taking place since the 1990s could be simply sidetracked and pigeonholed as new fields of expertise, declaring as "great" the diversification of the discipline while business continues to be conducted as usual. Indeed, it is always easier to forget or to ignore—and can one blame those who choose to do it? Frankly, it is a more benevolent environment for the development of practice, although not necessarily fruitful for attaining a project capable of breathing new life into architecture. But it is precisely that affirmation of life which constitutes the unmistakable ethics of the Generic Sublime.

Model

Resisting the impulse to turn its head from the windshield, the Generic Sublime leaves parametricism and its inflection behind as it abandons the entire rhetoric of negotiation. Computation had been conceptualized as a promising instrument with which to mediate between disparate interests, conjoin incongruent demands, facilitate dialogue, allow the resolution of legitimate yet conflicting concerns, or integrate data. Today, such promises have degraded into myths, able at most to sublate contradictory fragments into seamless compositions. Without cynicism, and deeply conscious of the historical role they have played, the Generic Sublime moves beyond those myths.

With procedural systematicity, technical consistency, and internal complexity as its *raison d'être*, the Generic Sublime's mode of engagement with its context can be defined as respectful local indifference. In the transformation of large swaths of urban territory, the Generic Sublime does not bow to or pay reverence toward external gravitational forces. Instead, its local indifference makes no assumptions or judgments about them. It does not recognize the value of precedents per se, nor does it revere communication unless the message is generic enough to be directed to the totality of the field of reception. Rather than striving for formal convergence and continuity, local indifference affirms autonomy, individuality, and performance. The Generic Sublime is the ultimate architectural regime of the multitude: an organization whose existence presupposes shared linguistic, cultural, and genetic codes from which it can only deviate in search of highly sophisticated, separate, and individualistic forms of consistency. Divergent, multifarious, and expansive, its über-urbanity exploits the material seamlessness that is characteristic of infrastructure to allow its parts the maximum degree of autonomy while they converge into a (tragic) whole.

Cutting its ties to its surroundings, the Generic Sublime nonetheless requires a driver for its highly differentiated body in its quest for singularity. What this means is simply that its reliance on the conceptual is more evident, if not more decisive, than that of its predecessor regimes. The Generic Sublime needs a richly interconnected cultural medium in order to thrive, for it has to import information from domains not readily accessible to an empirical survey. In that sense, it promises to become a truly accomplished form of posturban—even postnational—architectural sensibility. Which may amount to nothing less than a new incarnation of classicism.

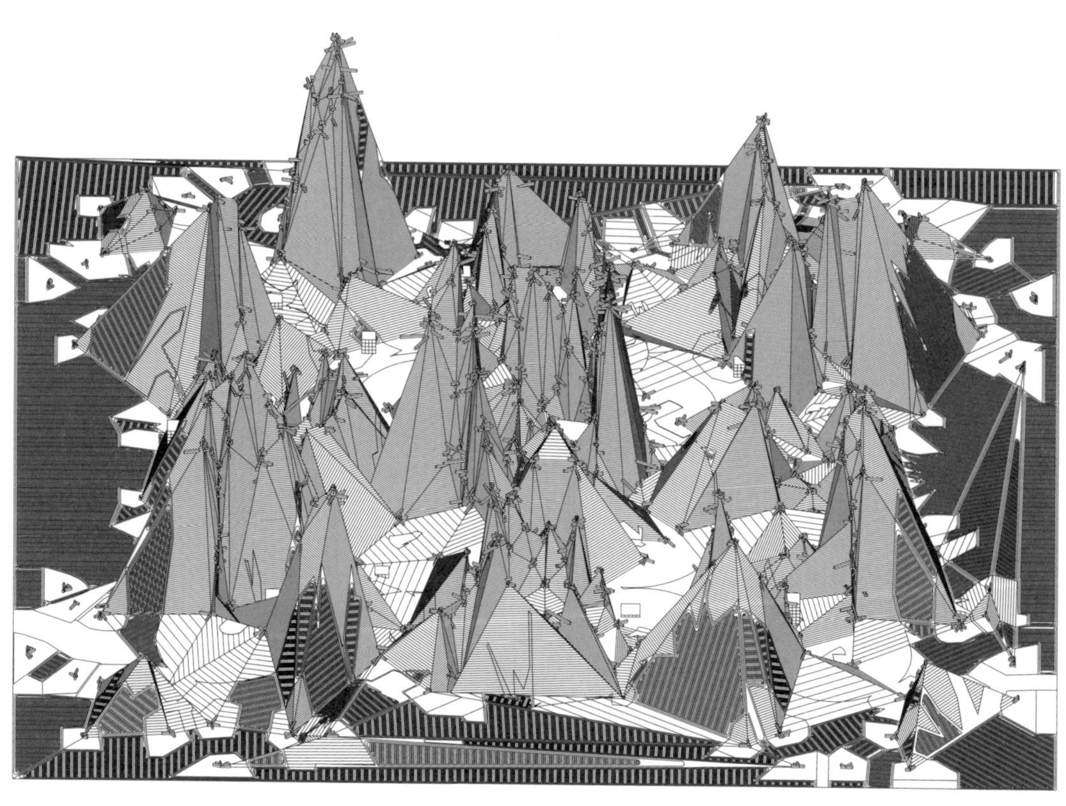

Worlds of Their Own

Ciro Najle

Currency, or the Fundamental Inevitability of the Generic

One step at a time and unwearyingly: this is how the Generic Sublime is constructed. Start by earnestly assuming and embracing the generic. This enlightened concept comes to architecture, as if naturally, through modernism and projects itself as the default condition of any contemporary architectural theory which holds that the ethical mindset and ideological framework of the discipline necessarily rest on architecture's universal capacity to generate transformation. Formed along the deterministic lineage, the generic comprises an all-encompassing organizational state in which adaptation to the contingent is seamlessly suppressed in favor of blankness and neutrality. This allegedly pure state is structured around the total erasure of hierarchies and the supremacy of homogeneity and repetition, and is characterized by indifference in tone, apathy in character, and insipidness in expression. Here, the classical premises of permanence, endurance, severity, and ubiquity in architecture are paradoxically refreshed through a model of total flexibility.

Profoundly embedded in the radical spirit of the modern, this genealogy feeds on the belief that the normal is that which lacks difference. Any gradual variation or qualitative diversity is carefully flattened. Any form of difference is melted away and reduced to plain quantity. Any nuance is either upgraded as indispensable and turned into a structural constituent of a building or deemed disturbing and disregarded as a superfluous extravagance. The generic claims a one-to-one correspondence between means and ends, perpetuating this claim by aligning the two through an automatism that restrains the unpredictable and sieves discontinuities, forcing them to appear absent. Collateral effects magically evaporate against the endless uniformity of organizations. The generic promises to contain uncertainties within a void of information so that the disorderly, unsustainable, and damaging consequences that they may bring into a system are barred in advance. The generic confines problems in the effort to prevent them from taking form: that is, until a threshold is exceeded and the normative system in place suddenly collapses.

Yet, until such a threshold is met, the generic appears as a second nature: a self-explanatory worldview that presents the full equivalence between a set of positive values and the concrete ways in which these values are articulated in an organization. The generic camouflages these values behind ever-new forms of the self-evident, by which the normal paradoxically perpetuates itself through imperceptible changes. This is its implacable force, its persuasive capacity, and the target of its reason: to incarnate the real as if it were obvious. The generic is a machine for the preservation of the same, at every turn taking on a new, advanced form. The carefully concealed paradox of permanence and change harmoniously holds the seeds for each potential update, which is only actualized when indispensable, favorable, or convenient, appearing as the by-product of progress.

By means of this self-contradictory mechanism, the generic evolves as an ever-renewed form of currency, growing in compliance and pliability via the exclusion of the other and the sedimentation of the superfluous from the essential. What constitutes this essence, and how it can be turned technically workable so that its omissions become assertive, remains impenetrable. In the underbelly of the generic resides a perpetual mystery.

Protocols, or the Explosive Peculiarity of the Normal

Protocols configure the abstract medium within which generic organizations are engineered and through which they establish their standards of normality. Protocols mediate between otherwise unconstrained systems and manage their potentially disruptive effects by ensuring that system behaviors are balanced and remain stable over time under predictable conditions. Protocols inherently set the variables of system fluctuation, rationalize their ranges of performance, and regulate their relationships, thereby guaranteeing the overall stability of operational and ethical frameworks. In generic organizations, where systems are reduced to an absolute minimum in terms of quantity and complexity, protocols enforce a minimum of variability. Zero is their ultimate condition. This standard is globally assumed as a search for—and an idealization of—invariance. Although far from natural, invariants are regarded as a given and create an atmosphere of demonstrability, the seemingly solid logic of which can never be questioned as there is nothing outside with which to challenge it.

In spite of this ideological conundrum, no matter how generic an organization is, or how invariable it appears, its composition is irreducible to pure nothingness. It must continually exorcize thresholds and negotiate boundaries to remain controlled. Suppression and inhibition drive problems away: the less the variety and variability of systems in an organization, the tighter its order and the farther afield its unwanted states. Yet curiously, the tighter these principles are, the higher the organization's global propensity toward radical change becomes. This is the basis for the double radicality of the generic. On the one hand, difference is profoundly exacerbated precisely by the implausible attempt to reduce it: the less the difference is, the more passionate that difference becomes. On the other hand, as the threat that operates as the primal condition of existence in the generic increasingly tightens, its potential tragedy actually strengthens: the more reductive the organization, the higher the danger of its breakdown. Intensity and tension concur behind the veil of organizational invariance.

Organizational wisdom here can be associated not so much with the primal will of a generic organization toward nothingness but with the cautious management of power relationships between difference and indifference, which, guided by conservatism and absoluteness, either administers or increases the potential for accidents that might escalate in impact through deviations, fissures, and fractures. Protocols are thus driven by the goal of reducing power relationships to zero, but more importantly, of compensating their imbalances. Yet it is precisely through this dual endeavor that generic organizations load themselves, consciously or unconsciously, with potentially volatile forces. Consequently, the normal works not merely as a barrier to the dysfunctional but as the very device that handles its potential energy. Control confines undesirable difference inasmuch as it holds latent transformation, the power of which is liberated as soon as an organization reaches its limits of performance: no sooner, and no later.

Rather than celebrating, fearing, invoking, or disregarding these confined forces, the whole territory that results from their inhibition and suppression must be claimed as the ultimate space of work for architecture. This tight, often invisible, but extremely fertile space must be engaged without moralistic faith in its promise, regulated without blind belief in its efficacy, contained without fear of the other, managed without anxiety toward the well ordered, and secured without gravity. Its embedded, self-escalating potential is a matter of serious irresponsibility.

Alienation, or the Insatiable Escalation of Difference

It is well known that, when far from equilibrium, systems acquire unpredictable behaviors of their own, rendering cause-and-effect relationships irreversible. What is not equally clear is how to arrive at this state of nonlinearity steadily and progressively, and how to artificially embed its outcomes in the process of managing difference: how to come in and out of this state with suppleness, and how to stay within it in an untroubled, creative manner. Similarly, while it is known that the irreversibility of this process breeds ineffable conditions, as if magically, within organizations, it is not apparent in advance how these conditions can be controlled, nor what specific opportunities they will bring about. As a consequence it becomes comfortable to fall back on simplifications and mystifications at a discursive level, and to build apparatuses of indeterminacy at an operative one. How to engender machines to nurture desirable (rather than merely surprising) qualitative shifts out of common conditions remains elusive.

It is therefore decisive to refrain from jumping too rapidly into simplistic oppositions, taking positions on one side or the other. The inner creativity of protocols lies in the possibility of delaying automatisms by slowly deviating their instructions, betraying initial premises precisely through that slowness. Switching a rationale can happen by registering variability and breeding seepages out of linear patterns. Variability, in turn, results from systematizing nuances, and this follows from the understanding that any deviation is a potential propensity. Shades in patterns are constituted by a multiplicity of trends, and these have to be dissected, one from the other, and activated. It could even be said that the tone of a generic organization, no matter how pure or detached it pretends to be, lies in how these trends are integrated in an unknown but already latent behavior. That is the mood of the generic: its disposition to become something else.

Constituents can be broken down and filtered at a preconceptual level, creating a plane of consistency out of what at first appears insipid. Properties can be intuited at once, either from the common understanding that generic organizations carry, or from the image that they project, or simply from the traces of sympathy that they broadly entertain. Deviations lie at the core of gradations, and this is where a customary but explicit sensibility becomes a precise but open-ended sensitivity. Once deviations are identified and decoded, protocols shift from operating as switches in a rigid control panel to working as tools in a platform through which an entirely artificial behavior may unfold. Through the radical intensification of variation and its continuous escalation to extreme conditions, material determinations, organizational constraints, and even norms start speaking in foreign tongues, shouting out precise curves and rhythms and bursting with ingenious conditions: the utmost emerges out of the regular; the unspeakable, out of the common; the indefinable, out of the well known.

There is no need to induce indeterminacy as an external force: detecting unsettled states, preliminary deviations, unresolved errors, indistinct voices, hesitations, and vague zones is sufficiently disruptive. The minimum angle of declination is a potential line of fugue, a route to noise. Far from being the linear outcome of progress, novelty is a whole other form of order by which systems consistently self-alienate. By thoroughly following their fault lines and by actively systematizing their variation, organizations differentiate into what they latently contained but had failed to acknowledge.

Novelty, or the Singular out of the Generic

This second form of order does not necessarily imply a desire for indeterminacy but, more generally, a drive toward a higher level of organizational intelligence. The systematic management of difference allows an organization to overcome the status whereby, in order to endure, it must frantically eradicate difference. Furthermore, a higher-level organization emancipates itself not only from the association of order with uniformity but, more importantly, from the underlying opposition between order and difference, now denaturalized. This emancipation does not simply contradict the affirmative logic of its predecessor but constructs the plane within which its inner creativity snowballs and bursts.

Once potentials are detoured out of the neutral ground within which they lie in latency, generic systems grow weird, perverse, even hilarious, and overwhelm themselves. Difference is steered by agitation and change rather than concealed by desperation and suppression. Willfulness becomes will, determination becomes desire: generic organizations, in this advanced, empowered form, do not exclude variety or propagate sameness but align variations and synthesize change. Nuances encounter patterns where former irregularities become trends with hierarchies, which, progressively stronger, eventually acquire structural status, not only taking over the ethos of naturalized homogeneity but also constructing new qualities and more advanced performances.

Unlike the mild idea of variation operating as an inflection within a continuum of repetition, qualitative differences configure distinct forms out of the continuum of variation in which they dwell, thus introducing a change in the system's overall logic. These are not mere peculiarities, motifs, or undulations in an otherwise insipid background that eventually remains the same. They are not merely adjectives or enhancing traits. Beyond such mannerisms, these differences actually make a difference: they raise the status of variation to a new form of value, which they identify for themselves and outline as an affirmative rationale. A whole judgment criterion is lifted up from convention and acquires a form. A context of relevance is created anew.

Yet, inasmuch as variation does not assure by itself the alienation of values, the value system that it nurtures does not simply derive, as if naturally, from the deviation of concealed nuances as such. A variation manifold requires the parallel consolidation of a platform onto which to put at play the rationalization of these newly acquired structures of order. This platform and this structure—this form—involve the use of difference not only as a means of nourishing forces but also as the medium for the substantiation of a higher level of organizational thinking, which itself exerts forces. Novelty therefore does not just emancipate an organization from its generic ground but redefines at its root what the generic virtually is: a source of new types of order for architecture.

And while, at a basic level, generic organizations can still be seen as primitive devices of reduction, at higher levels they operate as forms of knowledge that persist while betraying themselves. By recognizing and escalating internal differences, generic organizations acquire multifariousness without loosing any of their integrity. The generic overcomes several thresholds in this process, each time encountering new challenges and solving them by heightening their very notion of order, thus growing in multivalence as a whole. The model of generality based in nonspecificity and indifference progressively shifts into one of overspecificity and multiplicity: the singular evolves out of the generic.

Uniqueness, or the Irresistible Ubiquity of the Singular

No opposites here, and a single way out: forward, with greater complexity. The will for robust forms of order expands the spectrum of disparateness and incompatibility that generic organizations are capable of integrating. Through this, the generic overcomes the illusion of flexibility grounded in organizational neutrality and formlessness to project new forms of imagination. Singularized, it still preserves its conventional ground, but it also constructs forms of value that transcend its assumptions. What is at stake here is no longer a model that segregates generalities and individuations, norms and cases, rules and samples, systems and versions: these are brought together in a single, persuasive model characterized by the vitality and wealth of architectural form, the performative multifariousness of which coincides with their formal irresistibility.

During the past decades, much has been said about differentiation, but little has been settled in terms of constructing more advanced forms of value by its own means. The rhetoric of difference has been encapsulated within an unrestricted gymnastic of form, with little discussion about the role of complex form as a model of knowledge. If architectural technique simply rejects thought and withdraws into a realm of over-technified formalism and free-floating speculation (both of which misinterpret experimentation as mere exploration and turn research into a commodity), then it only reinforces the conditions for reactionary discourses to arise and for escapades into form as entertainment to endlessly multiply, further deteriorating the disciplinary scene and depleting its cultural authority. Various retreats into superficial forms of ideology, excursions into allegedly urgent architectural concerns, or regressions into formal palettes of the recent past are assumed to circumvent this vacuum. Decorative declinations, shortcuts into figuration, and self-mystifying theories are adopted as blind and self-destructive (albeit delightful) getaways to form-making for its own sake. In the midst of this explosive but fundamentally vulnerable panorama (the significance of which remains vague), the generic resets a discussion about the problematic integration of architectural theory and form, where each simultaneously grows and respectively overcomes its ideological or conventional premises without creating, as a consequence, a representational gap.

The singular status of the generic conceptualizes differentiation as it happens, without straightjacketing its openness but without falling into a discursive void either. For this, formal variables are tightly associated with performance-driven aptitudes, convention-oriented restrictions, and organization-related accountabilities, so that their meaning is not detached from the rational frameworks on which they rest. Differentiation understood as a formal construction grounded on organization differs radically from both the visual hedonism and the technocratic optimization of form we frequently find within practice and academia today. The differentiation process is neither an update of form-finding methods nor an advanced form of technology: instead, it is a thorough procedure designed to breed organization and engender new forms of the real. Neither a poignant icon nor a memorable statement, the singular—in its uniqueness and irreducibility—perfectly coincides with the extensive and ubiquitous vision of the generic. Architectural knowledge is potentiated by artificially constructing archetypes out of this coincidence, capable of engaging other fields, times, and scales out of specific disciplinary principles and figures, which architecture cannot risk relinquishing. The inverse of the interdisciplinary is not autonomy but rather the construction of new forms of the disciplinary.

Metatypes, or the Amoral Nature of Multiplicities

If under extreme differentiation the generic first encounters and then constructs for itself the status of the singular, the multiplication of these singularities stimulates the advent of the sublime. By operating in the context of building collectives, the latent differences that are contained in generic organizations not only deviate and escalate upward, through the unfolding of nuances in protocols and the construction of rules of differentiation, but also vibrate horizontally, through the proliferation of transversal relationships between protocols of organizations in principle autonomous and segregated. These reverberating relationships, in turn, not only endorse internal exchanges, configure articulated hierarchies, and calibrate the adaptation of the organization to the environment but also challenge the discreteness of internal, individual building entities, short-circuiting their organizations and establishing direct exchanges between their performances and figurations. Well beyond collage and its estranging effect as an architectural technique, such vibration between otherwise unrelated protocols introduces informational promiscuity and radical change at an organizational level. Here we have both diverged from modernism's willful ethics of transformation and bypassed the rhetoric of its ideological critique, thus overcoming the sterile opposition of the two.

Collective organizations introduce the unprecedented potential of a self-constructed, self-instantiated, and self-determined architecture. When participating at large scale—be it of the site, the urban, the natural, the infrastructural, or the territorial—architecture has traditionally exhibited an aptitude for crossbreeding. Historically evident and to a large extent ethically forceful, this aptitude has commonly been overshadowed by discussions of context, the city, the landscape, the network, or the region—all of which are alternately regarded as the natural purview of architecture. Often idiosyncratic and even deviant, these transversal relationships have been continually acknowledged and embraced, but only when socially necessary, aesthetically pleasing, or morally important—that is, when understood as the inherent preconditions of architectural goodness in response to the environment. Yet frequently these large-scale forms fail to create challenging or stimulating individuations, blinded as they are by the will to assure agreeable spatial situations, historically appropriate types, and common architectural verbiage, and focused as they are on smoothing out the frictions unfairly exerted over buildings.

What recent large-scale architectural typologies have brought into this panorama is the challenge for architecture to overcome its allegedly essential impulse toward goodness by amorally integrating these externalities into new forms of building collectives: clusters, sets, and series of large buildings; agglomerations of disparate formations, wild encounters of types, incorporations of types within types, accumulations of incompatible forms, dramatic changes of scale, and unnatural enlargements of structures; internalizations of public space, open space, or landscapes; unexpected infrastructural formats; unusually long, super-tall, or extra-fat buildings; superblocks, fat-mattresses, and porous, spongy, hollow, terraced building masses; building-like urban districts, purpose-built landscapes, expansive performance sheds housing stations, airports, or parking lots; and so many other massing or organizational variants. Within such aberrant agglomerations and weird coexistences, buildings are not only driven to nicely resolve their relationship to externalities but also compelled to create mediums to embrace these externalities and integrate their multiplicity into a new kind of architectural form.

The Virtual Megalomania of the Generic Sublime

To push generic organizations away from the mandate of nonspecificity and toward greater organizational intelligence—away from the concealment of differences under homogeneous conditions and toward the construction of singularities that turn difference into a source of robustness—and then urge them to integrate the diversity of the many within the complexity of the one: this is the virtual megalomania of the Generic Sublime. At this second stratum of differentiation, the escalation of difference into singular organizations becomes of a completely different order, where the need for adaptation and endurance develops into a will toward magnanimousness and expansiveness. Here, in order to adapt to external conditions, systems dare to put in jeopardy the very possibility of their global sustenance, assuming evolution as an inner force rather than a simple condition of survival. Multiplicity, architecture's contemporary expression of the classical striving toward ubiquity, thus overcomes the limited framework of sheer systemic convenience and finally embraces the full potentiality of the singular—architecture's contemporary manifestation of its classical desire of transcendence. The Generic Sublime is a multiplicity-thing: a miniature extra-extra-large organization that belongs to no site, projects its logic into any site, and is itself a site.

The sublimation of the generic results from escalating contingencies two times over: first, to the status of a singularity, and second, to the status of a multiplicity. The Generic Sublime is an amusing form of absoluteness: a non-oppressive whole characterized by the alliance between the one and the many. Both blank and voluptuous, severe and indulgent, the Generic Sublime is a trans-systemic organization with endless systemic reverberations and a nonfigurative cultural imprint. Often characterized by hugeness and a coarse symmetry, it is blunt and fragile, crude and sophisticated, robust and delicate. The Generic Sublime is a friendly monster, shy and perplexing, tender and horrifying, bold and sensitive, grandiloquent and naive. It is spatially and systemically high-minded, even spiritual, in its organization. Its amoral ethics—an ethics completely beyond purpose—is grounded on turning problems into advantages—or miracles—where systemic redundancy becomes organizational generosity.

Within the Generic Sublime, exceptionally incompatible components—mismatched typologies, clusters of elevator cores, multiple circulation loops, branches, and shortcuts, manifolds of embedded artificial landscapes, abyssal private interiors, highly assorted infrastructural modes, unpleasantly explicit technologies, abstract territorial figures, cartoonish motifs, and eccentric ecologies—coexist in a three-dimensional armature with a slippery aesthetic. It formulates a mindset of believable implausibility, exploiting the logic of commercial benefit to project hyper-real forms of the far-fetched. The Generic Sublime is not attached to any prejudice (let alone an *architectural* one): instead it projects forms and tones of judgment of its own, the very ground zero of its models. The escalation of difference is here literally a process of building up complexity until it reaches a critical mass of turbulent austerity, whose timeless appearance is the consequence of merging virtual consistency with literal structure.

The Generic Sublime is a self-indulged form of order, steeped in cultural resonances but ultimately unfamiliar. It brings a less-shock-and-more-awe plan to the globalized world, which it assumes as a second nature and onto which it projects its horrifying yet inoffensive image. With the resolution of a tragedy, it formulates models beyond the paradigm of robustness and away from the paradigm of indeterminacy.

One or Many Models

The Generic Sublime surpasses the prototypical condition of the generic and amasses a self-standing model. This model overwhelms the very limits of the discipline and illuminates other realms of culture without jeopardizing its disciplinary specificity. Generic Sublime models are structured architectural multiplicities that rigorously approximate unknowable futures, each time with a specific set of principles and tools, and each time with a newly persuasive prospect.

Sublime because of their innocent appearance of dominance, these models do not merely analyze, reproduce, or simulate phenomena but build a supra-reality that is only describable through grandiose architectural means operating as an otherness to the real—the utmost expression of the difference-within of its generic predecessors. Generic Sublime models do not evoke forms of anticipation or fiction as much as they amalgamate the oscillating logics of differentiation, singularization, and sublimation of the ordinary. They contain systematic methods that, although precise and communicable, are not moralizing or didactic and cannot be extrapolated without being redefined at their core.

The techniques of the Generic Sublime do not make claims for universality; nor do they aspire to being all encompassing, extensive, or unbiased. And yet, the ad hoc condition of the Generic Sublime does not preclude its knowledge from being translatable to other disciplines. It is precisely the irreducibility of the nonlinear that is capable of propagating the notion of generality in architecture (redefined beyond mechanical reproducibility) outward, albeit without giving up its disciplinary specificity. The very notion of the architectural model (an abstract construct embedded in buildings and capable of transcending the limits of the disciplinary) radically explodes. Without losing its wider applicability (what makes a model a model), it resists reducing its values and standards to automatizing means and predicting outcomes. Instead, it upgrades them to a regime of the ineffable, where rules are precise but upshots appear as unique.

Therefore, Generic Sublime models do not disseminate allegedly neutral methodologies in the traditionally modern way but radiate singular method-forms in the plural. Their generality is ingrained in their overspecificity, and their canon is not rooted in objectivity but in a particular form of persuasion and belief. Their rationale consists of the vicissitudes of their modalities, and their orthodoxy is constructed on their irreducibility to premises. This plurality does not fragment knowledge but rather obscures its figures and elevates its effects, thus freeing it from the straightjacket of mere commonsensical understanding.

The virtual megalomania of the Generic Sublime is, at its core, the candid way in which architectural imagination takes reason by force. Its earnestness should not be seen as a moral but rather as a way in which a consciously infantile worldview recognizes in everything—no matter how absurd, how constrained, or how dull—the potential to become a model. This worldview cannot but be literal and rigorous, these being its operative preconditions. Architecture unassumingly confronts itself with its most ancient dream: changing the world by means of a moving representation. The miniature-like appearance of Generic Sublime models, frightening but innocent, gigantic but shy, is nothing but the unaffected expression of this simple yet extraordinary fact.

Flickering Grandeur, or the Materialism of Wonder

The grandeur of the Generic Sublime inevitably flickers candidness, and that is its ultimate force. It radiates self-contradiction, absurdity, inoffensiveness, pomposity, excess, naivety, and comedy. It launches new forms of humor. This is how it overcomes both the rigid, insipid mandate of neutrality and the benign and ultimately dull mandate of robustness with a well-mannered and cold-blooded paradigm. This is also how the setting aside of indeterminacy opens up the space for a sharper political agenda. Call it mood: mood of the many-in-one that tempers the world with a blunt stimulation; mood that paints the world with its own colors and permeates a peculiar feel; mood that creates the conditions for an unsolicited change.

Beyond the poignancy of images, the Generic Sublime sparks its inner force along a multitude of microscopic transformations. In other eras, such as the Baroque, and in other domains of culture, such as functional music, artists have achieved this level of ubiquity where the conditions of production by themselves empower artistic practices beyond the threshold of social relevance and impel them into the realm of pure and direct emotion. By boldly deserting correctness and embracing higher forms of creativity, by compulsively assigning success to apparently banal outcomes and feeding their achievements back into the standards of production (instead of censuring their lack of criticality), the scope of the practice expands without losing specificity. Through the rapid proliferation of the mechanisms of generation, the imagery of the discipline becomes effervescent, escalating into the frantic realm of the Generic Sublime. At such speed and scale, architectural imagination vibrates to such a level that capturing it within teleological discourses becomes not only flawed but also insufficient. Its impact on thought becomes, in this context, inevitable and almost natural. It seems incredible that increasing the rate of oscillation in and out of the generic can construct singular forms of architectural will so threatening and so liberating. Even harder to accept is that these singularities, simply constructed through an excess of consistency, invent a rationale of their own and project this rationale onto the world.

The Generic Sublime constitutes a class of order in which the regimes of organizational complexity have been embedded in architectural procedure to the point where the most banal intelligence merges with the highest of emotions. This condition is beyond the meltdown of discourse and does not critically stop in the midst of this danger. Rather, it uses this danger as a liminal condition within which the practice acquires access to today's forms of the absolute, invoking not just the transformation of the real but its sublimation in an architectural object. Architecture's slowness here becomes an invaluable asset, as it overcomes the sheer consumption of the energy that nurtures it by means of the meticulous singularization of the passion that it inexorably unfolds. Continuity with the real is thus taken to a threshold of intense discontinuity, where the ruthless dynamic of developmental phenomena—huge, rapid, excessive, multiple, incongruent, and overtly generic—breeds, at its climax, the conditions for the appearance of a new architectural phenomenon. The Generic Sublime—the regime of the extraordinary out of the ordinary—once again opens up a space for optimism (nowadays a curiously underrated artistic force) through a materialism of wonder.

Generic Sublime Forms

Project **John Hancock Center, Chicago, IL, USA, 1970**
Architect **Skidmore, Owings & Merrill**
Site area: 9,661 sqm
Gross floor area: 260,128 sqm
Maximum building height: 344 m
www.som.com/projects/john_hancock_center

Blank icon. Scaleless, formally contained, primeval super-skyscraper, with a square plan, linearly diminishing as it goes up to form a truncated pyramid. Deep black glass facades with an obscured floor rhythm, barely distinguishable mechanical floors, and a flattened cross-bracing skin frame. Set back behind a shallow public plaza crater, four lobbies interconnected through a tortuous ground-level commercial area, with four points of access. Interior observatory at top, with bar, restaurant, and a theatrical view of the lake.

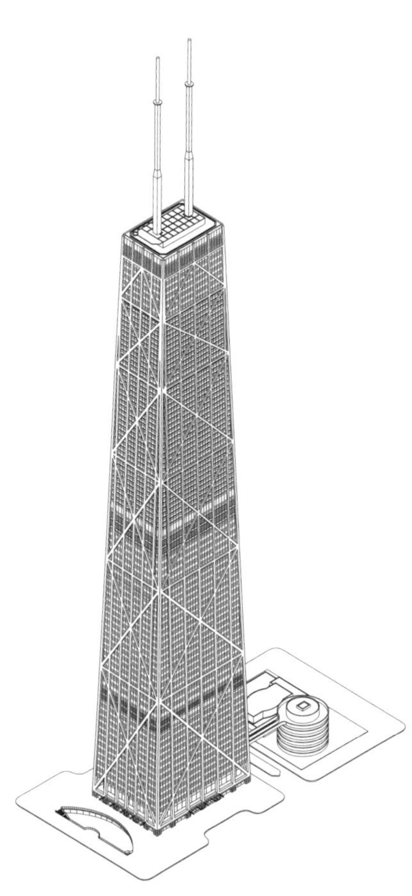

Project **Willis (Sears) Tower, Chicago, IL, USA, 1974**
Architect **Skidmore, Owings & Merrill**
Site area: 12,140 sqm
Gross floor area: 413,961 sqm
Maximum building height: 442 m
www.som.com/projects/willis_tower_formerly_sears_tower

Stepped skyscraper or pack of adjacent slender towers. Irregularly pyramidal, tubular tower manifold resulting from the upward extraction of modules from a nine-square-grid plan. Variable floor plan around a central core with multiple elevators. Double-height mechanical services, double-antenna rooftop. Lateral setback plaza, frontal sculpture garden, triple-level retail interior plaza, attached semicylindrical public lobby, and office entry esplanade with cantilevered canopy.

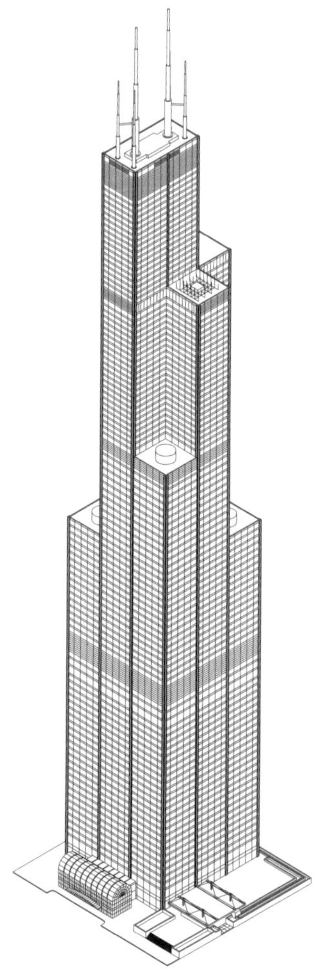

Project **Jin Mao Tower, Shanghai, China, 1999**
Architect **Skidmore, Owings & Merrill**
Site area: 23,257 sqm
Gross floor area: 287,000 sqm
Maximum building height: 421 m
www.som.com/projects/jin_mao_tower

Fat super-skyscraper with an exponentially striated skin, containing stacked, independent interior organizations. Square plan, octagonal central core, perimetral columns, regularly distributed mechanical levels, dense stainless-steel curtain wall. Six-story podium, attached entry canopy, landscaped open-air courtyard, encircling reflecting pool. Crown roof with spire top, sky hotel lobby, cylindrical atrium with double spiral interior balconies. Business offices, conference centers, public parking, mall, ballrooms, meeting rooms, restaurants, bars, clubs, fitness centers, swimming pools, spas, cinemas, and exhibition halls.

Project **One World Trade Center, New York, NY, USA, 2014**
Architect **Skidmore, Owings & Merrill**
Site area: 6,905 sqm
Gross floor area: 325,160 sqm
Maximum building height: 541 m
www.som.com/projects/one_world_trade_center

Single, fat tower above a massive memorial ground. Tall office tower with square base, rotated square top, and variations of octagonal plans transitioning between the two. Reflective curtain wall envelope forming eight elongated triangular facets, shimmering. Service core at center, evacuation cores at corners, chamfered edges. Cubic embedded plinth with concrete wall and glass fins. Four axial lobby accesses, gallery and event spaces, public ground surface, memorial plaza, underground transport connectivity. Central broadcasting antenna, sky lobby, observation deck, shops, kiosks, restaurants, cafes, and bars.

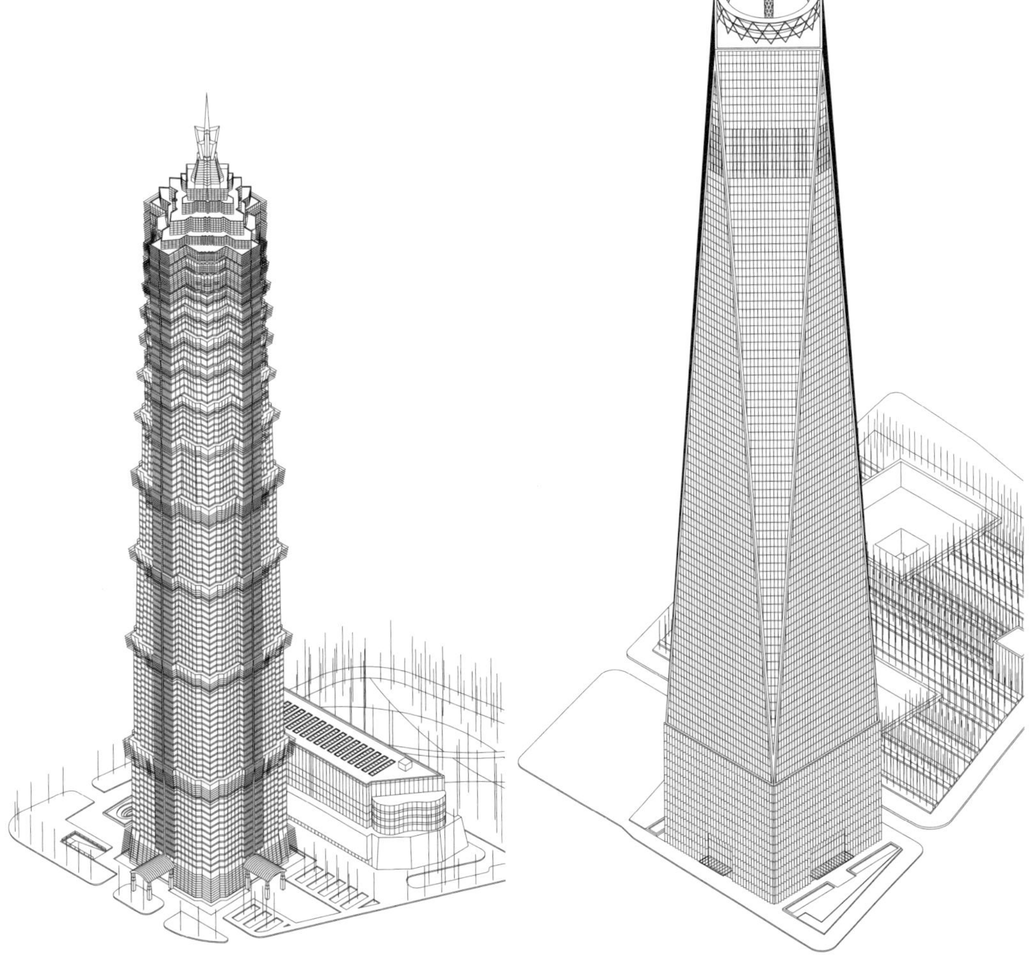

Project **Hyatt Regency Hotel, San Francisco, CA, USA, 1973**
Architect **John Portman & Associates**
Site area: 7,804 sqm
Gross floor area: 80,210 sqm
Maximum building height: 77 m
en.wikipedia.org/wiki/Hyatt_Regency_San_Francisco

Atrium shell on a plinth. Wedge-shaped, deep-plan, hollow building consisting of L-shaped, medium-height bars and a terraced stack, broken in plan along the diagonal. Central semipyramidal atrium, cylindrical observation deck at top corner. Elevated hotel lobby, interior public plaza, bullet elevator core, cantilevered interior balconies, linear skylight. Ground-floor double-height access lobby, plinth with ballrooms, meeting rooms, exhibition halls, and event spaces, publicly accessible roof garden, and private basement parking. Shops, kiosks, restaurants, cafes, fitness centers, and gyms.

Project **Marriott Marquis Hotel, Atlanta, GA, USA, 1985**
Architect **John Portman & Associates**
Site area: 14,569 sqm
Gross floor area: 162,580 sqm
Maximum building height: 51 m
www.portmanusa.com/en/projects/hospitality/atlanta-marriott-marquis-hotel/

Gradually opening, blown-up building bar on prismatic podium. Dry, repetitive exterior and rich, voluptuous atrium interior, transitioning from rectangular to elliptical in plan. Podium-level ballrooms, meeting rooms, conference centers, restaurants, cafes, swimming pools, and exhibition halls. Recessed rooms with regular floor depth. Mid-height, maximally recessed conference lobby. Cylindrical concrete core with bullet elevators and filleted diagonal bridges. Inner vertical garden, sky-lit roof, and ground-level drop-off roundabout.

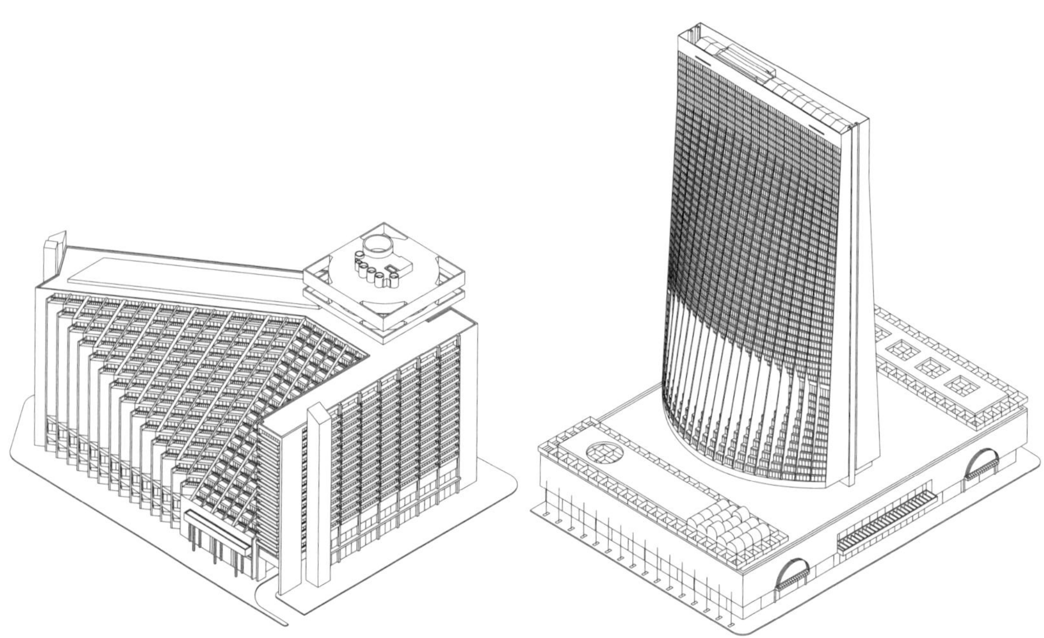

Project **Hyatt Regency Hotel, Atlanta, GA, USA, 1967**
Architect **John Portman & Associates**
Site area: 7,774 sqm
Gross floor area: 75,976 sqm
Maximum building height: 95 m
www.portmanusa.com/en/projects/hospitality/hyatt-regency-atlanta/

Cubic cloister of displaced building bars around a cubic interior atrium. Variegated commercial plinth containing stores, kiosks, meeting rooms, restaurants, cafes, fitness centers, and outdoor pools, adjoined by a low ballroom shed and parking structure. Repetitive concrete modular facade with recessed hotel interiors. Colossal interior, histrionically traversed by a cylindrical battery of bullet elevators. Roof of crisscrossing skylights, crowned by semispherical, monumentalizing rotating restaurant. Artificially landscaped balconies and stay areas lubricating the dry atrium.

Project **Marriott Marquis Hotel, New York, NY, USA, 1985**
Architect **John Portman & Associates**
Site area: 6,880 sqm
Gross floor area: 171,390 sqm
Maximum building height: 175 m
en.wikipedia.org/wiki/New_York_Marriott_Marquis

Manhattan block with two parallel hotel bars and a central, vertically receding atrium containing shops, restaurants, and cafes. Greenhouse sky-lobby bridges, cylindrical central core with bullet elevators. Eight-level buffer podium with conference rooms, large axial ballroom, semicylindrical stage, and urban billboard. Artificially lit, free-plan plaza on ground level with vehicular access and drop-off area. Horizontally striated longitudinal volumes framing a central, stepped glass facade. Rotating restaurant above.

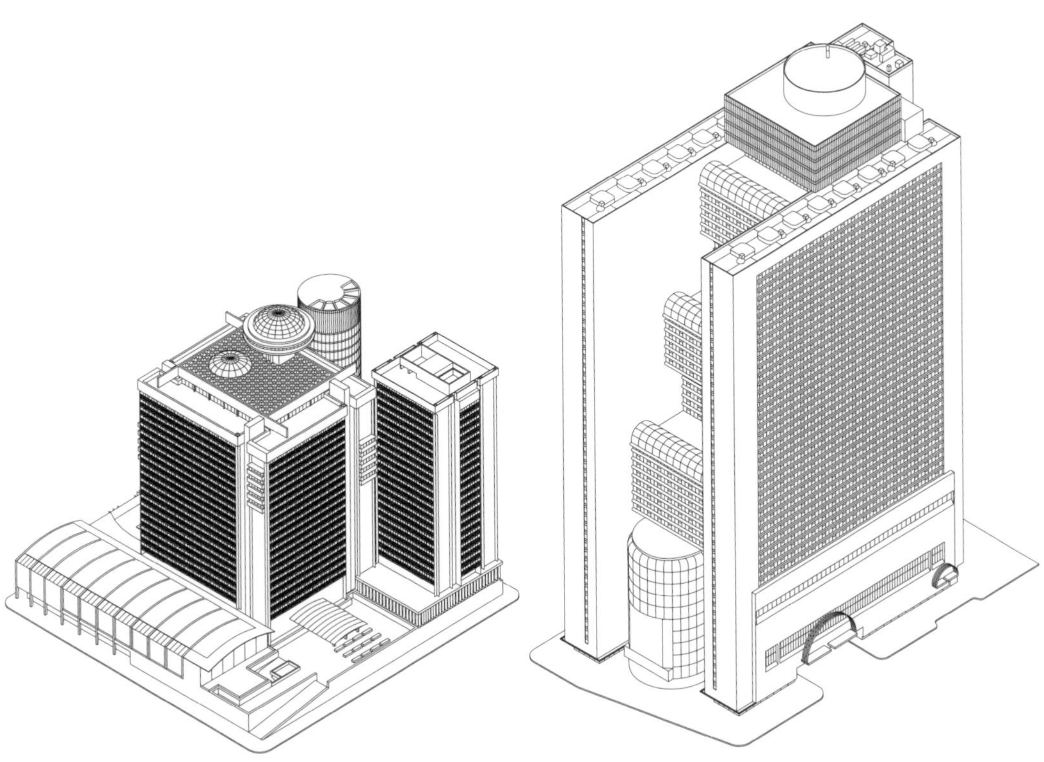

Project **World Trade Center, New York, NY, USA, 1973**
Architect **Minoru Yamasaki Associates**
Site area: 68,796 sqm
Gross floor area: 1,114,836 sqm
Maximum building height: 530 m
www.archdaily.com/504682/ad-classics-world-trade-center-minoru-yamasaki-associates-emery-roth-and-sons

Cluster of two super-tall towers, three low-rise office buildings, one mid-rise linear building bar, and one off-site mid-rise building, monumentally distributed as an open cloister around a grand, square plaza above an underground commercial and infrastructural basement. Twin towers with square plan, chamfered corners, and narrow vertical openings in a tube-frame structural system. Double-height ground floor lobby and two mechanical, elevator-transfer sky lobbies. Open office plan with central, multiple-battery core. Restaurants, stores, observation decks, museums, and exhibition halls.

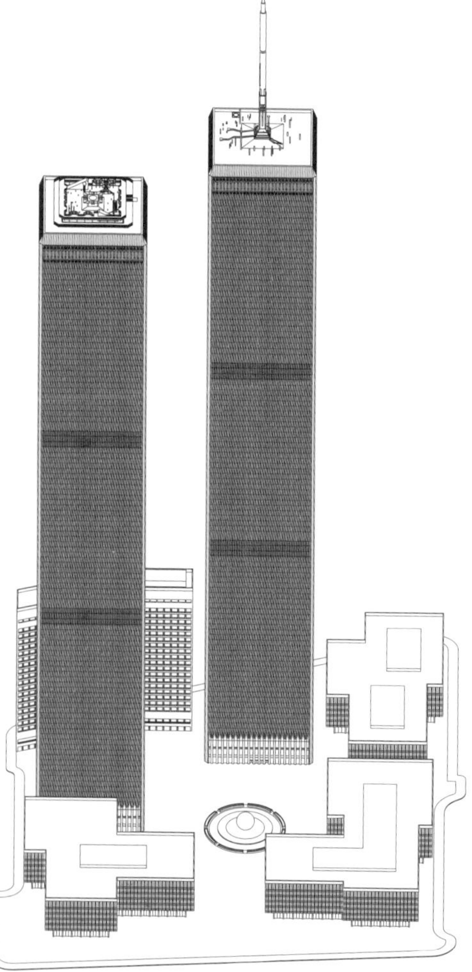

Project **Petronas Towers, Kuala Lumpur, Malaysia, 1997**
Architect **Pelli Clarke Pelli Architects**
Site area: 57,263 sqm
Gross floor area: 341,760 sqm
Maximum building height: 452 m
www.pcparch.com/project/petronas-towers

Twin cylindrical office towers symmetrically organized along a local urban axis. Corrugated circular perimeter configured by an eight-pointed star plan with alternating rounded protuberances maximizing compactness and exposure. Formal autonomy of towers, consolidated through telescopic setbacks, horizontal cladding, and sphere-needle antennas, and tensioned by a slim sky pedestrian bridge, an atrium-mall plinth with cultural institutions, two appendicular, cylindrical conference-center towers flanking the set, and exhibition halls following the overall axial urban design.

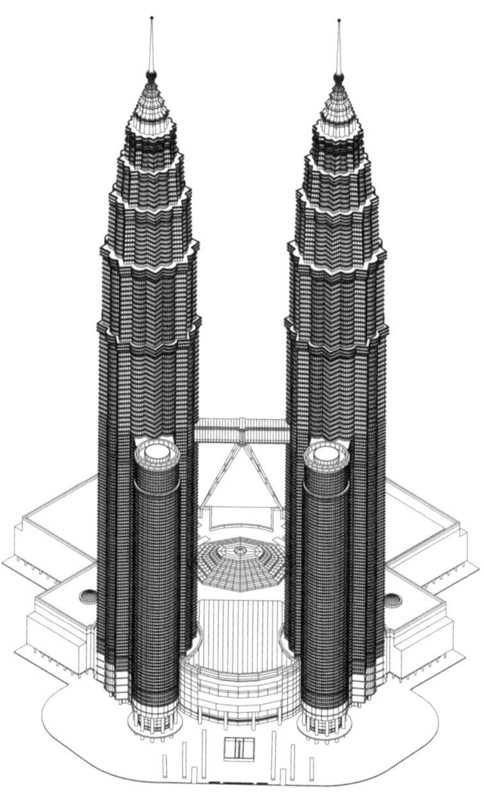

Project **Metropolitan Government, Tokyo, Japan, 1991**
Architect **Tange Associates**
Site area: 42,941 sqm
Gross floor area: 380,504 sqm
Maximum building height: 243 m
www.tangeweb.com/popup.php?id=26&lang=en

Bulky amalgam of two symmetrical, square-plan monolithic towers, a transversal megalithic office bar, and a rectangular plinth with a semicircular monumental plaza inside. Rotated tower tops, modular recesses, open corners, and varying window proportions, managed by a flat, grid surface-textured continuum. Nuanced yet strong, heavy-handed, compact mass. Podium with a semicircular arcade, traversed by lobby opening and road bridge. Broadcast drum crowns.

Project **Beijing Yintai Center, Beijing, China, 2008**
Architect **John Portman & Associates**
Site area: 31,629 sqm
Gross floor area: 350,000 sqm
Maximum building height: 250 m
www.portmanusa.com/en/projects/mixed-use
/beijing-yintai-centre/

Trio of square-plan towers. A hotel and high-end residential building at the center, flanked by two symmetrical, set-back office buildings escorting the former on either side. Public area buffer, frontal shopping plinth, and basement parking. Offices, residences, and rooms organized around a central core. Gridded facade and window modules varying only at corner bays. Ruthless homogeneity altered by hollow structures at the mechanical floors, sky lobby levels, and top crowns.

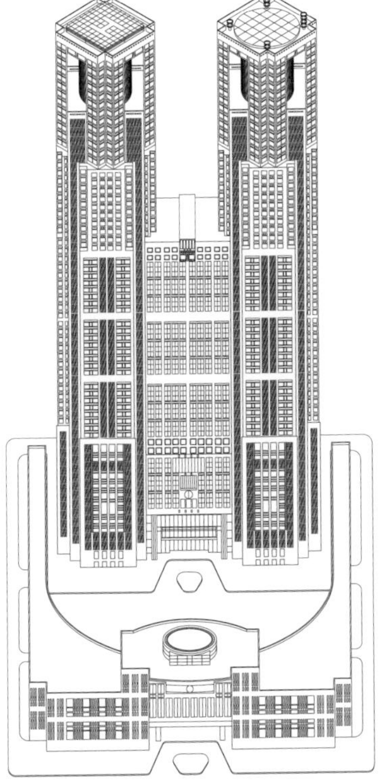

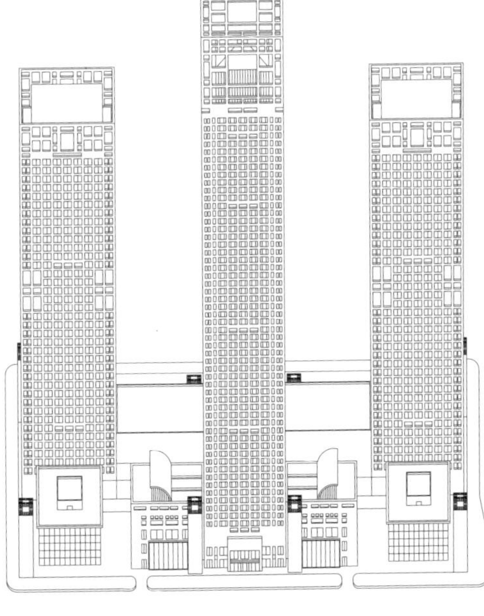

Project **Grande Arche de la Fraternité, Paris, France, 1989**
Architect **Johan Otto von Spreckelsen**
Site area: 10,000 sqm
Gross floor area: 12,096 sqm
Maximum building height: 110 m
www.grandearche.com

Massive, fine-grain space-frame matrix, volumetrically a cube and figuratively an arch, integrating two parallel office bars with a mechanical roof bridging between them above and a thick infrastructural ground connecting them below. Internalized urban axis with through-perspectives and a public podium/plaza. Rotated grid pavement, frontal urban staircase, axial highway tunnel underground, cylindrical skylight, and public foyer. Suspended tensile structure, symmetrical semicylindrical entrance halls, and external elevator cores. Smooth outer glass facades and textured interior concrete facades, both with square grid. Frontal 45-degree facets stressing the cubic geometry.

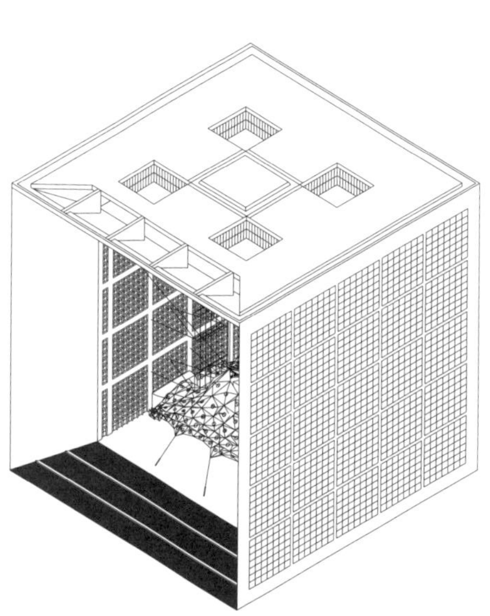

Project **One WTC, Bundle Towers, New York, NY, USA, 2002**
Architect **Foreign Office Architects**
Site area: unknown
Gross floor area: 884,000 sqm
Maximum building height: 500 m
www.farshidmoussavi.com/node/105
www.azpml.com/#/projects/6333

Tower collective of vertically meandering and interconnecting structural tubes. Hexagonal matrix regulating the undulating trajectory of implausibly slim towers, paired at regular intervals and leaning on one another. Horizontally rigid structure through dispersal of building mass in a tubular net, self-similar with the building's own diagonal grid skin structure. Variable location of elevator cores in relation to individual circular plans. Sky lobbies at kissing points. Central exterior atrium, open above and at regular vertical intervals.

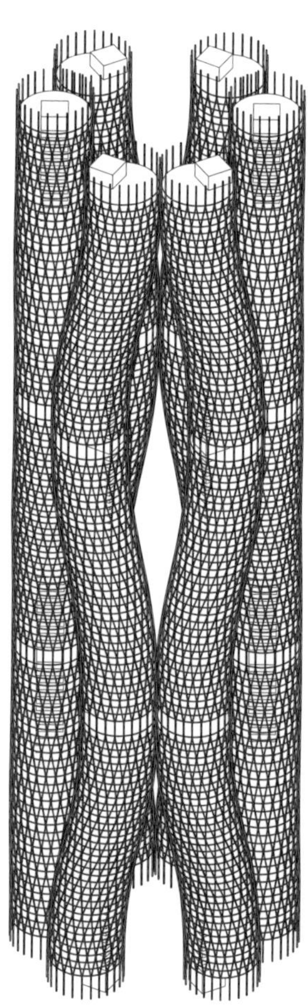

Project **CCTV Headquarters, Beijing, China, 2012**
Architect **Office for Metropolitan Architecture**
Site area: 25,600 sqm
Gross floor area: 473,000 sqm
Maximum building height: 234 m
www.oma.eu/projects/cctv-service-building

Instant iconic figure, alternatively a void cube, two office towers connected by a jagged cantilevered bridge, a portal, a consecutive set of six L-shaped building segments and a crooked, segmented loop of business and administration offices, conference centers, meeting rooms, broadcast facilities, restaurants, cafes, and fitness centers. Triangulated steel tubes, varying in density across a common diagonal structural grid, texturing the otherwise subdued expression of the mass. Spatial continuum, functional autonomy. Full-block plinth, elevated urban plaza, and artificial roof garden. Vertical lobbies, elevator cores to the underground, horizontal datum of sky walkways. Virtually a public loop/promenade.

Project **Shenzhen Stock Exchange, Shenzhen, China, 2013**
Architect **Office for Metropolitan Architecture**
Site area: 16,000 sqm
Gross floor area: 265,000 sqm
Maximum building height: 256 m
www.oma.eu/projects/2006/shenzhen-stock-exchange/

Apparently straightforward prismatic tower surrounded by a primitively lifted, monumentalized cantilevering podium, with a covered urban plaza below and a void atrium in between. Shallow plinth, tall basement, and private roof garden. Blunt stacking of rental, staff and executive offices, information technology, conference centers, restaurants, and canteens running across typological distinctions. Sky lobbies imperceptibly striating the mass. Grid-skin structure at the tower, grid-skin and truss at the atrium, and patterned skin and truss at the plinth.

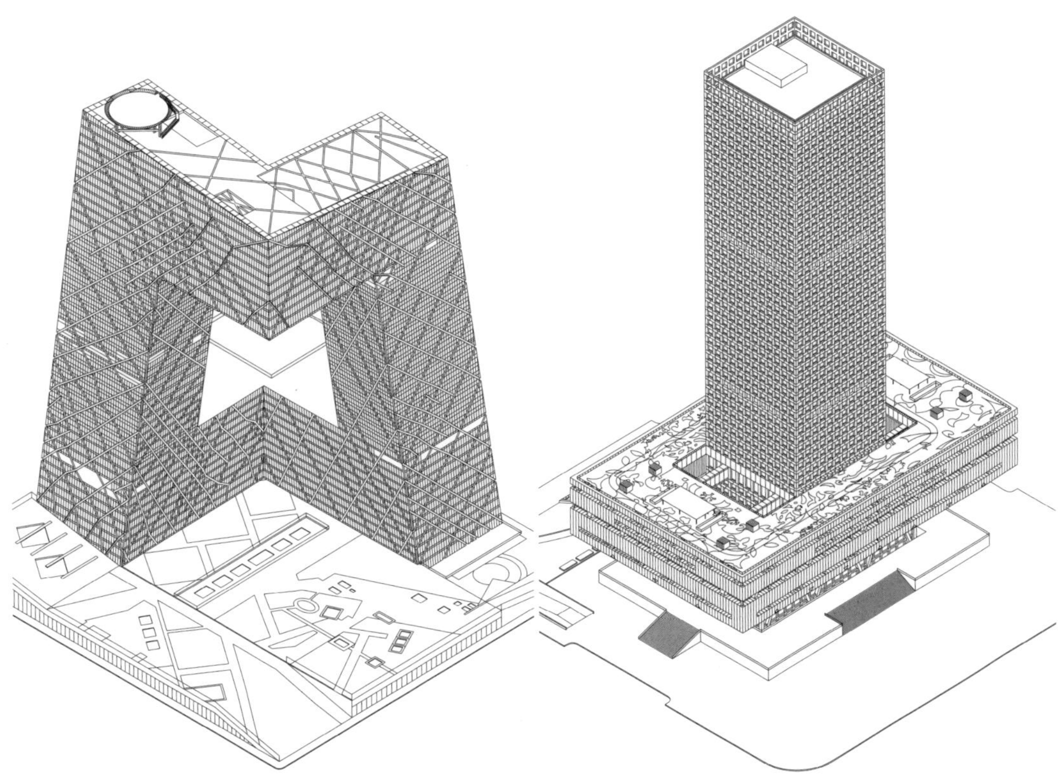

Project **Marina City, Chicago, IL, USA, 1968**
Architect **Bertrand Goldberg Associates**
Site area: 11,148,000 sqm
Gross floor area: 225,527 sqm
Maximum building height: 179 m
www.marinacity.org

Twin apartment and parking towers, placed over a civic urban plaza and a marina plinth. Skating rink, theater building, commercial ground and lobby plinth, office basement podium, and free-plan underground marina. Towers finely striated in floor levels and horizontally stratified in programmatically distinct bands. Balcony apartments and intermediate, double-height level above open parking plates with internal helix ramp. Radial housing organization with an erratic modularity of interior partitions. Semicircular balconies, perimetral living areas, corridor and service internal rings, and central circular core.

Project **New York by Gehry, New York, NY, USA, 2010**
Architect **Gehry Partners LLP**
Site area: 3,800 sqm
Gross floor area: 93,000 sqm
Maximum building height: 265 m
www.newyorkbygehry.com

T-shaped tower with a vibrant wrapping surface on an ordinary plinth. Axial elevator battery, longitudinal and traversal corridors flanked by perimetral rental apartments with inner service spaces. Erratically glowing stainless steel facades with vertically continuous, undulating edges, variable window panels, variegated bay windows, varyingly widened parapets, and tiny balconies. Medium-scale terrace breaks with double-height spaces and long balconies. Flat front facade. Block plinth with lateral pedestrian access, a public square, parking, school, shops, playrooms, medical facilities, fitness centers, and swimming pools.

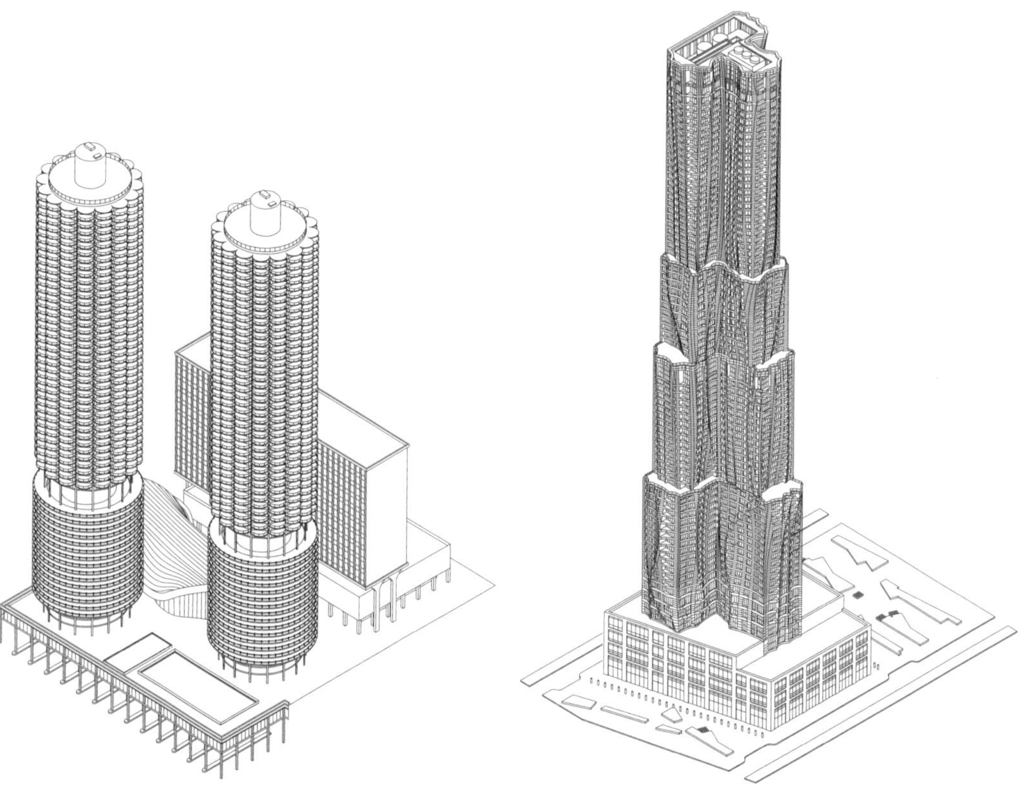

Project **56 Leonard Street, New York, NY, USA, 2016**
Architect **Herzog & de Meuron**
Site area: 12,954 sqm
Gross floor area: 217,170 sqm
Maximum building height: 245 m
www.herzogdemeuron.com/index/projects/complete-works/301-325/305-56-leonard-street.html

Thin-layered building with haphazardly stacked glass house-like apartments, promoted as 145 unique residences made of building fragments organized according to various vertical alternation modes. Central service core, transparent domestic facades, random terracing, covered and open balconies, and alternative vertical window modules. Cross-axial apartment distribution, through-view horizon-framing galleries, and flat floor plates. Lower level amenities including library lounge, indoor/outdoor theater, infinity-edge lap pool, landscaped outdoor sundeck and hot tub, fitness center, yoga studio, steam room, sauna, private dining salon, catering kitchen, and conference center.

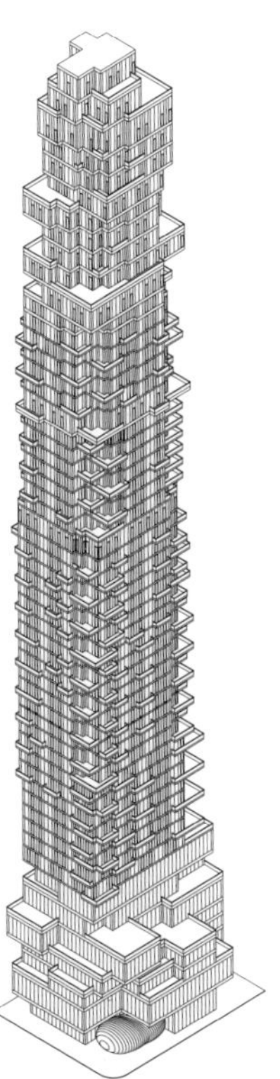

Project **432 Park Avenue, New York, NY, USA, 2015**
Architect **Rafael Viñoly Architects and SLCE Architects**
Site area: 3,100 sqm
Gross floor area: 38,335 sqm
Maximum building height: 426 m
www.432parkavenue.com

Extraordinarily slender, super-tall luxury apartments tower, both hard-core and comic, with a central dual symmetrical core. Full-floor, half-floor, and third-of-a-floor residences of two, three, five, or six bedrooms, with square-proportioned spaces. Regular square-grid structure with large, repetitive square openings, framing the cityscape at increasing heights. Bare, double-level mechanical floors and residential terraces. Tower set back for maximum height. Front cantilevered access canopy, triple-height ground-floor lobby. Divided retail and amenities plinth with playrooms, meeting rooms, restaurants, storage, health centers, lounges, swimming pools, and gyms.

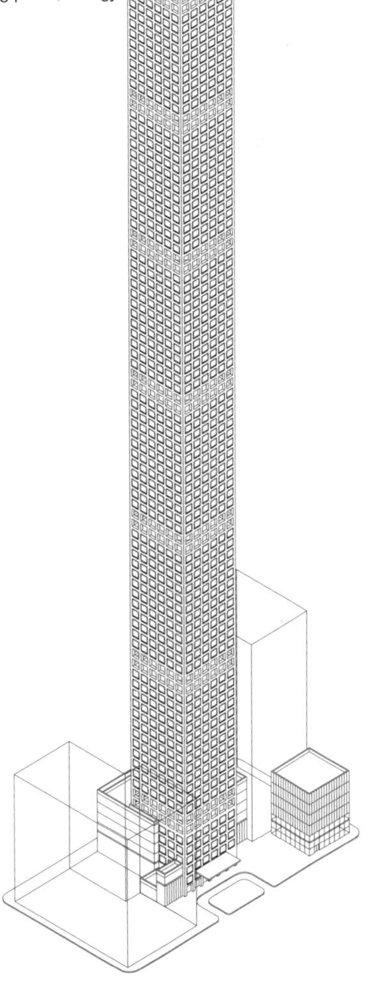

Project **Time Warner Center, New York, NY, USA, 2004**
Architect **Skidmore, Owings & Merrill**
Site area: 13,875 sqm
Gross floor area: 260,128 sqm
Maximum building height: 228 m
www.som.com/projects/time_warner_center

Twin, parallel, shifted towers with set-back volumes adapted to the zoning envelope. Compact, six-floor mixed-use podium etched by a roundabout. Horizontally striped, full-block lateral facades with vertical urban gardens. Axial six-story atrium with a bifurcating shopping arcade and lateral access lobbies. Cantilevering glass-box corner, public underground access. Business offices, hotels, condominiums, public parking, shopping mall, restaurants, cafes, broadcast facilities, and exhibition halls.

Project **Roppongi Hills, Tokyo, Japan, 2003**
Architect **Kohn Pedersen Fox with Jerde Partnership**
Site area: 114,930 sqm
Gross floor area: 724,000 sqm
Maximum building height: 238 m
www.jerde.com/regions/place113.html

Hollow, double-skin, fat office tower with a deformed square plan placed on a massive new district crust. Twin, medium-height residential towers, surrounded by low office towers and grounded by four-level crescent-shaped podium containing retail promenade. Television station drum. Topographic green roof, curvilinear avenue tunnel, interior peripheral streets, small adjoining parks, curvilinear bridges, and deck plaza. Business offices, apartments, hotels, public parking, observatory decks, restaurants, cafes, museums, cinemas, outdoor theaters.

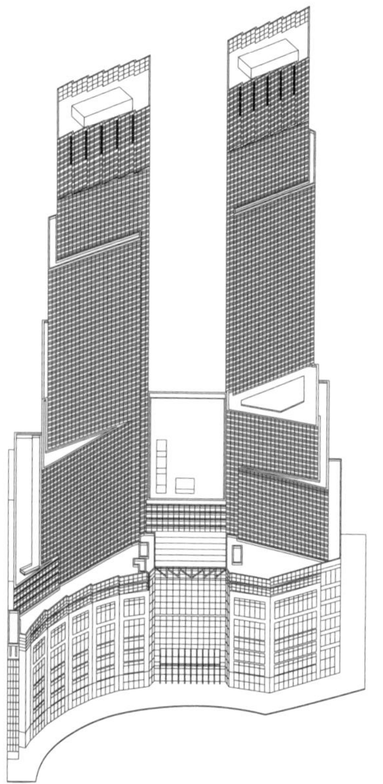

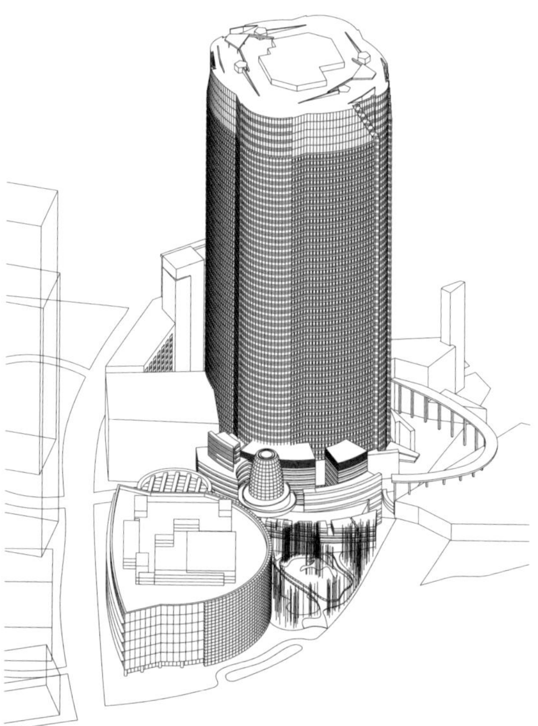

Project **Kanyon, Istanbul, Turkey, 2006**
Architect **Jerde Partnership**
Site area: 29,946 sqm
Gross floor area: 255,000 sqm
Maximum building height: 40 m
www.jerde.com/featured/place10.html

Meandering, sectionally oblique, terraced, tri-level interior street carved as a canyon along a compact yet variegated building mass. Windy, open-air shopping mall, with a longitudinally tiered housing bar, a fat office tower, and a carved semispherical performance amphitheater. Rooftop sports fields, interior garden, water-edged plaza, tensile canopy, and basement-level public parking. Inclined concrete-and-glass parapets, linear-garden guardrails, and curved bridges articulating the texture and scale of the interior. Meeting rooms, restaurants, bars, kiosks, fitness centers, cinemas, and theaters.

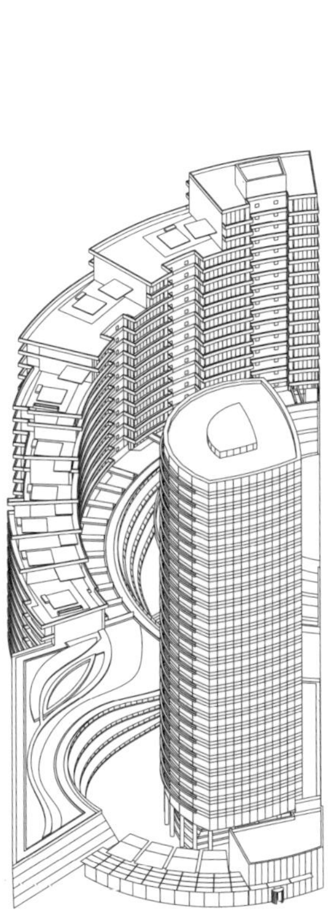

Project **Aldar Central Market, Abu Dhabi, UAE, 2006**
Architect **Foster and Partners**
Site area: 700,000 sqm
Gross floor area: 1,967,053 sqm
Maximum building height: 382 m
www.fosterandpartners.com/projects/aldar-central-market/

Two alike but dissimilar towers on a thick mat-building with interior market-like boutique shops rhythmically distributed along public walkways and courtyards, crossed by bridging alleyways, covered by sliding roof panels, and textured with varying facade patterns. Office-apartment and hotel-and-serviced-apartment towers, with undulating glass facades and diagonally sliced roofs. Central cores, sky lobbies, terraced gardens, public parking, leisure facilities, and venue spaces.

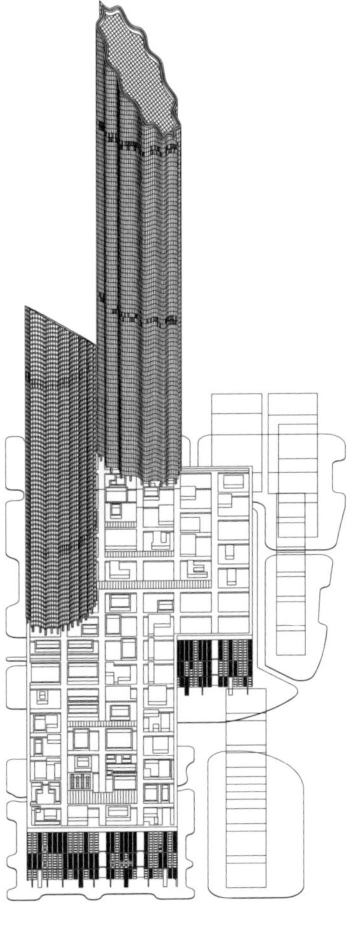

Project **Mirador, Madrid, Spain, 2005**
Architect **MVRDV**
Site area: 10,000 sqm
Gross floor area: 18,300 sqm
Maximum building height: 70 m
www.mvrdv.nl/projects/mirador

Donut-shaped housing superblock made of independent apartment building types, stacked and juxtaposed around a sky courtyard. Internal community spaces, interior sky lobbies and spatial buffers, and semipublic elevated plaza. Vertically and horizontally segmented continuous-circulation loop, central longitudinal corridor, and cantilevered staircases. Contiguous, heterogeneous facades varying in the size and proportion of openings and flattened in a patchwork of architectural languages. Hybrid of regular-span and bridge structures. Raw surrounding landscape plaza.

Project **1111 Lincoln Road, Miami Beach, FL, USA, 2010**
Architect **Herzog & de Meuron**
Site area: 2,510 sqm
Gross floor area: 22,575 sqm
Maximum building height: 38 m
www.herzogdemeuron.com/index/projects/complete-works/276-300/279-1111-lincoln-road.html

Open, flat-slab concrete structure with public parking of varying ceiling heights and a thin-edged perimeter standing on bidirectional, bifurcating columns of sophisticatedly raw material resolution. Apartment condominium block with retail, restaurants, cafes, and event spaces. Continuous semipublic space integrating a central, open-stair promenade, pedestrian shopping street, residential and bridging terraces, interior balconies, outdoor seating, observatory decks, public parking, and car circulation ramps.

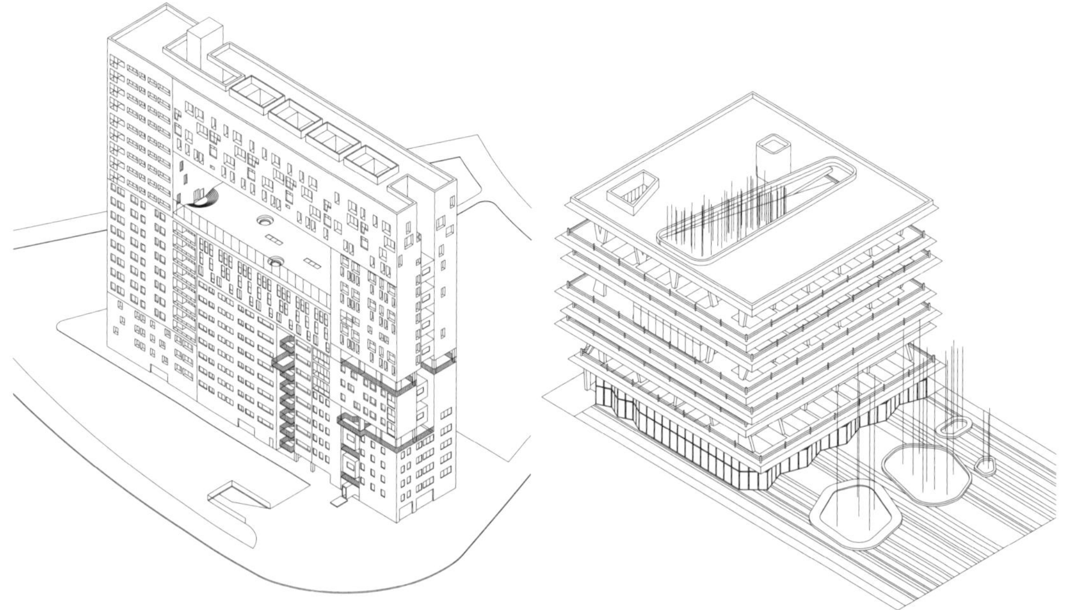

Project **Cross-Towers, Seoul, South Korea, 2012**
Architect **Bjarke Ingels Group**
Site area: 20,996 sqm
Gross floor area: 96,534 sqm
Maximum building height: 214 m
www.big.dk/#projects-yon

Two square-plan towers, diagonally displaced, supporting two interlocking, bridging horizontal bars at disparate heights, with a central courtyard atrium and cantilevering rooftop sky gardens and playgrounds. Orthogonally gridded structural facades with various shading elements and window recesses. Ground-level arrival bar, roof garden, underground courtyard, and landscaped urban plaza. High-end residences and amenities including library, gallery space, kindergarten, public parking, and exhibition halls.

Project **The Interlace, Singapore, 2012**
Architect **Office for Metropolitan Architecture**
Site area: 81,000 sqm
Gross floor area: 170,000 sqm
Maximum building height: 90 m
www.oma.eu/projects/2009/the-interlace/

Apartment block network organized through a hexagonal matrix of stacked housing bars, intertwined with and articulated by vertical cores at their ends. Six central four-level cores, fourteen peripheral three-level cores, two remote two-level cores. Triangular courtyards and linear corridors interconnected by continuous multiple-level intertwinement of outdoor spaces, covered sky plazas, terraced roof gardens, topographical landscapes, and sparse balconies. Sports facilities, meeting rooms, communal facilities, ground-floor canopies, and public parking, surrounded by an external circulatory loop.

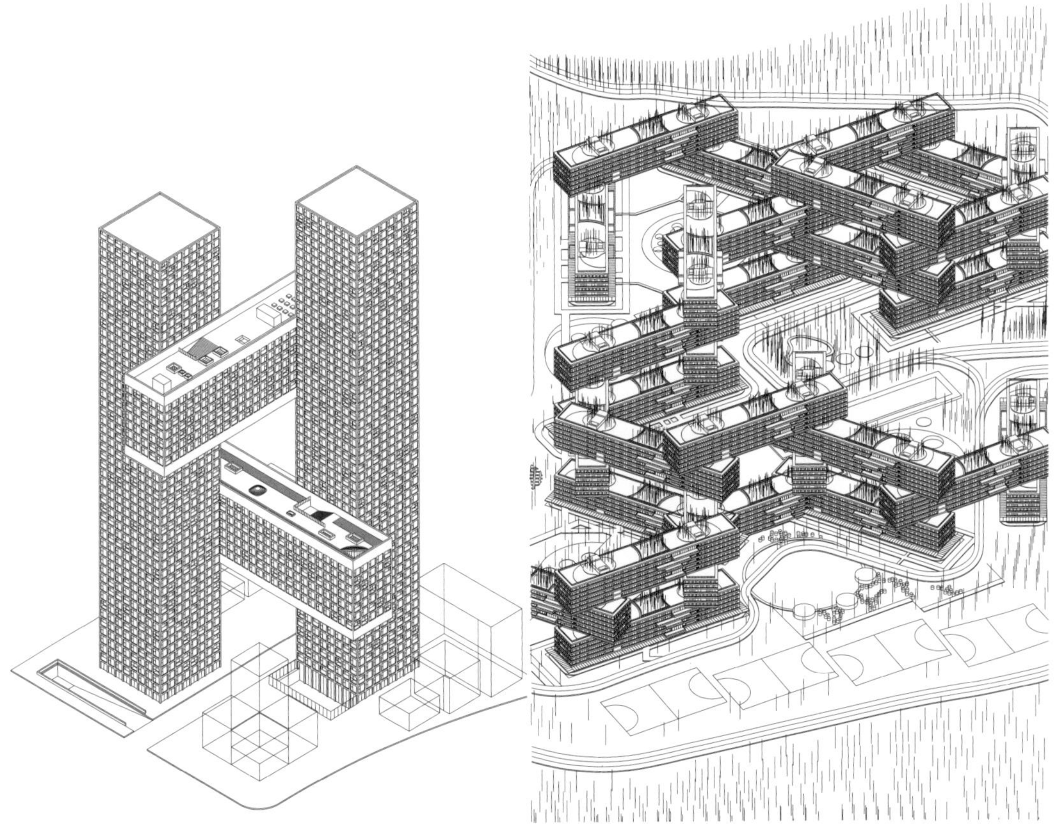

Project **Polestar, Gothenburg, Sweden, 2019**
Architect **Skidmore, Owings & Merrill and Entasis**
Site area: 143,000 sqm
Gross floor area: 1,500,000 sqm
Maximum building height: 230 m
www.som.com/projects/polestar, http://entasis.dk/2662

Four slim towers, integrated into a single, fat, square-plan tower, surrounded by several short towers on a continuous podium containing peripheral tower-podium combinations. Twisting curtain-wall facades with balconies in-between, interior terraces, internal atrium core, and cubic, hollow, lantern-like garden tops. Single-story, duplex-apartment, and loft-like units. Podium roof decks, observatory decks, landscape corridors, pedestrian walks, restaurants, cafes, bars, and gyms.

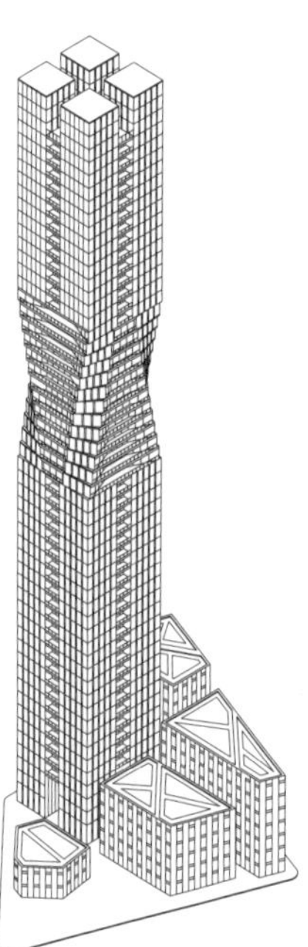

Project **Al Hamra Tower, Kuwait City, Kuwait, 2011**
Architect **Skidmore, Owings & Merrill**
Site area: 10,000 sqm
Gross floor area: 195,000 sqm
Maximum building height: 412 m
www.som.com/projects/al_hamra_tower

Open-courtyard prismatic office tower with opaque inner facade and curtain-walled outer facade, a shifting void, oblique cuts, and rounded corners. Internal street court, perimetral frame structure, subtly spiraling lateral walls, stone-clad continuous ribbon. Attached retail podium with horizontally stripped, undulating roof surfaces wrapped around shopping malls, meeting rooms, restaurants, cafes, and a heath club. Twenty-meter-tall structurally expressive lobby.

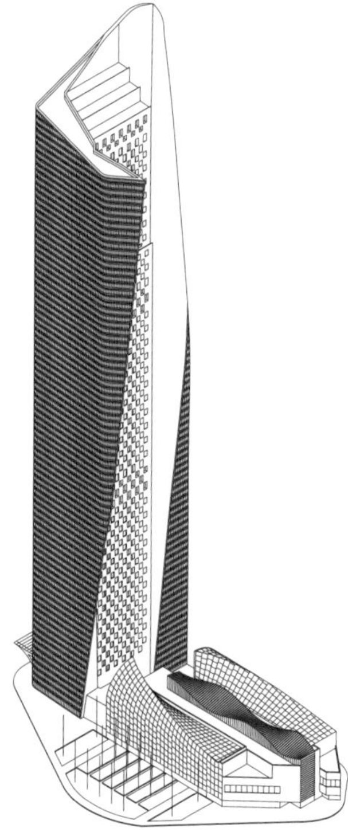

Project **Burj Khalifa, Dubai, UAE, 2010**
Architect **Skidmore, Owings & Merrill**
Site area: 104,210 sqm
Gross floor area: 454,249 sqm
Maximum building height: 828 m
www.som.com/projects/burj_khalifa__mep

Three-wing tower with petal-like, spirally arrayed, receding wings, triangular triple-battery central elevator and service core, and axial circulatory corridors. Symmetrically organized boutique hotel rooms, one- and two-bedroom apartments, private luxury residences, offices, and corporate suites. Gleaming glass and stainless-steel cladding behind thin vertical partitions. Regularly distributed mechanical levels with dense horizontal stainless-steel railing. Lake peninsula with patterned urban plaza, peripheral support pavilions, drop-off area, water's edge promenade, pedestrian boulevards, water features, and parking. Pinnacle roof with public observatory, sky lobbies, and terraces. Fitness facilities, swimming pools, and meeting spaces.

Project **Incheon 151 Tower, South Korea, 2010**
Architect **John Portman & Associates**
Site area: 6,070,238 sqm
Gross floor area: 621,700 sqm
Maximum building height: 600 m
www.portmanusa.com/en/projects/mixed-use/incheon
-151-tower-at-songdo-landmark-city/

High-rise twin office and apartment towers, joined by three bridge structures at regular intervals and by a high-rise building and a wedge-shaped lobby with multiple levels of access at their base. Center of a roundabout monumental plaza with a thick retail, conference, and entertainment basement and a concentric underground plinth, a diamond-shaped unifying roof structure, axial vehicular bridge access, a transport nodal interchange, and connection to a new subway system. Landscaped peripheral ring and circular water edge.

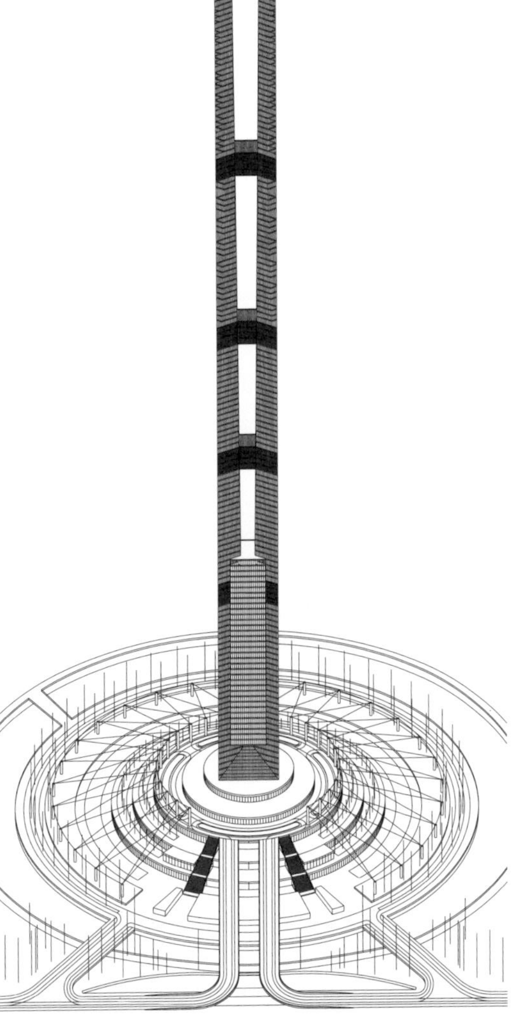

Project **Marina Bay Sands, Singapore, 2011**
Architect **Safdie Architects**
Site area: 249,843 sqm
Gross floor area: 929,000 sqm
Maximum building height: 207 m
www.msafdie.com/#/projects/marinabaysands

Three double-bar towers aligned along a curved longitudinal axis running along a bay, open at lower levels with a continuous internal corridor/atrium mall. Tower-to-tower flyover bridge-like platform with a long, ship-shaped cantilever at one end, containing a sky park, open-air pool, and terrace promenade with palm trees. Plinth with theater, casino, convention center, and exhibition block. Arcaded waterfront promenade, glass pavilion peninsula, round museum peninsula, event plaza, art installation squares, shopping malls, restaurants, and bars.

Project **Sliced Porosity Block, Chengdu, China, 2012**
Architect **Steven Holl Architects**
Site area: 39,019 sqm
Gross floor area: 306,580 sqm
Maximum building height: 150 m
www.stevenholl.com/project-detail.php?id=98

Sliced courtyard block of business offices, serviced apartments, and hotels with large openings, elevated terraces, and bridging structures clustered around a monumentalized public plaza. Abstract skeletal-frame structure with diagonal reinforcements, regular openings, irregular outline, and lateral curtain-walled facades. Three plaza levels with central skylights, wide ramps, punctured staircases, and terraced ponds. Six-floor shopping basement, double-front perimetral shops, restaurants, cafes, and public parking.

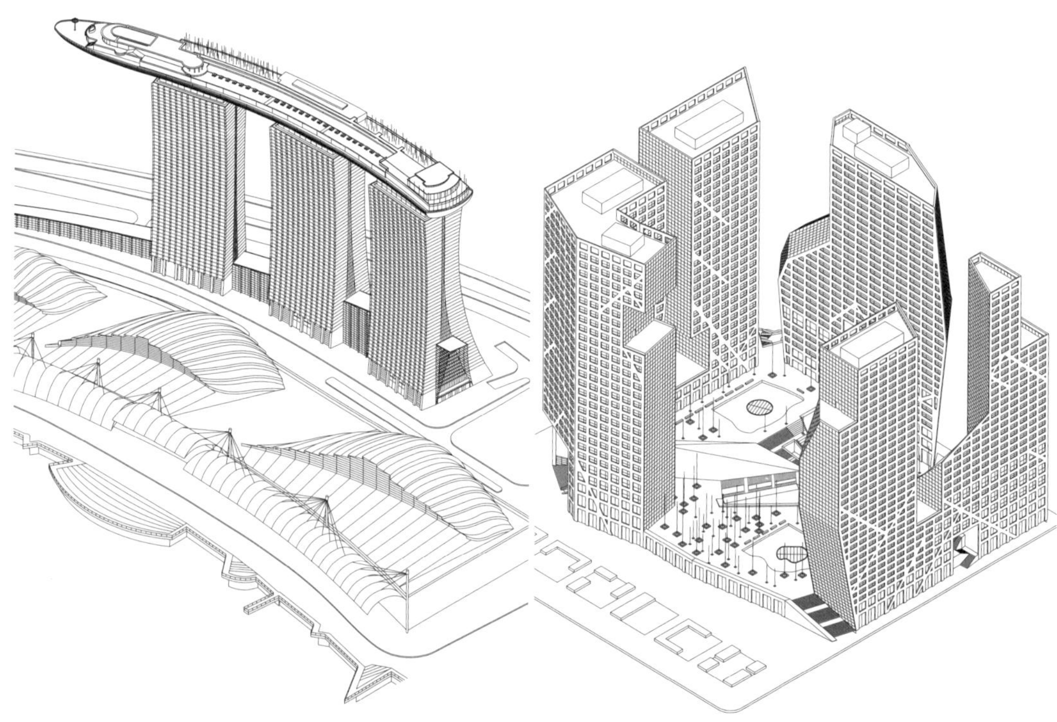

Project **De Rotterdam, Rotterdam, Netherlands, 2013**
Architect **Office for Metropolitan Architecture**
Site area: 3,852 sqm
Gross floor area: 162,000 sqm
Maximum building height: 150 m
www.oma.eu/projects/1997/de-rotterdam/

Set of three contiguous, partially shifted, interlocked, interconnected towers, running longitudinally along a common elevated plinth with lobbies and a waterfront promenade. General traffic hub, parking buffer, public ground floor, leisure levels, and service terrace floor. Vertically striated, double-skinned facade, exterior atrium-like vertical gaps between buildings, and three aligned compact elevator cores. Business offices, conference centers, apartments, hotels, shops, restaurants, cafes, and fitness centers.

Project **Dubai Pearl, Dubai, UAE, 2018**
Architect **SAA Schweger Architekten**
Site area: 167,225 sqm
Gross floor area: 2,043,867 sqm
Maximum building height: 300 m
www.schweger-architects.com/en/architecture/dubai-pearl

Multilevel arcade with four towers organized in two perpendicular sets, a long rectangular podium, and a three-story, rooftop bridge with a central rectangular void. Roundabout infrastructural node containing mid-rise residential and commercial building conglomerates with domestic character and local scale, orthogonally distributed fashion ateliers, retail units, small hotels, sport clubs, offices, and residential blocks. Front square and lateral water fountains, perimetral jogging trail, leisure activities, public parking, malls, and restaurants.

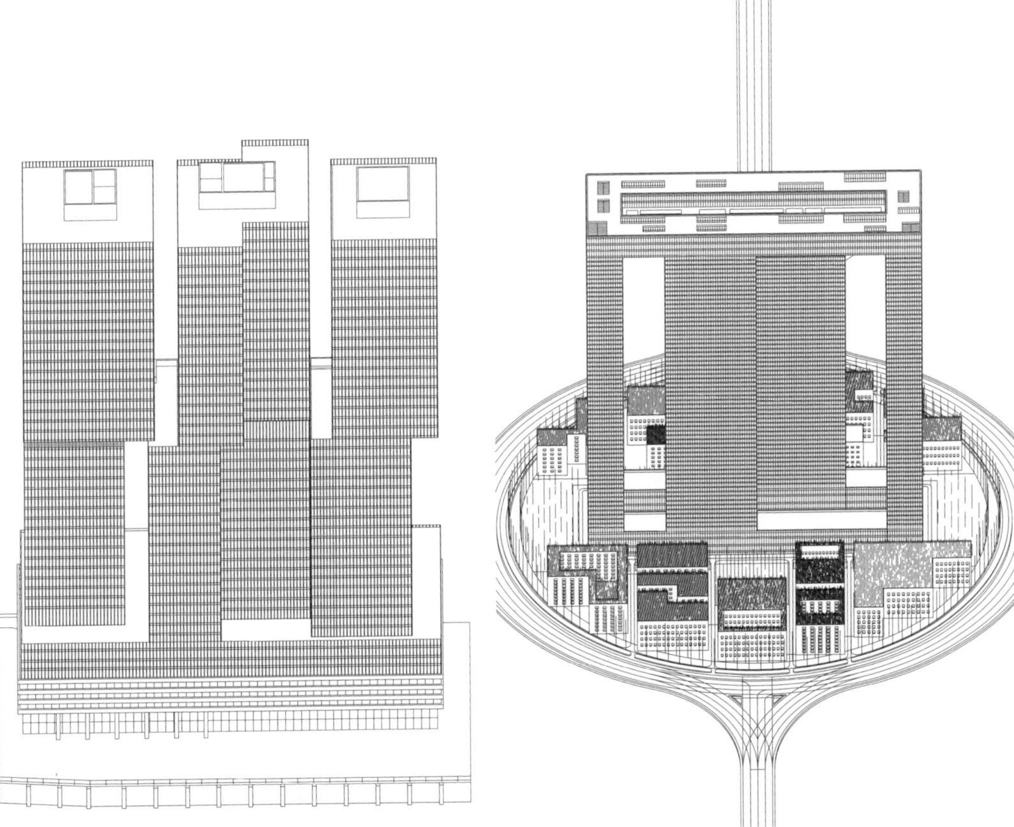

Project **Peruri 88, Jakarta, Indonesia, 2012**
Architect **MVRDV, Jerde Partnership, and Arup**
Site area: 40,000 sqm
Gross floor area: 360,000 sqm
Maximum building height: 400 m
www.mvrdv.nl/projects/peruri-88

Seemingly irregular but hierarchically stacked collage of office and housing typologies, including office towers, mid-rise live/work space, lofts, terraced apartment buildings, and luxury hotel, with a tall tower on top crowned by a domestic building. Semipublic roofs with parks, gardens, patios, playgrounds, landscapes, and observatory platforms. Multidirectional facades with variegated balconies and a sky courtyard. Five vertical cores, bridging floors, and escalators. Podium with central plaza, water bodies, sunken garden plaza, and lush jungle. Outdoor auditorium, sports fields, cinemas, theaters, events spaces, restaurants, cafes, shops, swimming pools, spas, and gyms.

Project **Museum Plaza, Louisville, KY, USA, 2008 (on hold)**
Architect **REX**
Site area: unknown
Gross floor area: 141,800 sqm
Maximum building height: 214 m
www.rex-ny.com/museum-plaza/

Tower clusters branching up and down off a raised cultural datum. Stack of tall buildings on a thick urban platform, presented as an island, containing a contemporary art institute with swimming pool, auditorium, ballroom, gyms, bars, restaurants, and retail. Luxury condominiums, loft apartments, and hotel and office towers. Thick parking basement, elevated public plaza, roof garden, diagonal elevator, vertical opaque bare core, ring corridor, ground-floor free-plan sculpture garden.

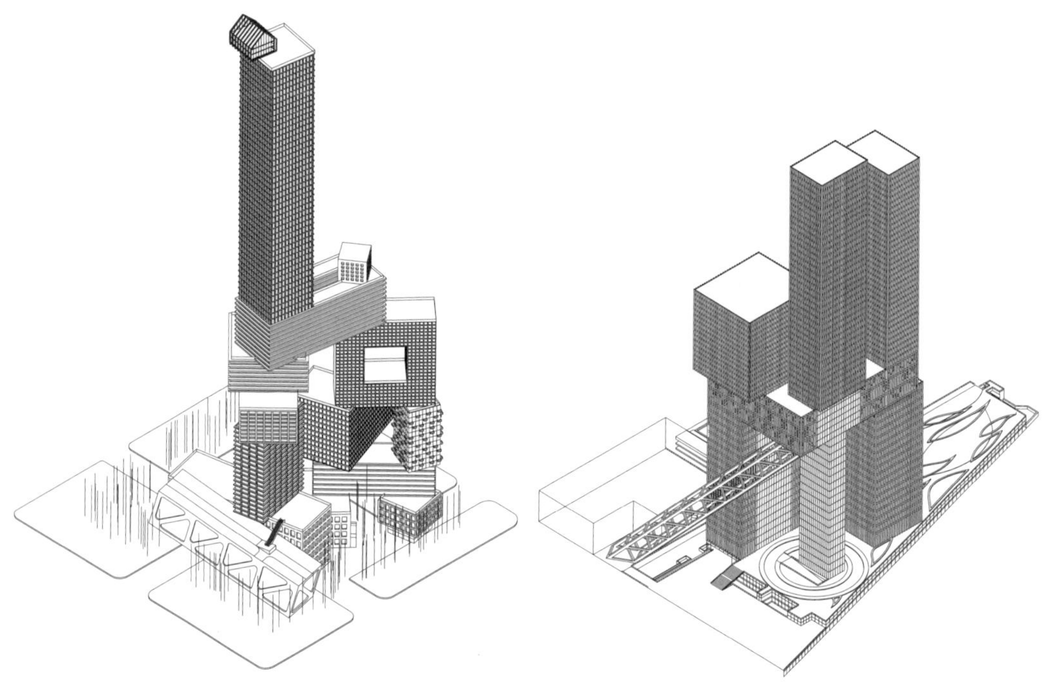

Project **Hyperbuilding, Bangkok, Thailand, 1995**
Architect **Office for Metropolitan Architecture**
Site area: 5,000,000 sqm
Gross floor area: 11,420,000 sqm
Maximum building height: 1,000 m
www.oma.nl/projects/1996/hyperbuilding/

Self-contained city of bold building forms, explicit technologies, and miniaturized urban infrastructures. Off-the-shelf assembly of towers, bars, plinths, plazas, basements, screens, and shafts. High-tower streets, thick-plate parks, interlocked-volume districts, tubular diagonal boulevards, cable car gondola elevators, high- and low-speed vertical connections, ground-to-rooftop promenades, artificial landscapes, and gigantic billboard facades. Office buildings, industries, condominiums, public parking, shops, restaurants, cultural and educational institutions, and leisure and medical facilities.

Project **Crystal Island, Moscow, Russia, 2007**
Architect **Foster and Partners**
Site area: 440,000 sqm
Gross floor area: 2,500,000 sqm
Maximum building height: 450 m
www.fosterandpartners.com/news/archive/2007/12
/foster-partners-presents-a-new-mixed-use-destination-for-moscow/

Megastructural diagonal-grid envelope integrating a spiraling tent-like building volume and a geometrically rigid, artificial landscape. Cultural, exhibition, and performance facilities, hotels, apartments, offices, shops, and educational and sport facilities, embedded in a live/work loop within a continuously active public interior. Escalating series of tiers, terraces, and winter gardens transitioning and climatically buffering the interior. Multitude of panels nuancing the structural frame and allowing light control and energy management. Platform at summit revealing open panoramas of Moscow.

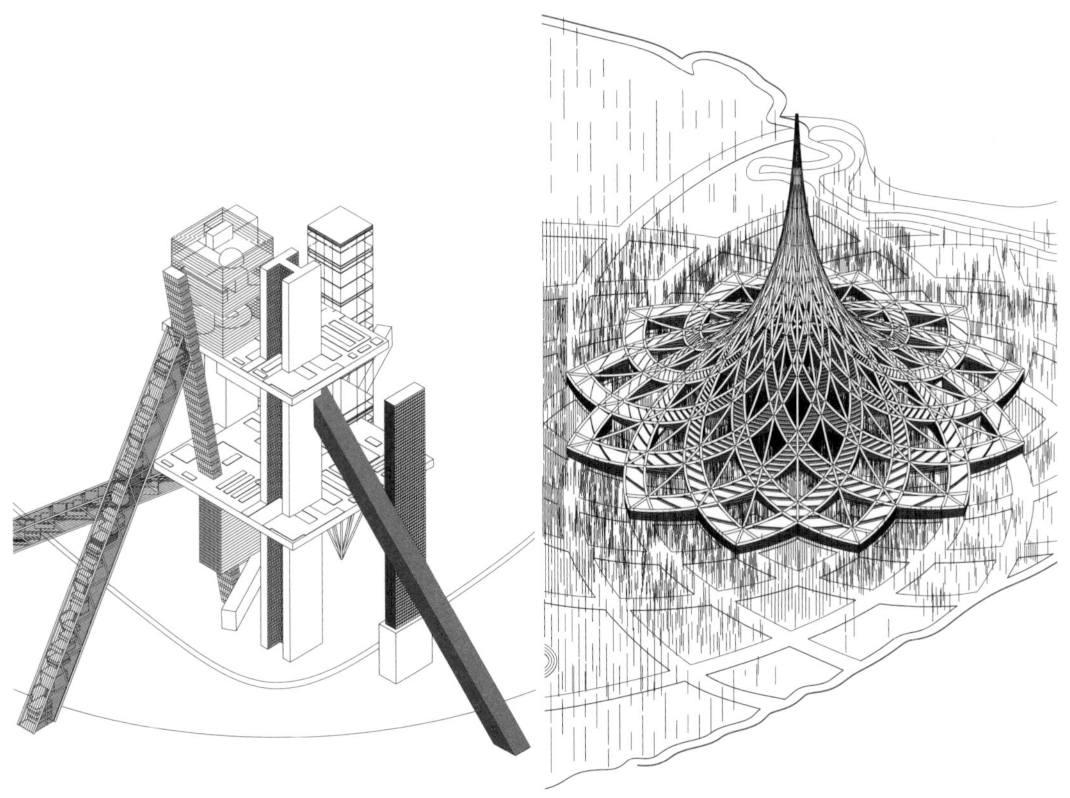

Project **Desert Highlands, Scottsdale, AZ, USA, 1980**
Architect **Lyle Anderson**
Site area: 3,439,828 sqm
Gross floor area: unknown
Maximum building height: unknown
www.deserthighlandsscottsdale.com

Central rocky hill, as if purpose built, surrounded by a gated community organized around an elongated, double-looped, spotlessly green golf course branching down and a meandering road system with dead ends and pockets branching up. Dry, rugged natural ground covered by a rich, smooth artificial landscape. Perimetral and insular neighborhoods with plots of three to five sides. Low-density, low-rise, expansive residences, high-density repetitive row houses. Administration offices, communal facilities, private parking, shops, restaurants, fitness centers, swimming pools, and sports fields.

Project **Nordelta, Buenos Aires, Argentina, 2000**
Architect/Developer **Julián Astolfoni y Eduardo Costantini**
Site area: 8,500,000 sqm
Gross floor area: unknown
Maximum building height: unknown
www.nordelta.com

Gated conglomerate of gated neighborhoods, arranged along both sides of a continuous circulatory loop running around a common artificial lagoon. Mildly corrugated water's edge of branching neighborhoods with dead-end cul-de-sacs and private water access. Central neighborhoods made of chunky, combed, crescent, radial, gridded, concentric, T-shaped, golf-buffered, and finger peninsulas. Peripheral neighborhoods around mid-size lagoons. Mid-rise town-houses, condominiums, hotels, shopping malls, food courts, education facilities, medical facilities, communal facilities, administration offices, cinema complexes, and health centers. Private parking, bicycle facilities, marinas, swimming pools, golf courses, and sports fields.

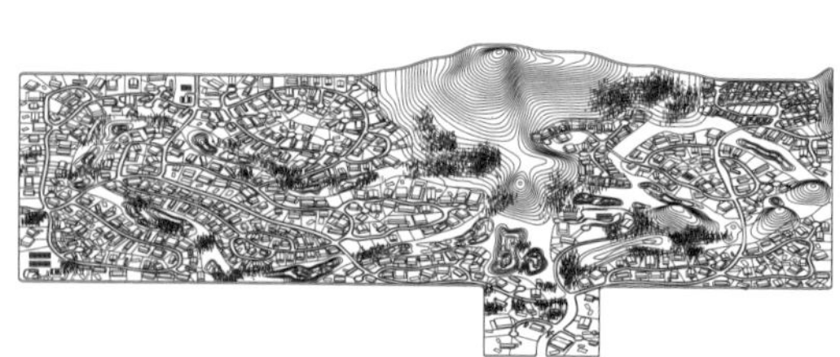

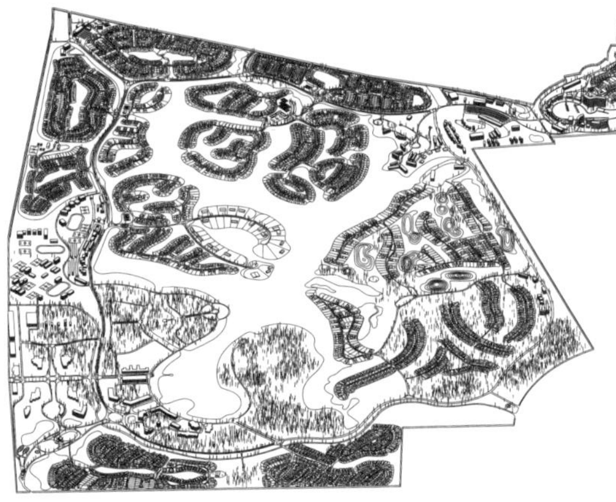

Project **The Palm Jumeirah, Dubai, UAE, 2002**
Architect/Developer **Nakheel**
Site area: 5,600,000 sqm
Gross floor area: unknown
Maximum building height: unknown
www.nakheel.com/en/communities/palm-jumeirah

Branching, palm-like peninsular neighborhood with dead-end cul-de-sacs, a surrounding crescent, and a protection edge branching out from a high-density circulatory axis connecting to the main land. Icon in plan. Road-to-shore private lots and villas with beach access. Condominiums between branches. Axial high-rise service buildings, hotels, office towers, luxury apartments, and mid-rise buildings aligned on waterfront. Public parking, shopping malls, restaurants, cafes, bars, leisure and medical facilities, swimming pools, and sports fields.

Project **Durrat al Bahrain, Bahrain, 2004**
Architect/Developer **Atkins Global**
Site area: 20,000,000 sqm
Gross floor area: unknown
Maximum building height: unknown
www.durratbahrain.com

Circular road connecting a necklace of six courtyard-like community atolls with semicircular private residential crescents, five fish-shaped islands each with an elliptical, private residential loop and a public beach at its end, and a central half-moon hotel island. Coastal double-peninsula bay with towers, golf course, and semicircular entertainment marina. Inner protected beaches, outer low-rise residential arrays. Undulating roads with side gardens. Pre-designed villa types, condominiums, and luxury apartments. Offices and commercial buildings, public parking, leisure and medical facilities, fitness centers, and swimming pools.

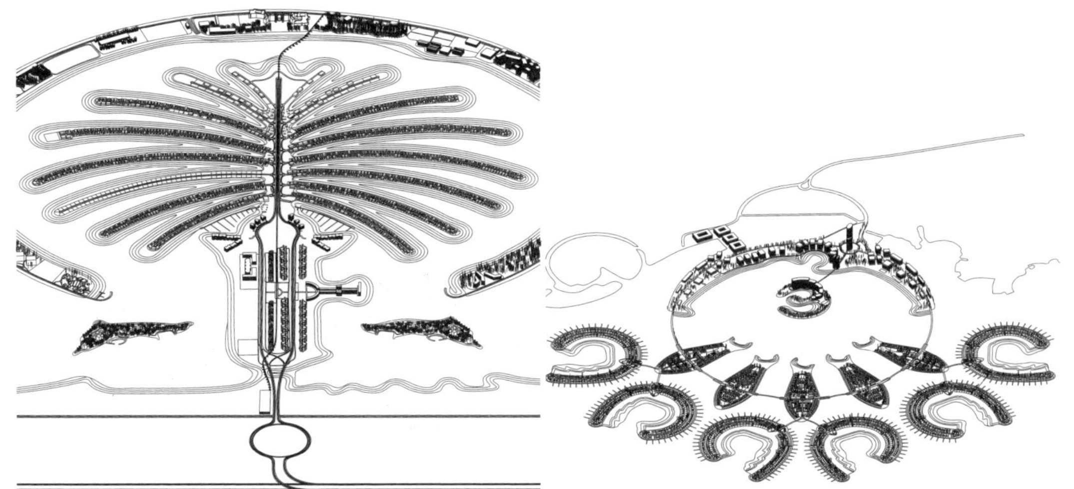

Project **Jebel al Jais Mountain Resort, Ras al Khaimah, UAE, 2005**
Architect **Office for Metropolitan Architecture**
Site area: 10,000,000 sqm
Gross floor area: 881,015 sqm
Maximum building height: unknown
www.oma.eu/projects/2006/jebel-al-jais-mountain-resort/

Small-scale urban fragments linearly scattered and tortuously aligned across a rough topography. Linear road with topographic interruptions, haphazard building dispositions, repetitive villas with staggered terrace configurations, integrated roof gardens, wedge-shaped public squares, building enclaves, courtyard buildings, clustered modular units, descending circulatory ramps, vertical connections, narrow alleys, stair networks, bridges, cantilevers, and a dam. Apartments, villas, hotels, shops, observatory decks, leisure and communal facilities, swimming pools, sports fields, and event spaces.

Project **City in the Desert, Hameem, UAE, 2005**
Architect **Office for Metropolitan Architecture**
Site area: 1,204,200 sqm
Gross floor area: 994,600 sqm
Maximum building height: unknown
www.oma.eu/projects/2006/city-in-the-desert/

Square city plan with two orthogonal central axes and external satellite building clusters. Singular public buildings and wide variety of building types scattered and mashed together according to zones in a grid. Central lagoon, low-rise central area, and high-rise peripheral bands, with green fields and public spaces in between and mid-rise buildings beyond. Ground-level road circulation grid and elevated quick-transit circulation supergrid. Government and administrative offices, apartments, hotels, industrial and commercial buildings, leisure and education facilities, health centers, and cultural institutions.

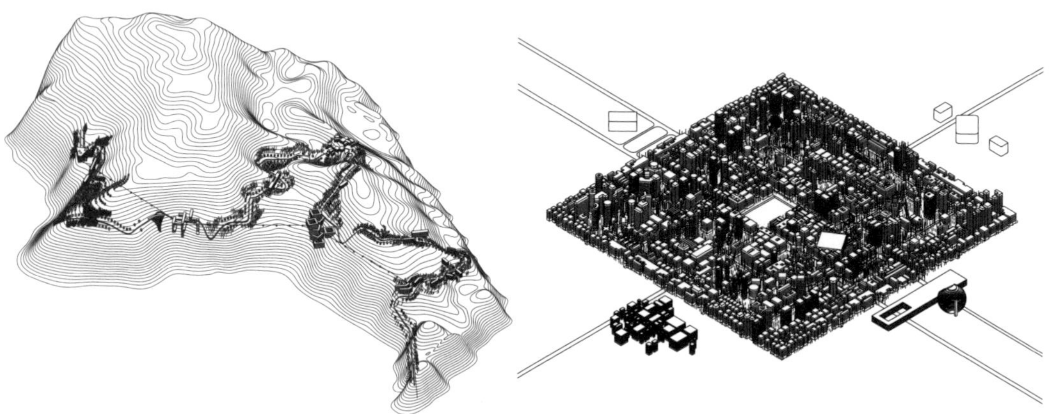

Project **Waterfront City, Dubai, UAE, 2007**
Architect **Office for Metropolitan Architecture**
Site area: 11,800,000 sqm
Gross floor area: 1,710,000 sqm
Maximum building height: unknown
www.oma.eu/projects/waterfront-city

Central, square artificial island surrounded by linear neighborhoods and enclaves. Regular five-by-five-block city fabric, spherical mixed-use building at the corner edge facing the open sea, a series of clustered high-rise and mid-rise towers, several iconic interventions, central park, and perimetral park with circulation loop. Four bridges crossing perimetral water bodies: three connecting to a peripheral ring road, a boulevard, a linear beach park, and a series of aligned mid-rise plinth towers on the mainland, the fourth connecting to an irregular pedestrian street fabric with a dense housing cluster opposite a tall, spiral tower. Business and administrative offices, convention halls, hotels, condominiums, apartments, residences, restaurants, clubs, malls, public parking and transport, marinas, leisure, educational, and medical facilities, fitness and health centers, swimming pools, sports facilities, museums, theaters, and exhibition halls.

Project **Masdar Development, Abu Dhabi, UAE, 2007**
Architect **Foster and Partners**
Site area: 6,400,000 sqm
Gross floor area: 82,000 sqm
Maximum building height: unknown
www.fosterandpartners.com/projects/masdar-development/

Two square-plan cities, one major and one minor. Orthogonal street grid over a continuous basement slab, single-cabin underground train, diagonal linear park, and transversal green corridors. Street-level building colonnades, shaded streets, narrow walkways, and courtyards with fountains. Compact mat-building and multileveled atriums. Business and administrative offices, conference centers, convention halls, industries, apartments, hotels, public parking and transport, malls, swimming pools, sports fields, theaters, cultural institutions, exhibition halls, and trade fairs.

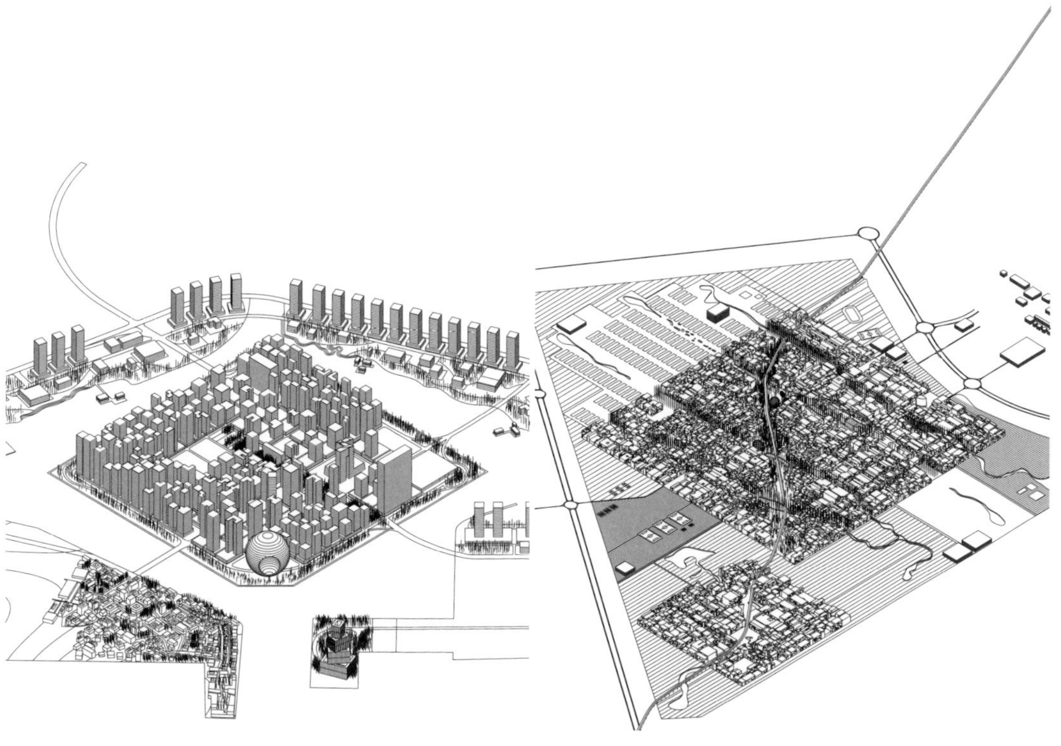

Generic Sublime Models

Karst Palace, Ana María Flor Ortiz and Rodia Valladares Sánchez.
Field. Organization. Suburban karst masterplan. Physical model perspective sector.

The Fantasy Landscape Model

Karst Palace is a synthetic construct that integrates karst geomorphologies and palace typologies within a single model. Positioned at the waterfront of congested city centers, it sits on an unstable ground characterized by changing river dynamics. It proposes a model for the expansion of large cities into untouched lands next to their core. The model claims this space for the projection of metropolitan desires and fantasies.

The rules and constraints of the model establish a network of public parks within which inhabitable surfaces proliferate and bifurcate. Tension lines determined by proximity to water sources activate a tessellated field and trigger the creation of sinkholes. Beyond certain thresholds, basins subdivide and a global reconfiguration of the landscape takes place. Clusters of living units become embedded within the water management topography: organized across its oblique triangular surfaces, they run upward and downward from a common horizontal datum. Adjacent surfaces are either concave or convex, and consequently the inhabitable clusters are either extroverted or introverted.

A first order of topographic modulation defines the geometry of basins and the location of sinks and summits. A second order regulates underground water distribution. A third order manages the organization of housing and vegetation. A fourth order determines the circulation network, based on several regimes of speed. The autonomous but interconnected lagoons exploit the fragility of environmental equilibrium, their contained condition providing a breeding ground for anomalous ecosystems, which flourish.

A glowing decadence characterizes this artificial (and artificially flavored) reservoir, created from the rubble of demolished buildings and highways and reconfigured as a miniature karst form. Over a brief period of time, the transplanted debris mixes with the by-products of river sedimentation and activates the growth of incompatible ecological and biological forms. Exotic species progressively take over the area. The pseudo-natural character of the model is paradoxically enhanced by this highly improbable habitat and nurtured by wild recreation activities, turning upside down the naturalized connection between the preservation of the environment and the security of a gated neighborhood. Public access is here not merely the result of an urbanism of good intentions but the means for a fantasy model to persist and succeed through liveliness, in a state of perpetually worn-out gloss.

In accordance with its character, the model offers the potential to test new forms of living based on the integration of natural and artificial structures. By introducing a system of water management that operates as a network of basins, natural ecosystems are embedded within palace structures and potentiated as their implausible amenities. Karst Palace embodies the active colonization of vacant urban spaces, the fostering of collective desires, the nurturing of strange ecologies, and the synergetic democratization of gated space, offering the mutually disrupted realization of the ideal of integrating high-density urban living with weird forms of nature. Karst Palace is a new state of exception—the world of the shabby fantastic.

Model. Differentiation. Karst formation simulation. From top left to bottom right: first, second, and third iterations of process of sink formation: maximum reach of sinks, basins competition and adjustment of limits, tension lines adjusted, center's movement at shortest drainage path, basins combined through absorption of neighboring sinks, basin size threshold, segregated sinks. Plans.

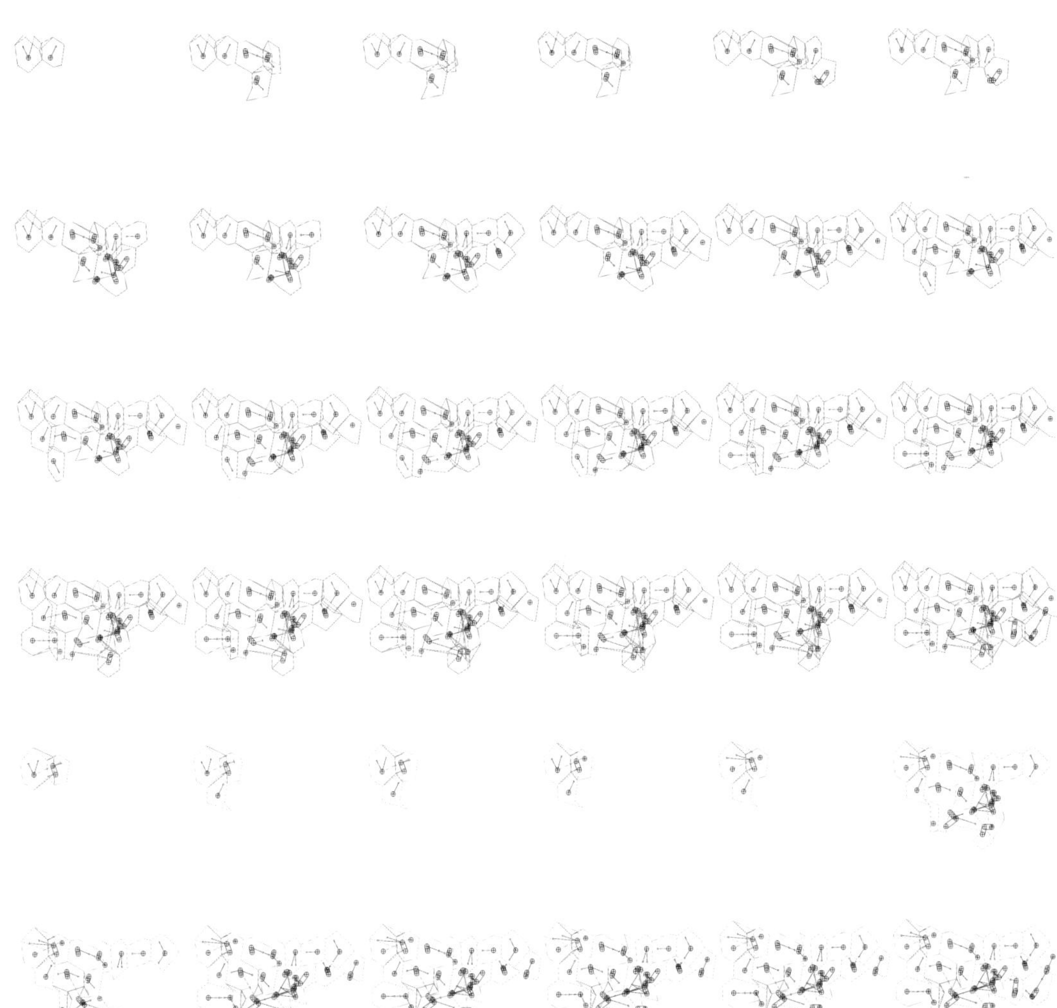

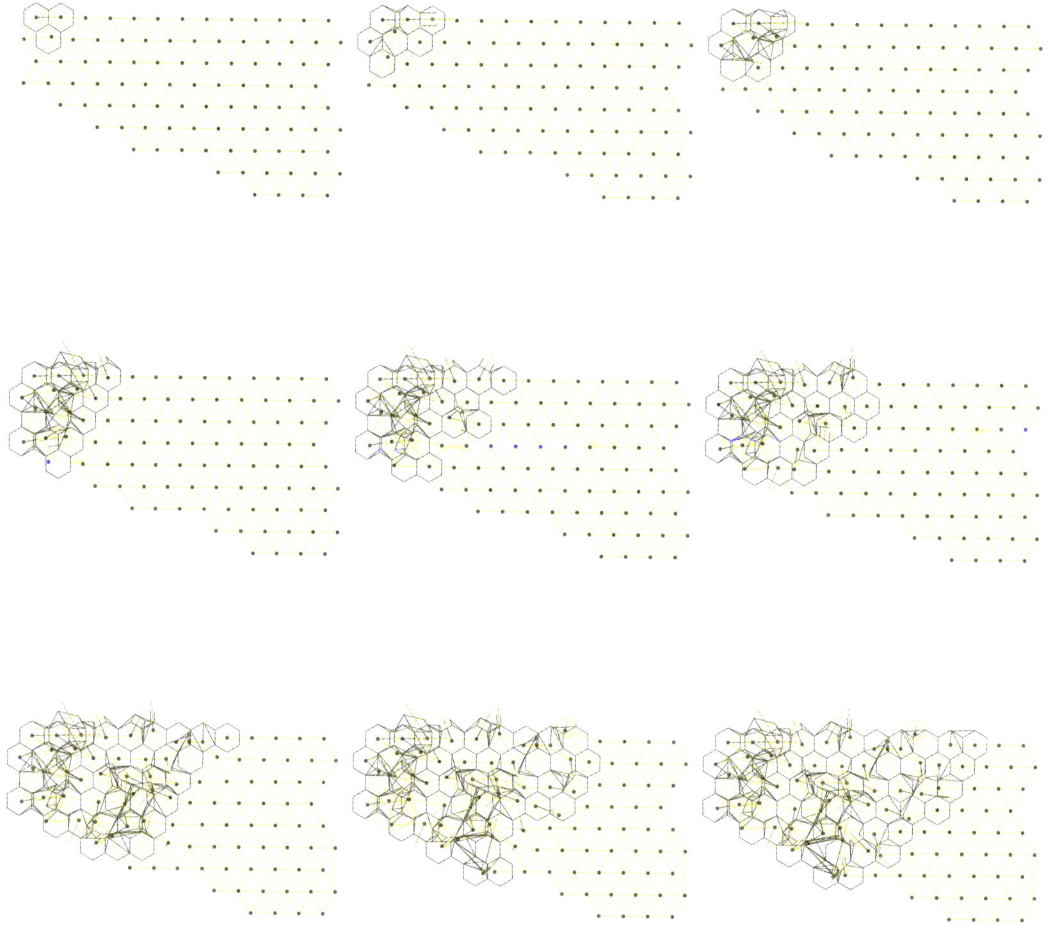

Field. Differentiation. Suburban karst construction. From top left to bottom right: first, second, and third iteration of process of sink formation responsive to flood capacity: maximum reach of sinks, basins competition and adjustment of limits, tension lines adjusted, centers movement at shortest drainage path, basins combined through absorption of neighboring sinks, basin size threshold, segregated sinks. Plans.

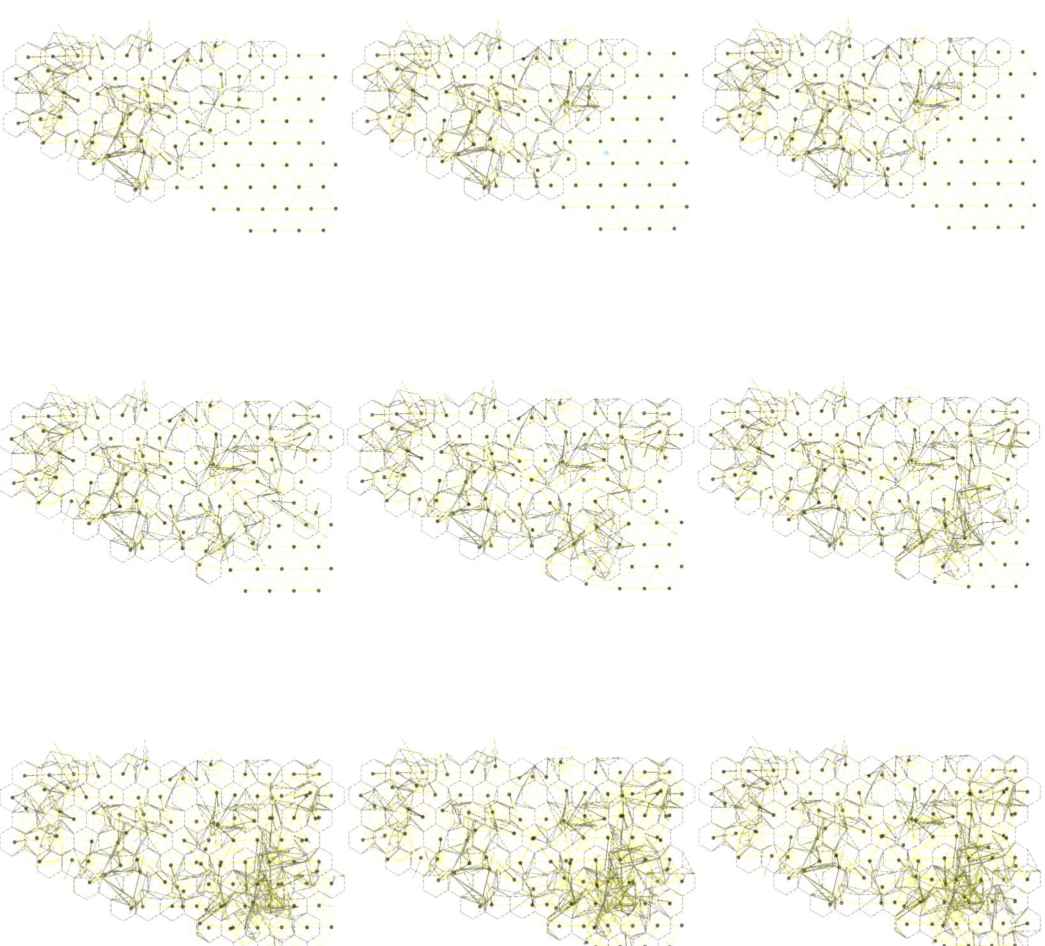

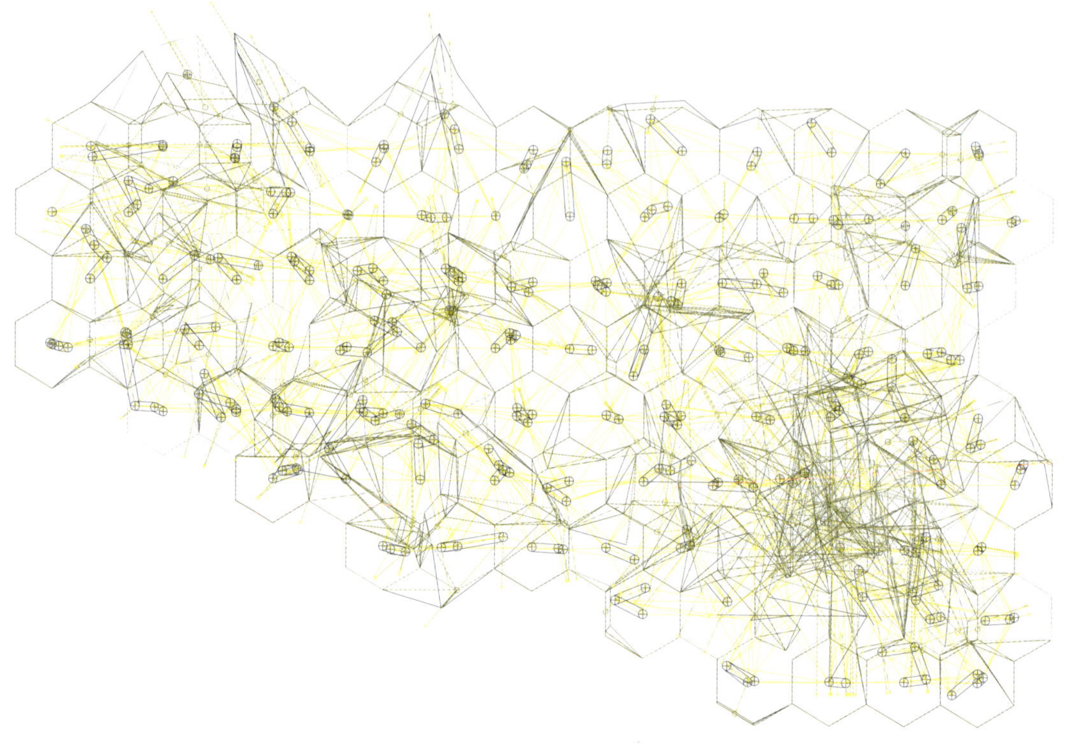

Field. Organization. Suburban karst matrix. Emergent order of sinks resultant of the response to flood capacity and of the interaction of neighboring relationships between sinks and summits. Plan.

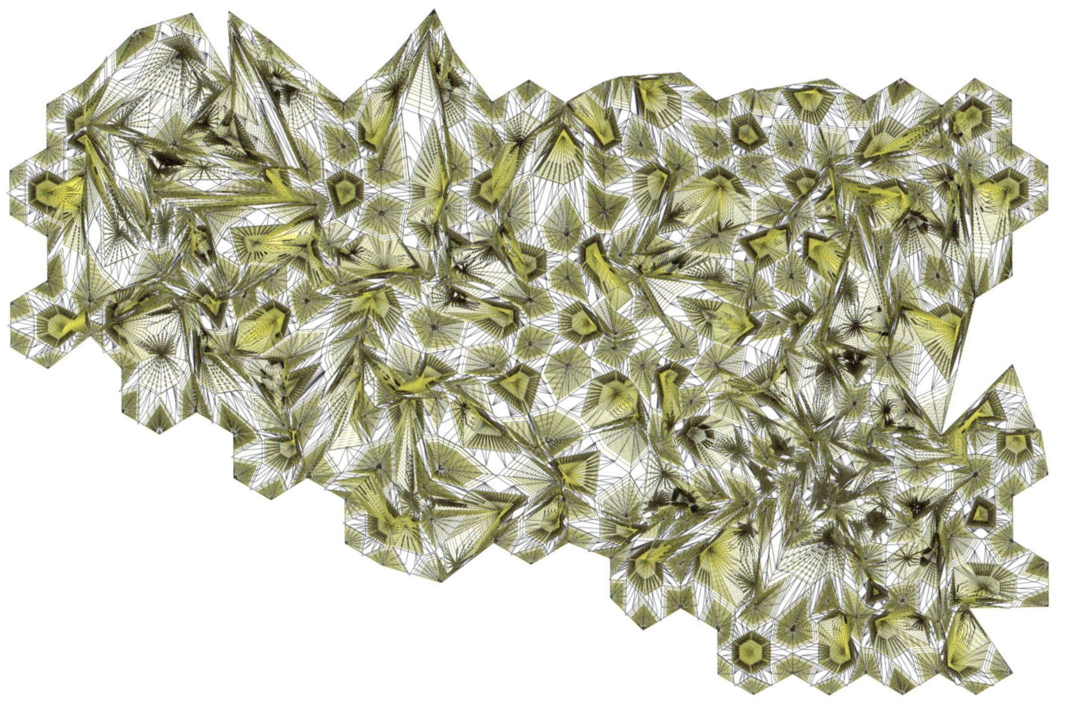

Field. Organization. Suburban karst masterplan. Emergent order of sinks populated by systems: circulation systems, paths and routes, basins and sinks, summits and pinnacles, interior room units, water systems, lagoons, landscape, plantation lines. Plan.

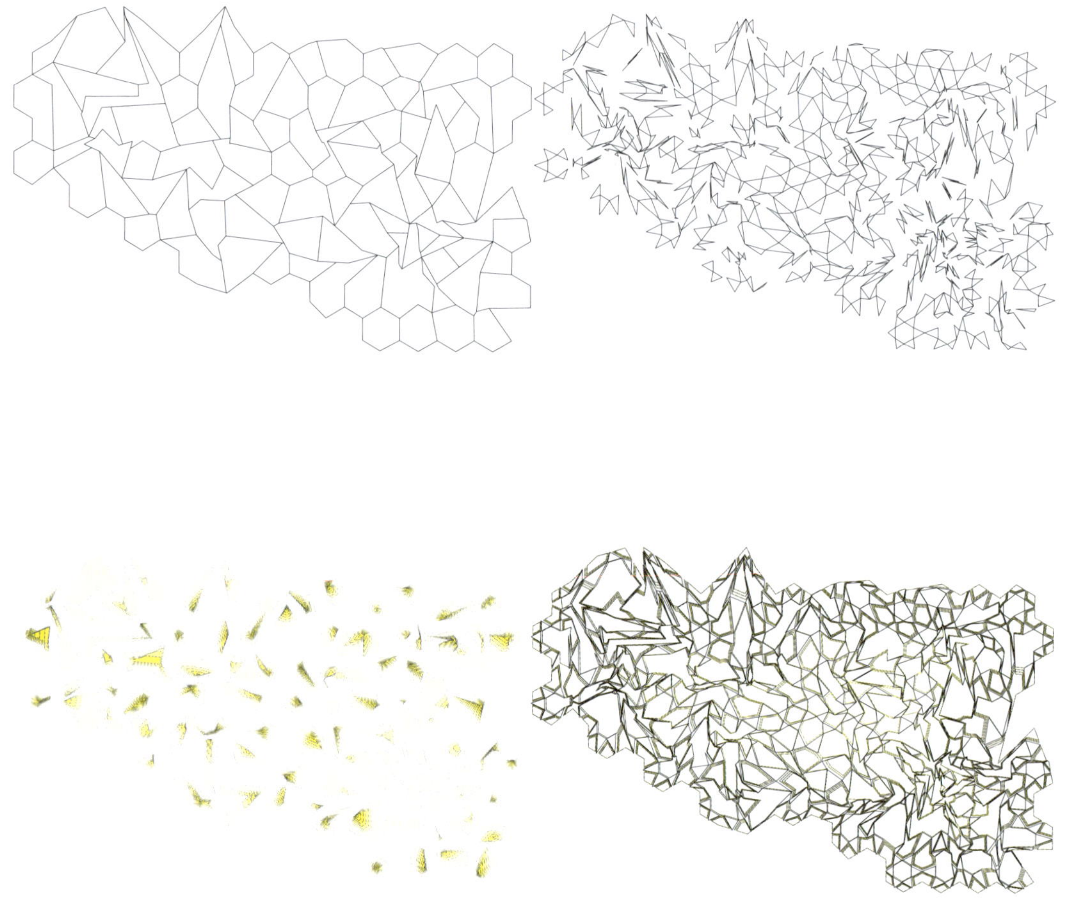

Field. Diversification. Suburban karst matricial systems. From top left to bottom right: hexagonal matrix, triangulated matrix, basins and ponds, fast and slow paths. Plans.

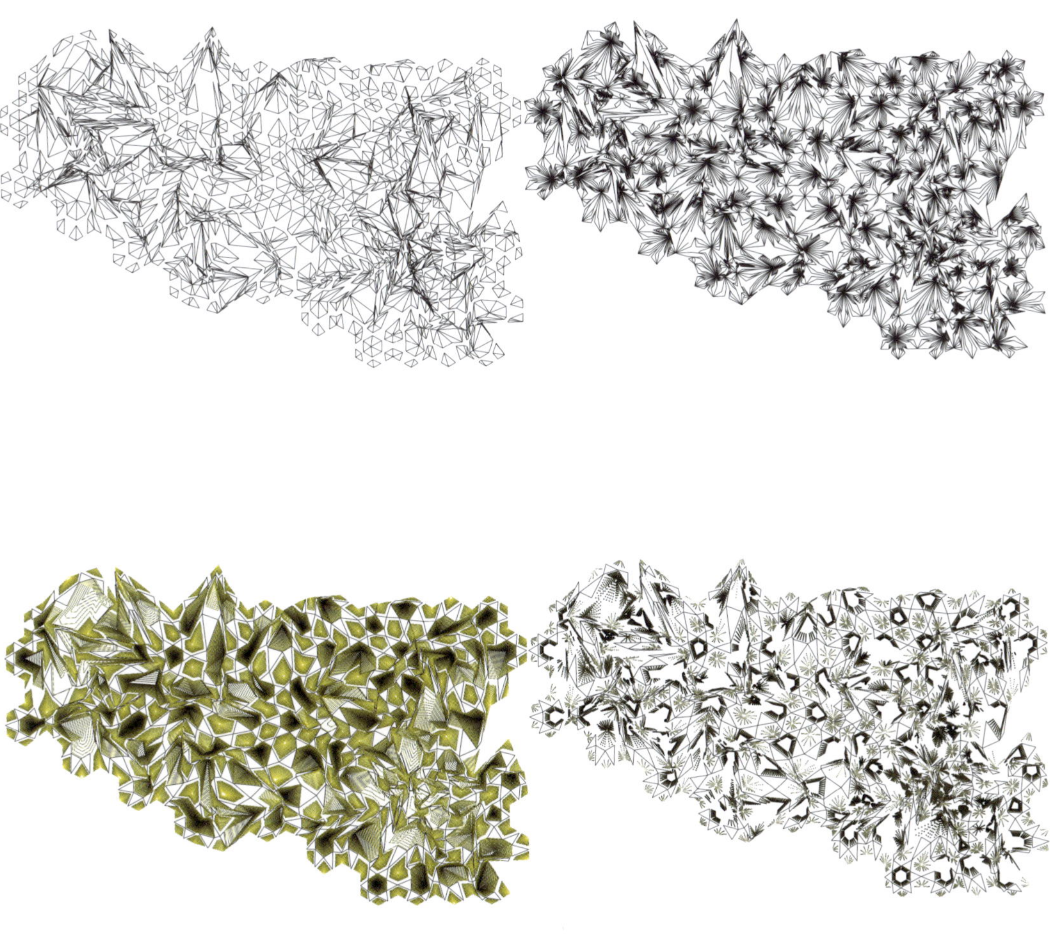

Field. Diversification. Suburban karst public datum systems. From top left to bottom right: summits and sinks, plantation lines, topographic contours, room units. Plans.

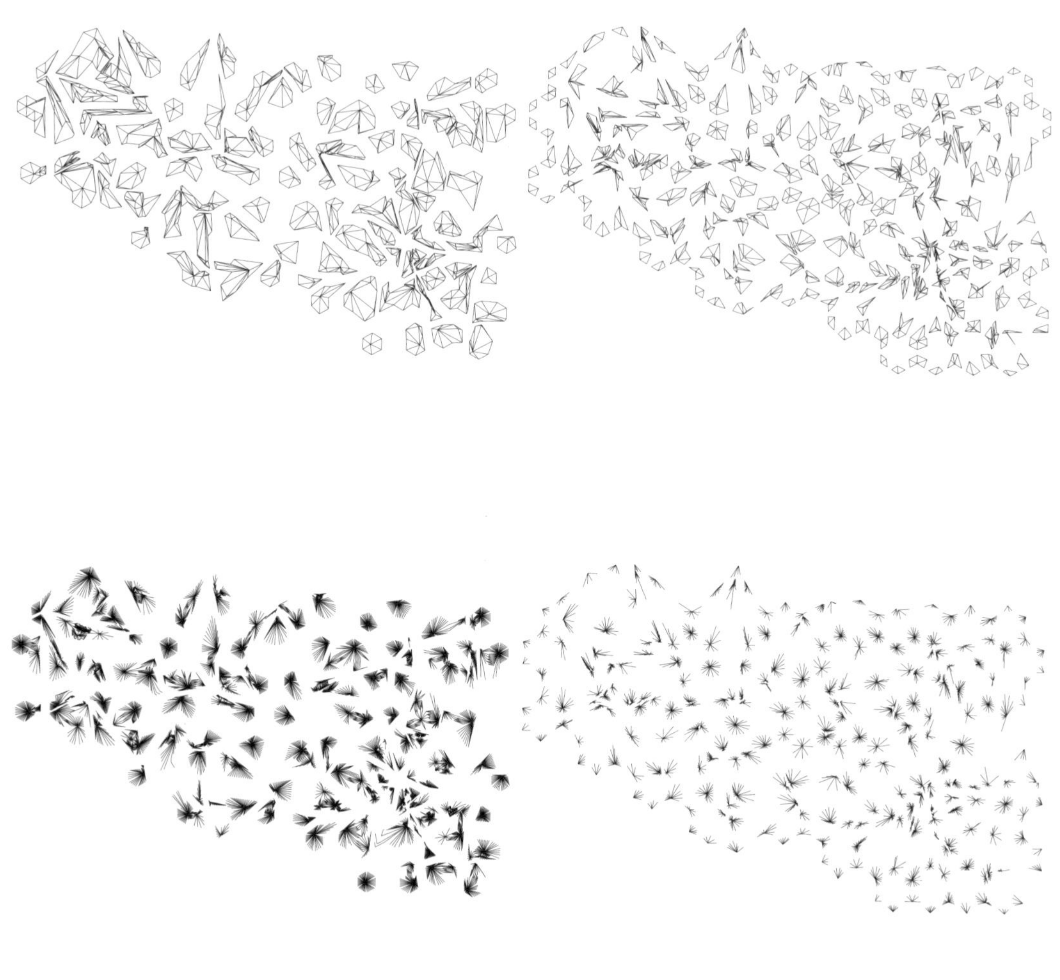

Field. Diversification. Suburban karst landscape systems. From top left to bottom right: summits, sinks, summits plantation lines, sinks plantation lines. Plans.

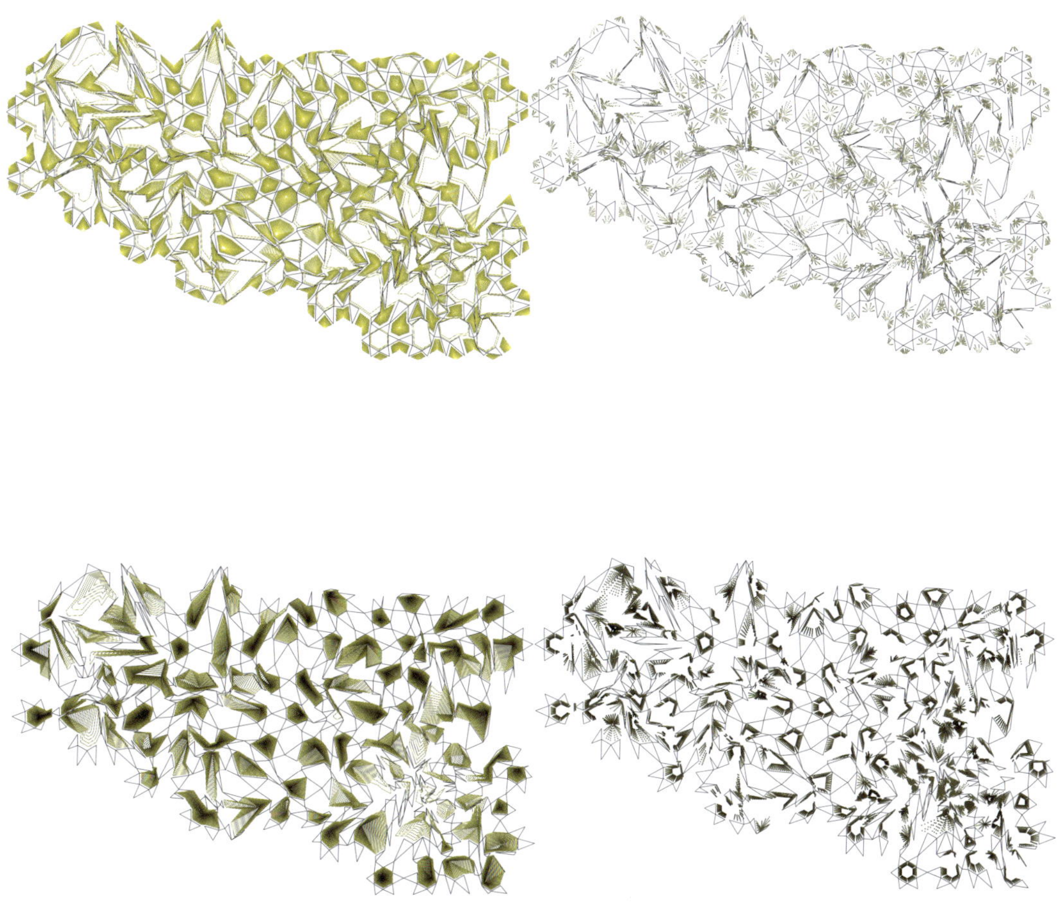

Field. Diversification. Suburban karst housing systems. From top left to bottom right: summits topographic contours, sinks topographic contours, summits room units, sinks room units. Plans.

Field. Organization. Suburban karst masterplan. Physical model plan sector.

Field. Organization. Suburban karst masterplan. Physical model plan sector zoom.

Alluvial Ecospheres, Kaz Yoneda.
Field. Organization. Braided urban archipelago. Physical model plan sector zoom.

The Bare Ecosphere Model

Alluvial Ecospheres integrates the organizational protocols of a high-rise housing collective with a series of nested geometries that simulate the behavior of a braided river system. An extensive, ecologically constrained model of island formation prescribes the dimensional and directional characteristics of tower manifolds. The closed, *hof*-like housing sequences contain and condition the environmental performance of an archipelago of open parks, synchronizing leisure, living, research, and curiosity-driven appropriations of nature.

The main channel of a flat-plain river system divides into multiple waterways as its flow encounters alluvial deposits, forming islands along the way. An interconnected pattern emerges as the trajectories of bifurcating channels converge with and diverge from their immediate neighbors. Rhomboidal island-bars form and constitute the basic alternating components of a dynamic diagonal grid, covering large territories through transversal proliferation. The larger the floodplain and the slower the currents, the larger the islands and the wider the channels; the lower the density, the higher the connectivity, and the smaller the ecological pockets. Stable ground is progressively created, exerting an influence on the performance of ecosystems and on the material characteristics of the isolated environments. The braided pattern can be easily observed from great distances but is less recognizable up close. However, as the size of islands diminishes, rivers narrow and the gradient of the topography increases, configuring, at extreme levels, meandering landscapes with systematic picturesque characteristics.

Tower manifolds, made of independent but contiguous high-rise, high-density residential bars, are aligned longitudinally and surround these formations. Each bar has a vertical core and two wings of apartments containing varying numbers of bedrooms. They are organized as curvilinear segments of a round megatower form. The sparse center of the form varies in location and number of focal points depending on the directionality and intensity of area flow dynamics. The free plan of the ground level accommodates small vessels of condominium residences. A public plaza coordinates the vessels' navigation along streams with pedestrian access to the leisure amenities that carefully populate the restricted ecological environments. Connecting the two sides of these soft edges, a series of environmental corridors cut across the tower manifold through openings and displacements.

The overall permeability of the model is managed in one direction by the braided islands pattern and in the other through the variation of density in the array of housing bars, up to a density that makes the islands impenetrable. By controlling the permeability of edges, the model sieves the circulation of people and living species through the field. Tidal cycles provide periodic cleansing. As lagoons naturally drain, species dependent on them grow increasingly at risk, thus requiring a methodic management of fresh water across the field through gentle ecological thresholds. Human circulation, in principle concentrated along the edges, does not generally penetrate into the ecological cores: when it does, the alluvial ecospheres are laid bare.

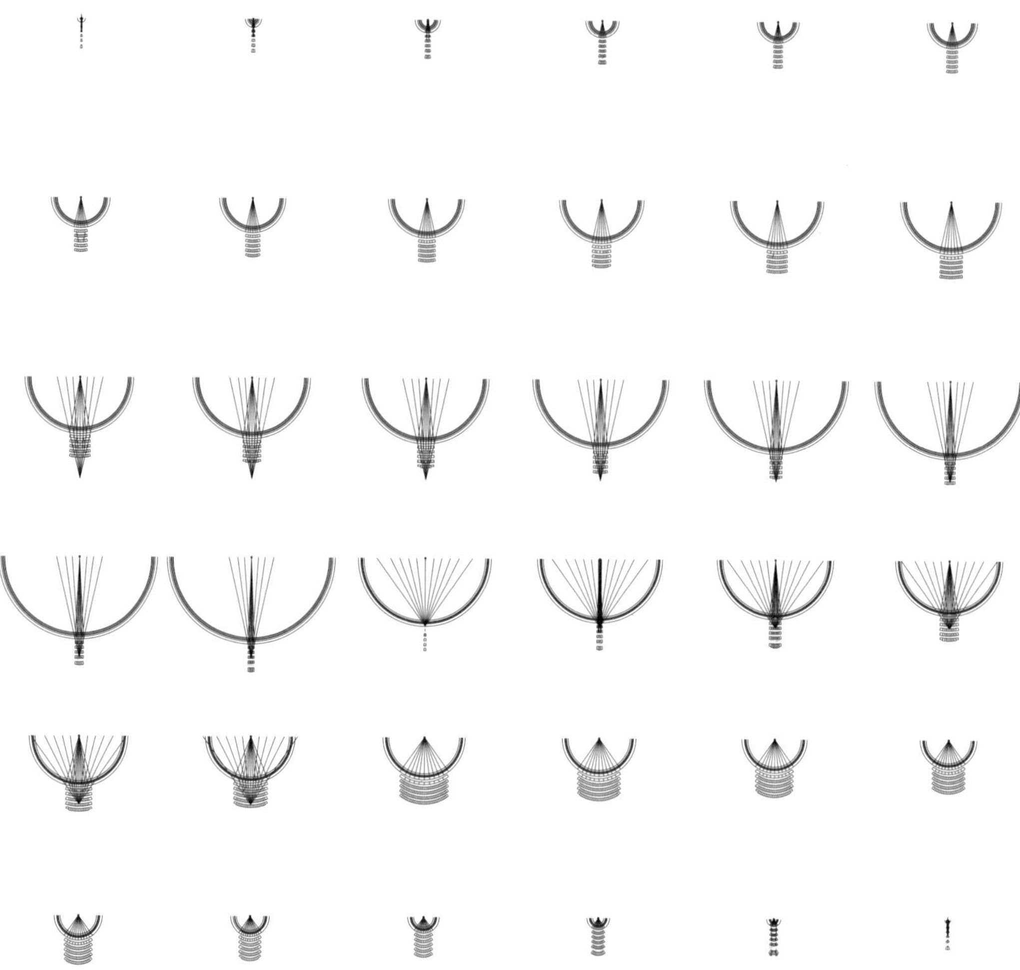

Modality. Variation. Housing bars variation and differentiation. Variation of number and radius of radiating lines, squeezing of repetitive housing units, evaluation of spatial overlaps, compensatory expansion and reduction of housing unit sizes, introduction of new housing units. Plans.

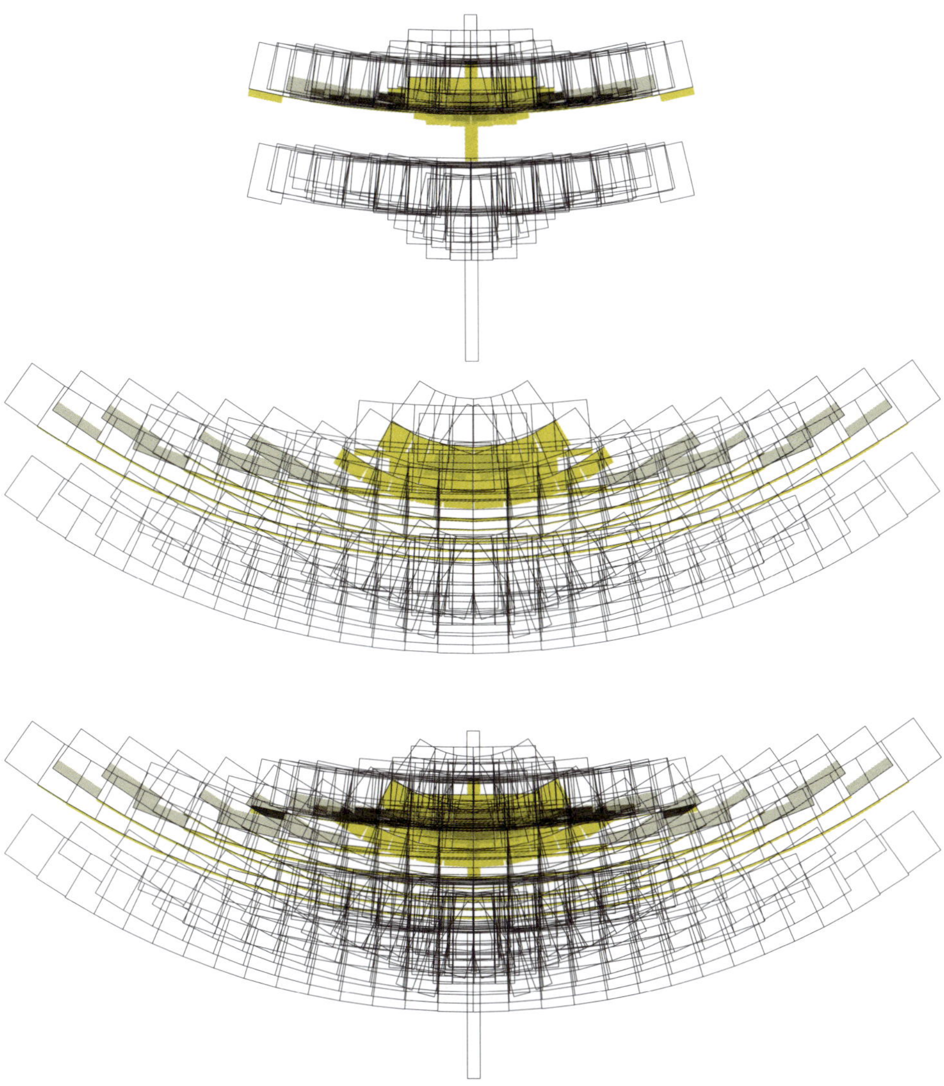

Modality. Variability. Housing bars variation and differentiation spectrum. Spectrum of variation of number and radius of radiating lines, squeezing of repetitive housing units, evaluation of spatial overlaps, compensatory expansion and reduction of housing unit sizes, introduction of new housing units. Plans.

Model. Organization. Braided river system spectrum. Spectrum of variation of central bar size and orientation, lobe size and orientation, protrusion height and flow deflection, stages of formation of bottlenecks, flow overruns, surface erosion, chute cut-offs. Plan.

Model. Organization. Braided river system population. Association of central bar and lobe formation stages with housing arrays, heights, depths, quantities, and radius variations. Plan.

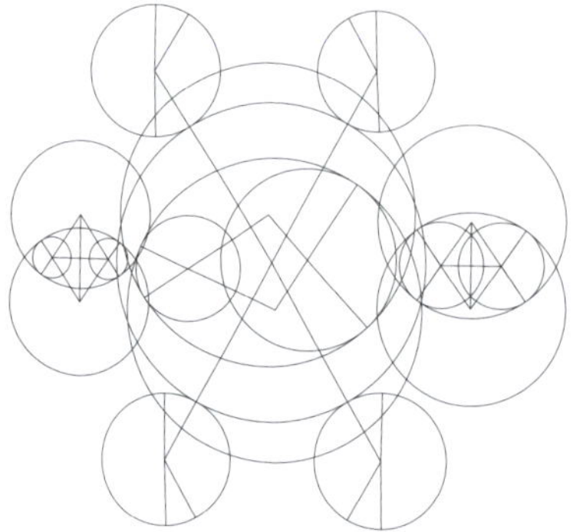

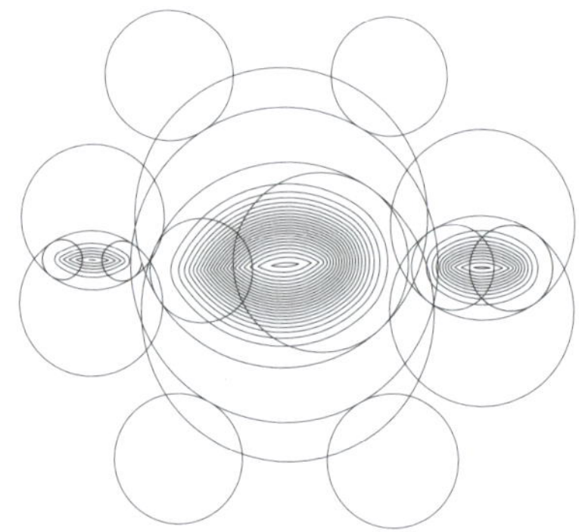

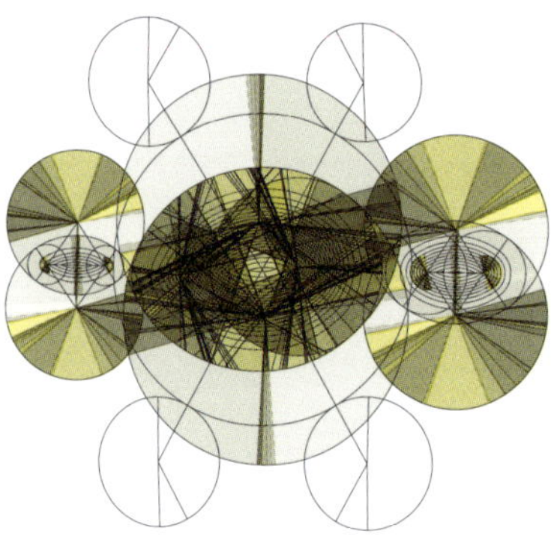

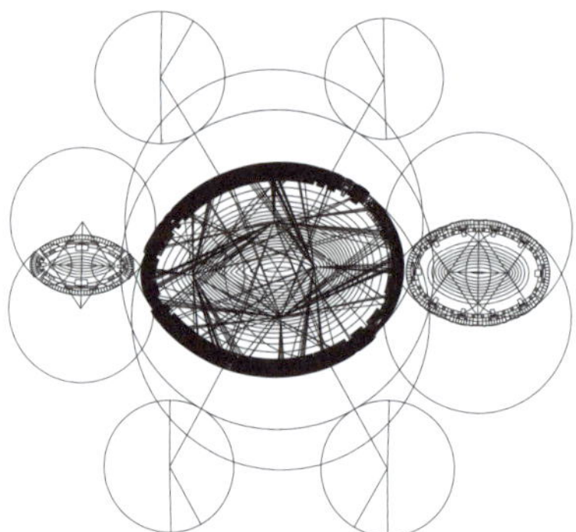

Prototype. Diversification. Braided urban island-set environmental strategy. From top left to bottom right: landform outlines, topographic contours, transversal ecological corridors, high-rise housing bars. Plans.

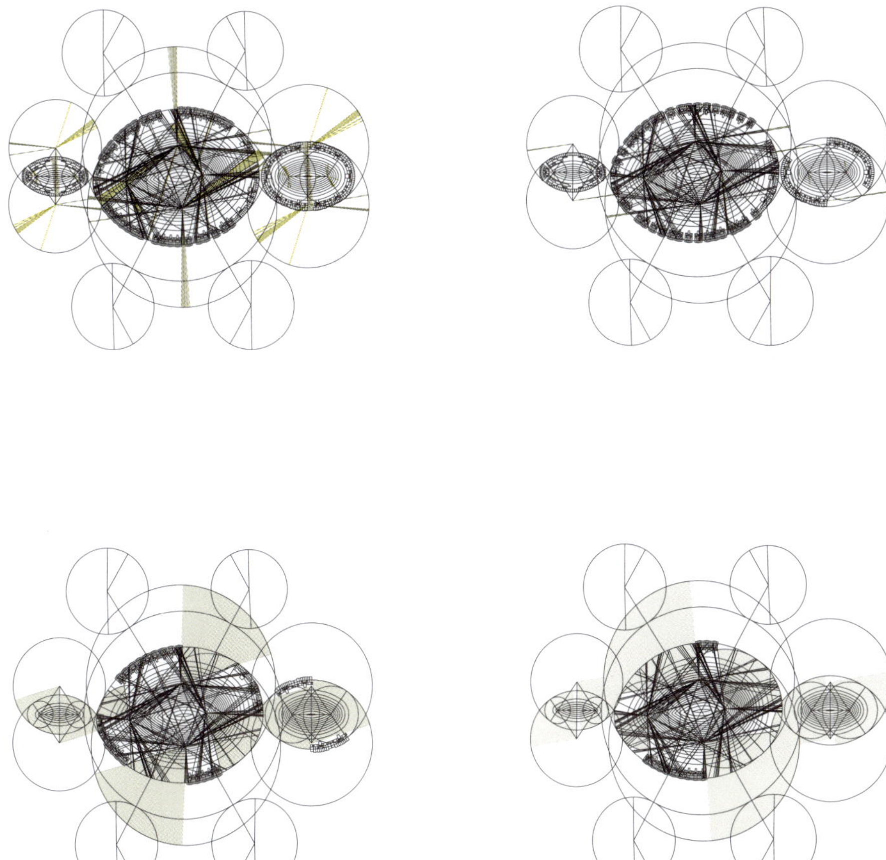

Prototype. Diversification. Braided urban island-set massing process. From top left to bottom right: high-rise housing bar selection variants according to transversal ecological corridors. Plans.

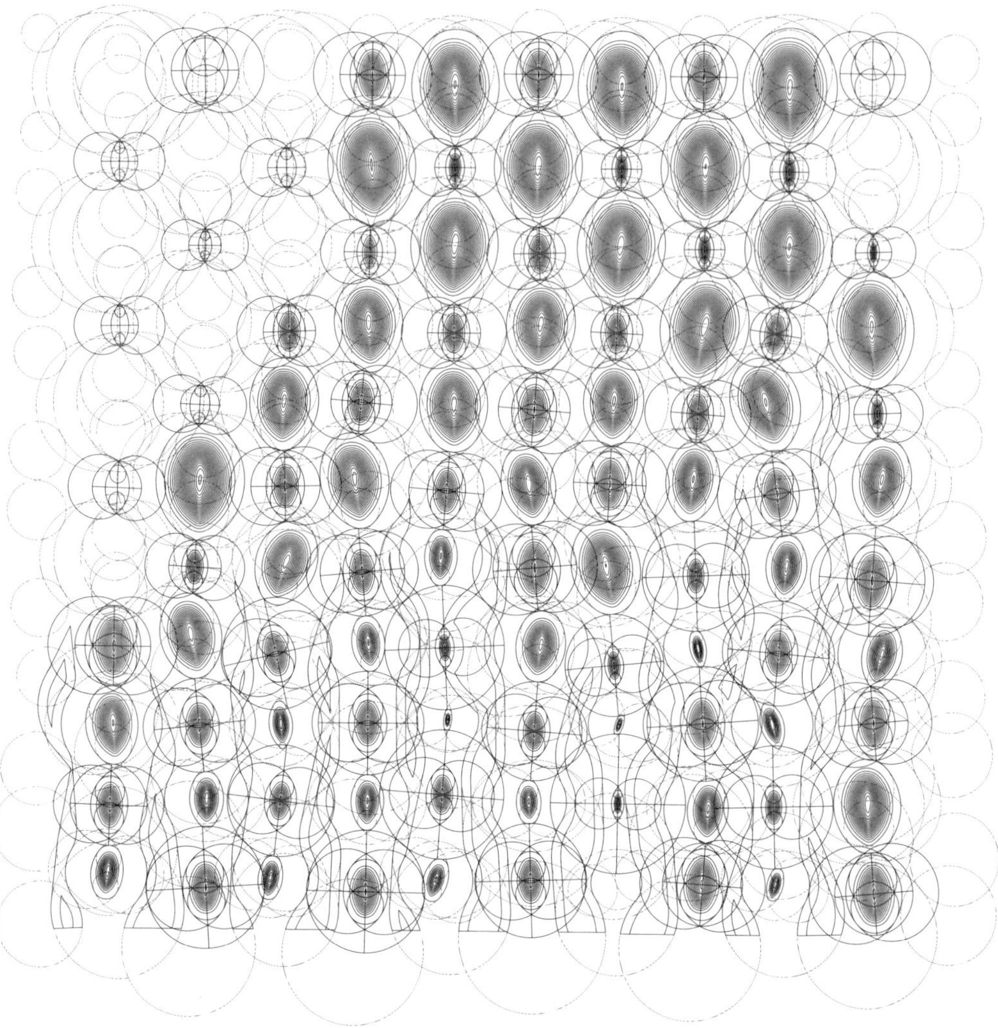

Field. Matrix. Braided urban archipelago indexical construction. Landform outlines and topographic contours. Plan.

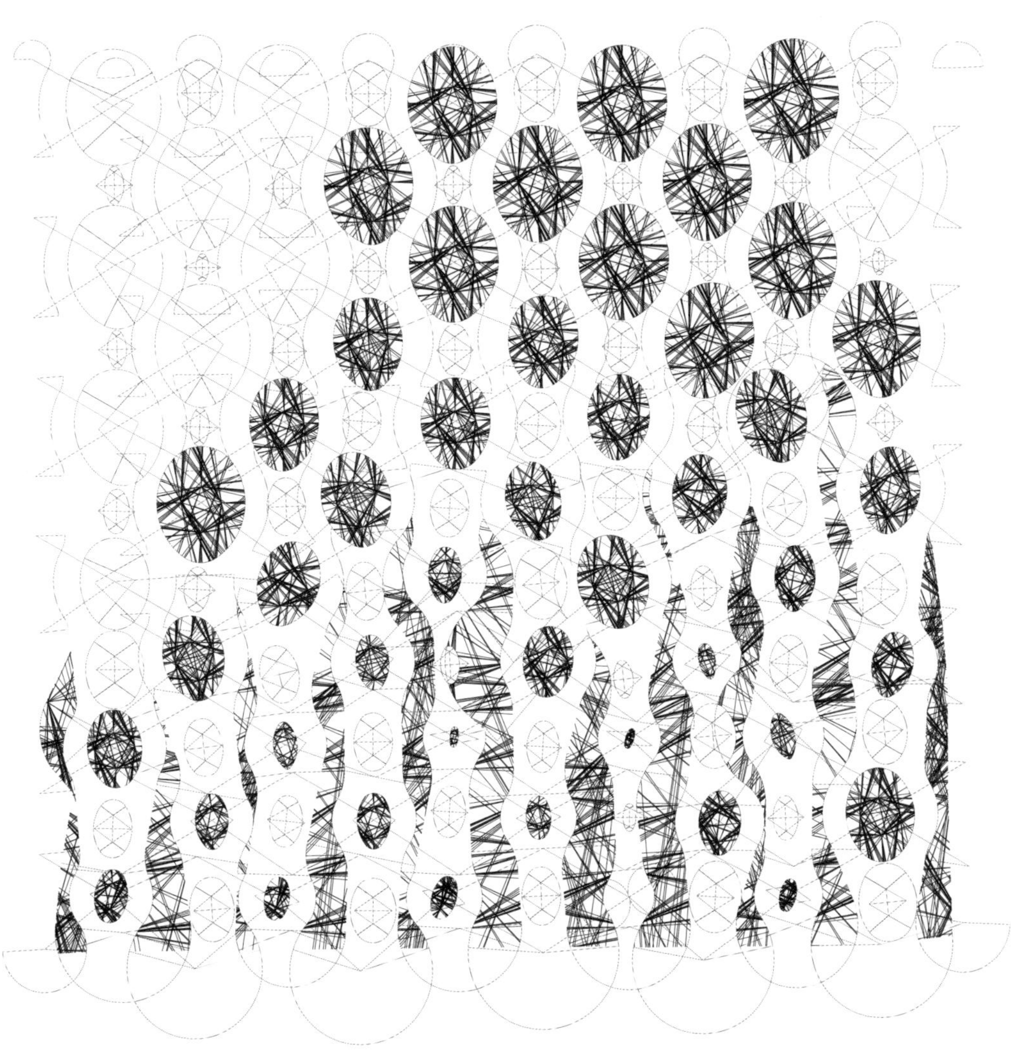

Field. Matrix. Braided urban archipelago indexical construction. Landform outlines and transversal ecological corridors. Plan.

Field. Organization. Braided urban archipelago ground and massing organization. Topographic contours, and high-rise housing bar organization resultant of the interaction with river currents and topographic drainage. Plan.

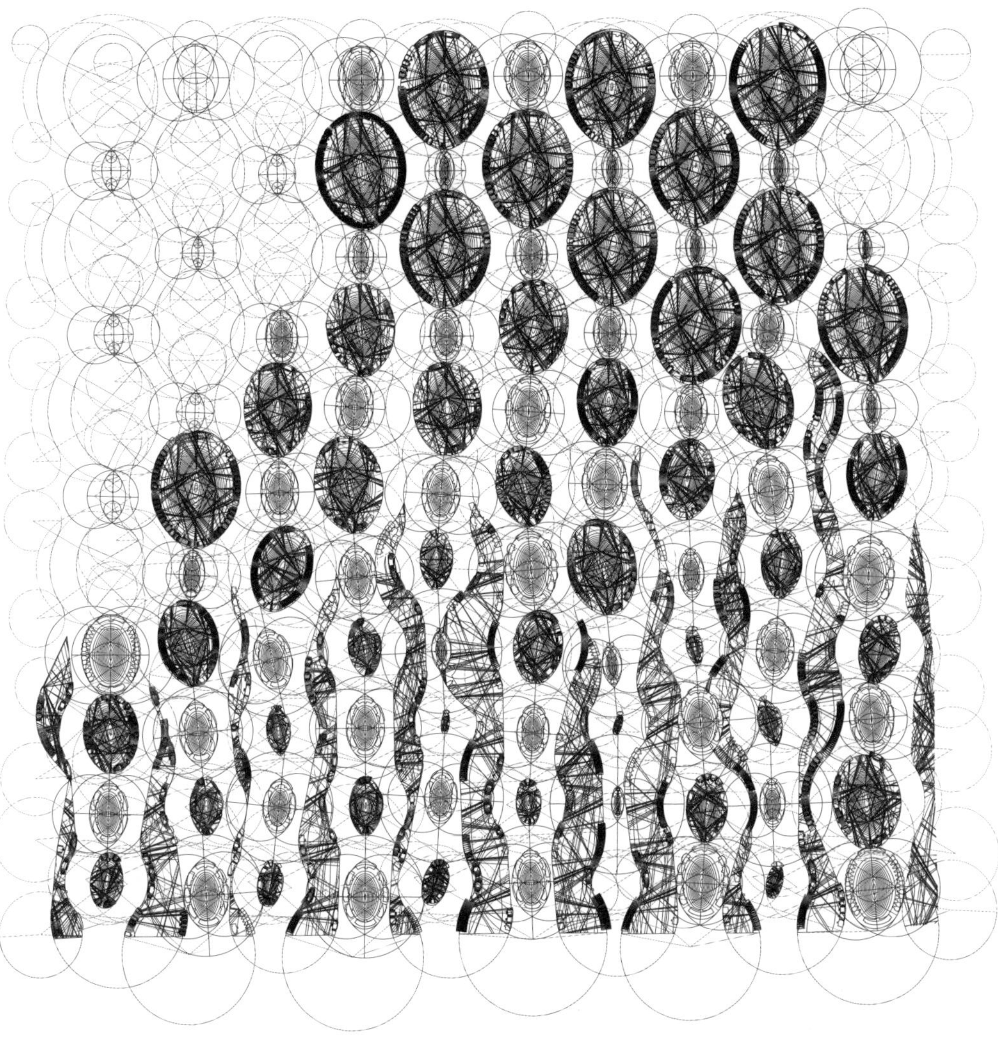

Field. Organization. Braided urban archipelago indexical construction, and ground and massing organization. Landform outlines, transversal ecological corridors, topographic contours, and high-rise housing bar organization resultant of the interaction with river currents and topographic drainage. Plan.

Delirium Atrium, Dongjae Cho and Fred Chung.
Prototype. Variability. Atrium building lineage. Physical model plans.

The Meta-Antiurban Model

Delirium Atrium introduces a new stage in the evolution of the atrium building by integrating its modalities to configure spectacular interiors, organize meandering circulations, manage relationships with urban infrastructure, and construct iconic figures at the scale of the city.

Delirium Atrium merges these modalities in a model constituted by the horizontal displacement and vertical bifurcation of vertical circulation, shared programs, and internal voids. The model is controlled through a series of five horizontal strata that emanate from a virtual datum located in the middle of the building. The strata are offset vertically to control the distribution of an increasing number of components across the elevation. Bifurcations grow and extend the atrium upward and downward at varying rhythms and rates.

The atrium becomes a laboratory of forms of interiorized urban exteriority, located at the core of an extra-extra-large tower. The space ranges from the monumental to the domestic, from the hyperactive to the peaceful, from the frightening to the blank, and from the spectacular to the neutral. A trans-scalar void-making apparatus, Delirium Atrium works as a Klein bottle, through which the lobotomy of skyscraper interiors swallows the scales of the urban environment into the building's spatial configuration. The horizontal and vertical expansion of office space through higher configurations and deeper plans fuels the interior's escalation in complexity, giving birth to a form of atrium capable not only of bringing light and air into the building and of assuring the fluency and variability of its inner circulation, but also of articulating the spectacular condition of the space and of strengthening the iconic poignancy of the structure. The singularity of these higher forms of interior is not simply determined by the requirements of what they serve or by the uninterrupted transition from the exteriority on which they allegedly depend. Rather, this fully contained, independent architectural artifact, despite its generous appearance, influences and overpowers both the public and the private through its will, and hence creates an artificial atmosphere within which the notion of "public" becomes a construct.

Delirium Atrium suspends any sense of destination and creates an autonomous form of orientation through the same transparency of organization that it conceals. The bold but devious presence of the section as a public spectacle both exposes and hinders the linear spatial sequence of the whole. Delirium Atrium identifies the characteristics on which the uniqueness of these intensely autonomous spaces stands, evaluates their size, form, location, and organizational capabilities, and turns them into a system that provides the conditions for both breeding singularity and absoluteness into the antiurban interior and managing its diversification beyond its recent tradition.

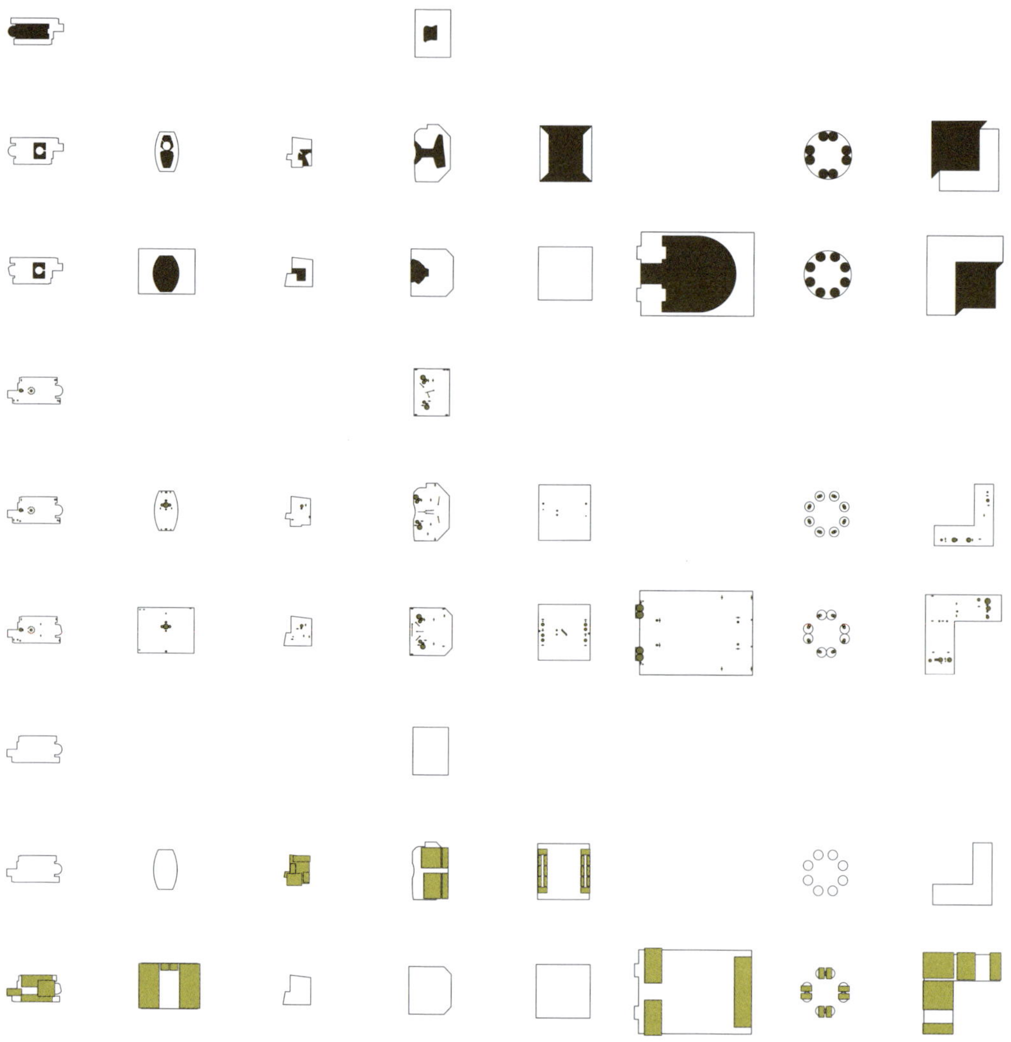

Typology. Reduction. Atrium building systems. From top to bottom: interior and exterior atriums; elevators, escalators, and service cores; hotel units, office spaces, and commercial spaces. From left to right: inner spectacle type (John Portman & Associates, Marriott Marquis Hotel, New York, NY, USA; John Portman & Associates, Marriott Marquis Hotel, Atlanta, GA, USA); meandering circulation type (Behnisch, Genzyme Center, Cambridge, MA, USA; Jerde Partnership, Mega Box, Hong Kong, China); urban infrastructure type (Otto Von Spreckelsen, Grande Arche de la Fraternité, Paris, France; Tange Associates, Tokyo Metropolitan Government, Tokyo, Japan); cityscape icon type (Foreign Office Architects, Bundle Tower, New York, NY, USA; Office for Metropolitan Architecture, CCTV, Beijing, China). Plans.

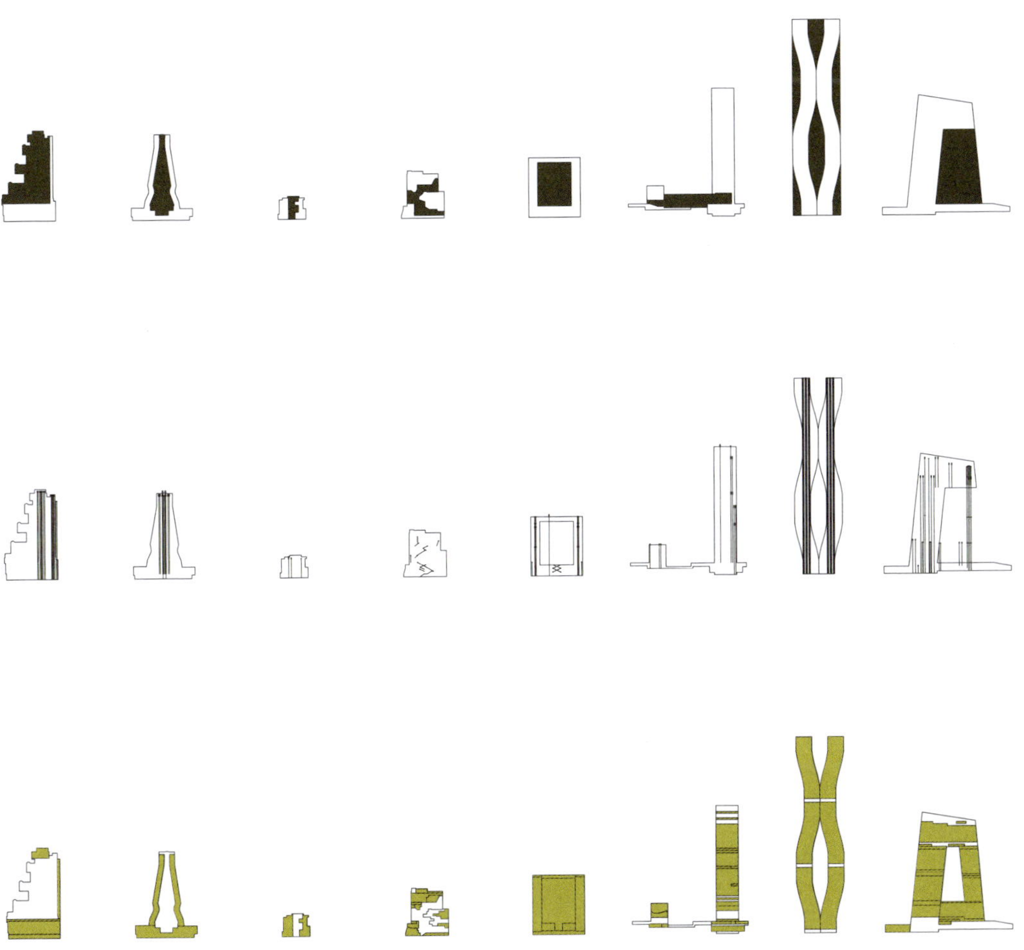

Typology. Reduction. Atrium building systems. From top to bottom: interior and exterior atriums; elevators, escalators, and service cores; hotel units, office spaces, and commercial spaces. From left to right: inner spectacle type (John Portman & Associates, Marriott Marquis Hotel, New York, NY, USA; John Portman & Associates, Marriott Marquis Hotel, Atlanta, GA, USA); meandering circulation type (Behnisch, Genzyme Center, Cambridge, MA, USA; Jerde Partnership, Mega Box, Hong Kong, China); urban infrastructure type (Otto Von Spreckelsen, Grande Arche de la Fraternité, Paris, France; Tange Associates, Tokyo Metropolitan Government, Tokyo, Japan); cityscape icon type (Foreign Office Architects, Bundle Tower, New York, NY, USA; Office for Metropolitan Architecture, CCTV, Beijing, China). Elevations.

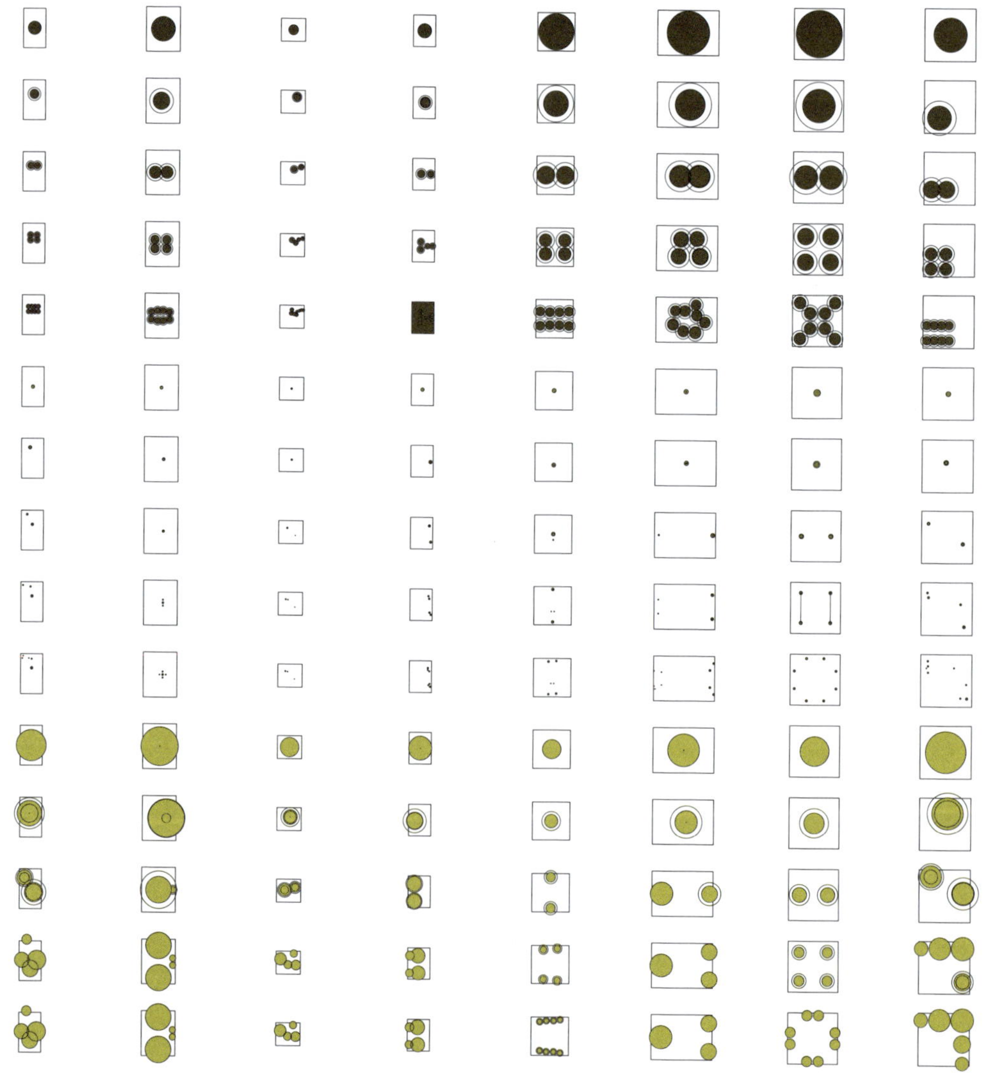

Modality. Generalization. Atrium building systems datum abstraction. From top to bottom: interior and exterior atriums; elevators, escalators, and service cores; hotel units, office spaces, and commercial spaces. From left to right: inner spectacle type (John Portman & Associates, Marriott Marquis Hotel, New York, NY, USA; John Portman & Associates, Marriott Marquis Hotel, Atlanta, GA, USA); meandering circulation type (Behnisch, Genzyme Center, Cambridge, MA, USA; Jerde Partnership, Mega Box, Hong Kong, China); urban infrastructure type (Otto Von Spreckelsen, Grande Arche de la Fraternité, Paris, France; Tange Associates, Tokyo Metropolitan Government, Tokyo, Japan); cityscape icon type (Foreign Office Architects, Bundle Tower, New York, NY, USA; Office for Metropolitan Architecture, CCTV, Beijing, China). Plans.

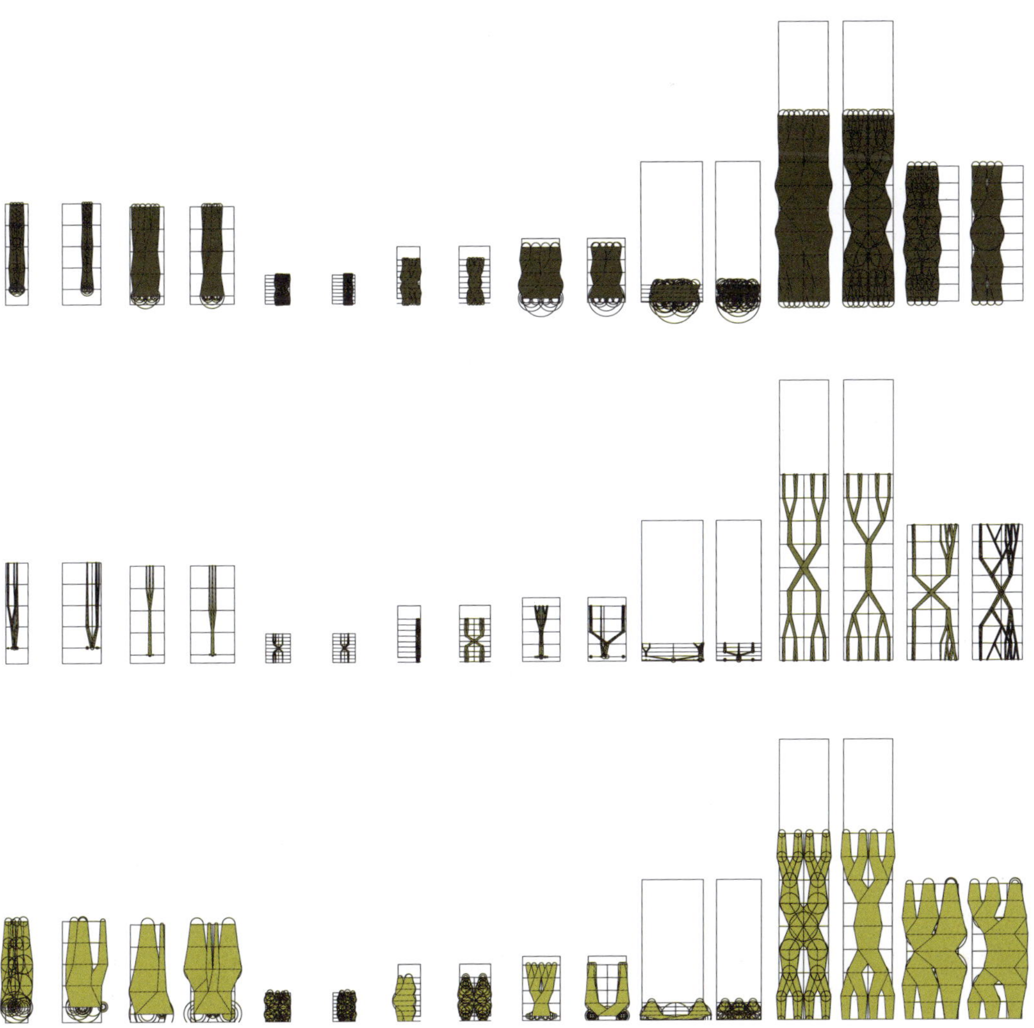

Modality. Generalization. Atrium building systems datum abstraction. From top to bottom: interior and exterior atriums; elevators, escalators, and service cores; hotel units, office spaces, and commercial spaces. From left to right: inner spectacle type (John Portman & Associates, Marriott Marquis Hotel, New York, NY, USA; John Portman & Associates, Marriott Marquis Hotel, Atlanta, GA, USA); meandering circulation type (Behnisch, Genzyme Center, Cambridge, MA, USA; Jerde Partnership, Mega Box, Hong Kong, China); urban infrastructure type (Otto Von Spreckelsen, Grande Arche de la Fraternité, Paris, France; Tange Associates, Tokyo Metropolitan Government, Tokyo, Japan); cityscape icon type (Foreign Office Architects, Bundle Tower, New York, NY, USA; Office for Metropolitan Architecture, CCTV, Beijing, China). Elevations.

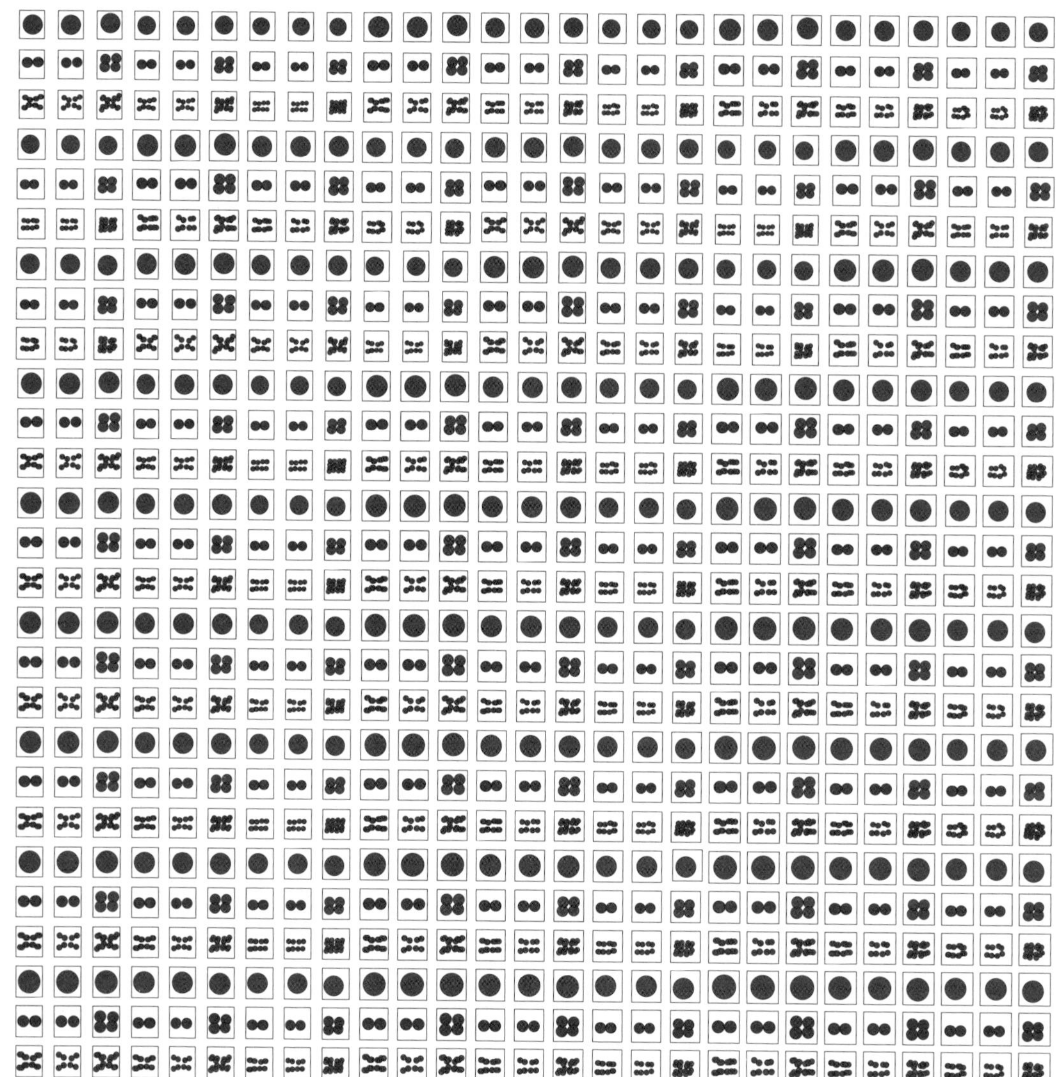

Model. Variability. Atrium systems reconstruction. Modalities of variation in size, displacement, and splitting of interior and exterior atriums at horizontal datums, depending on type. Plans.

Model. Variability. Atrium systems reconstruction. Interior and exterior atriums bifurcations at regular intervals according to modalities of variation in size, displacement, and splitting at horizontal datums, depending on type. Elevations.

Model. Variability. Circulation systems reconstruction. Modalities of variation in size, displacement, and splitting of elevators, escalators, and service cores at horizontal datums, depending on type. Plans.

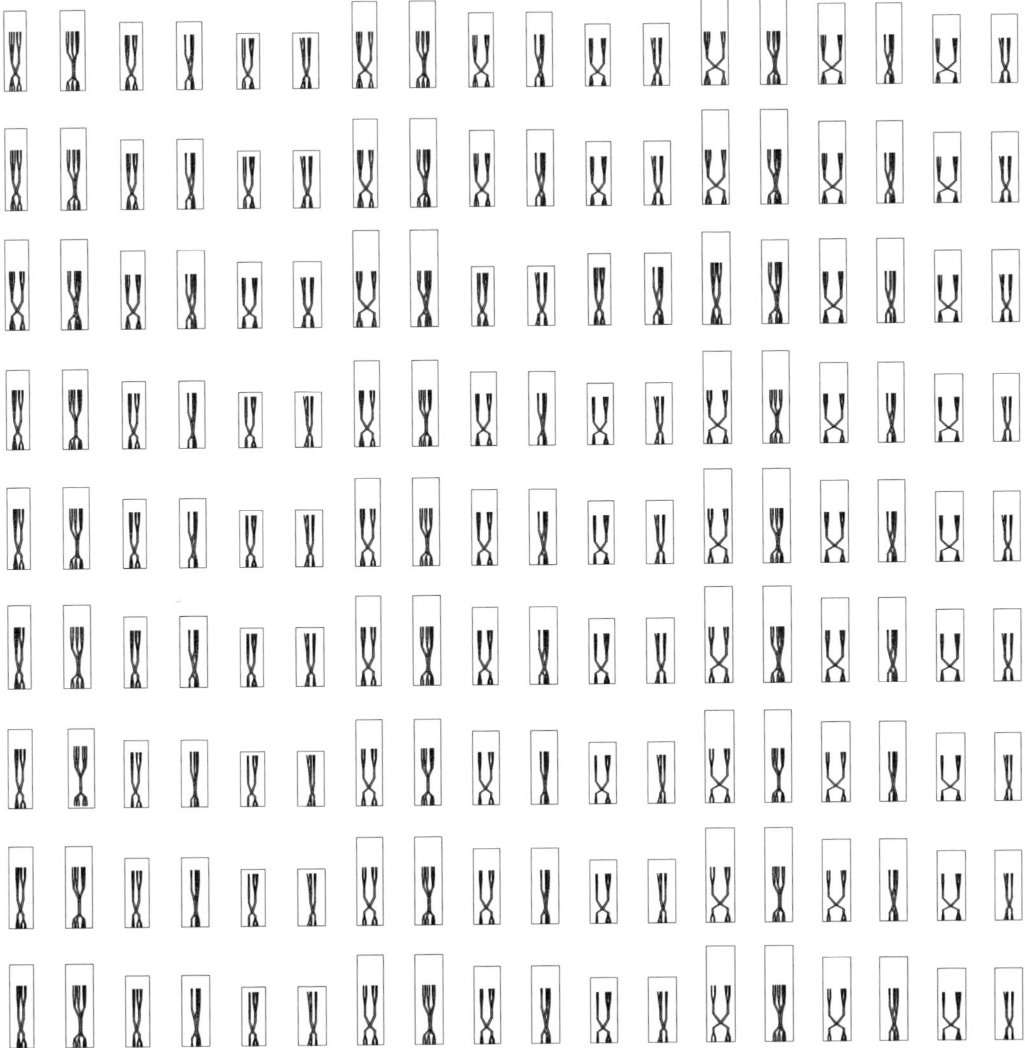

Model. Variability. Circulation systems reconstruction. Elevators, escalators, and service core bifurcations at regular intervals according to modalities of variation in size, displacement, and splitting at horizontal datums, depending on type. Elevations.

Model. Variability. Programmatic systems reconstruction. Modalities of variation in size, displacement, and splitting of hotel units, office spaces, and commercial spaces at horizontal datums, depending on type. Plans.

Model. Variability. Programmatic systems reconstruction. Hotel unit, office space, and commercial space bifurcations at regular intervals according to modalities of variation in size, displacement, and splitting at horizontal datums, depending on types. Elevations.

Prototype. Differentiation. Deep plan differentiation process. From top left to bottom right: iterative process of territorial distribution, negotiation of adjacencies, definition of internal connectivity, integration of vertical circulation, programmatic diversification, and spatial subdivision. Plans.

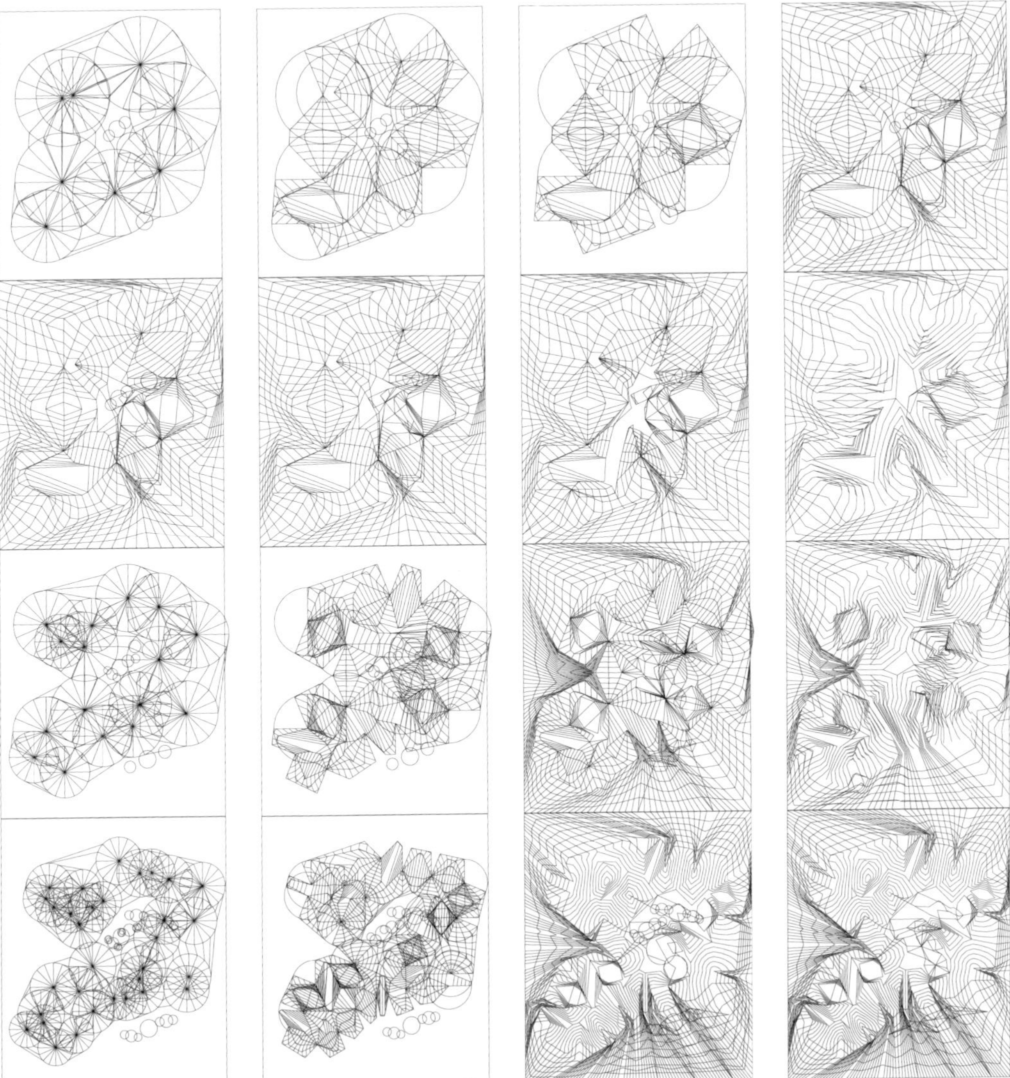

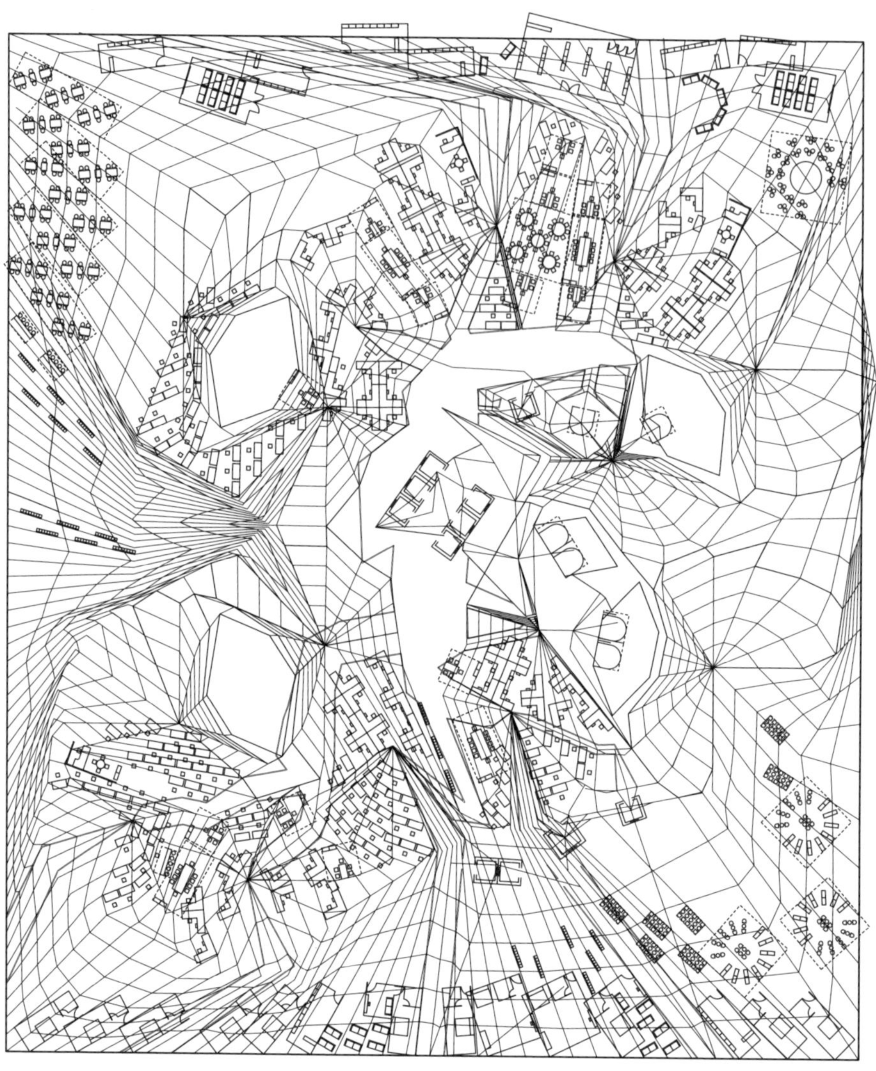

Prototype. Organization. Atrium Building, fourth datum spatial variegation. Atriums, lobbies, and local lobbies; elevator cores, courtyards, shafts, storage areas, and terraces; open lounges, exhibition areas, meeting areas, food courts, round tables, auditoriums, projection rooms, and classrooms; office units; open and linear workspace; hotel rooms. Plan.

Prototype. Organization. Atrium building, fifth datum spatial variegation. Atriums, lobbies, and local lobbies; elevator cores, courtyards, shafts, storage areas, and terraces; open lounges, exhibition areas, meeting areas, food courts, round tables, auditoriums, projection rooms, and classrooms; office units; open and linear workspace; hotel rooms. Plan.

Data-Form, Lucas Correa-Sevilla and Zhou Wu.
Prototype. Variability. Mixed-use data massing lineage. Physical model plan.

The Big Data Model

Data Form weaves together a set of mixed-use islands within a matrix of internal commercial connectedness. The mixed-use building—a self-segregated city within a city—is so unique and irresistible that it effortlessly attracts inhabitants into a limbo of shared distraction. It engenders a field of numbness characterized by its appealing adequacy and its uncritical relevance, which hides the extreme vulnerability of the user under the illusion of his/her overpowering by sheer consumption.

Data Form is an entangled archipelago of islands characterized by determined indeterminacy, uprising their machinery for generating totally unnecessary information by means of an internal web that frantically produces difference for the sake of difference. A manifold of mixed-use buildings acts as the infrastructural spine that integrates independent commercial masses within a single artifact. The more congested this spine, the more numerous its internal connections, the more open the exchanges, and the more indifferent to the outside world.

A set of common behavioral rules relates programs across a set of mixed-use buildings, in the attempt to foster programmatic coexistences and induce them to transform each other. The rules result from the quantification of variables across a mixed-use taxonomy, the recognition of patterns across those variables, the construction of internally consistent behaviors, and the configuration of relations that work as gradients in an informational continuum. This manifold of mutual destabilizers paradoxically constructs a highly static universe, the vibrating programmatic heterogeneity of which is dispersed to the point of becoming a rigorous, indeterminate order. Variables are organized by the unfolding of cores within a set of mixed-use buildings, arranged as a sequential logic of number of programs per core. Various levels of complexity are achieved based on the following variables: total surface area per core, total surface area per program per core, average floor area per program, spatial height per program, plan depth per program, distance of programs to the ground, surface area of core per program, surface area of hallway per program, and vertical and horizontal connectivity between programs. The gradient of organizational diversity that emerges from the mixed-use mix is conditioned by the intertwinement of variations, and a series of mixed-use manifolds is constructed through the integration of this web.

The accumulation of these incompatible spatial conditions configures a mountain of mutually displaced pyramidal sections with interstitial plateaus that build up a single cumulative structure. The blunt reification of information creates the basis for the rugged megaform, which both systemically and allegorically piles up the informational debris indexed along its generation. The pyramidal sections of this pile configure a manifold of pinnacles. Consumption reaches its maximum density in the central, highest point, which radiates the internal logic outward, reaching its ultimate amplification when the interior releases its containment and projects itself as a singular totality.

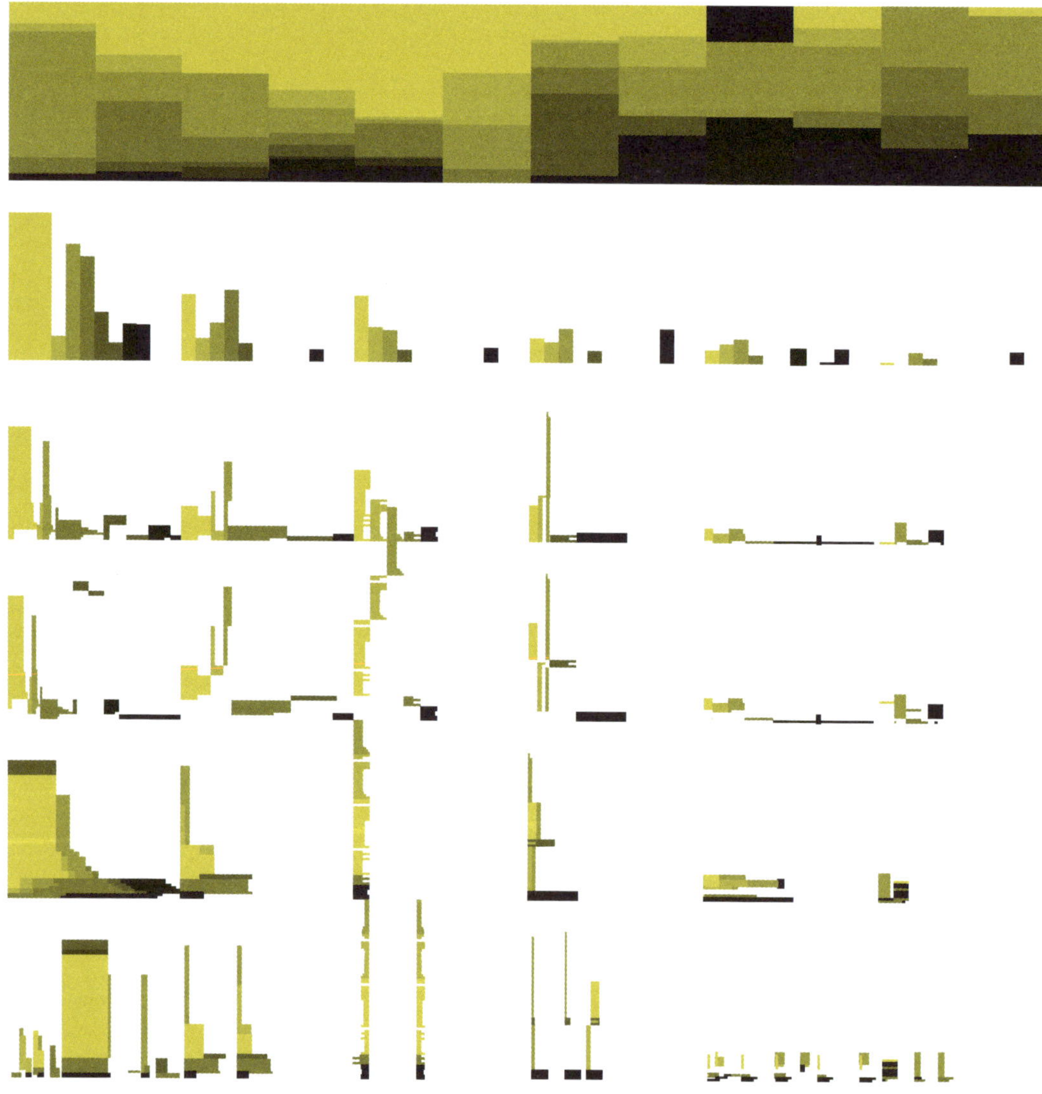

Typology. Abstraction. Mixed-use vertical programmatic distribution. From top to bottom: relative programmatic distribution, absolute programmatic distribution, programmatic distribution by height and area, programmatic distribution in elevation, programmatic overlay in elevation, programmatic plug-ins along vertical spines. From left to right: Minoru Mori, Roppongi Hills, Tokyo, Japan; Skidmore, Owings & Merrill, Time Warner Center, New York, NY, USA; Jean Nouvel, Tour Signal, Esplanade de la Defense, Paris, France; REX, Museum Plaza, Louisville, KY, USA; Steven Holl, Vanke Center, Shenzhen, China; Herzog & de Meuron, 1111 Lincoln Road, Miami, FL, USA. Elevation charts.

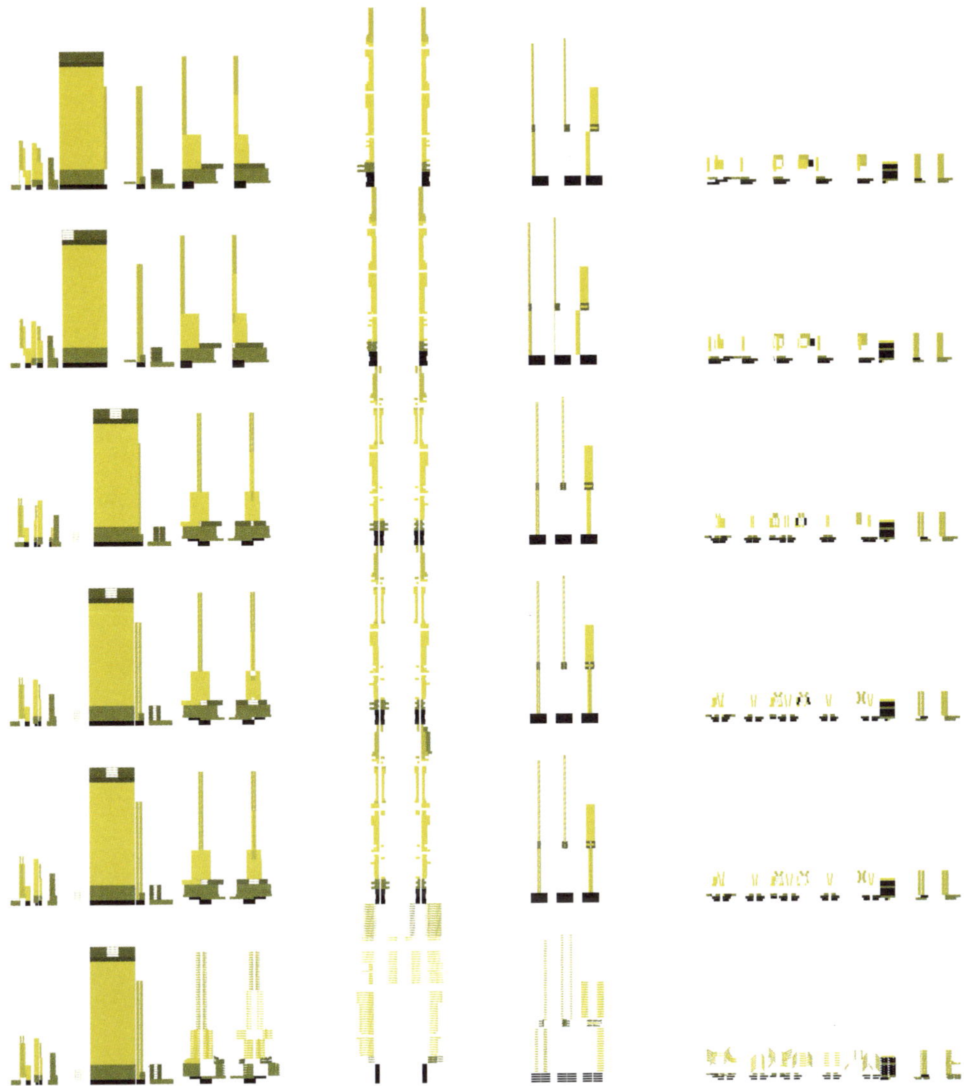

Typology. Abstraction. Mixed-use vertical programmatic distribution. From top to bottom: scaling of core spine, programmatic reorganization, programmatic distribution per core, introduction of horizontal circulatory components, recognition of inner voids, unfolding of slabs. From left to right: Minoru Mori, Roppongi Hills, Tokyo, Japan; Skidmore, Owings & Merrill, Time Warner Center, New York, NY, USA; Jean Nouvel, Tour Signal, Esplanade de la Defense, Paris, France; REX, Museum Plaza, Louisville, KY, USA; Steven Holl, Vanke Center, Shenzhen, China; Herzog & de Meuron, 1111 Lincoln Road, Miami, FL, USA. Elevation charts.

Modality. Evaluation. Mixed-use relative variation of programmatic areas. From top to bottom: core sequence by proximity, plan unfolding, number of programs per core, total surface area per core, total surface area per program per core, average floor surface area per program. From left to right: Minoru Mori, Roppongi Hills, Tokyo, Japan; Skidmore, Owings & Merrill, Time Warner Center, New York, NY, USA; Jean Nouvel, Tour Signal, Esplanade de la Defense, Paris, France; REX, Museum Plaza, Louisville, KY, USA; Steven Holl, Vanke Center, Shenzhen, China; Herzog & de Meuron, 1111 Lincoln Road, Miami, FL, USA. Elevation charts.

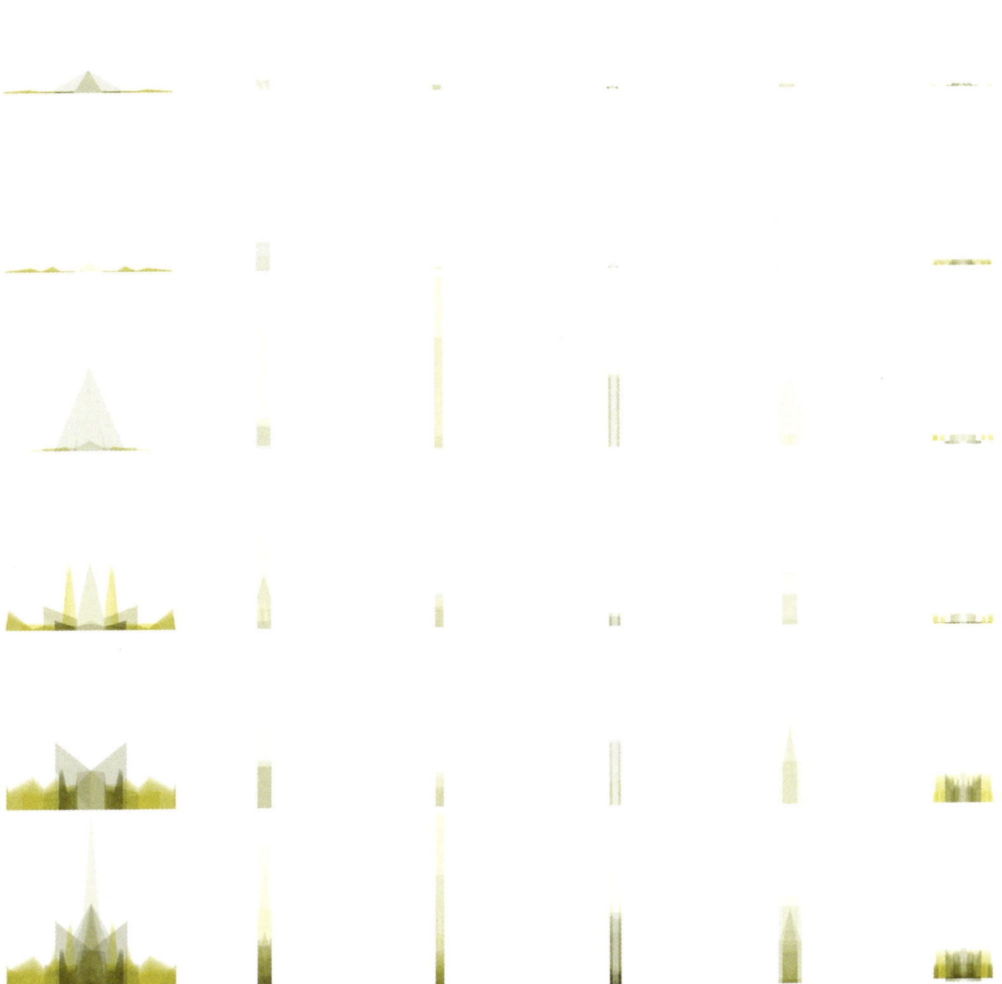

Modality. Evaluation. Mixed-use relative variation of programmatic areas. From top to bottom: floor area of core per program, floor area of hallway per program, elevation from ground per program, vertical depth variation per program, horizontal depth variation per program, composite of variations. From left to right: Minoru Mori, Roppongi Hills, Tokyo, Japan; Skidmore, Owings & Merrill, Time Warner Center, New York, NY, USA; Jean Nouvel, Tour Signal, Esplanade de la Defense, Paris, France; REX, Museum Plaza, Louisville, KY, USA; Steven Holl, Vanke Center, Shenzhen, China; Herzog & de Meuron, 1111 Lincoln Road, Miami, FL, USA. Elevation charts.

Model. Assemblage. Data sectional integration. Sectional composite of programmatic variations across cases. Elevation.

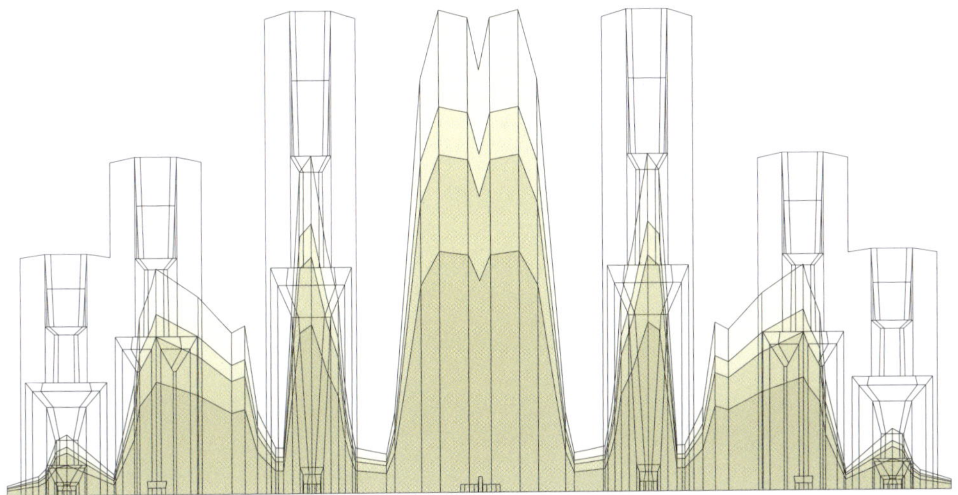

Model. Assemblage. Data sectional construction. Massing determined by average number of programs per core, by total surface area per program per core, and by average floor surface area per program. Elevation.

Prototype. Organization. Data plan programmatic matrix. Distribution of office programs, hotel programs, residential programs, retail programs, cultural programs, education programs, industrial programs, and parking programs. Plan.

Prototype. Differentiation. Data plan differentiated matrix. Incorporation of rapid and mid-range elevator cores, escalators and staircases, hallways and lobbies, service cores, and atrium spaces. Plan.

Prototype. Organization. Mixed-use data massing samples. Samples of massing by average total surface area per core, samples of typological dominance. Rendered elevations.

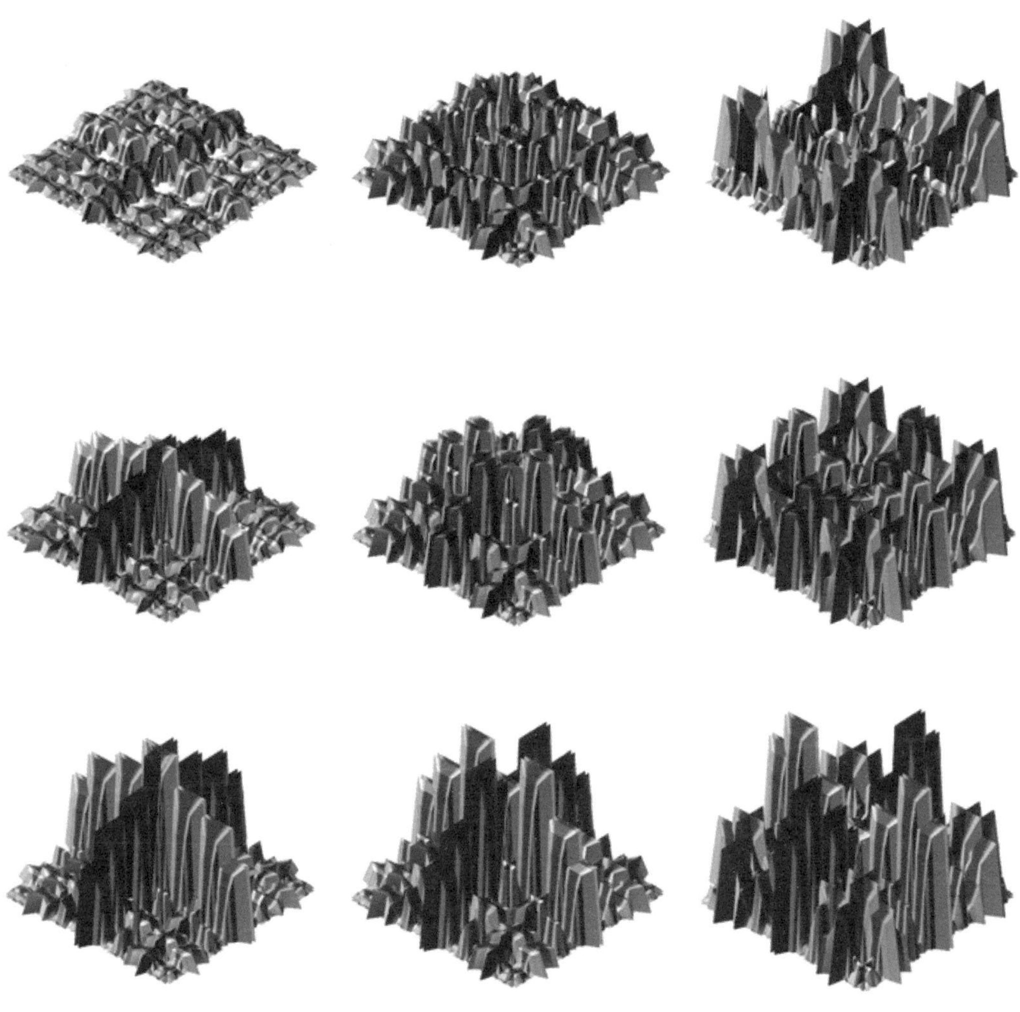

Prototype. Variability. Mixed-use data massing lineage. Variations of massing by average total surface area per core. Rendered axonometrics.

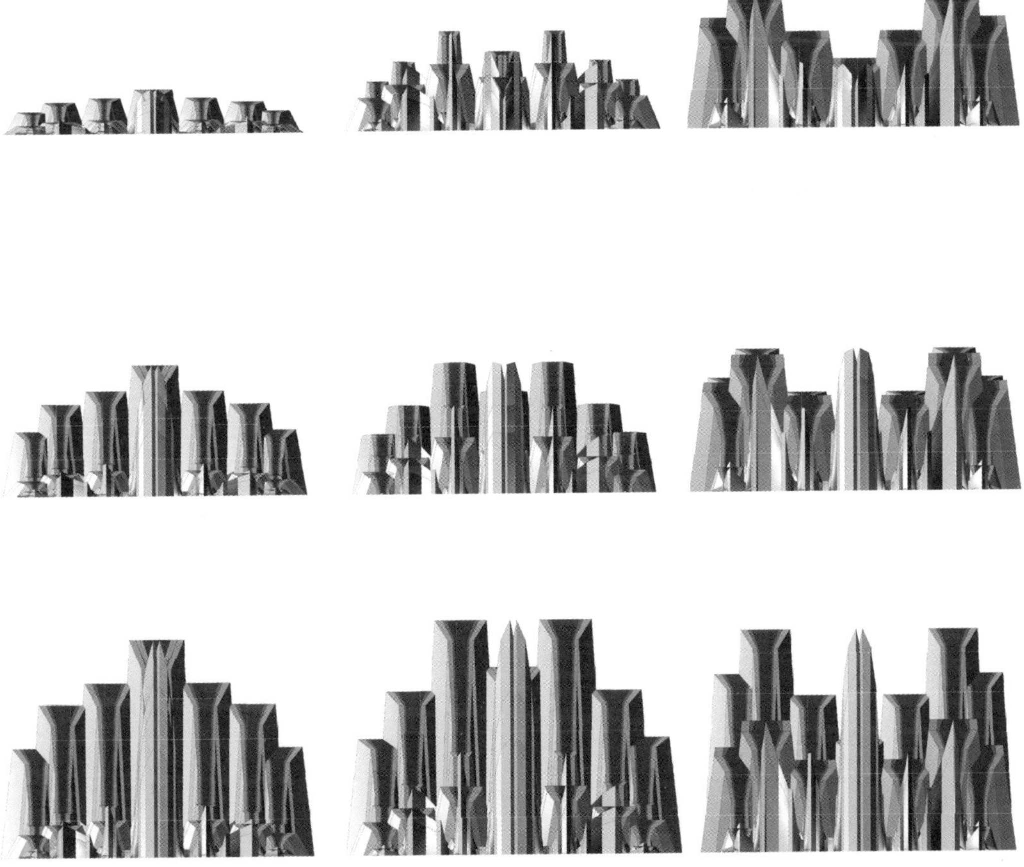

Prototype. Variability. Mixed-use data massing lineage. Variations of massing by average total surface area per core. Rendered elevations.

Irresistible Synthetic, Day Jiménez and Ostap Rudakevych.
Prototype. Organization. Gated community land lineage. Physical model plan.

The Surface Enclave Model

Irresistible Synthetic is initiated by the simple act of enclosing a large piece of land and cropping a surface. The square frame that defines the territory and the grid that stands for its density establish a radically neutral, endless subdivision. The geometry describes, in a similarly insipid way, homogeneous arrays of houses and amenities—golf courses, park spaces, bodies of water, swimming pools, gatehouses, tennis courts, clubhouses, and peripheral services.

The scalar uniformity of these layered arrays yields an ideal distribution with no variation, no relationship, no hierarchy, and no distinction, except quantity. The banal appearance, dubious interior feel, suspiciously friendly neighborliness, and ill-conceived idea of intimacy of the gated community are grounded in this indifferent set up, where everything shares the same volatility of real value. In this context, difference, no matter how nuanced, has the potential to affect all other locations, as if spreading a virus through a medium characterized by a capricious sensitivity toward entertainment. It is, however, through the playful, pragmatic management of whimsical differences that gated communities unexpectedly generate higher forms of value, which are rapidly capitalized by the appeal of the market to target specialized segments of desire. The consumption of desires stimulates the general illusion of a supernatural condition, working under the formula of an ever-renewed promise of diversity.

The seductive component of this equation is introduced in between the repetitive layers through the differentiated proportions of houses and amenities and their chronically slippery proximity, which establish an inherent imbalance in the whole, like a flickering. Each monotonous distribution operates as a force field in respect to the others, locally displacing components to assure easy access. The sequence by which this is done creates a different arrangement each time: each community in the lineage is formally driven to ensure maximum proximity between houses and amenities, revealing a variable organizational web that manages the range and tendency of the irresistible. The distribution of amenities, in turn, creates variation in the topography. Steepness comes to compensate for imbalances and brings back proximity (or distance) where it is lacking, thus generating a communal form of promiscuity.

To survive the indifference that it creates by default, Irresistible Synthetic turns the forcefully enclosed territory into its absolute extreme: nature as amenity. The gated community is equipped with paraphernalia that distorts the real through an ideology that hides, under the gloss of politeness and adequate civility, the open and desperate competition between neighbors. Through the systematic conversion of anything natural into a service, the gated community configures its assets and becomes a self-contained enclave, where the idyllic blends with the hysterical.

Modality. Indexing. Cumulative relational residential distribution. From left to right: uniform residential distribution, redistribution resultant of the proximity to golf courses, clubhouses, parks, water bodies, swimming pools, tennis courts, gatehouses, and peripheral amenities (ordered from large to small in each case), redistribution trajectories, final organization. From top to bottom: Sun City, Phoenix, AZ, USA; Niguel Shores, Monarch Beach, CA, USA; Scottsdale House, Phoenix, AZ, USA; Desert Highlands, Phoenix, AZ, USA; Frenchmen's Creek, Palm Beach Gardens, FL, USA; Nordelta, Tigre, Buenos Aires, Argentina. Plans.

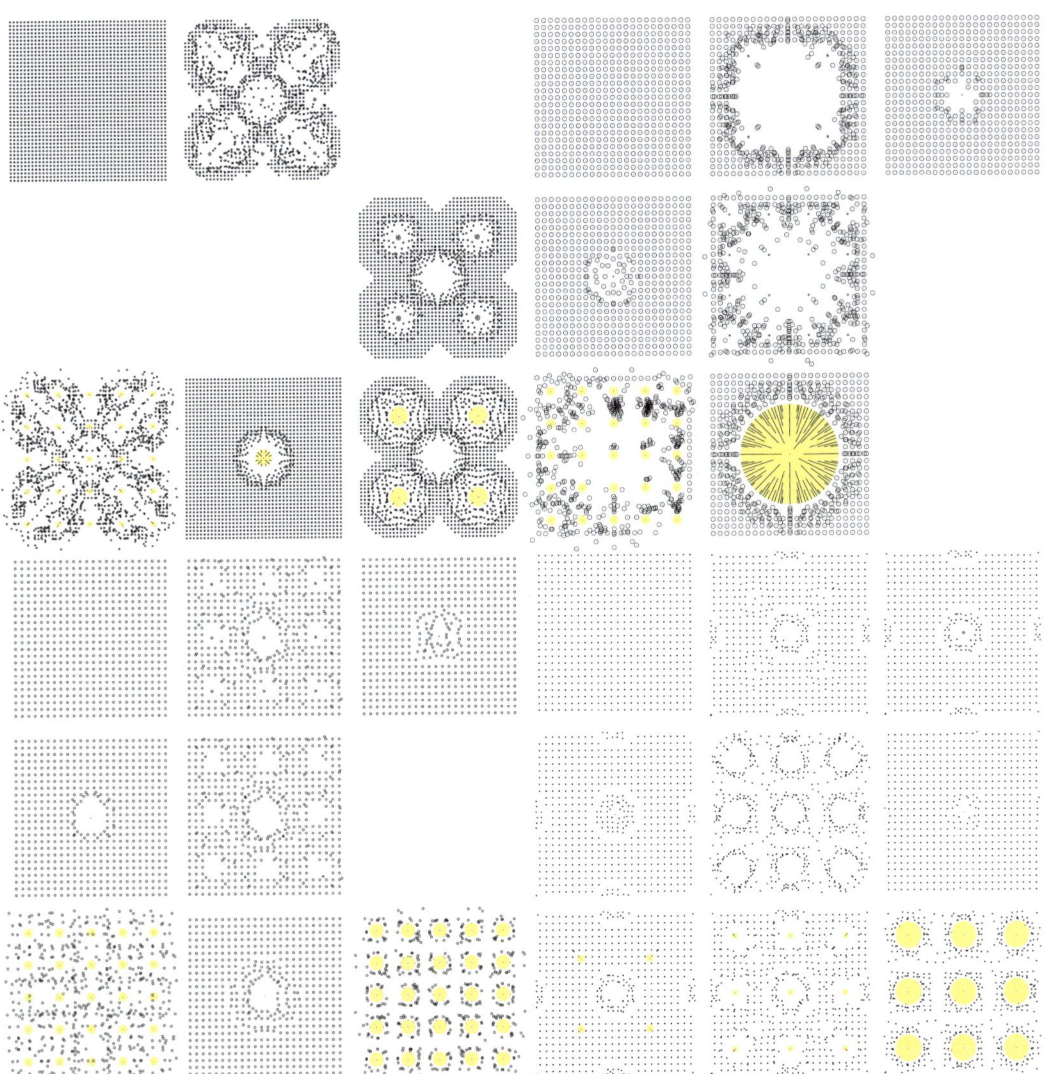

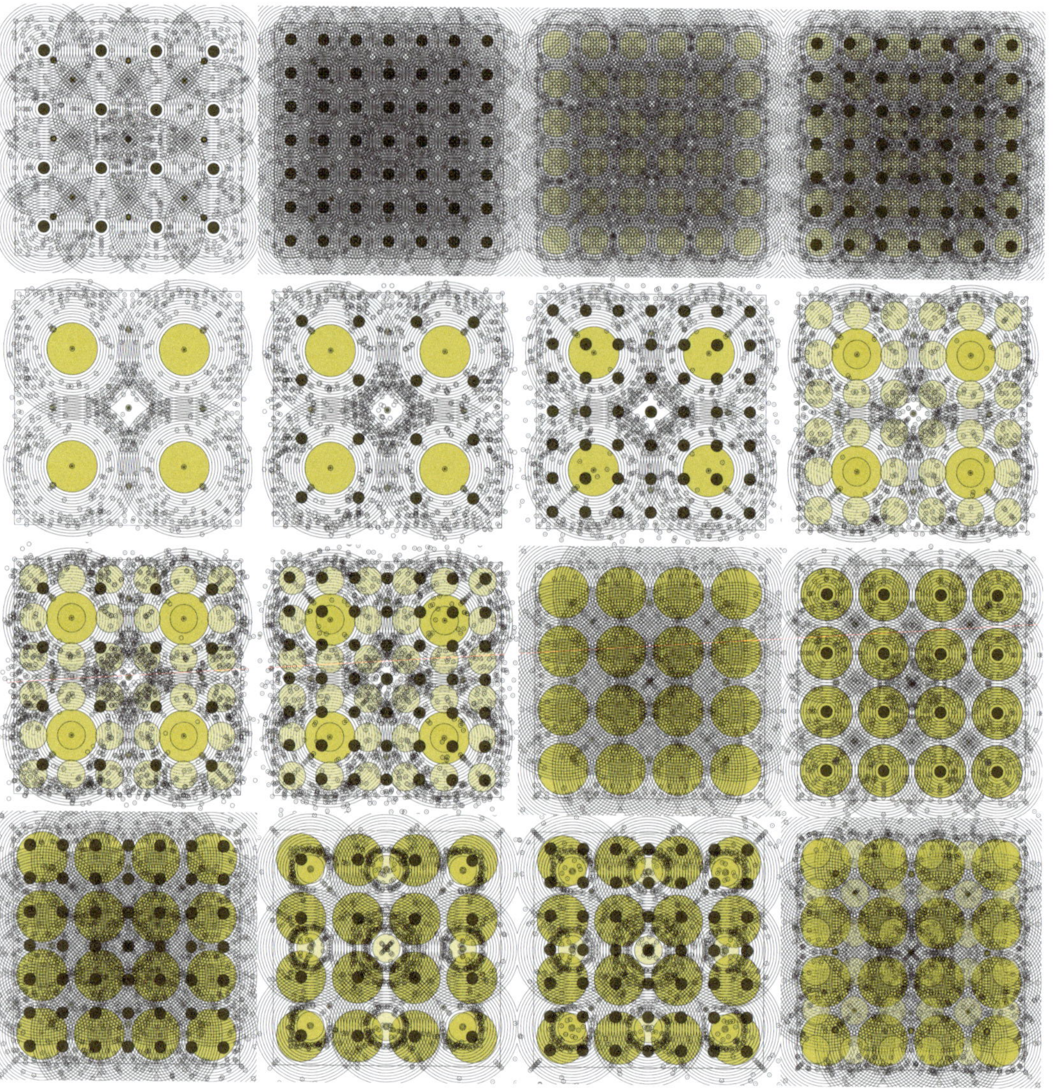

Model. Integration. Residential distribution matrix lineage. Residential distribution resultant of the integration of proximities of residential units to swimming pools, gatehouses, peripheral amenities, tennis courts, and clubhouses, with variations resultant of several combinations of proximities to parks, water bodies, and golf courses. Plans.

Model. Integration. Residential distribution trajectories lineage. Distribution trajectories of the cumulative integration of proximities of residential units to swimming pools, gatehouses, peripheral amenities, tennis courts, and clubhouses, with variations resultant of several combinations of proximities to parks, water bodies, and golf courses. Plans.

Model. Differentiation. Territorial subdivision lineage. Triangulation of residential distribution resultant of the integration of proximities to swimming pools, gatehouses, peripheral amenities, tennis courts, and clubhouses, with variations resultant of several combinations of proximities to parks, water bodies, and golf courses. Plans.

Model. Differentiation. Territorial subdivision lineage. Tessellation of residential distribution and definition of buildable residential areas, plot areas, and semipublic areas resultant of the integration of proximities to swimming pools, gatehouses, peripheral amenities, tennis courts, and clubhouses, with variations resultant of several combinations of proximities to parks, water bodies, and golf courses. Plans.

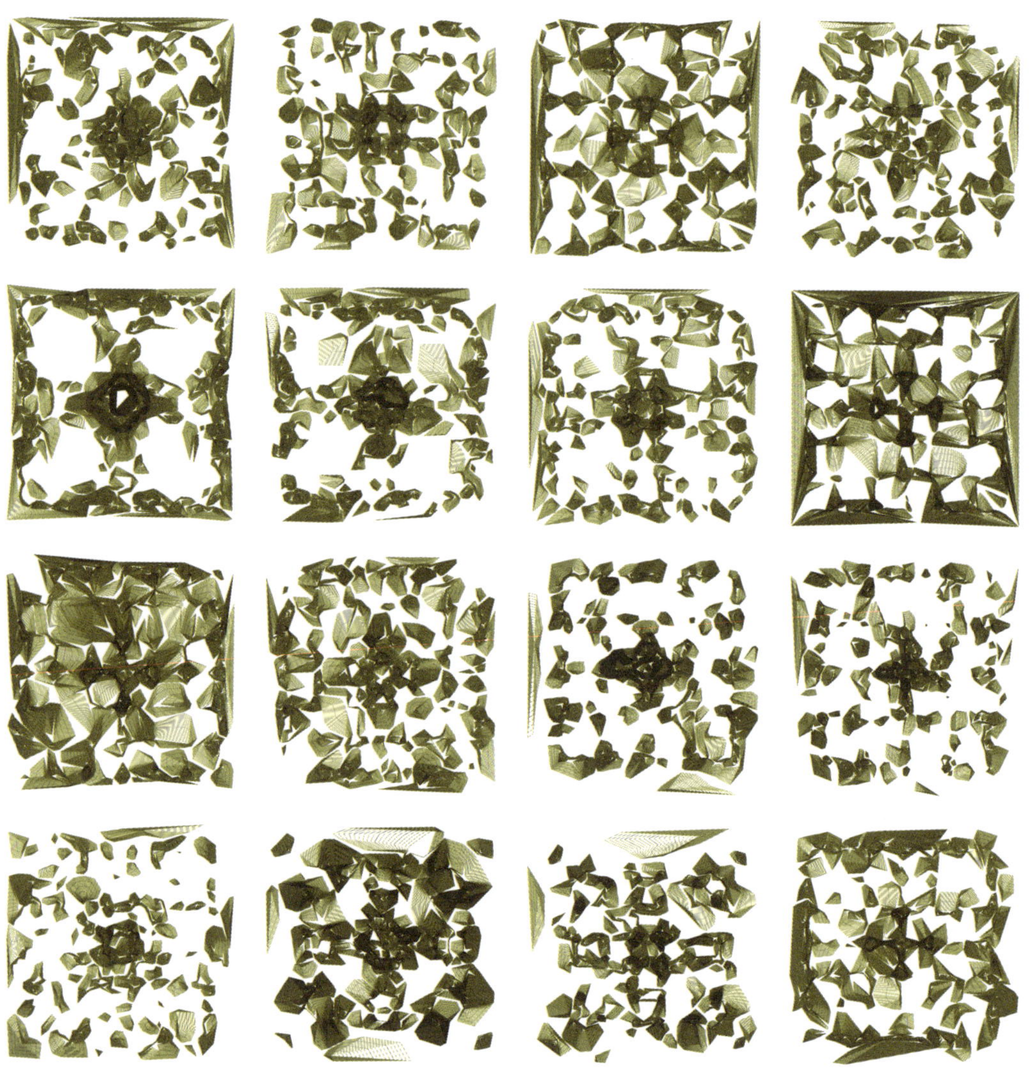

Model. Differentiation. Gated community topographic construction lineage. Vertical displacement of residential unit heights, inversely proportional to their mutual proximity. Plans.

Model. Differentiation. Gated community circulation systems lineage. Branching circulation systems as shortest outward routes from amenities along tessellation edges. Plans.

Model. Differentiation. Gated community residential distribution lineage. Residential units located at upper triangulation vortices, with wings along and proportionate in length to triangulation edges. Plans.

Model. Differentiation. Gated community amenities distribution lineage. Parks, water bodies, golf courses, swimming pools, gatehouses, peripheral amenities, tennis courts, and clubhouses as wideners of tessellated edges in lower-density areas. Plans.

Prototype. Organization. Gated community land samples. Samples of territorial distribution of residential units, topographic contours, circulation systems, parks, water bodies, golf courses, swimming pools, gatehouses, peripheral amenities, tennis courts, clubhouses. Plan.

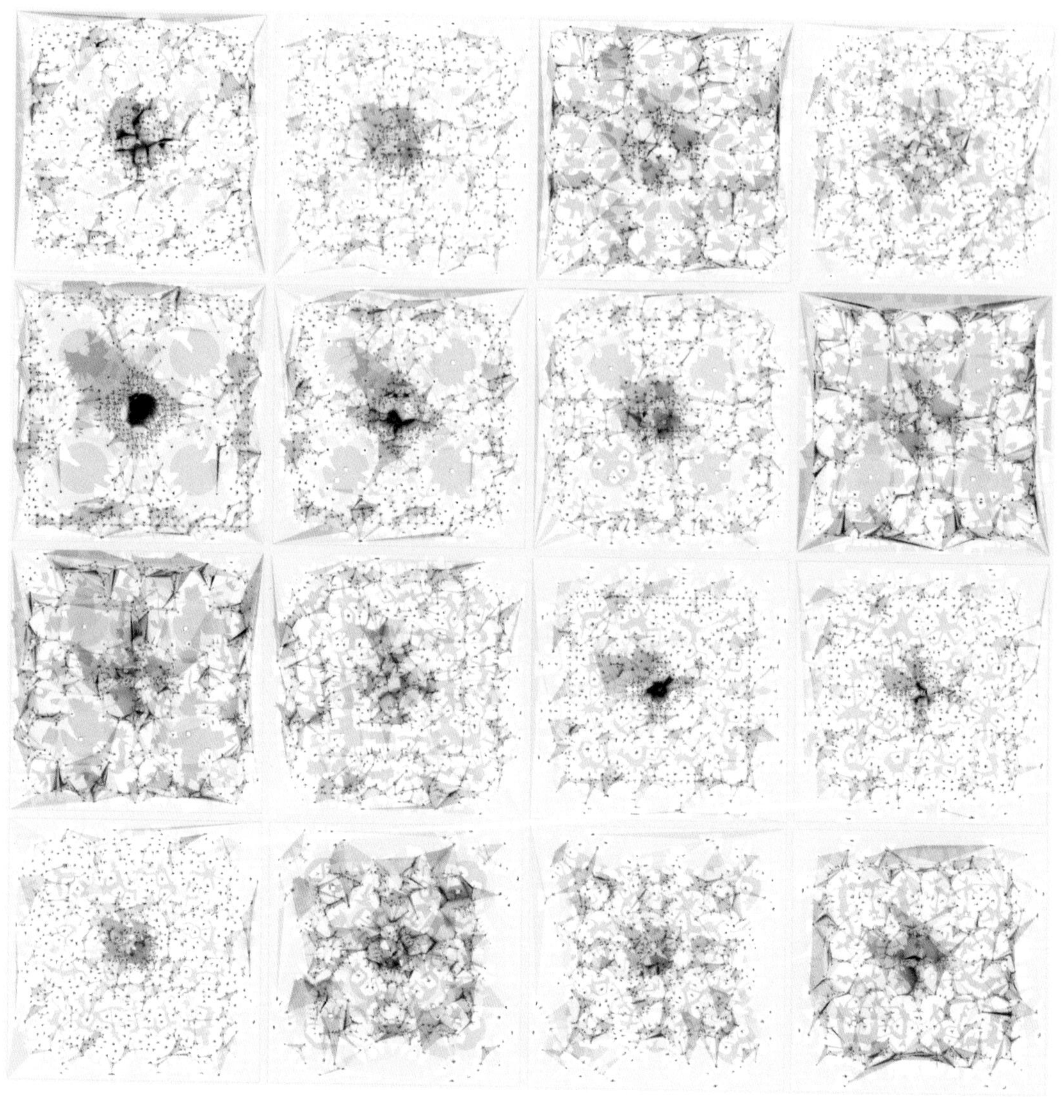

Prototype. Variability. Gated community land lineage. Variations of territorial distribution of residential units, circulation systems, and ground systems. Rendered plans.

Prototype. Variability. Gated community land lineage. Variations of territorial distribution of residential units, circulation systems, and ground systems. Rendered perspectives.

Prototype. Variability. Gated community land lineage. Variations of territorial distribution of residential units, circulation systems, and ground systems. Rendered perspectives sectors.

Territorial Schism, Mariusz Klemens and Steven Yingnien Chen.
Prototype. Organization. Territorial metropolis lineage. Physical model plan.

The Territorial Metropolitan Model

Territorial Schism is a matrix structure with repetitive floor plates, fueled by the metropolitan drive toward density and seemingly able to expand in escalating vertical forms, where spatial freedom comes into being accompanied by its irreparable burden: rampant urban congestion. It is within this dual structure that an unprecedented parallel between the metropolitan drive and the satellite city develops.

Satellite cities are frequently characterized by the segregation of needs in a schematic urban form, reduced to a simplistic formal template. This template is capable of fulfilling the need for a quick, overall legibility but dramatically fails to instill a genuine metropolitan character. The shock logic of the metropolitan is introduced in this context through a series of sudden interruptions, programmatic incongruences, and traverse fluxes at the scale of infrastructure. Major streets, highways, and landscape corridors are regarded as primary drivers for the development of such territorial metropolitanism. Through them, and by infusing their effects into the city fabric, satellite cities no longer remain in spiritual isolation.

If the erratic distribution of program within the skyscraper emphasizes the importance of connectivity to produce estrangement through unexpected organizational adjacencies, the distribution of urbanity in satellite cities is reconfigured as a systematically erratic construct by abstracting the manifold ways in which systems of transportation—vehicular roads, pedestrian paths, landscape corridors, and open spaces—introduce metropolitan catalysis. The radical autonomy of levels in the skyscraper is reincarnated at the scale of the city through the disconnectedness of territorial bands, and their sudden disruption by means of the elevator is recreated by the unexpected interconnections that infrastructural systems introduce in their organization. The vertical schism of the skyscraper is flipped horizontally and deployed as a matrix that induces the metropolitan condition in the satellite city. The system is loaded with linear schisms (the amount of programmatic changes along a corridor), cross schisms (the amount of programmatic changes across a corridor), variations of density (the ratio of number of floors to horizontally continuous programmatic areas), variations of programmatic intensity, and rhythms of transport intersection.

The composite constructs a pattern of metropolitan potential. Through the identification of the most differentiated sets and the engineering of their improbable coexistence within a fabric, the satellite city is reconstituted to promote specific modes of metropolitan life. The convergence of these modes results in surprising territorial forms—canyons, valleys, streams, ponds, mountain chains, rugged landscapes, flatlands, cracks, and crevices—which, on the one hand, instill metropolitan intensities in the aggregate and, on the other, construct a fine-grained geomorphology of building masses.

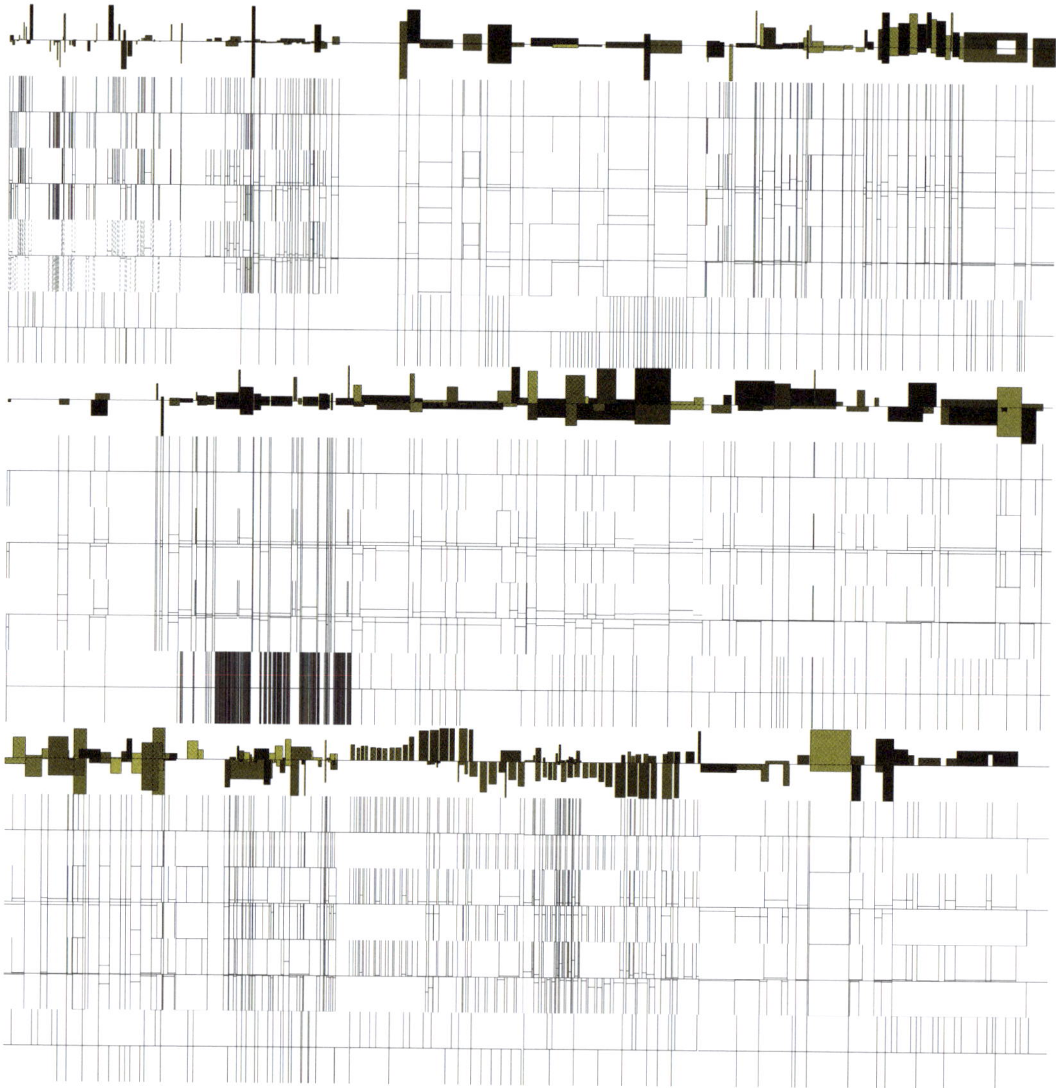

Typology. Abstraction. Metropolitan values recognition. Programmatic composition; linear schisms; average built height, built density, and rhythm of road intersections along infrastructural corridors. From top left to bottom right: Office for Metropolitan Architecture, City in the Desert, Hameem, UAE; Hisham Ashkouri, City of Light Development, Kabul, Afghanistan; Office for Metropolitan Architecture, Hanoi New Town, Hanoi, Vietnam; Office for Metropolitan Architecture, Jebel al Jais Mountain Resort, Ras al Khaimah, UAE; Foster and Partners, Masdar Development, Abu Dhabi, UAE; MKDC, Milton Keynes, Buckinghamshire, UK; Office for Metropolitan Architecture, Qianhai Port City, Shenzhen, China; Office for Metropolitan Architecture, Riga Port City, Riga, Latvia; John Portman & Associates, Songdo Landmark City, Incheon, South Korea. Plan charts.

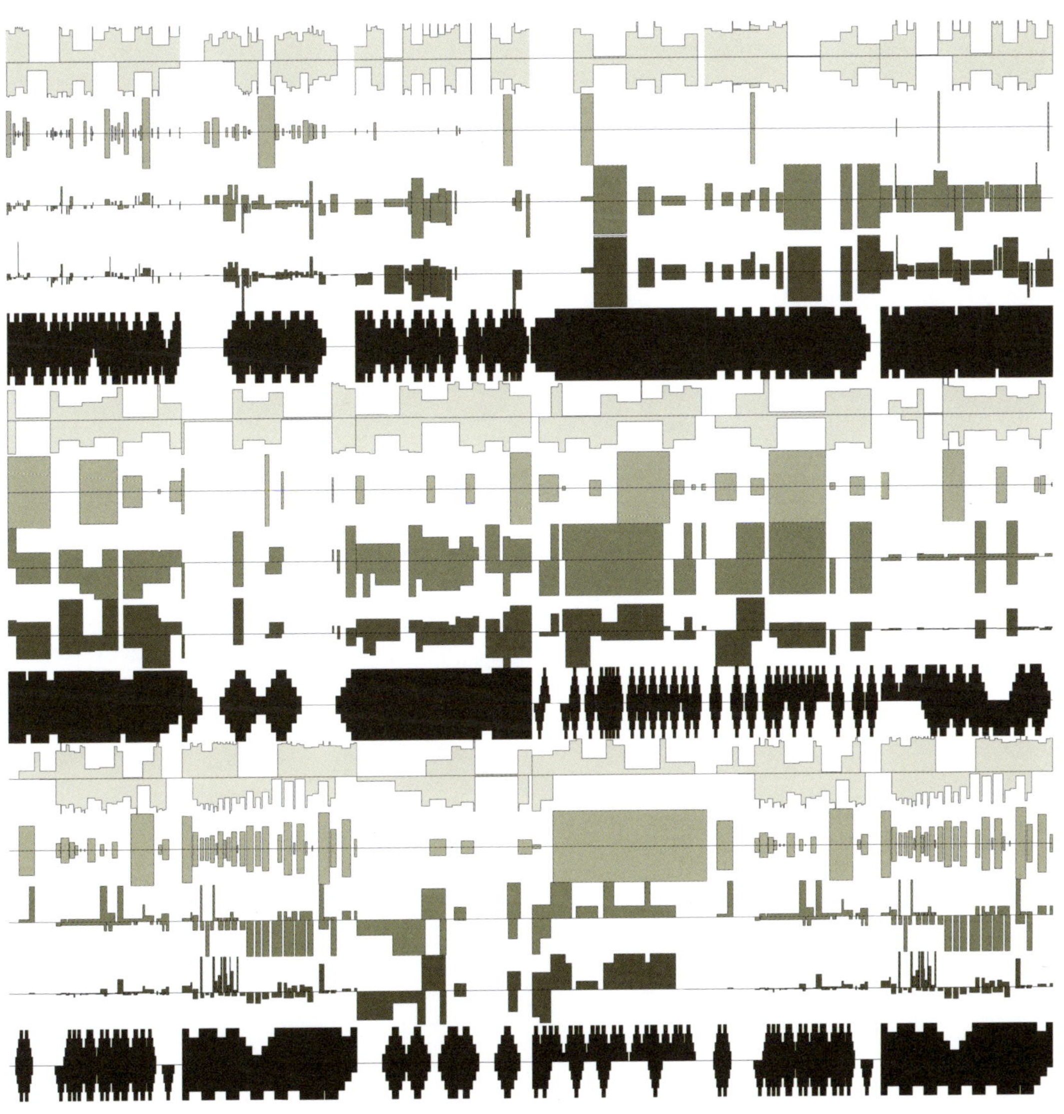

Modality. Generalization. Metropolitan intensity evaluation. Variation of linear schisms; average built height, built density, and rhythm of road intersections along infrastructural corridors. From top left to bottom right: Office for Metropolitan Architecture, City in the Desert, Hameem, UAE; Hisham Ashkouri, City of Light Development, Kabul, Afghanistan; Office for Metropolitan Architecture, Hanoi New Town, Hanoi, Vietnam; Office for Metropolitan Architecture, Jebel al Jais Mountain Resort, Ras al Khaimah, UAE; Foster and Partners, Masdar Development, Abu Dhabi, UAE; MKDC, Milton Keynes, Buckinghamshire, UK; Office for Metropolitan Architecture, Qianhai Port City, Shenzhen, China; Office for Metropolitan Architecture, Riga Port City, Riga, Latvia; John Portman & Associates, Songdo Landmark City, Incheon, South Korea. Plan charts.

Modality. Generalization. Metropolitan intensity regulation. Variation of linear schisms; average built height, built density, and rhythm of road intersections along infrastructural corridors. From top left to bottom right: Office for Metropolitan Architecture, City in the Desert, Hameem, UAE; Hisham Ashkouri, City of Light Development, Kabul, Afghanistan; Office for Metropolitan Architecture, Hanoi New Town, Hanoi, Vietnam; Office for Metropolitan Architecture, Jebel al Jais Mountain Resort, Ras al Khaimah, UAE; Foster and Partners, Masdar Development, Abu Dhabi, UAE; MKDC, Milton Keynes, Buckinghamshire, UK; Office for Metropolitan Architecture, Qianhai Port City, Shenzhen, China; Office for Metropolitan Architecture, Riga Port City, Riga, Latvia; John Portman & Associates, Songdo Landmark City, Incheon, South Korea. Plan charts.

Modality. Reification. Metropolitan pattern construction. Pattern of linear schisms; average built height, built density, and rhythm of road intersections along infrastructural corridors. From top left to bottom right: Office for Metropolitan Architecture, City in the Desert, Hameem, UAE; Hisham Ashkouri, City of Light Development, Kabul, Afghanistan; Office for Metropolitan Architecture, Hanoi New Town, Hanoi, Vietnam; Office for Metropolitan Architecture, Jebel al Jais Mountain Resort, Ras al Khaimah, UAE; Foster and Partners, Masdar Development, Abu Dhabi, UAE; MKDC, Milton Keynes, Buckinghamshire, UK; Office for Metropolitan Architecture, Qianhai Port City, Shenzhen, China; Office for Metropolitan Architecture, Riga Port City, Riga, Latvia; John Portman & Associates, Songdo Landmark City, Incheon, South Korea. Plan charts.

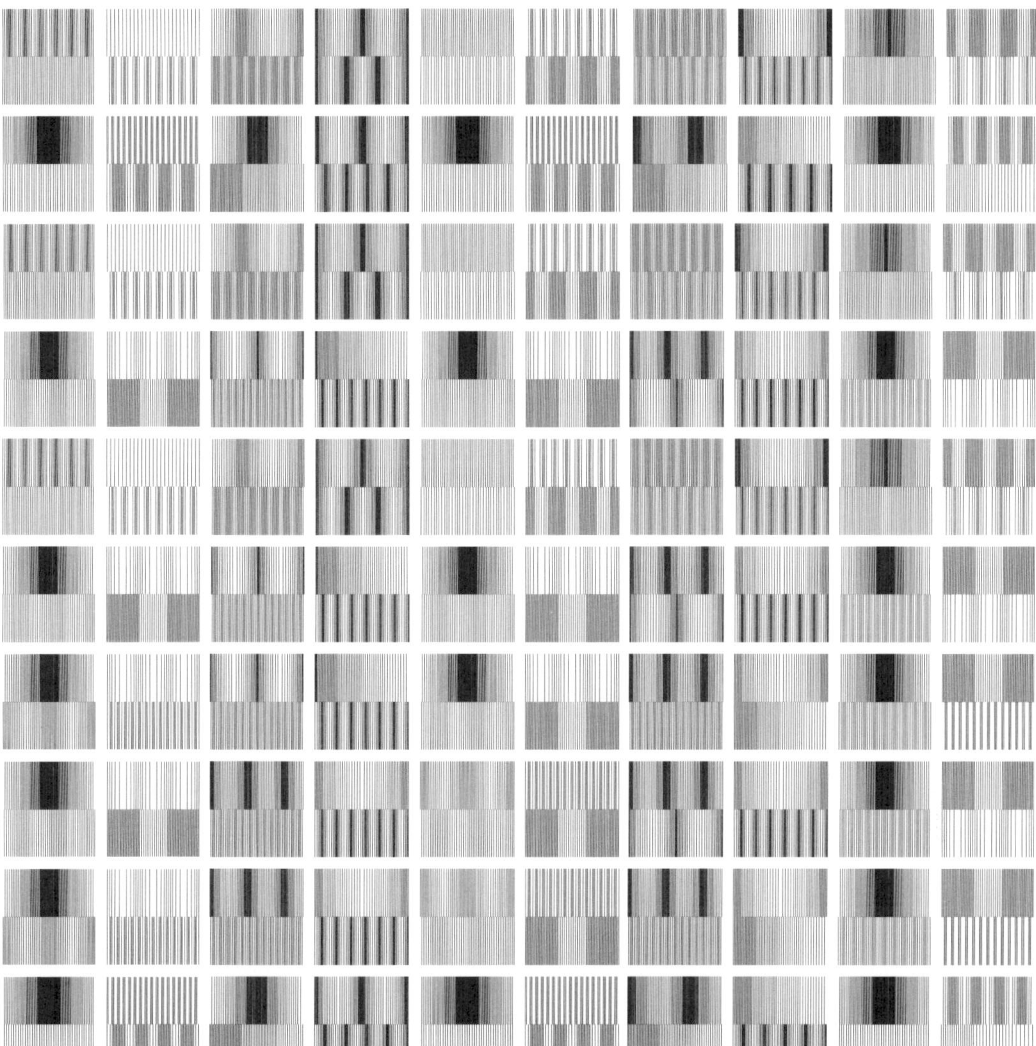

Model. Differentiation. Metropolitan pattern assemblage. From top to bottom: minor roads along major and minor road systems, major road and park systems, major and minor road systems, minor and minor road systems, and minor road and park systems. From left to right: variations of intensity. Plans.

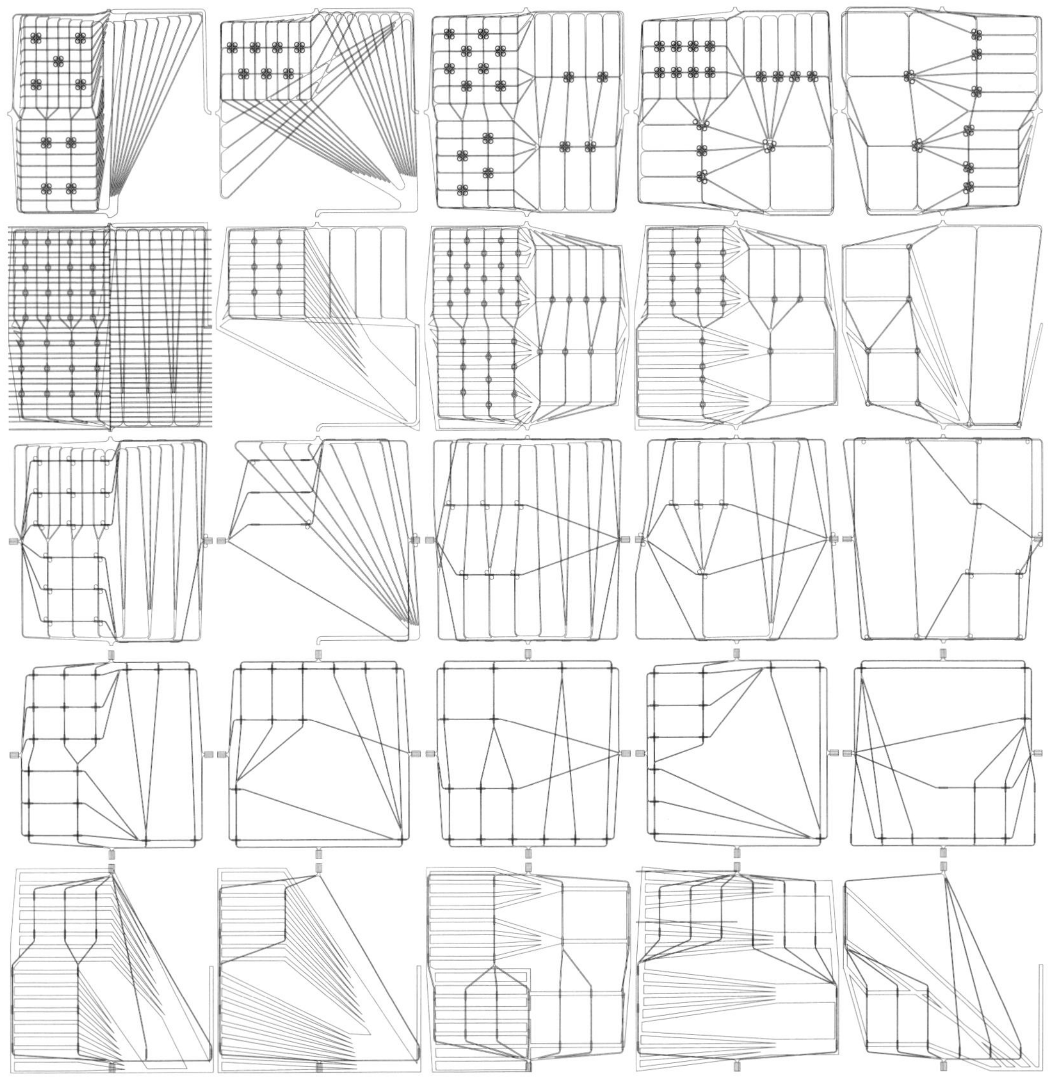

Model. Differentiation. Metropolitan pattern assemblage. From top to bottom: major roads along major and minor road systems, major road and park systems, major and minor road systems, minor and minor road systems, and minor road and park systems. From left to right: variations of intensity. Plans.

Model. Differentiation. Metropolitan pattern assemblage. From top to bottom: programmatic distribution and road systems along major and minor road systems, major road and park systems, major and minor road systems, minor and minor road systems, and minor road and park systems. From left to right: variations of intensity. Plans.

Model. Differentiation. Metropolitan pattern assemblage. From top to bottom: interstitial spaces and road systems along major and minor road systems, major road and park systems, major and minor road systems, minor and minor road systems, and minor road and park systems. From left to right: variations of intensity. Plans.

Prototype. Organization. Territorial metropolis built space assemblage. Programmatic distribution and road systems along major road and park systems. Medium intensity sample. Plan.

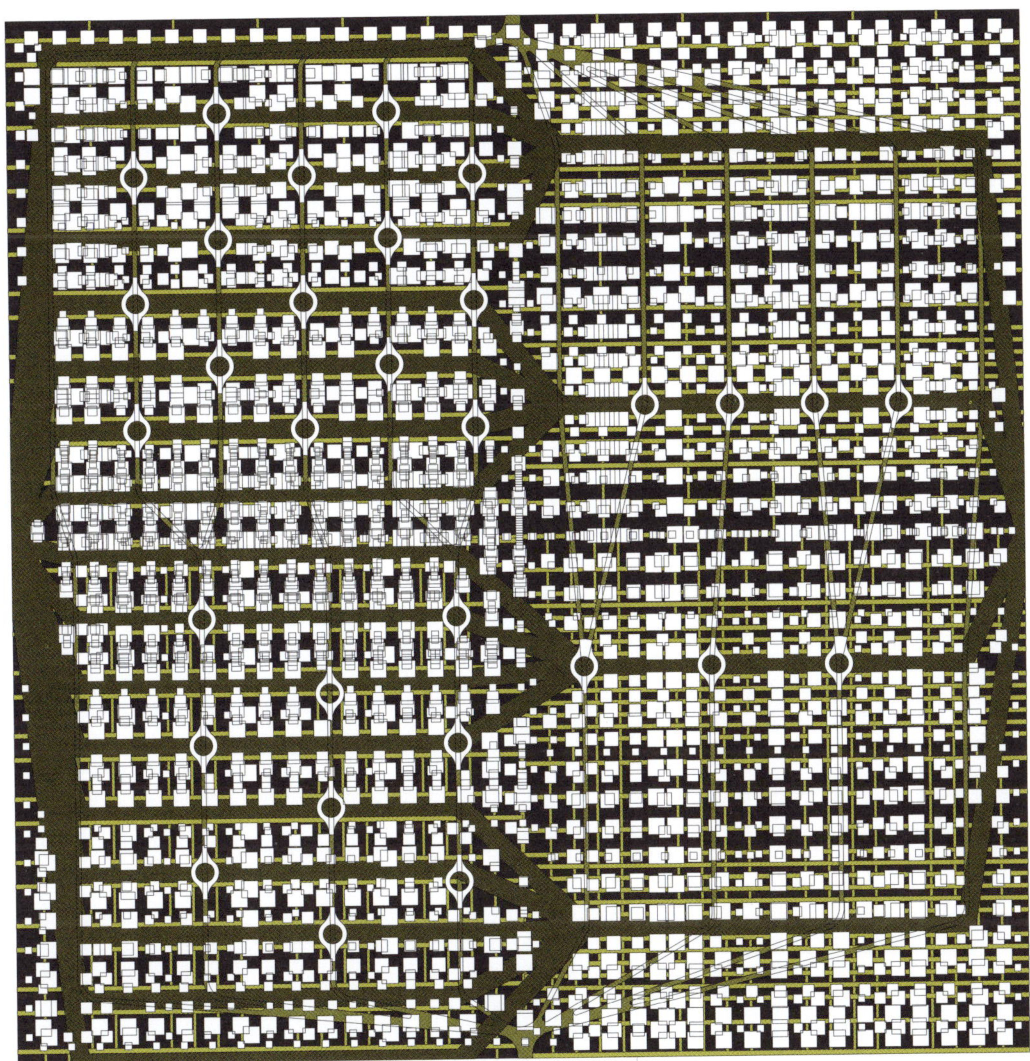

Prototype. Organization. Territorial metropolis interstitial space assemblage. Interstitial spaces and road systems along major road and park systems. Medium intensity sample. Plan.

Prototype. Evaluation. Territorial metropolis built space evaluation. Building clusters, elevator cores, and internal horizontal circulation. Plan.

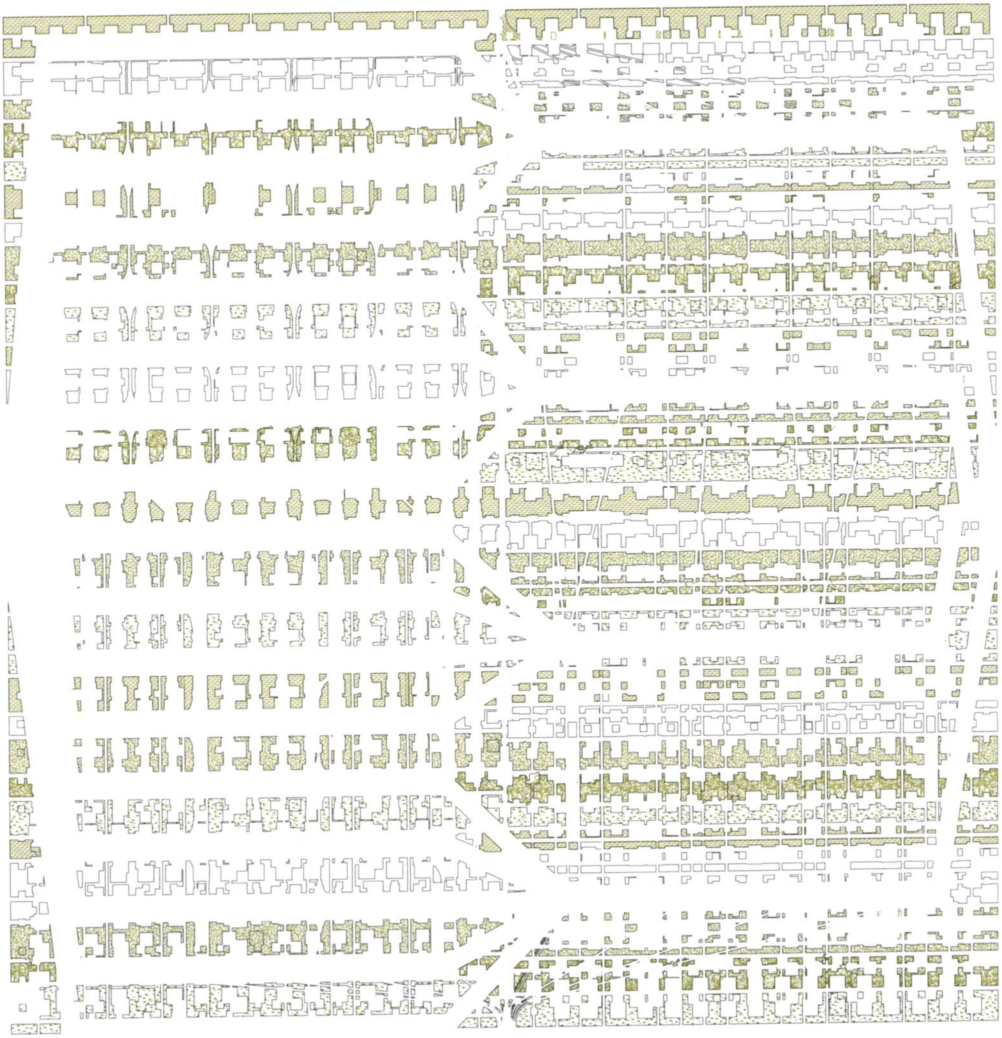

Prototype. Evaluation. Territorial metropolis interstitial space evaluation. Interstitial aggregates, landscape types, and surface contiguities. Plan.

Prototype. Organization. Territorial metropolis samples. Building clusters, elevator cores, and internal horizontal circulation; interstitial aggregates, landscape types, and surface contiguities; major and minor road systems. Plan sector.

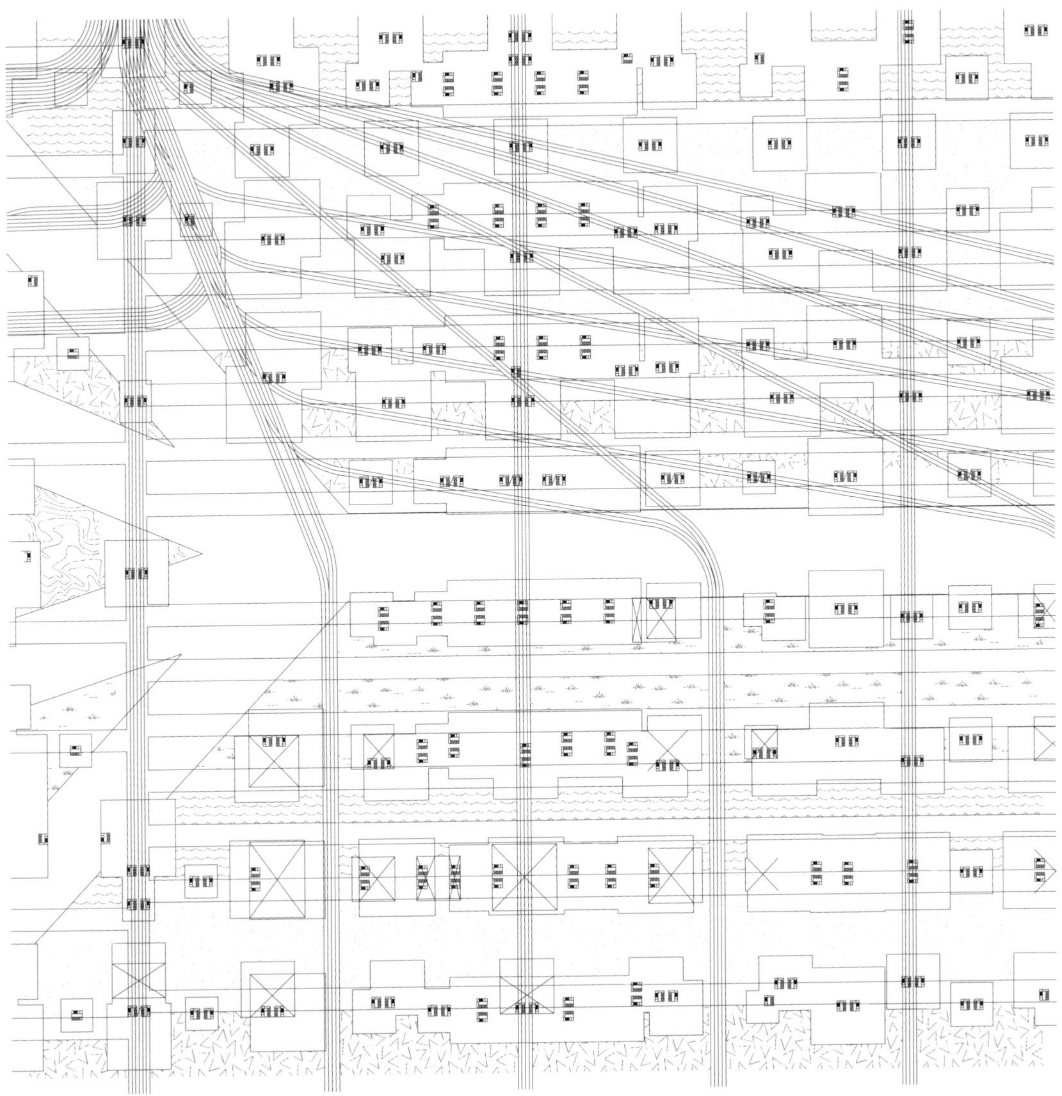

Prototype. Organization. Territorial metropolis samples. Building clusters, elevator cores, and internal horizontal circulation; interstitial aggregates, landscape types, and surface contiguities; major and minor road systems. Plan sector zoom.

Mahattanatomy, Pablo Barría Urenda and Mariano Gomez Luque.
Prototype. Organization. Generic model sample. Rendered axonometry.

The Open-Source Model

Manhattanatomy is an open source of primeval architectural models based on the decoding and recoding of concepts from Rem Koolhaas's *Delirious New York*. The retroactive manifesto, which purportedly makes evident the presence of an unconscious theory for the antiurban in the ruthless, pragmatic practice of Manhattan's early 20th-century culture of congestion, provides both a theoretical precedent and a repertoire of raw material to be transformed.

Manhattanatomy dissects Koolhaas's tract into a number of paradoxical statements, proliferates them in a set of fine-grained formulations, confronts them with a spectrum of extra-extra-large typologies, and turns them into a kit of explicit relational logics, without letting go of the humor and edge of the original. It claims these logics as the basis of operative mechanisms for contemporary development, differentiating the categorical and polemical character of the sources into precise yet open-ended design instruments.

Manhattanatomy constructs a toolbox of these instruments in the form of generic definitions, procedures, variations, and applications. This toolbox contains methods for transforming a tower of stacks into a tower of convergent floors, for establishing continuity between floors, for turning a tower into a globe and a globe into a tower, for simultaneously defining a globe and a tower cluster, for transforming a flat surface into a vertical structure, for turning towers into tower components, for dissolving office cores into programmatic continuums, for deriving building form from its surroundings, for transforming building skins into grids that merge inside and outside, for transforming towers into tower clusters, for reducing a massive building to an agglomeration of blocks, for defining a building that grows outward in equal proportion, for perpetuating urban spontaneity, for absorbing context, for multiplying the ground regardless of its vertical extrusion, for setting up a virtual grid of growth, for establishing progressive differentiation in urban structures, for evolving blocks into cities, for gaining freedom as approaching the ground, for isolating buildings from their surrounding, for weaving buildings, for transforming landscapes into buildings and buildings into landscapes, for articulating autonomous elements into three-dimensional frameworks, for reproducing nature inside self-contained globes, for preserving nature inside artificial environments, for extruding sections of natural or artificial environments, for turning exotic landscapes into endless strips, for building a city around a coveted center, for defining a self-destructing logic of growth, for defining disposable forms of urbanism, for turning single spaces into clusters and clusters into single spaces, for intertwining vectors of programmatic activity, for turning a collective into a superhouse, for merging disparate building components, for combining lobotomy and vertical schism in building skins, and for linking and yet separating. These methods are integrated in an operative open-source model-manifesto, projecting the organizational richness of the sources out of their retroactive framework and beyond their confinement within a critical body.

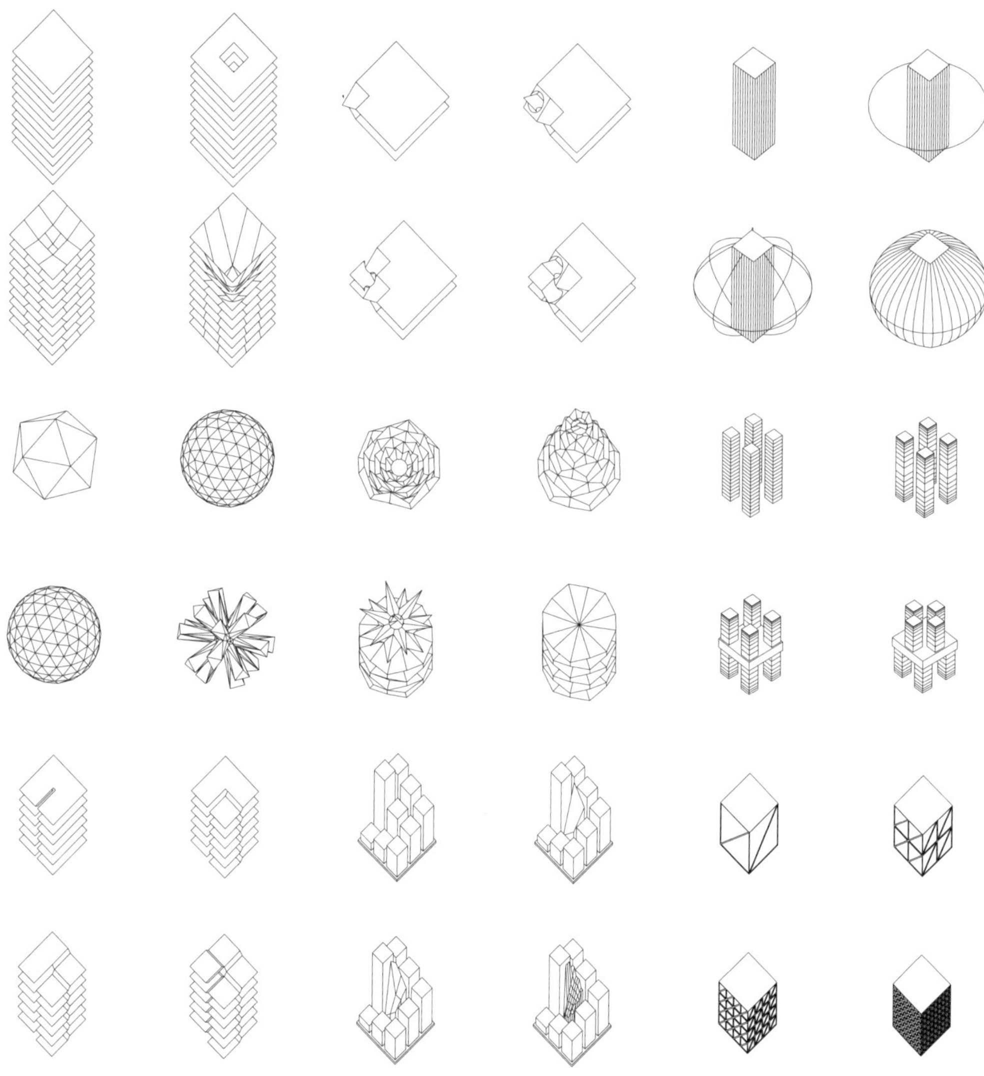

Modality. Variation. Generic model construction operations. Aleph Core, Phased Datum, Bubble Tower, Radial Skyline, Kirigami Plaza, Disconnective Chamber, Coreless Office, Compromise Envelope, and Lobotomy Grid. Axonometrics.

Modality. Variation. Generic model construction operations. Exponential Village, Porous Commune, Spherical Neighborhood, Surprise Grid, Black Hole Square, Saturated Plot, Spectral City, Domino-Effect Quadrant, and Fractal Block. Axonometrics.

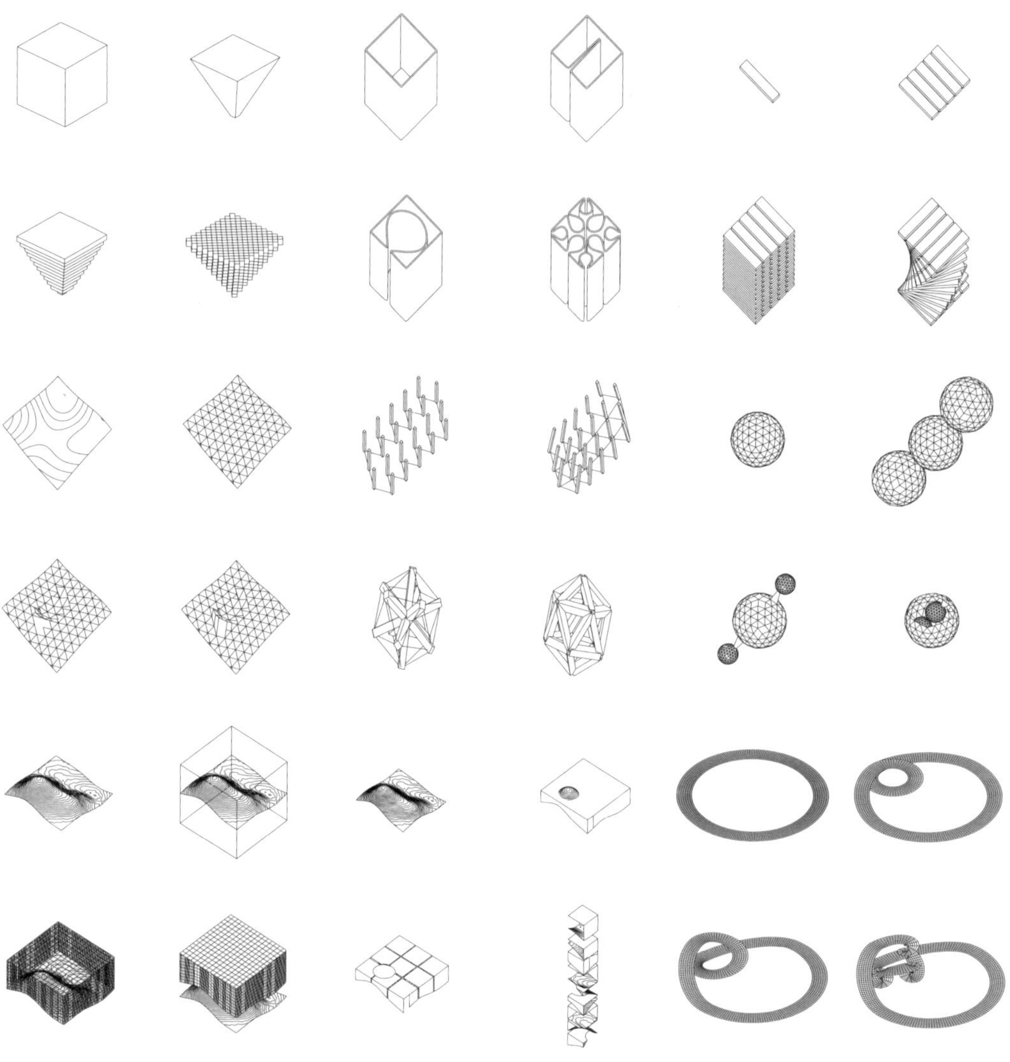

Modality. Variation. Generic model construction operations. Detached Condominium, Impervious Hotel, Congested Terraces, Landscape Building, Hyper Resort, Shell Retreat, Encapsulated Nature, Stacked Landscape, and 360 Beach. Axonometrics.

Modality. Variation. Generic model construction operations. Clogging Boomtown, Self-Destructing Borough, Canvas Polis, Folding Hive, Multi-Thread Inn, People's Palace, Manhattanist Stack, Manhattanist Skin, and Schizophrenic Spire. Axonometrics.

Model. Variability. Generic model variations. Aleph Core, Phased Datum, Bubble Tower, Radial Skyline, Kirigami Plaza, Disconnective Chamber, Coreless Office, Compromise Envelope, and Lobotomy Grid. Axonometrics.

Model. Variability. Generic model variations. Exponential Village, Porous Commune, Spherical Neighborhood, Surprise Grid, Black Hole Square, Saturated Plot, Spectral City, Domino-Effect Quadrant, and Fractal Block. Axonometrics.

Model. Variability. Generic model variations. Detached Condominium, Impervious Hotel, Congested Terraces, Landscape Building, Hyper Resort, Shell Retreat, Encapsulated Nature, Stacked Landscape, and 360 Beach. Axonometrics.

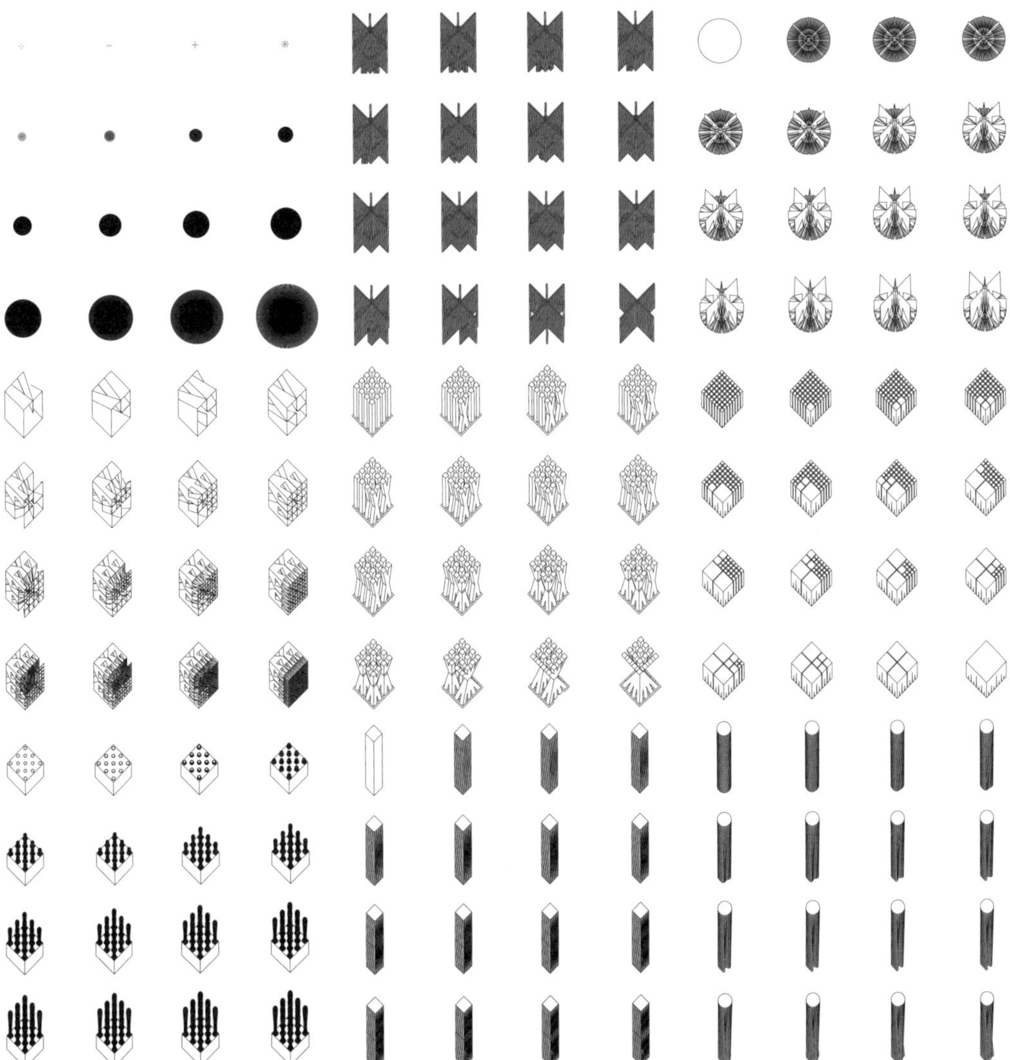

Model. Variability. Generic model variations. Clogging Boomtown, Self-Destructing Borough, Canvas Polis, Folding Hive, Multi-Thread Inn, People's Palace, Manhattanist Stack, Manhattanist Skin, Schizophrenic Spire. Axonometrics.

Prototype. Organization. Generic model samples. Aleph Core, Phased Datum, Bubble Tower, Radial Skyline, Kirigami Plaza, Disconnective Chamber, Coreless Office, Compromise Envelope, and Lobotomy Grid. Rendered axonometrics.

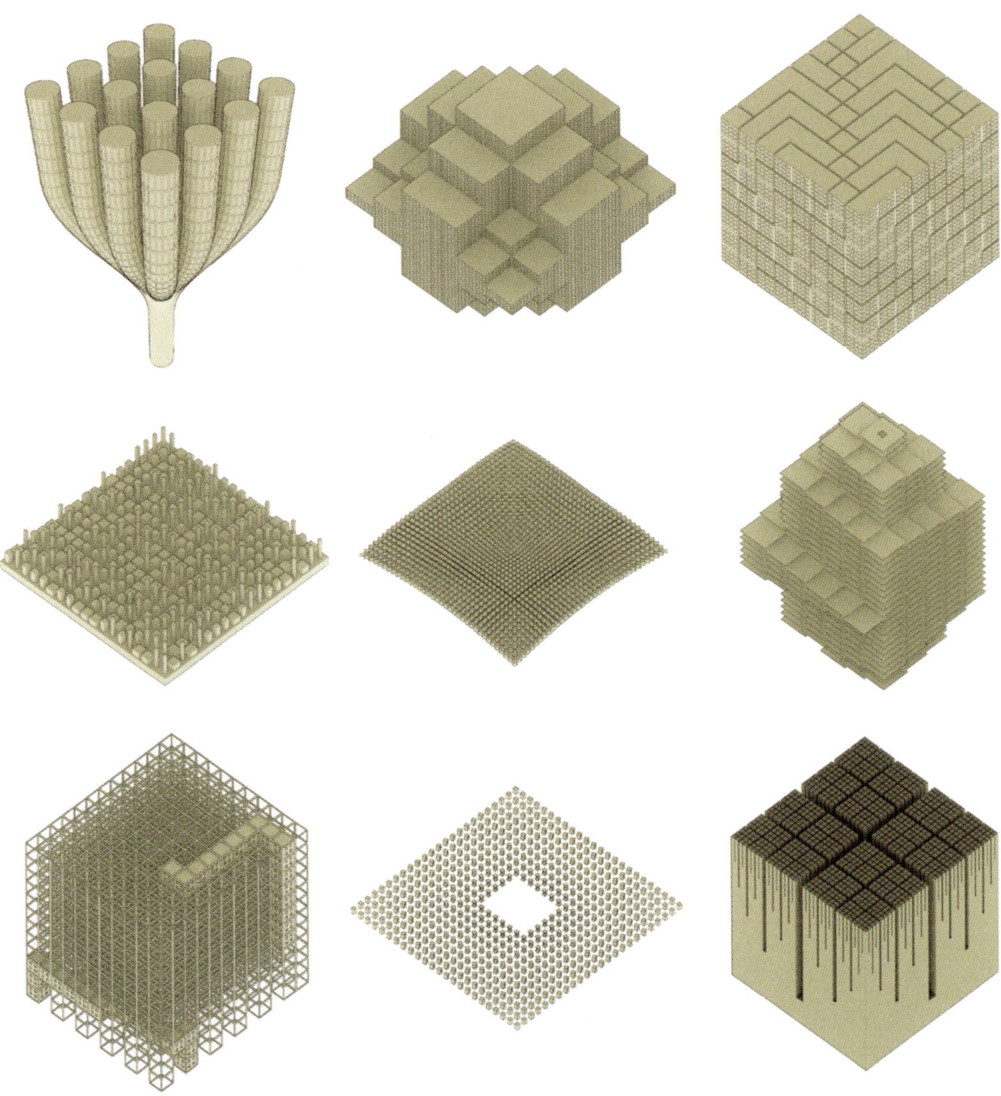

Prototype, Organization. Generic model samples. Exponential Village, Porous Commune, Spherical Neighborhood, Surprise Grid, Black Hole Square, Saturated Plot, Spectral City, Domino-Effect Quadrant, and Fractal Block. Rendered axonometrics.

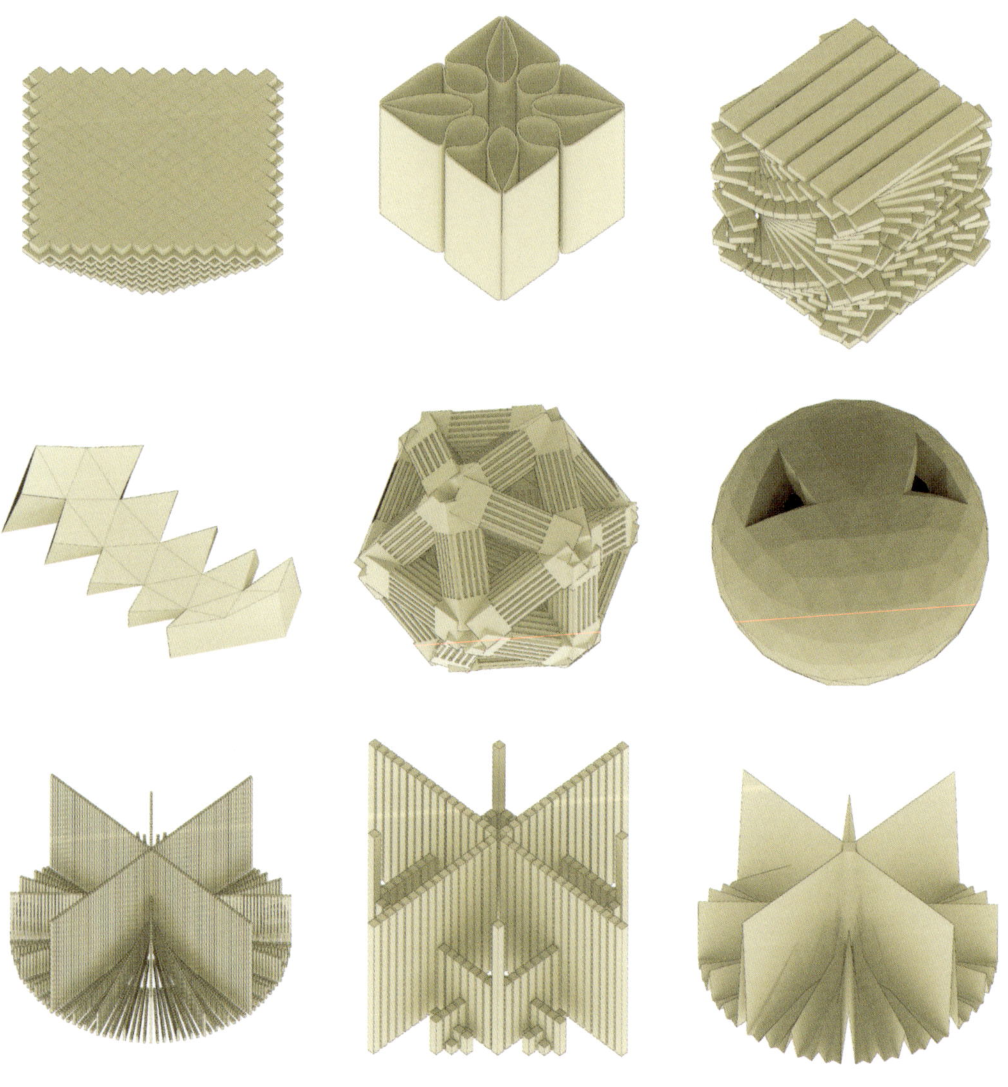

Prototype. Organization. Generic model samples. Detached Condominium, Impervious Hotel, Congested Terraces, Landscape Building, Hyper Resort, Shell Retreat, Encapsulated Nature, Stacked Landscape, and 360 Beach. Rendered axonometrics.

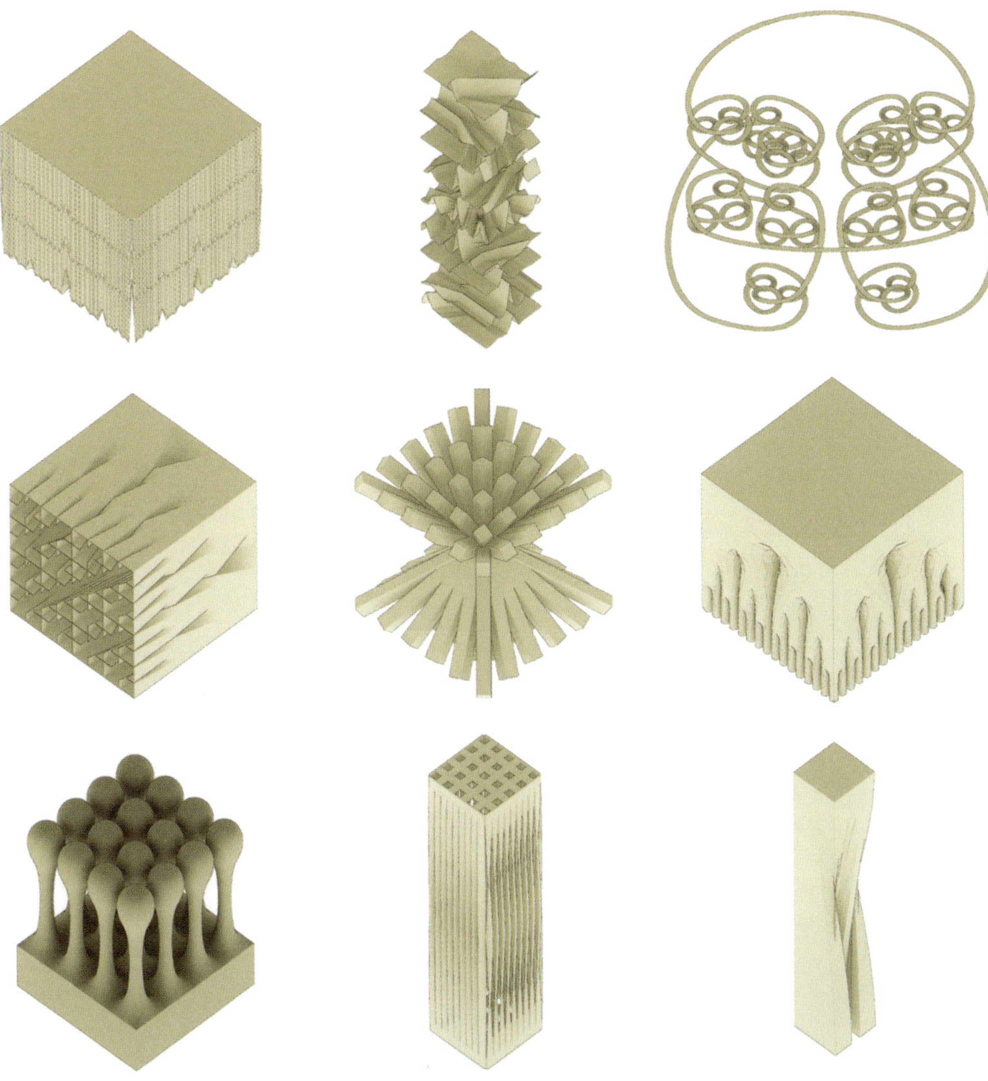

Prototype. Organization. Generic model samples. Clogging Boomtown, Self-Destructing Borough, Canvas Polis, Folding Hive, Multi-Thread Inn, People's Palace, Manhattanist Stack, Manhattanist Skin, and Schizophrenic Spire. Rendered axonometrics.

The Culture of Liberated Congestion, Nicholas Potts and Peter Zuroweste.
Prototype. Organization. High-rise housing stack. Physical model perspective sector.

The Value-Proliferation Model

The Culture of Liberated Congestion abstracts organizational principles embedded in tall Manhattan buildings and synthesizes them into a series of stacking modalities consisting of local cause-effect relationships between one level and the next of a vertical system, until the point of exhaustion. By analyzing floor-to-floor progressions across skyscrapers, the model formulates the rules for a self-stimulating process of land-value proliferation. The system responds in principle to the surface area of urban plots but grows through a blind, self-fueling, cumulative logic as the masses evolve upward.

Rather than understand the building as an autonomous object that installs itself, once and for all, onto apparently fixed conditions, the Culture of Liberated Congestion proposes a model grounded in a literal reading of Rem Koolhaas's Manhattanist theory by which "architecture is no longer the art of designing buildings so much as the brutal skyward extrusion of whatever site the developer has managed to assemble." Adopting this amoral stance and turning it into an autopoietic logic, the model speculates on the precise critical point where the carrying capacity of developable plots, subjected to the expansive pressure of capital, paradoxically renders its own premises archaic and obsolete. The Culture of Liberated Congestion searches for ever-higher extremes, wherein the logic of "commercial exhilaration where the maximum legally allowable is immediately translated into reality" undermines the internal stability of buildings, forcing them to become something other than single towers resultant of linear plot extrusion.

The model alternates between two basic forms of linear growth. The first, at the scale of the floor level, is based on linear mechanisms of replication, transformation, and limitation of levels in respect to their immediate lower neighbors, free from the restrictions resulting from the vertical projection of the plot. The second, at the scale of the sets, triggers switches in the modalities of proliferation when a given linear growth sequence finds its limits. These two modes activate one another, until the total mass reaches the realization of its full escalating potential. At that stage the organization redefines its conditions of possibility and projects them back down into the plot, now reconfigured as a complex normative form.

The Culture of Liberated Congestion both celebrates and supersedes Manhattan's 1916 Zoning Law, 100 years after its enactment. Stacked, terraced, proliferated, bifurcating, self-intersecting, cantilevering building masses invade and retreat from their lot limits, providing a base unit for collective intertwinements and helping imagine a city where the ground installs itself in the sky and is reproduced at multiple levels, without reaching out to any form of external imagery (iconic repertoires, allegorical forms, convoluted surfaces, spotless volumes), wild engineering gadgets (expressionist bridges, airborne vehicles, multiple-level infrastructures), or far-fetched versions of the fantastic (hanging gardens, elevated landscapes, flying ecologies). Rather, the Culture of Liberated Congestion self-stimulates and perpetuates basic plot-building dynamics through earnest, down-to-earth forms of civil architecture, made of discrete building masses in the air.

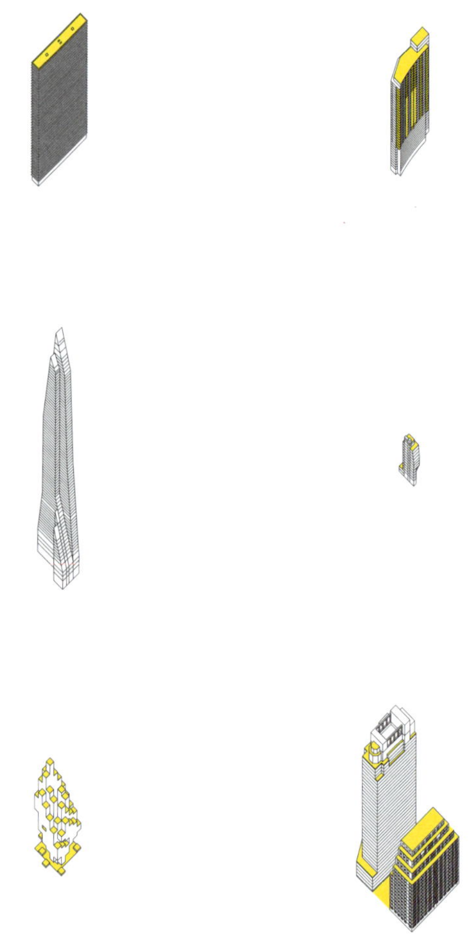

Typology. Evaluation. High-rise housing footprint and setback evaluation. From top left to bottom right: Jean Nouvel, Green Blade, Los Angeles, CA, USA; De Stefano + Partners, Riverbend Condominiums, Chicago, IL, USA; Herzog & de Meuron, 56 Leonard Street, New York, NY, USA; Office for Metropolitan Architecture, 111 First Street, Jersey City, NJ, USA; Office for Metropolitan Architecture, Rue de la Loi, Brussels, Belgium; Jean Nouvel, Tower Verre, New York, NY, USA; Neil Denari Architects, HL23, New York, NY, USA; Urban Works Architecture, Skyscape Condominiums, Minneapolis, MN, USA; Herzog & de Meuron, Elbephilharmonie, Hamburg, Denmark; REX, Songdo Landmark City, Incheon, South Korea; MVRDV, Skyvillage, Rodovre, Denmark; Robert A. M. Stern Architects, 15 Central Park West, New York, NY, USA; Studio Daniel Libeskind, 1 Madison Avenue, New York, NY, USA; Office for Metropolitan Architecture, 23 E 22nd Street, New York, NY, USA; Clinton & Russell, The Apthorp Apartments, New York, NY, USA. Axonometrics.

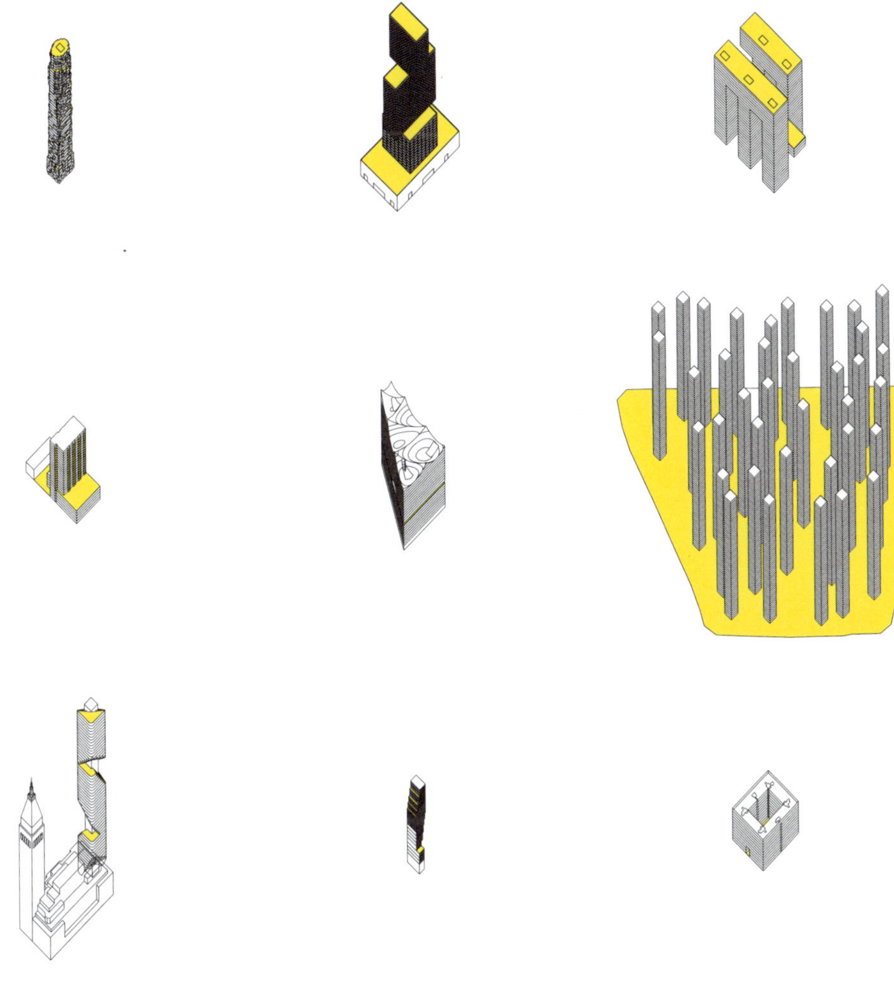

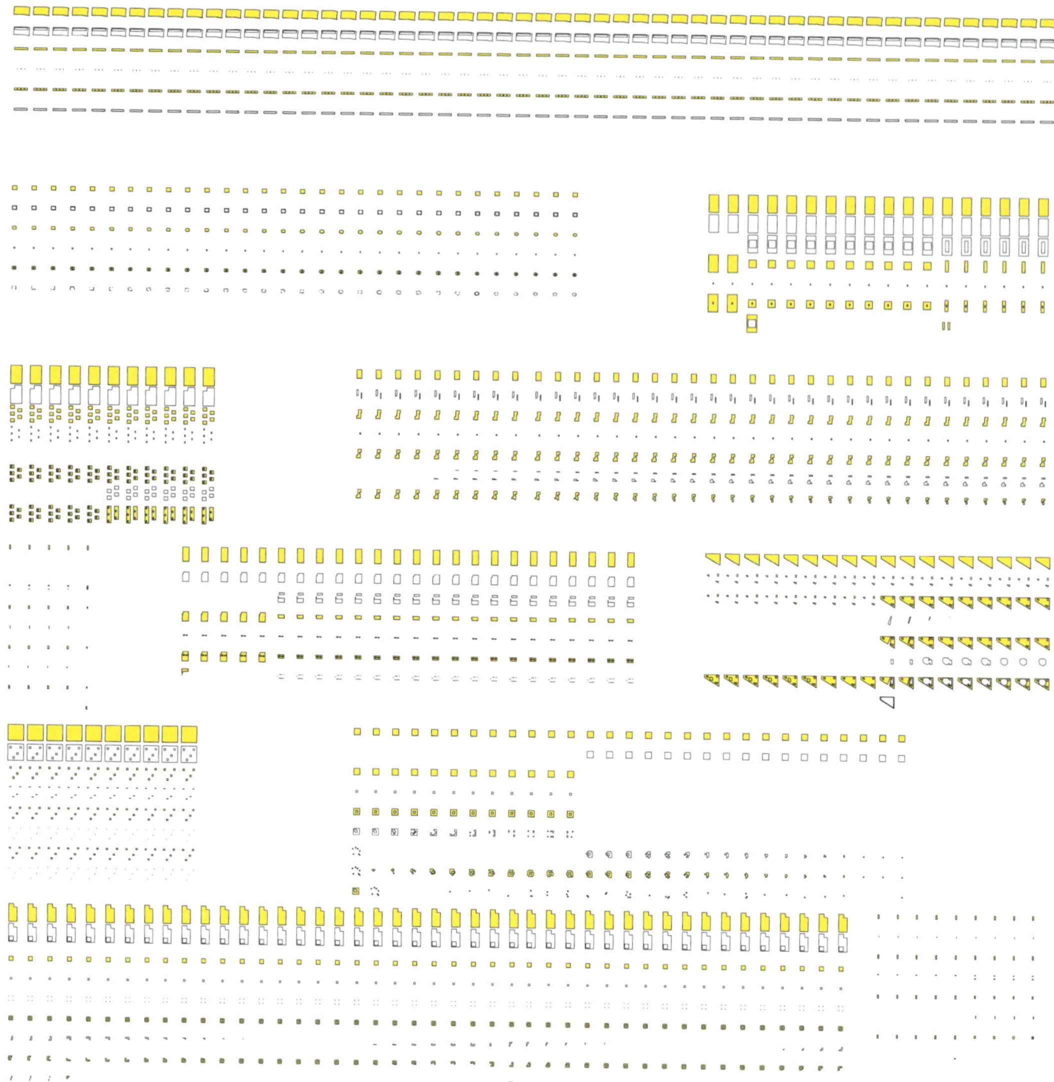

Typology. Evaluation. High-rise housing floor area and setback evaluation. From top left to bottom right: Jean Nouvel, Green Blade, Los Angeles, CA, USA; De Stefano + Partners, Riverbend Condominiums, Chicago, IL, USA; Herzog & de Meuron, 56 Leonard Street, New York, NY, USA; Office for Metropolitan Architecture, 111 First Street, Jersey City, NJ, USA; Office for Metropolitan Architecture, Rue de la Loi, Brussels, Belgium; Jean Nouvel, Tower Verre, New York, NY, USA; Neil Denari Architects, HL23, New York, NY, USA; Urban Works Architecture, Skyscape Condominiums, Minneapolis, MN, USA; Herzog & de Meuron, Elbephilharmonie, Hamburg, Denmark; REX, Songdo Landmark City, Incheon, South Korea; MVRDV, Skyvillage, Rodovre, Denmark; Robert A. M. Stern Architects, 15 Central Park West, New York, NY, USA; Studio Daniel Libeskind, 1 Madison Avenue, New York, NY, USA; Office for Metropolitan Architecture, 23 E 22nd Street, New York, NY, USA; Clinton & Russell, The Apthorp Apartments, New York, NY, USA. Plans.

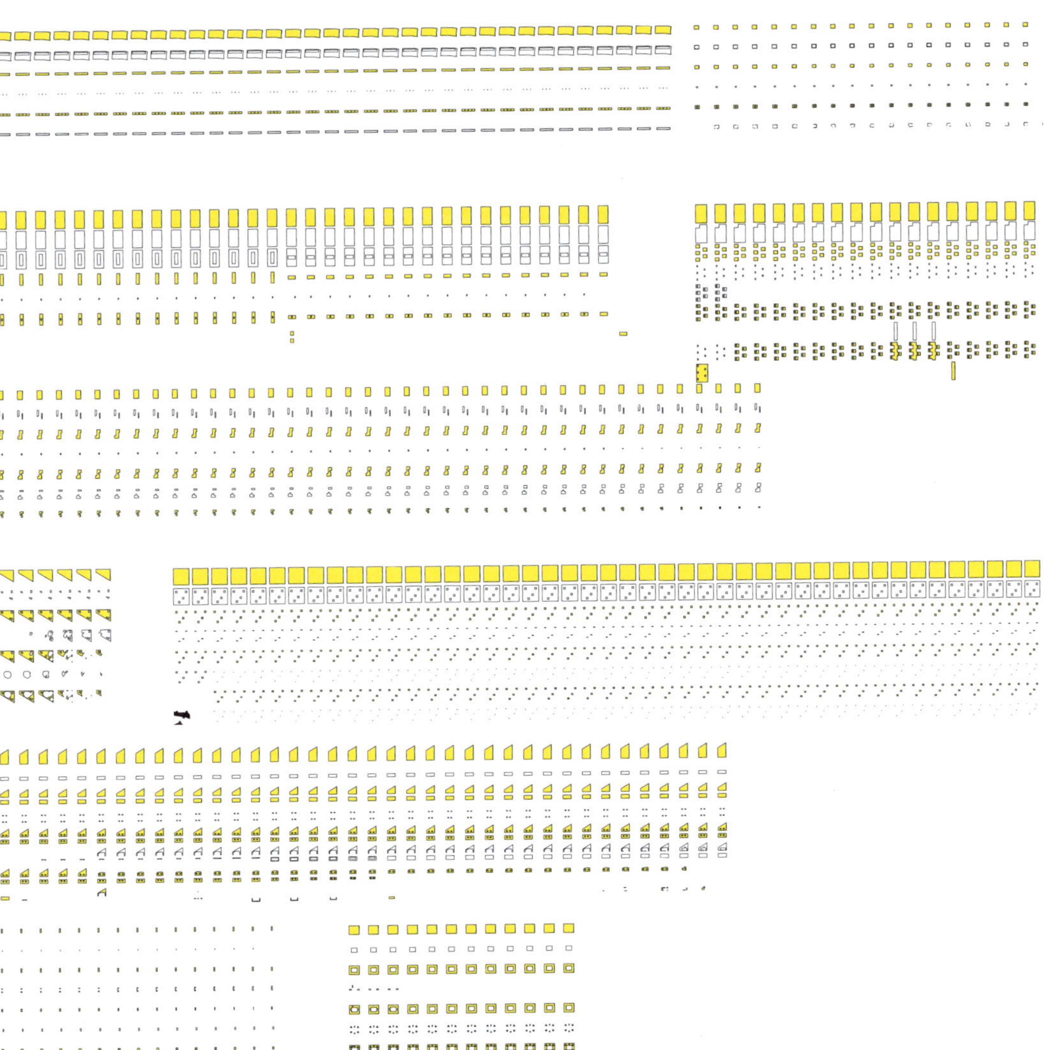

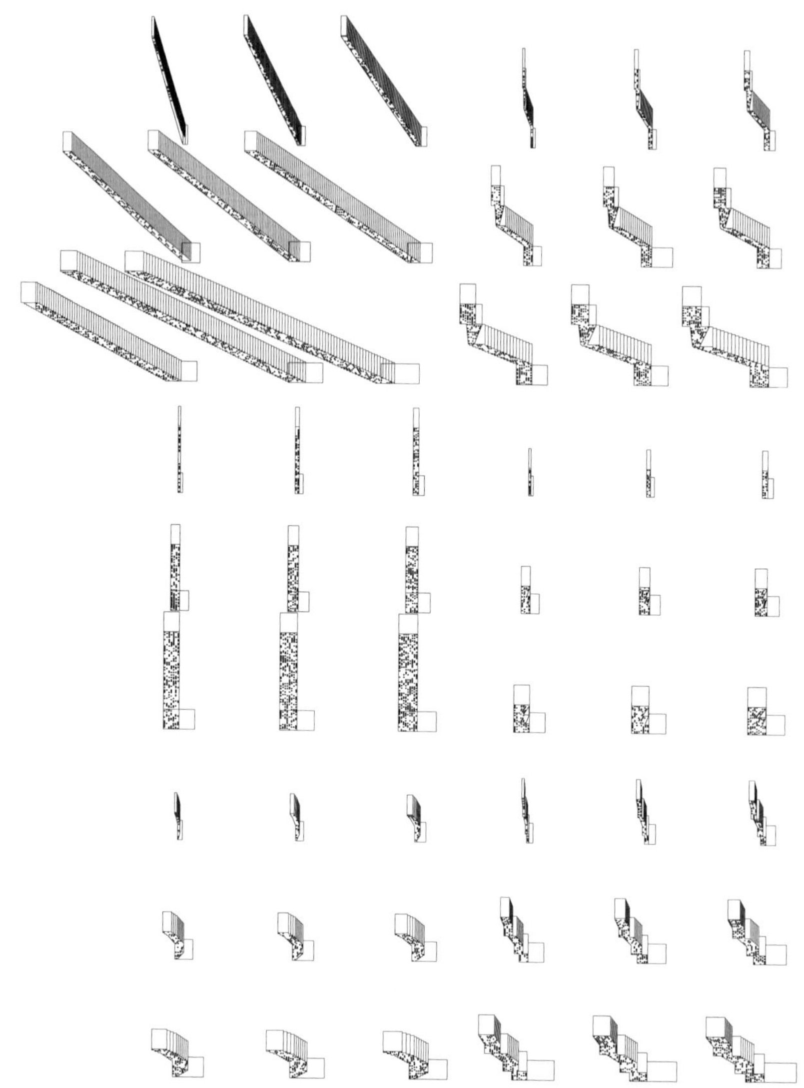

Modality. Variation. High-rise housing vertical proliferation. Modalities of replication, transformation, and limitation: variations of plan expansion relative to plot coverage and plot width. Axonometrics.

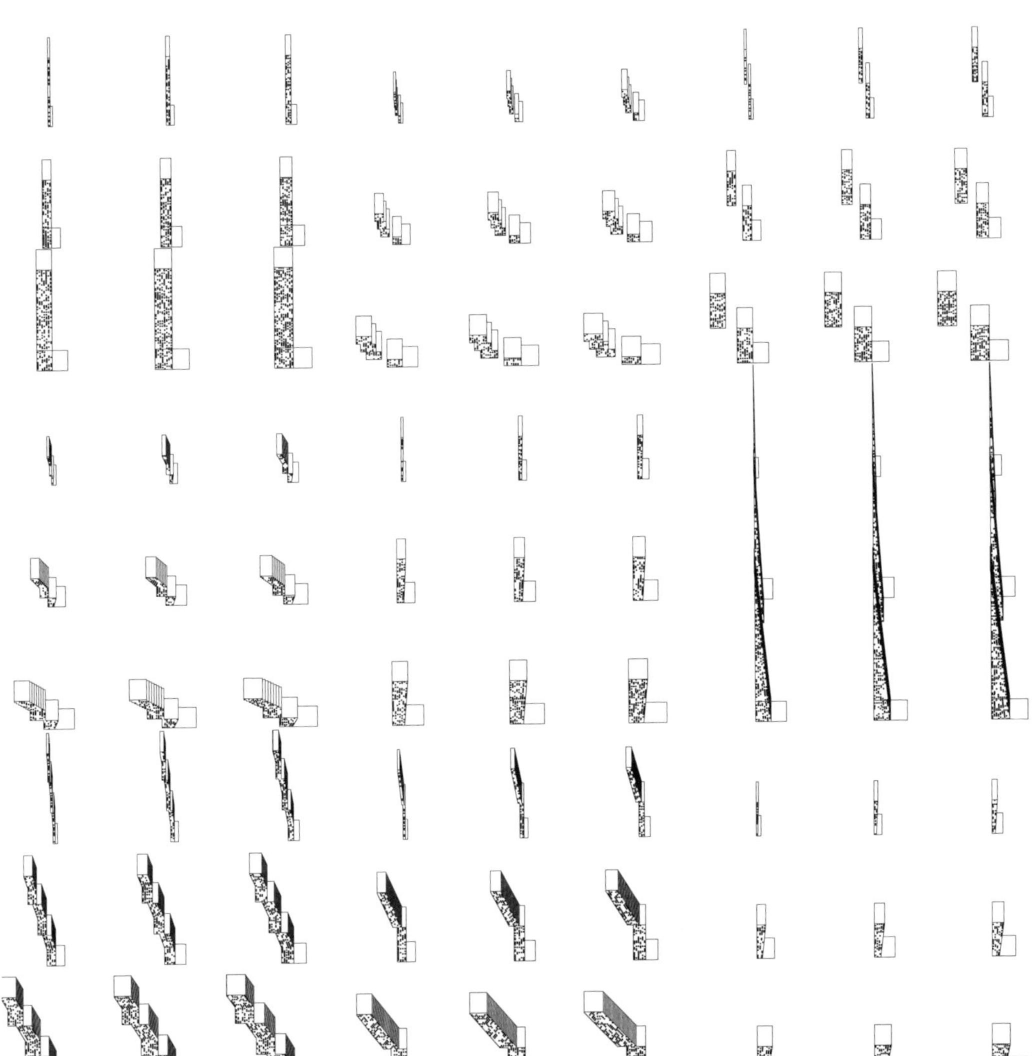

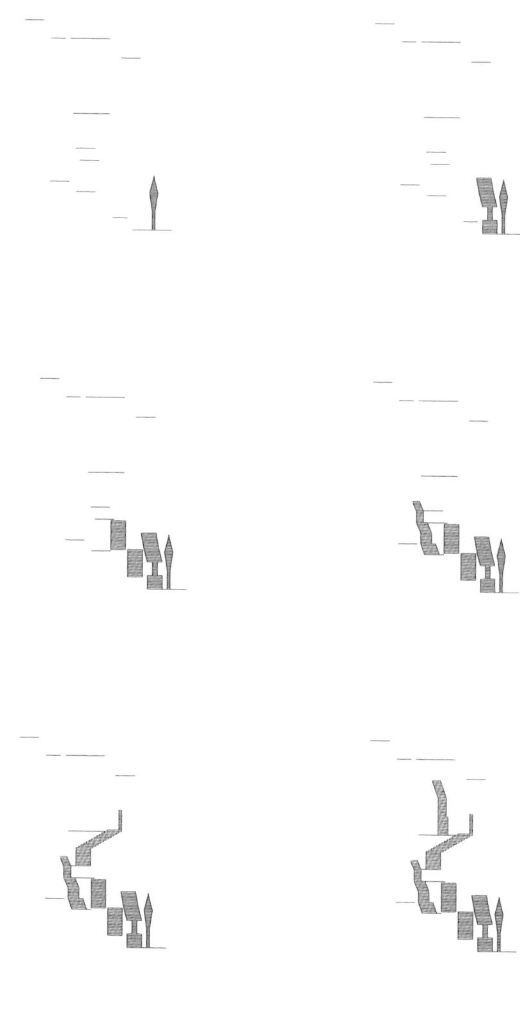

Model. Assemblage. High-rise housing stacking. Stacked sequence of modalities of replication, transformation, and limitation subsequently required by plot regeneration potential factors, cumulatively evaluated. Elevations.

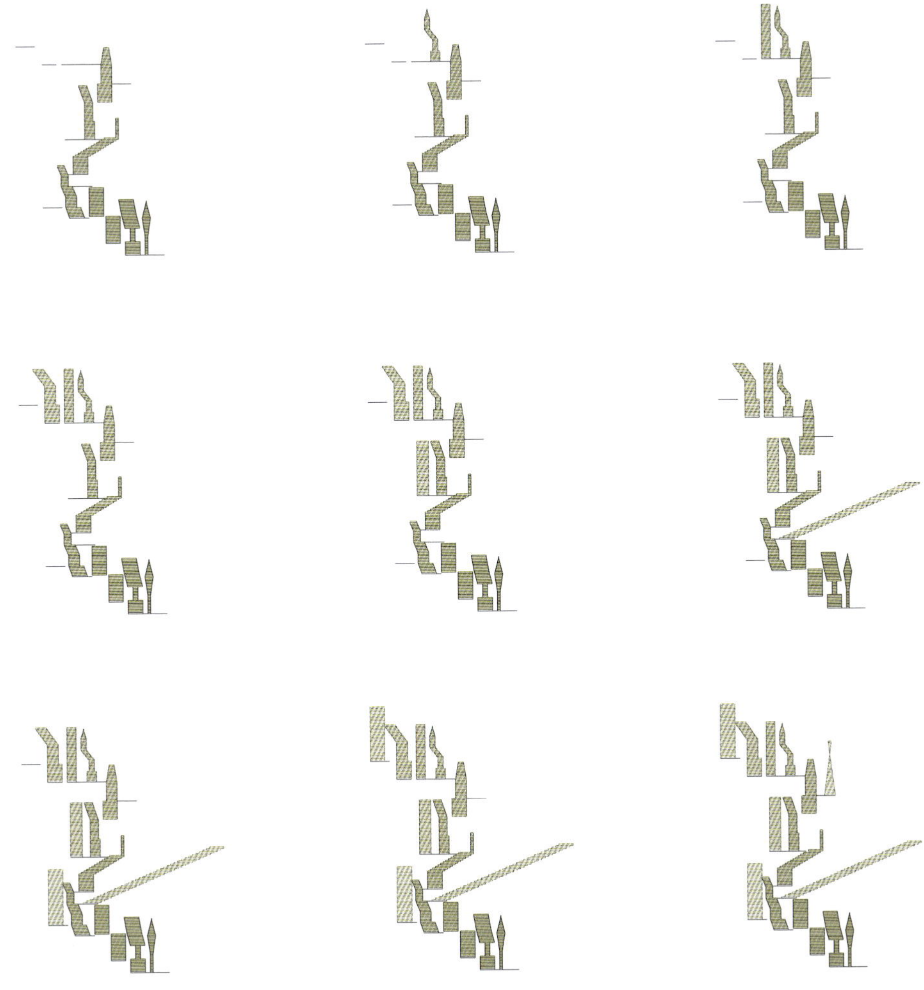

Model. Differentiation. High-rise housing stacking integration. Integrated stacked sequence of modalities of replication, transformation, and limitation. Axonometrics.

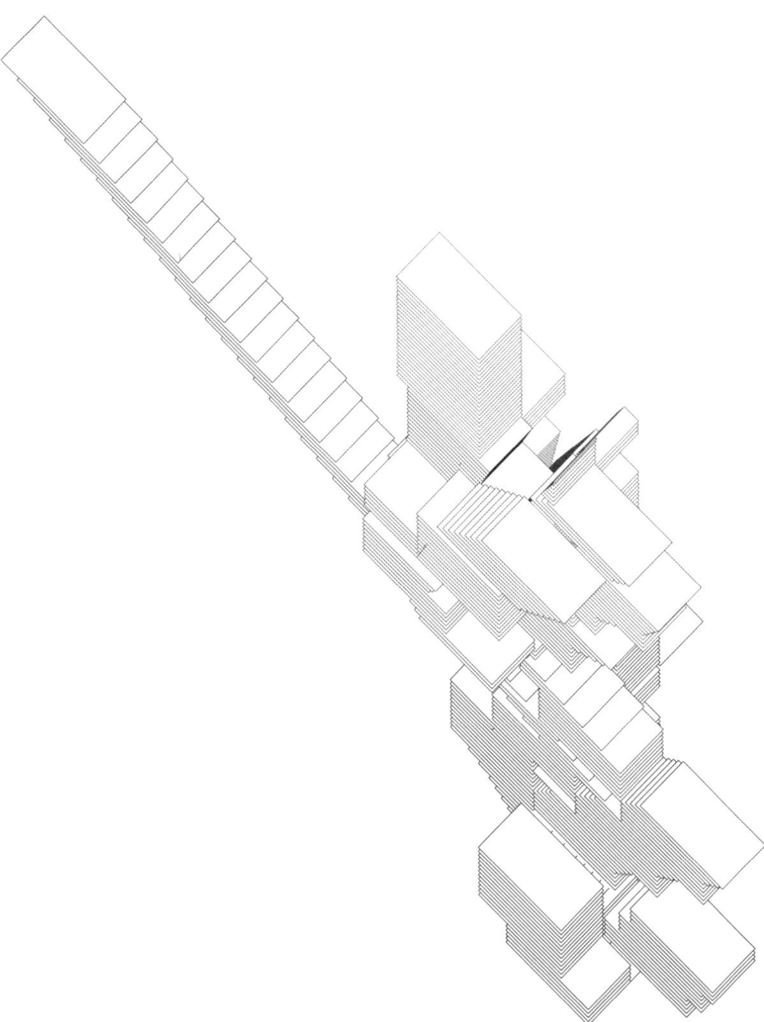

Prototype. Organization. High-rise housing integrated stack. Integrated stack of modalities of replication, transformation, and limitation. Axonometry.

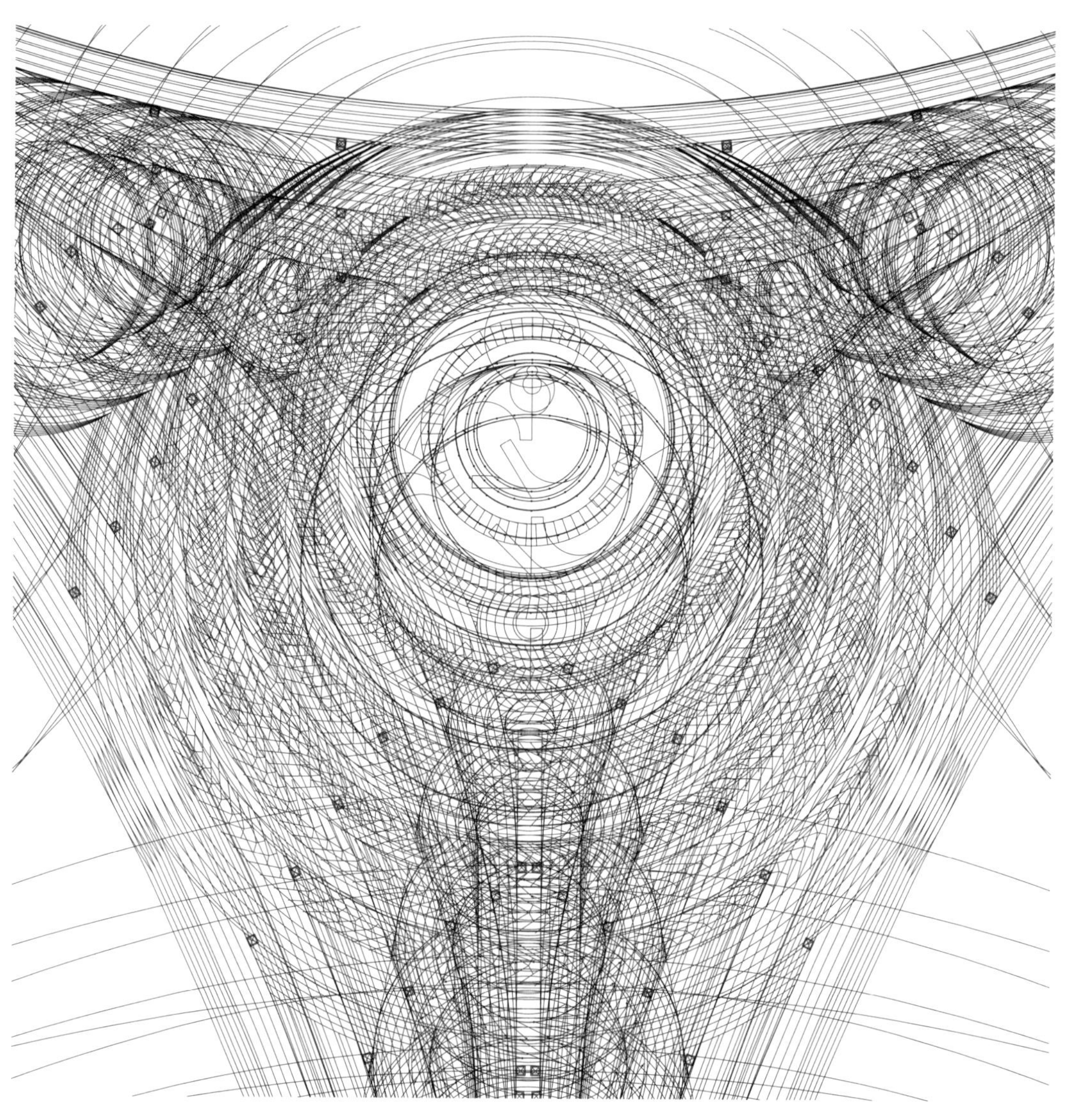

Obus Interchange, Max Wong.
Prototype. Organization. Territorial interchange atrium. Plan sector.

The Universal Interchange Model

Obus Interchange integrates housing and automobile infrastructure in a single urban/suburban building gradient. Le Corbusier's iterative proposals for skyscrapers and corridor buildings in Algiers are reverse-engineered to provide a synthetic model that manages the variation of housing unit sizes, pedestrian corridor widths, floor plan depths, and the rhythm of vertical connections, as well as the number, rotation, and internal splitting of wings, the height, position, and extension of free plans, the width and turning radius of vehicular lanes and pedestrian ways, and the variable filleting of circulatory intersections. By connecting these attributes to each other, the organization cascades the centrifugal effect resulting from the insertion of big-box retail stores into an interstate highway interchange, a three-dimensional roundabout with secondary loops, branches, and detours, parking areas, and pedestrian ways.

Obus Interchange softens and diversifies Le Corbusier's housing bar and expands its range of performance by engulfing within the building not only road infrastructure but the territory that is associated with it and is commonly disregarded as wasteland: landscape areas in between or contiguous to the detours, bridges, and loops of cloverleaf nodes. Frequently abandoned or occupied by suburban commercial programs and parking lots, these high-maintenance areas are often degraded. Le Corbusier's visual conquering of nature through panoramic views is upgraded by embedding the highway interchange and its surroundings within the corridor building, internalizing and exploiting the spatial benefits of these undermined landscapes. With sprawl having taken over nature at the scale of the region, Obus Interchange assumes that suburban culture must be incorporated into the high-density building structure. It proposes the highway node as the key to articulating network cities, freeing the territory in between and rendering all urban space a variant (at various scales) of the drive-in.

If the infrastructural network enables the urbanization of regions to overtake the natural environment, then modern housing is challenged to operate as the ultimate prototype of assimilation of the suburban. Instead of denouncing the interchange as a dysfunctional, overdeveloped entity, Obus Interchange embraces the redundancy of its form and reloads it with a more diversified palette of architectural properties to manage circulatory transitions across scales. Roads are segregated by speed limit and made continuous within a resilient and nuanced whole. The interchange becomes a medium of speed management, onto which blank buildings, vast parking lots, ancillary uses, and rest areas are piled up and absorbed. The knotted, triple-wing housing high-rise blows up, as if breathing, to ingest city sprawl, intertwine wastelands, and evacuate nature as quickly as possible, leaving in its place an architectural monument to the periphery, a universal interchange model for remote forms of urbanity.

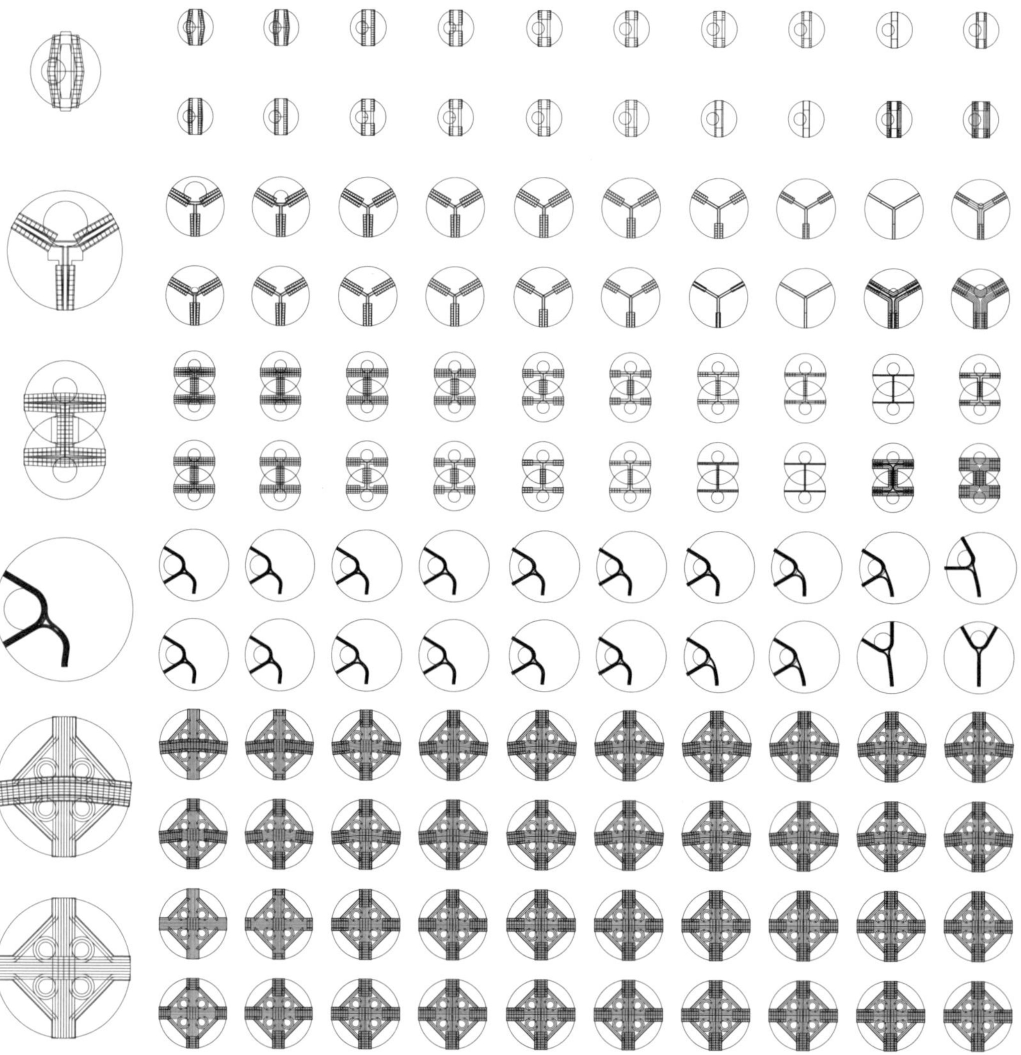

Modality. Variation. Corridor building reverse engineering. From left to right: zero-degree type, bar fillet chamfer radius variation, floor kink variation, floor length variation, floor depth variation, free plan extension variation, lane width variation, room length variation, corridor width variation, perpendicularity variation, stem size variation, cloverleaf scale variation, highway turning radius variation, branch rotation variation, mirroring, wing length variation, number of branches, primitive. From top to bottom: Le Corbusier, Obus Plan E, Algiers, Algeria, skyscraper bar; Le Corbusier, Obus Plan D, Algiers, Algeria, three-wing skyscraper; Le Corbusier, Obus Plans B and C, Algiers, Algeria, four-wing skyscraper; Le Corbusier, Obus Plan A, Algiers, Algeria, housing bars; Le Corbusier, Obus Plan A, Algiers, Algeria, cloverleaf interchange and housing bars; Le Corbusier, Obus Plan A, Algiers, Algeria, cloverleaf interchange. Plans.

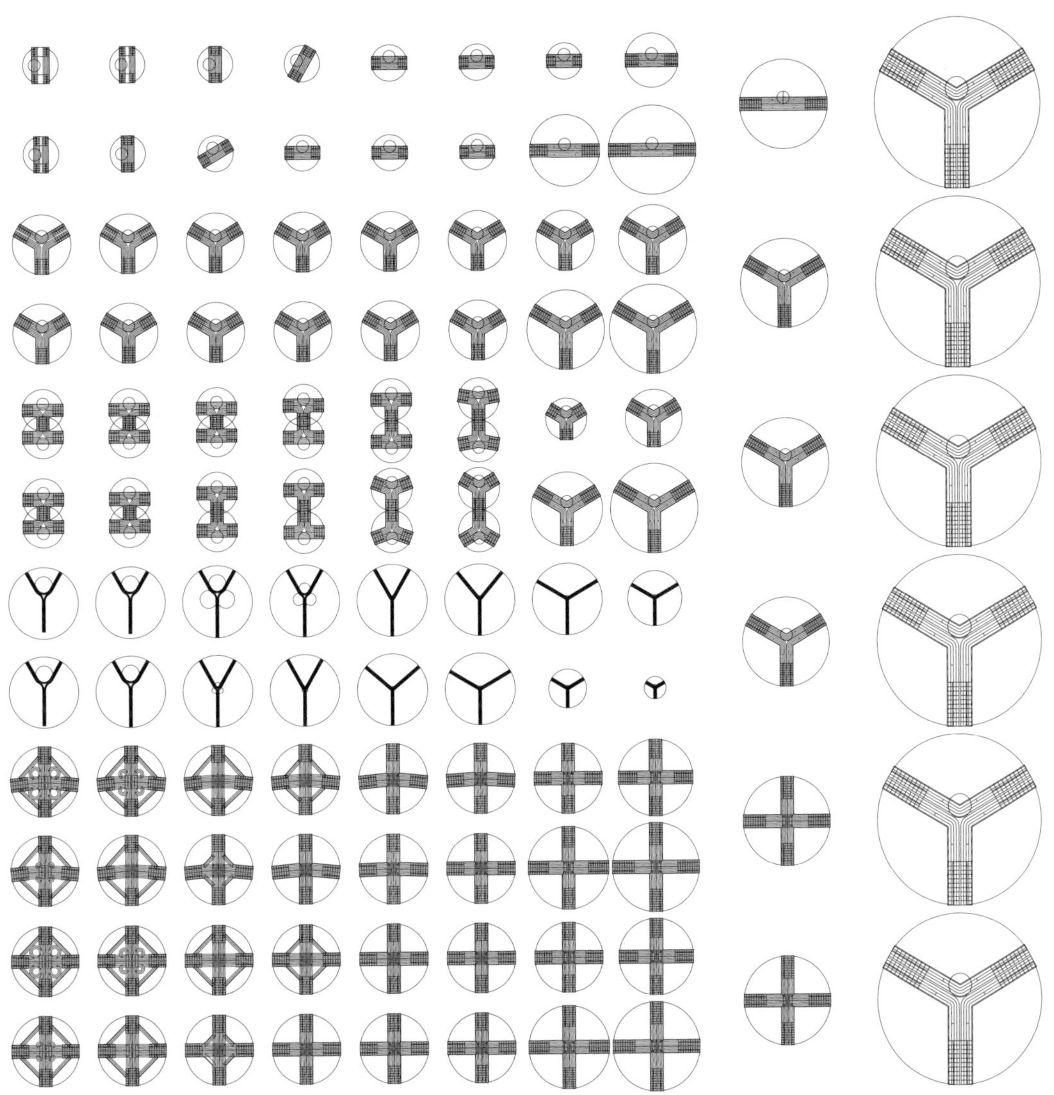

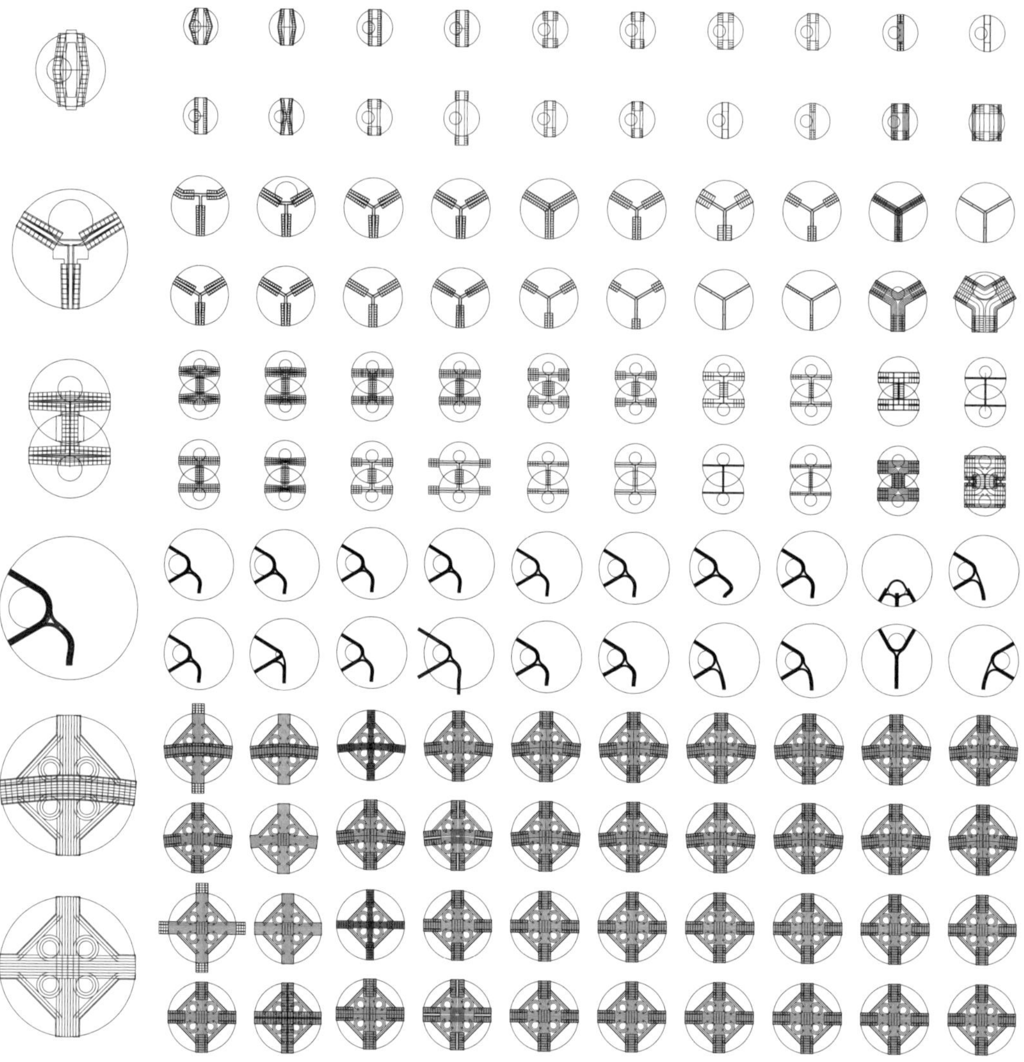

Modality. Variation. Corridor building exacerbated variation. From left to right: zero-degree type, bar fillet chamfer radius variation, floor kink variation, floor length variation, floor depth variation, free plan extension variation, lane width variation, room length variation, corridor width variation, perpendicularity variation, stem size variation, cloverleaf scale variation, highway turning radius variation, branch rotation variation, mirroring, wing length variation, number of branches, primitive. From top to bottom: Le Corbusier, Obus Plan E, Algiers, Algeria, skyscraper bar; Le Corbusier, Obus Plan D, Algiers, Algeria, three-wing skyscraper; Le Corbusier, Obus Plans B and C, Algiers, Algeria, four-wing skyscraper; Le Corbusier, Obus Plan A, Algiers, Algeria, housing bars; Le Corbusier, Obus Plan A, Algiers, Algeria, cloverleaf interchange and housing bars; Le Corbusier, Obus Plan A, Algiers, Algeria, cloverleaf interchange. Plans.

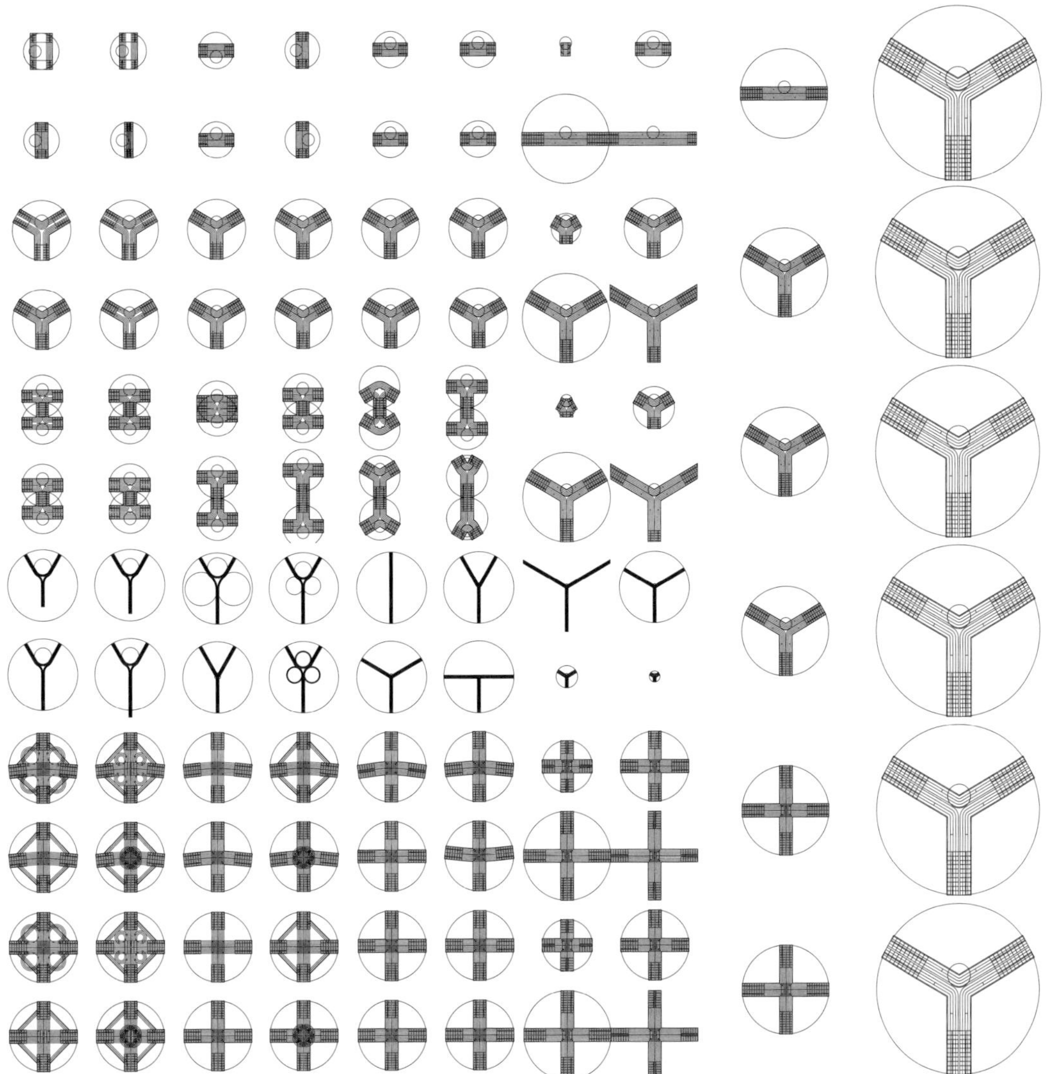

Model. Variability. Corridor building organizational variables. From left to right: bar fillet chamfer radius variation, tapering of floor plate variation, rest area expansion and contraction, housing expansion and contraction, floor depth widening and narrowing, plan depth widening and narrowing, vehicle and pedestrian lane widening and narrowing, retail and parking expansion and contraction, rest lane expansion and contraction, retail lane expansion and contraction, central corridor widening and narrowing, perpendicularity of intersections, rotation of branch pair, stem lengthening and shortening, cloverleaf widening and narrowing, turning radius increase and decrease, branch pair widening and narrowing, symmetrical doubling of units, scale increase and decrease, branch addition and subtraction, lane addition and subtraction, zero-degree corridor. From top to bottom: Le Corbusier, Obus Plan E, Algiers, Algeria, skyscraper bar; Le Corbusier, Obus Plan D, Algiers, Algeria, three-wing skyscraper; Le Corbusier, Obus Plans B and C, Algiers, Algeria, four-wing skyscraper; Le Corbusier, Obus Plan A, Algiers, Algeria, housing bars; Le Corbusier, Obus Plan A, Algiers, Algeria, cloverleaf interchange and housing bars; Le Corbusier, Obus Plan A, Algiers, Algeria, cloverleaf interchange. Plans.

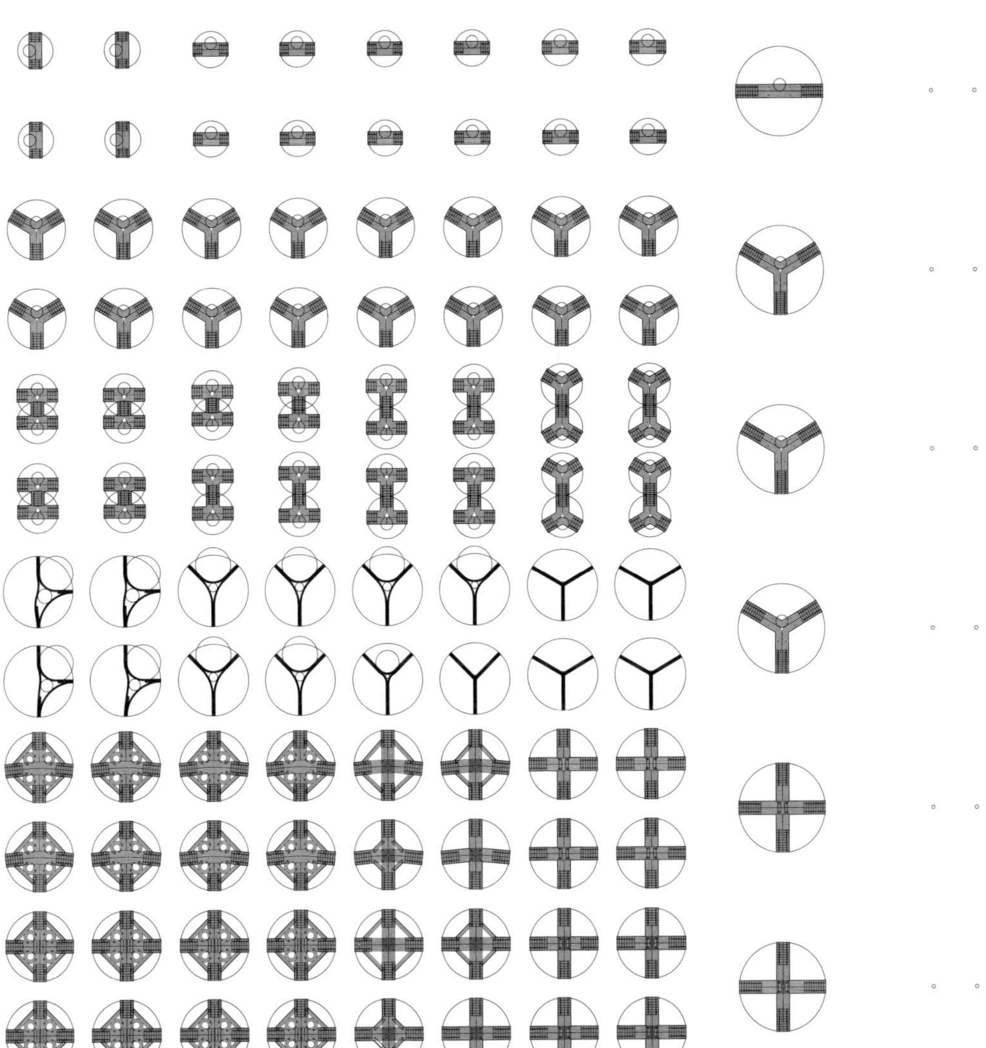

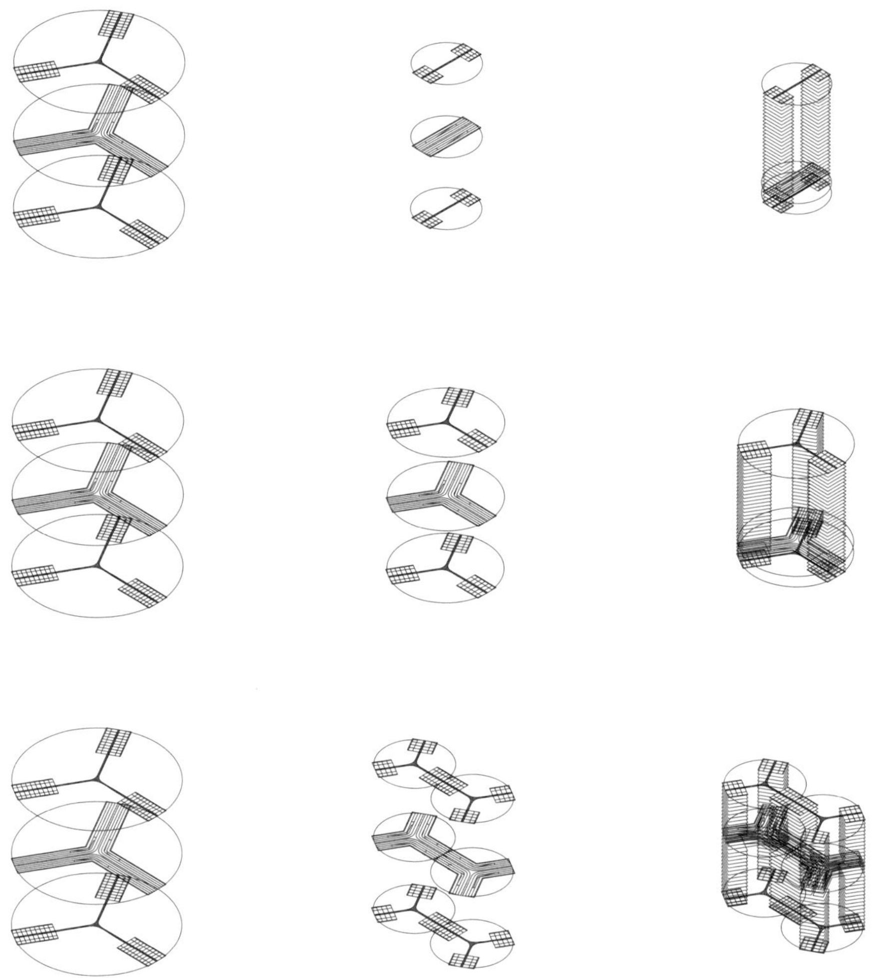

Model. Integration. Building-infrastructure assembly. From left to right: primitive; scaling, number of branches, and mirroring operations; sectional distribution; corridor width, lane width, symmetrical branch widening and narrowing, stem size, branch rotation, and free plan extension operations; highway turning radius, floor depth, floor length, bar fillet chamfer radius, and cloverleaf size operations; vertical connections. From top to bottom: Le Corbusier, Obus Plan E, Algiers, Algeria, skyscraper bar; Le Corbusier, Obus Plan D, Algiers, Algeria, three-wing skyscraper; Le Corbusier, Obus Plans B and C, Algiers, Algeria, four-wing skyscraper. Axonometrics.

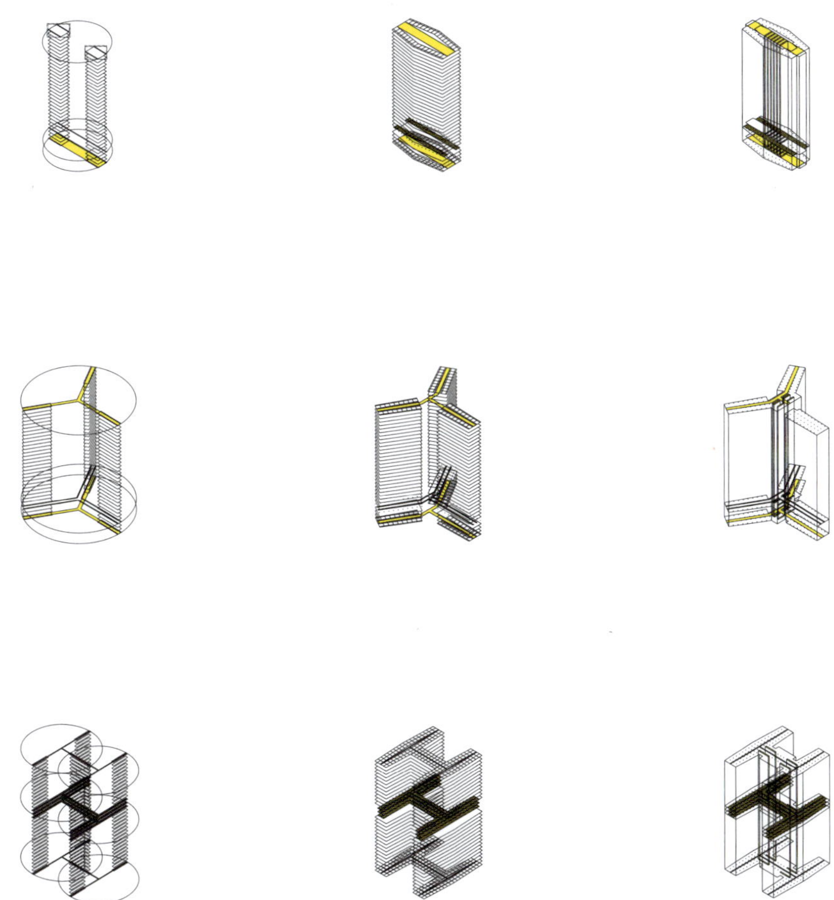

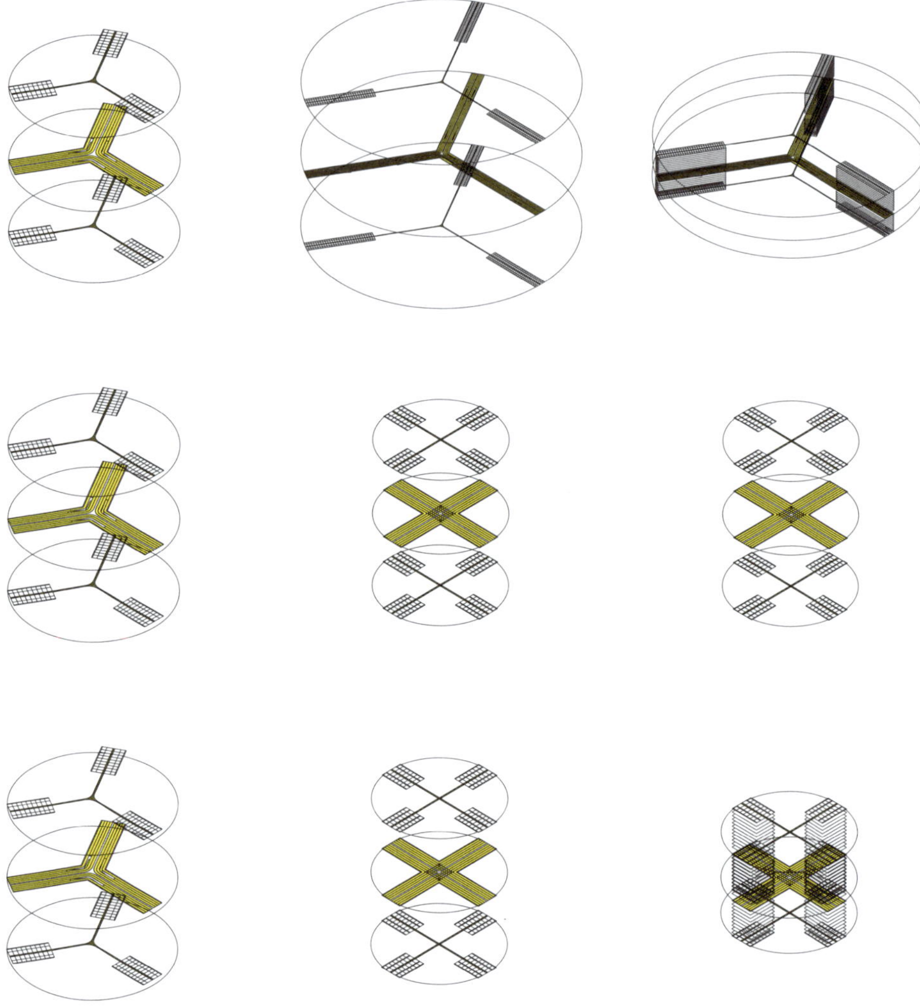

Model. Integration. Building-infrastructure assembly. From left to right: primitive; scaling, number of branches and mirroring operations; sectional distribution; corridor width, lane width, symmetrical branches widening and narrowing, stem size, branch rotation and free plan extension operations; highway turning radius, floor depth, floor length, bar fillet chamfer radius and cloverleaf size operations; vertical connections. From top to bottom: Le Corbusier, Obus Plan A, Algiers, Algeria, housing bars; Le Corbusier, Obus Plan A, Algiers, Algeria, cloverleaf interchange and housing bars; Le Corbusier, Obus Plan A, Algiers, Algeria, cloverleaf interchange. Axonometrics.

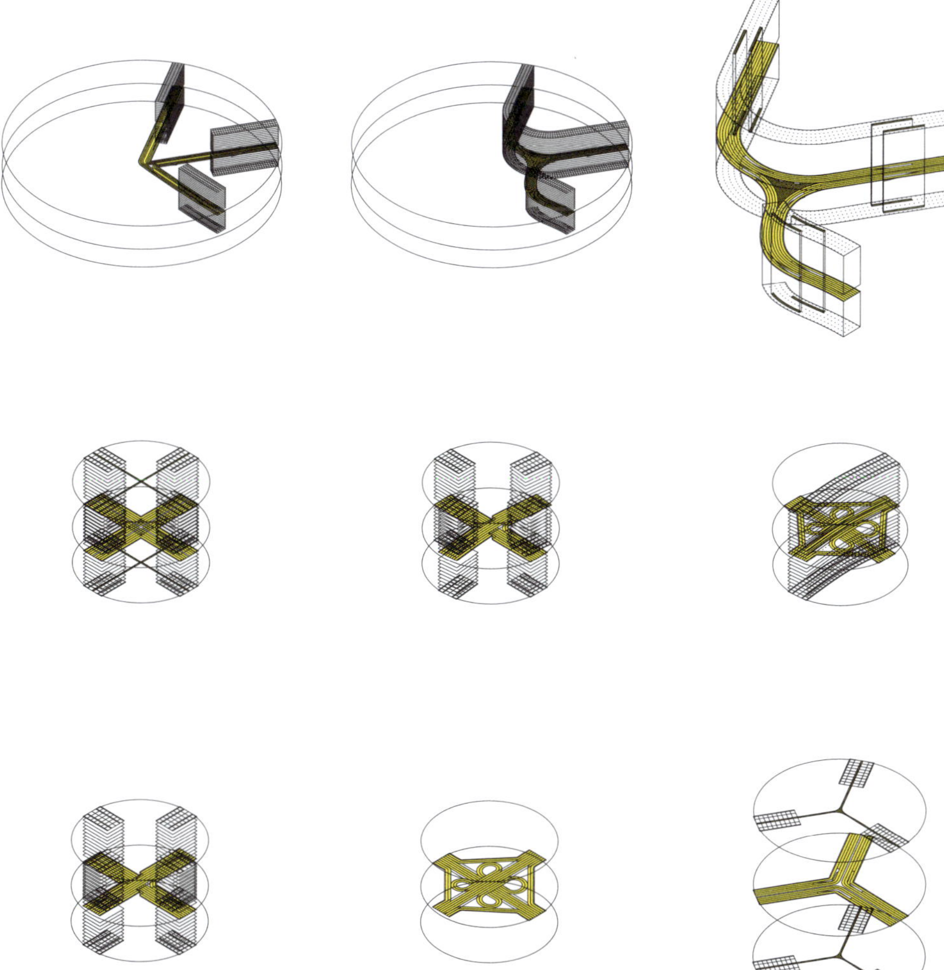

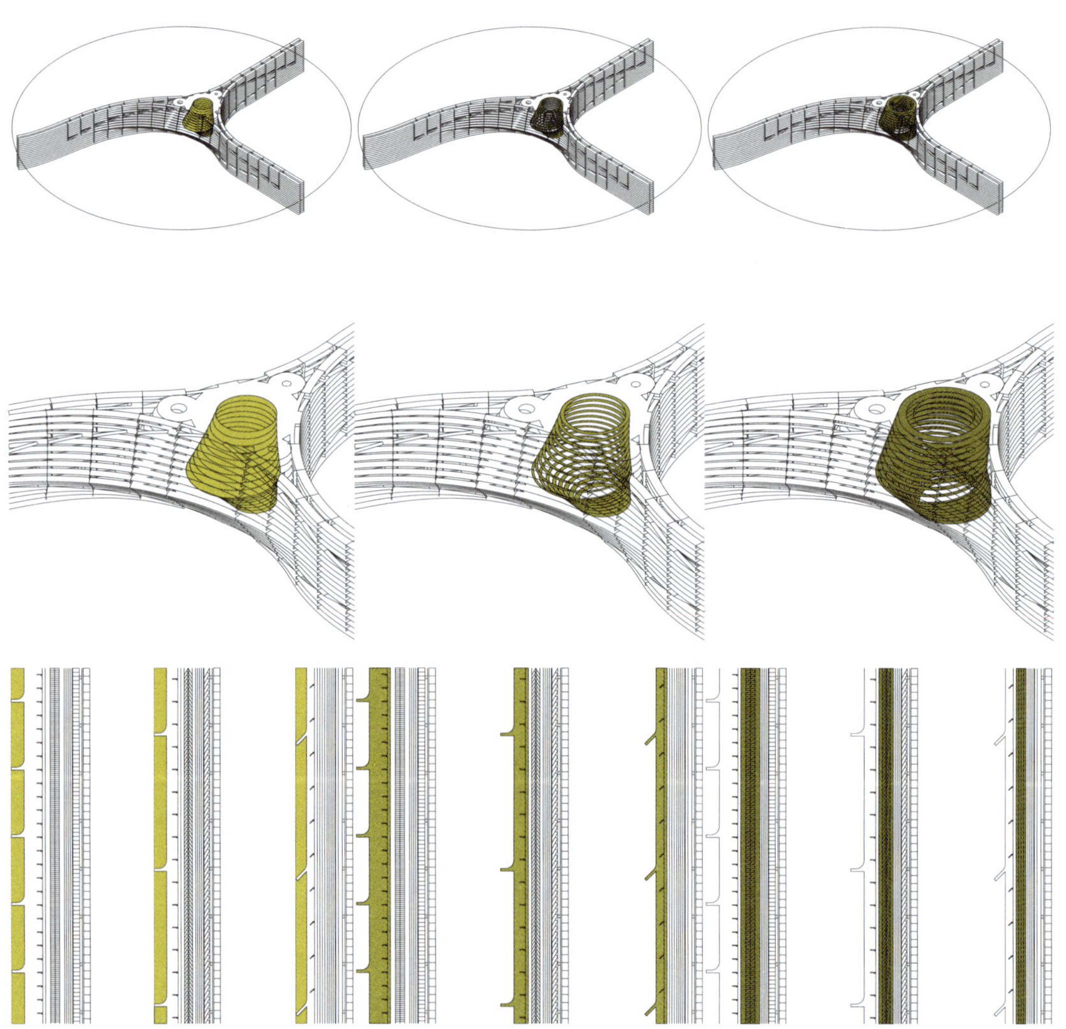

Model. Differentiation. Building-infrastructure systems. From left to right: loading, big-box retail, parking, highway, public rest and leisure areas, housing. From top to bottom: building organization; joint organization; variation of turning radius, design speed, and angle of parking. Axonometrics and plans sectors.

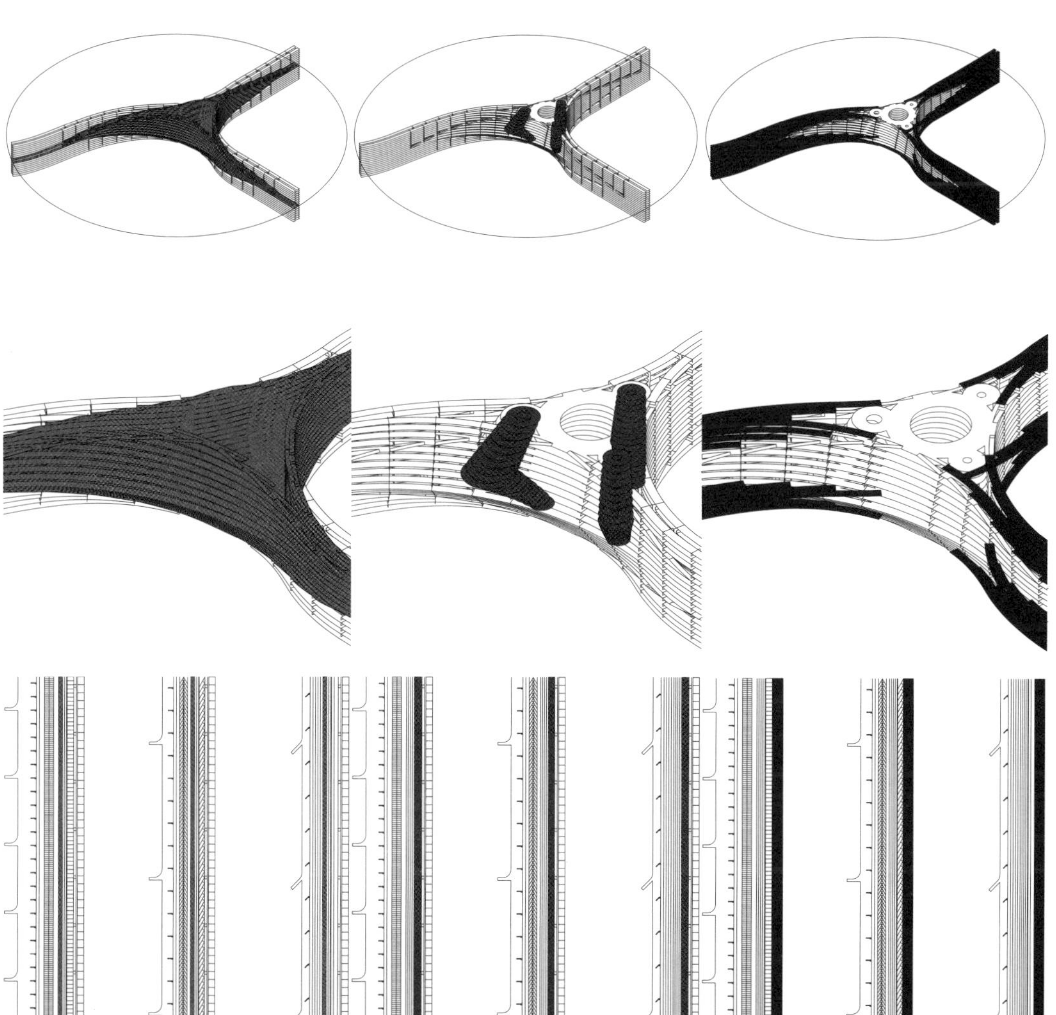

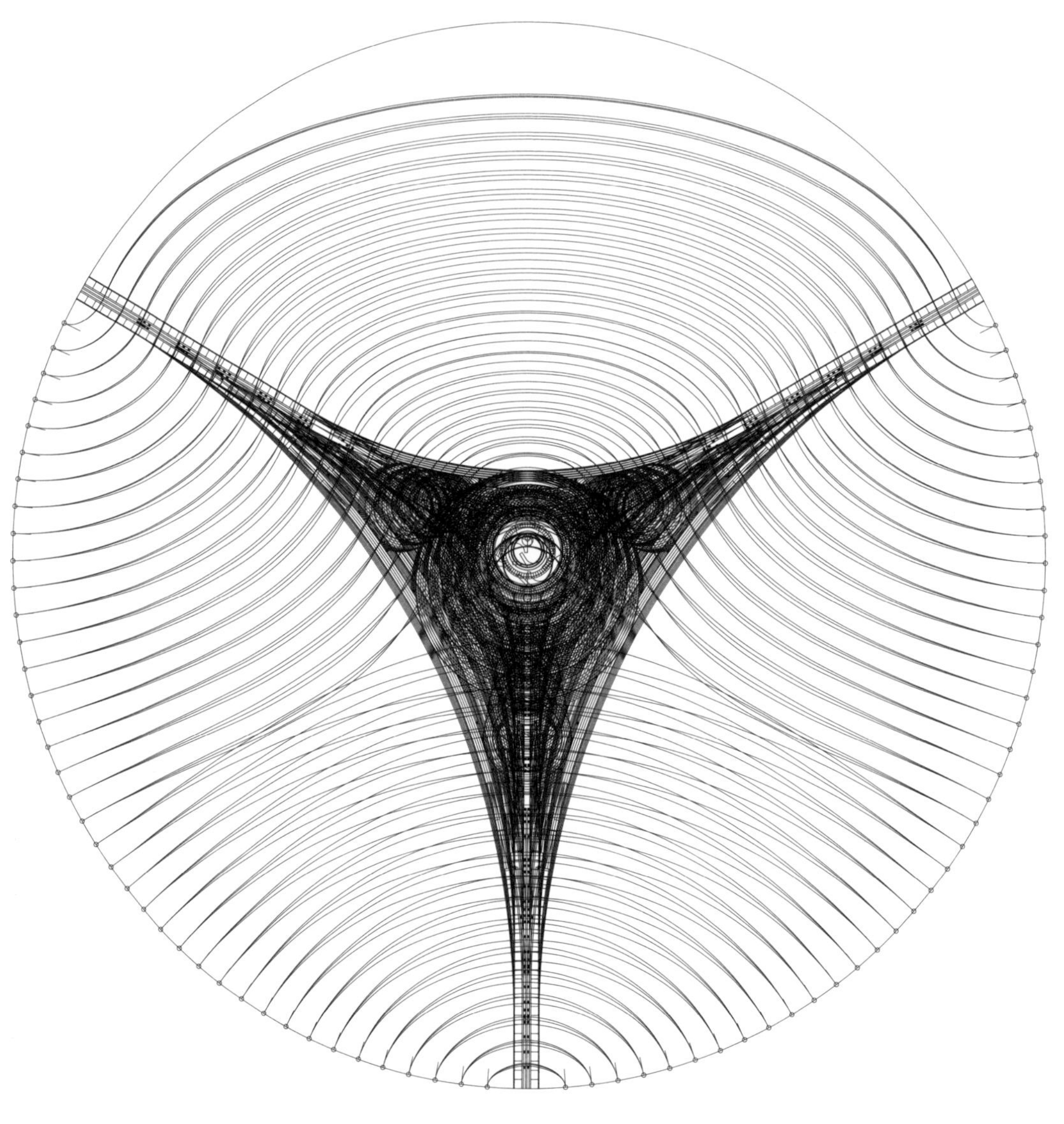

Prototype. Organization. Territorial building infrastructure. Variations of loading, big-box retail, parking, highway, public rest and leisure areas, housing. Plan.

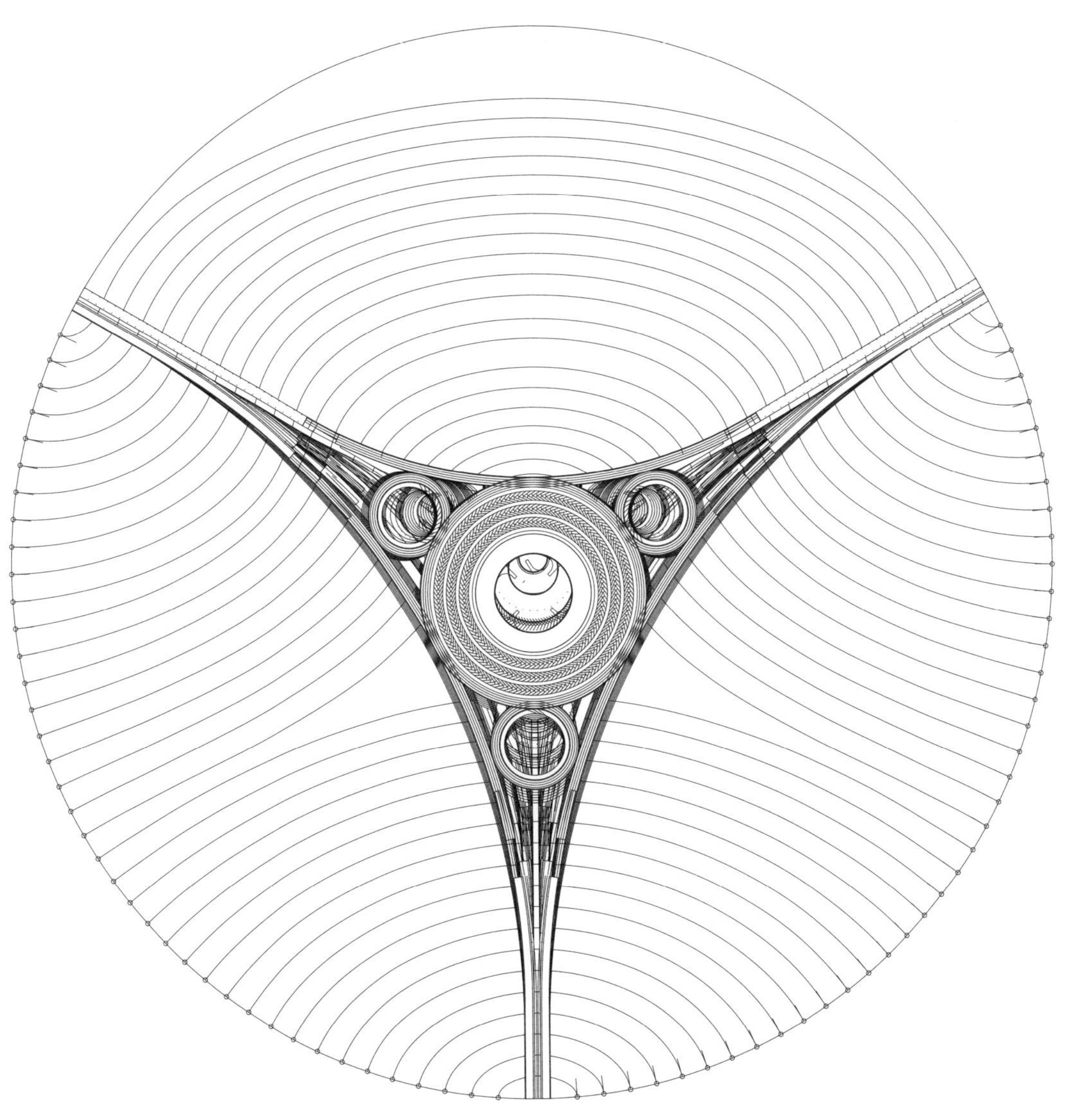

Prototype. Organization. Territorial interchange infrastructure. Loading, big-box retail, parking, highway, public rest and leisure areas, housing. Plan.

Ville Tropicale, Alessandro Boccacci.
Prototype. Organization. Megastructural stilt house. Physical model perspective.

The Differentiated Space-Matrix Model

Ville Tropicale awkwardly continues the genealogy of Yona Friedman's Ville Spatiale space-matrix projects and unexpectedly unifies them into a single, differentiated model. It fluently integrates all cases of the genealogy in a system of cumulative operations that manage the massing, density, height, elevation, directionality, and sectional characteristics of the spatial grid, the form, size, and distribution of its spatial units, and the degree of independence between the two, absorbing the peculiarities of Friedman's projects as the idiosyncratic variants of a synthetic differentiation lineage. The model therefore, at its basis, turns a series of autonomous but resonating projects into a single generative system.

In this context, Villa Tropicale overcomes the self-mystifying dichotomization between the rigid and the free, the orderly and the contingent, the total and the particular, the generic and the irreducible, the neutral and the unstable, by transitioning one into the other. The model evolves the detached, neutral understanding of megastructures—only possible by means of extra-large infrastructural pillars and extra-long spans—through a regionally sensitive structural collective that indexes changes in the conditions of the ground in its organization. A three-dimensional field, constituted by a structural grid running in all directions, is locally cleared up by a series of medium-scale intervals distributed regularly for the entrance of light. Instead of containing free-floating elements and being supported by a universal grid system, its structure converges and diverges, finding its own conditions of support. The specificity and irreducibility of local conditions, the regional variation and diversification of neighborhoods, corridors, and zones, the general orientation and distinction of areas, and the spatial hierarchies and segregation of components—ubiquitously present across Friedman's model—are made constitutive of a global/local continuum that gradually manages the balance, reciprocity, and correspondence of parts in a resilient whole.

This matrix can be overlaid onto any ground or ecology, its inner conditions can vary, and its structural organization can diversify, rendering obsolete both the need for the superstructural and the false identification of freedom with the erratic behavior of small architectural components. Fields of typological variations of pseudo-vernacular huts, systematically occupying ground formation processes, differentiate the repetitive structure and loose cell system of the free plan in a pliable vertical continuum, characterized by the progressive transition of the regular matrix down into the ground and of consistently distributed dwelling components into disparate configurations, affecting their variation and inducing their clustering in residential sets of varying complexity. Rather than its inevitable burden, its agent of freedom, its unpredictable threat, or its monstrous opponent, complexity becomes the ultimate condition of the ubiquitous—the very grain of the desire of architecture toward being everywhere and over anything.

Modality. Variation. Megastructural systems interdependence. From top to bottom: Yona Friedman, Administrative Center for the European Union; Yona Friedman, Spatial City over the City of Tunis; Yona Friedman, Bridge over the English Channel. From left to right: footprint, vertical structural components, space frame, dwelling units, circulatory corridors, systems overlay. Axonometrics.

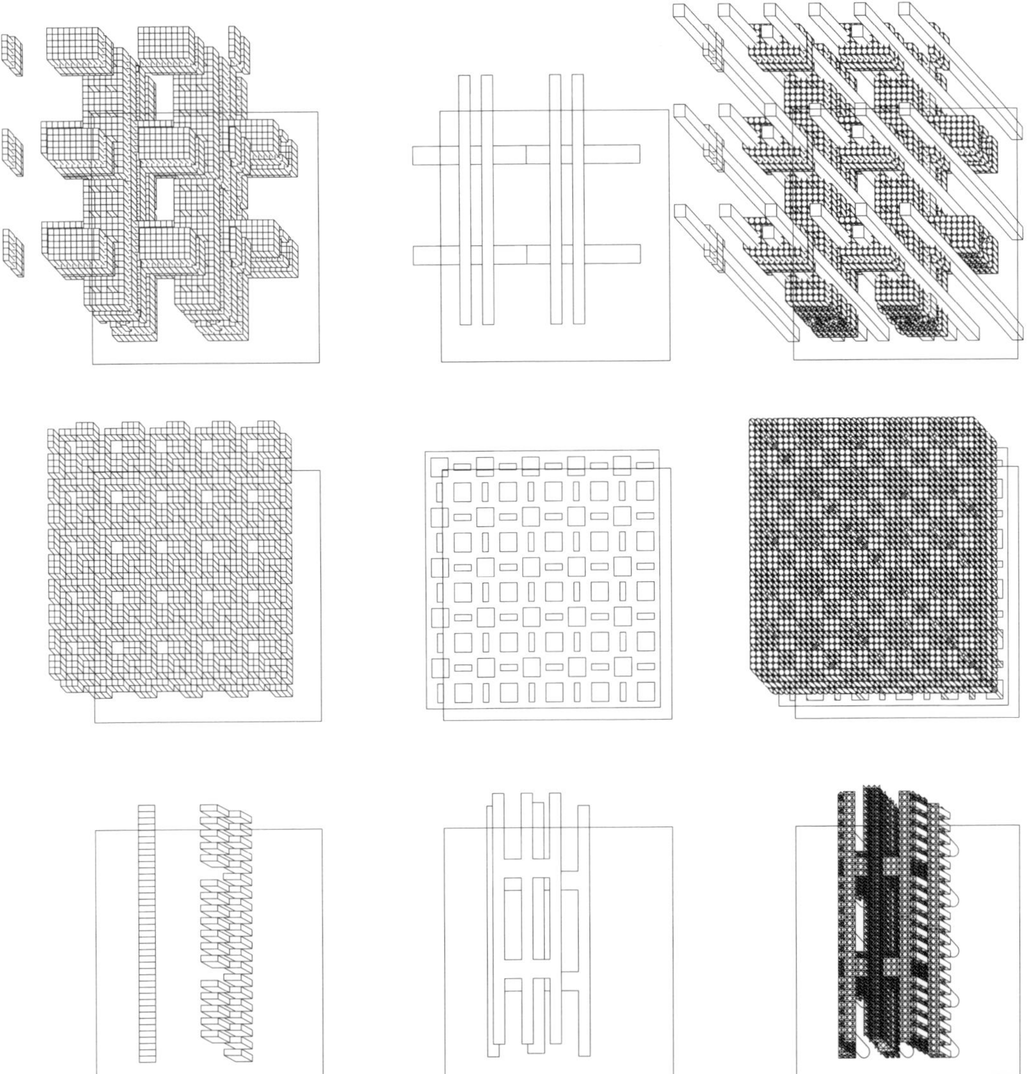

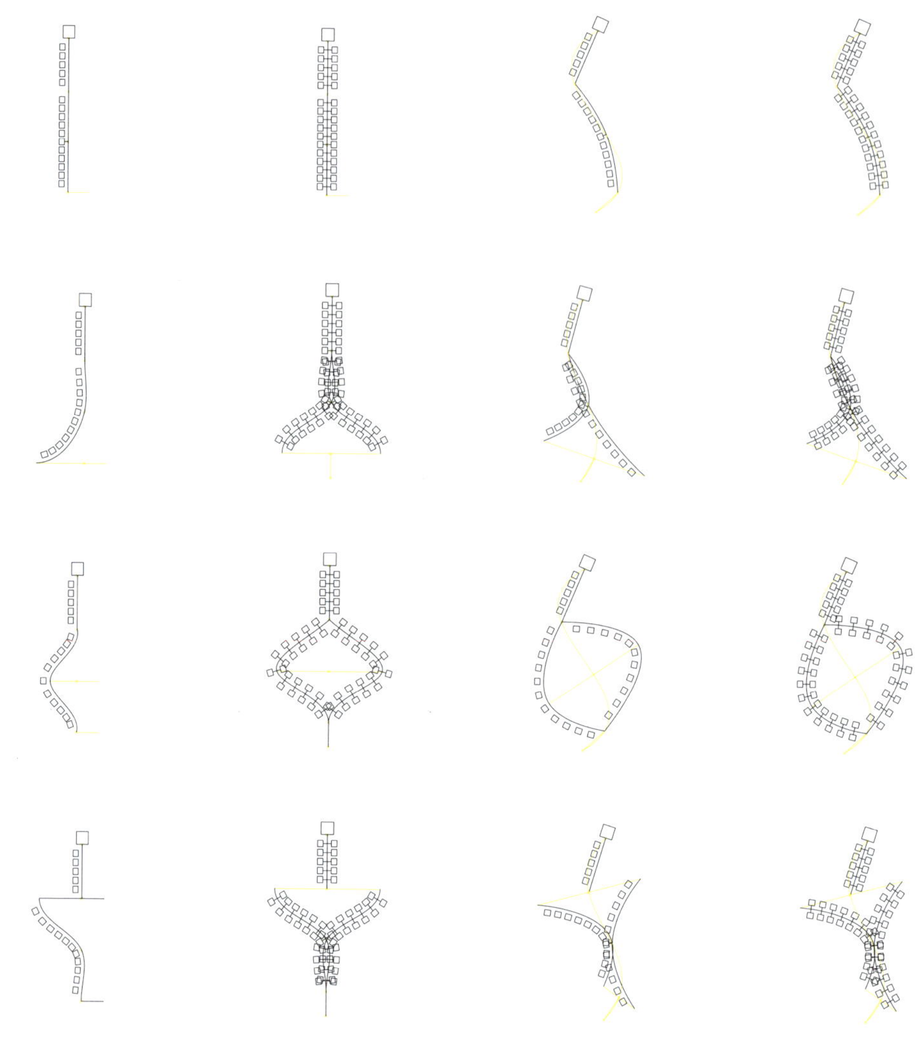

Modality. Variation. Stilt house typology variations. From top to bottom: linear type, curving type, bifurcating type, splitting type. From left to right: single continuous growth path, double continuous growth path, single broken growth path, double broken growth path. Plans.

Modality. Variation. Stilt house typology variations. From top to bottom: linear type, curving type, bifurcating type, splitting type. From left to right: double continuous growth path open at second segment end, open at second segment center, open at second segment start and end, open at second segment start. Plans.

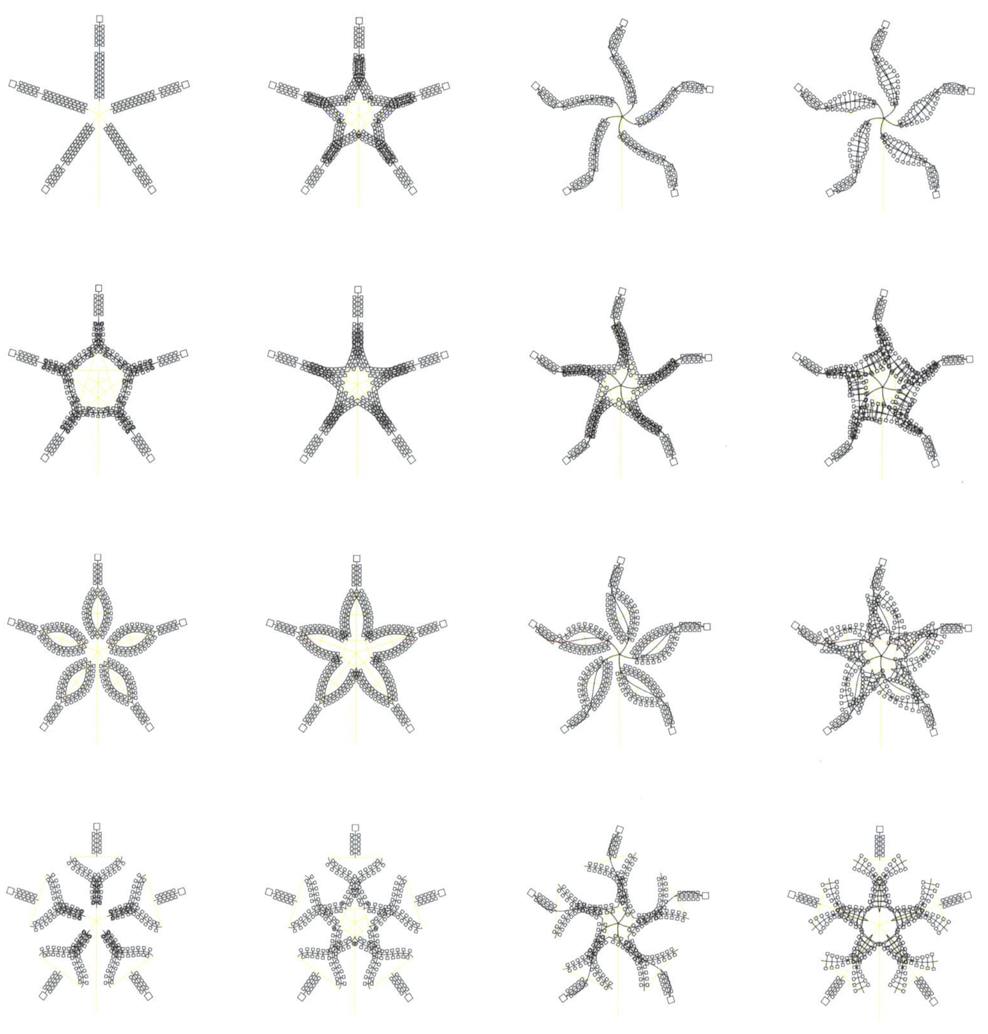

Modality. Variation. Stilt house typology variations. From top to bottom: linear type, curving type, bifurcating type, splitting type. From left to right: stellar manifold of single continuous growth path, stellar manifold of double continuous growth path, stellar manifold of single broken growth path, stellar manifold of double broken growth path. Plans.

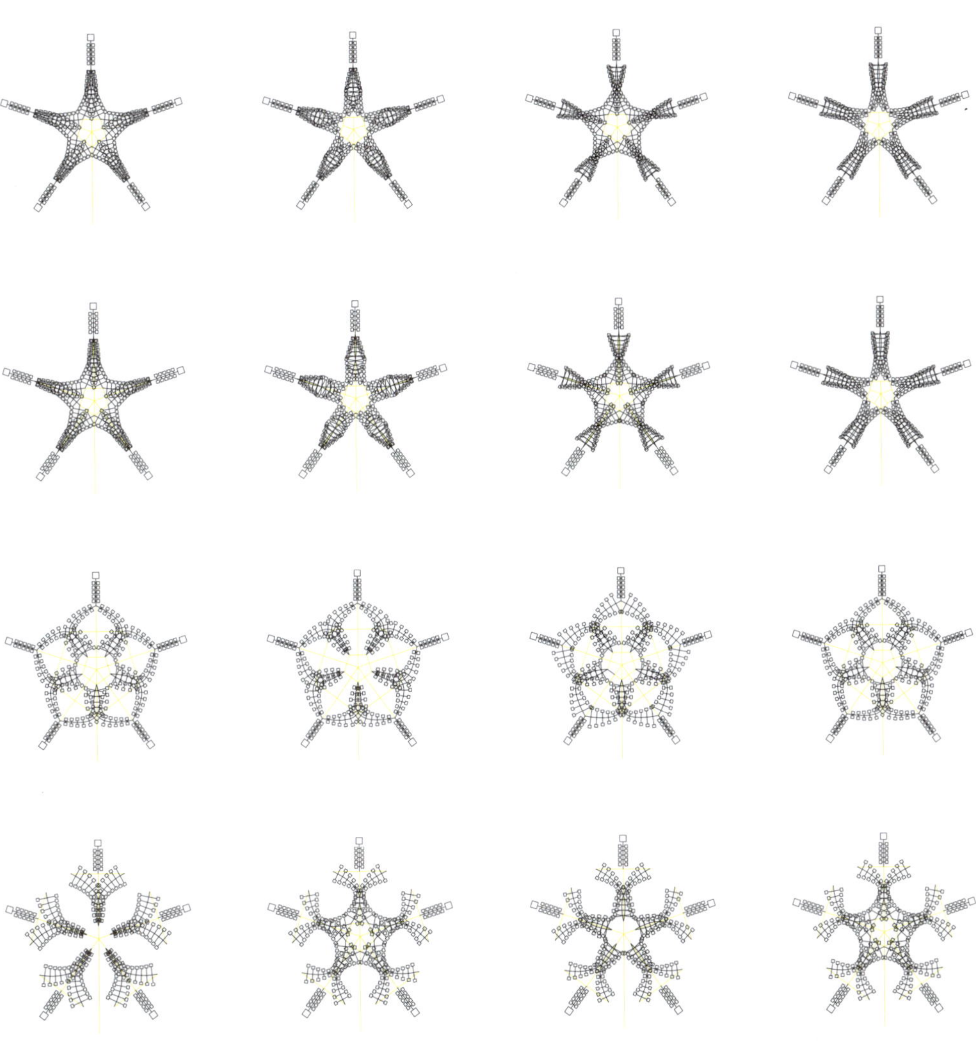

Modality. Variation. Stilt house typology variations. From top to bottom: linear type, curving type, bifurcating type, splitting type. From left to right: stellar manifold of double continuous growth path open at second segment end, open at second segment center, open at second segment start and end, open at second segment start. Plans.

Model. Differentiation. Megastructure differentiation process. From top left to bottom right: creation of a gridded field of points, determination of areas of exclusion, exclusion of points, overlay of gridded field over typological organization, connection of gridded field of points to closest points in typological organization, subdivision of connection lines in intermediate levels, construction of first set of square horizontal sections at subdivision points, rotation of first set of square horizontal sections. Plans.

Model. Integration. Megastructure-typology integration process. From top left to bottom right: connection of vertices of first set of square horizontal sections and definition of vertical structural components, construction of second set of square horizontal sections at subdivision points, rotation of second set of square horizontal sections, scaling of second set of square horizontal sections transitioning dwelling-unit size at upper grid level and at lower typological level, connection of vertices of second set of square horizontal sections and definition of vertical dwelling components, sectioning of vertical dwelling components in horizontal layers of dwelling units and offset of dwelling units at fourth layer, third layer, and second layer. Plans.

Prototype. Organization. Megastructural stilt house. Megastructure, dwelling units, circulation corridors, ground topography. Plan.

Prototype. Diversification. Megastructural stilt house systems. Dwelling units and circulation corridors. Plan.

Prototype. Diversification. Megastructural stilt house systems. Megastructure and dwelling units. Plan.

Prototype. Diversification. Megastructural stilt house systems. Dwelling units and ground topography. Plan.

Neon Sector, Elle Gerdeman.
Prototype. Organization. Indetermined entertainment megastructure. Physical model plan sector.

The Volatile Indexical Model

Neon Sector takes Constant Nieuwenhuys's paradoxical, indeterminate megastructure to an extreme level of determination, turning the revolutionary potential of the *dérive* into an intensive organizational system capable of transcending itself. Following the tactics of its source, the system sits at the inner fringes of the city, but here it operates through a series of tightly controlled interactions between its form, segmentation, modular size and angles, buildable height, rhythm, density and orientation, and the mapping of proximities with highways, railways, parks, major roads, cemeteries, and the central city core.

The model describes trajectories of various gradations of sensitivity to urban contingencies, articulated systematically as specific, irreducible situations. It indexes and responds to these conditions in degrees, so that its pattern and density as a field vary depending on them. The model proceeds from a fundamental will of detachment and freedom from the given. However the revolutionary looseness and radical escape from control become here parameters of organization in and of themselves. Instead of instigating their self-defeating capability toward the transformation of routines and the free definition of space, the maniac forces and darker impulses of pure play catalyze and turn into a system. Shamelessly blunt, the strategy results from the conflagration of a series of urban decoding tactics, rendered as rules of change and operating under the apparently inoffensive logic of a responsive system. Candidness becomes the ultimate form of determination; delicacy, the concealed formula for ruthlessness; and emancipation, the counterintuitive instrument of development.

The *dérive* is also redefined into a method to construct a continuous medium for the unique. Formerly a means of liberation, it becomes a device of wild entrepreneurial development, which through excess (and not through seepage) frees itself from convention. Neon Sector employs the radical but evanescent traces across the liberating fragments of the city as the vectors that structure an organizational system through indexical determinations. The volatile spatial conditions, the abrupt directional shifts, the slippery continuities and odd discontinuities, and the displacements, overlaps, disjunctions, and sudden changes in scale that these vectors stimulate activate a joyful atmosphere of forms, structures, and spaces and create the rugged conditions of an elevated datum of pure play.

The thick surface contains a continuous casino space, retail perimeter garlands, reception terraces, open-air lobbies, drop-off areas, and valet parking to accommodate the frantic gamblers' and curious tourists' arrivals. The interior atmosphere shows itself through terraces, oblique surfaces, irregular star-shape swimming pools, and endless cascades. Below, the infrastructure extends the casino ambiance. The surface connects at seemingly irregular intervals to the ground through diagonal structural components, around which bundles of lifts and spiraling car ramps are organized. While the casino infrastructure projects down into the indeterminate interiority of the elevated ground, the hotel building bars above playfully float over the pattern, inheriting its directions and worshiping the gleaming view of the space-frame landscape.

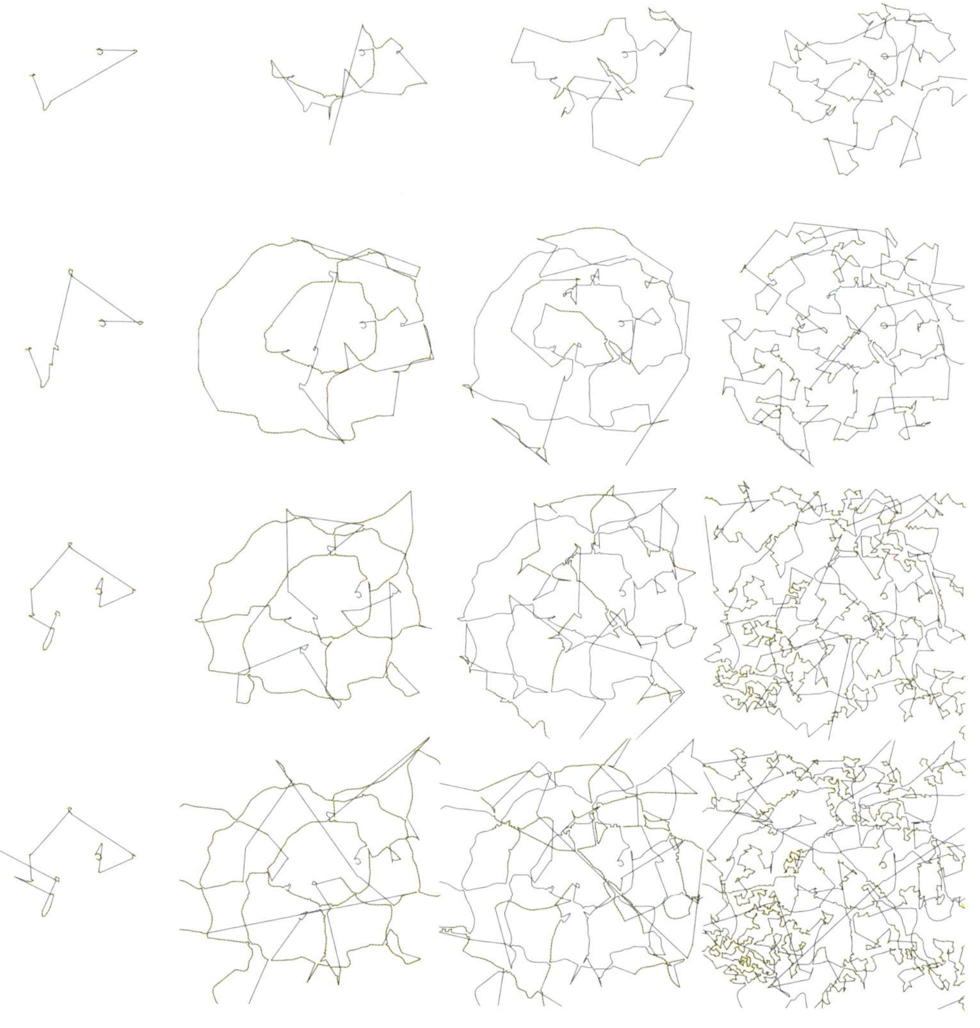

Field. Indexing. *Dérive* system trajectories. From top to bottom: index sensitivity variations. From left to right: proximity to cemeteries, proximity to highways, proximity to railways, proximity to parks, exclusion of medieval city, calibration to major roads, calibration to minor roads, truss integration. Plans.

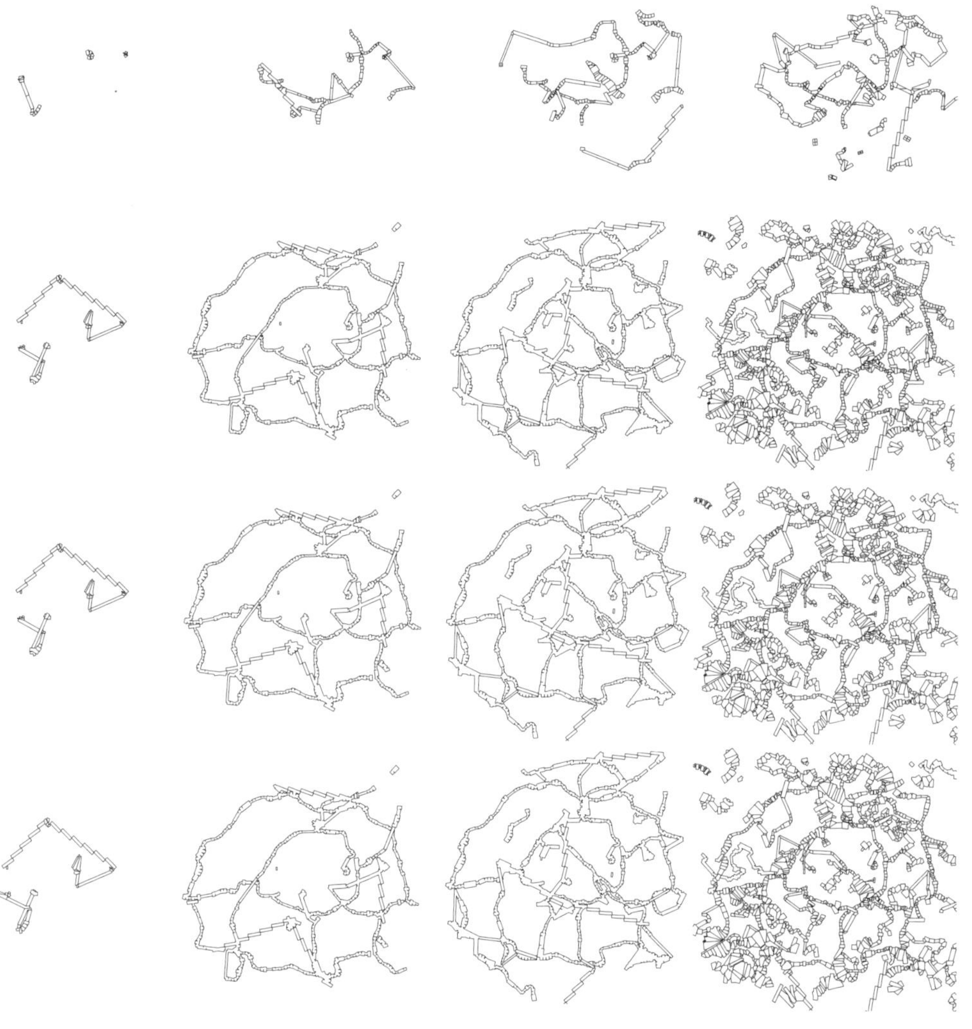

Field. Differentiation. *Dérive* system patches. From top to bottom: index sensitivity variations. From left to right: proximity to cemeteries, proximity to highways, proximity to railways, proximity to parks, exclusion of medieval city, calibration to major roads, calibration to minor roads, truss integration. Plans.

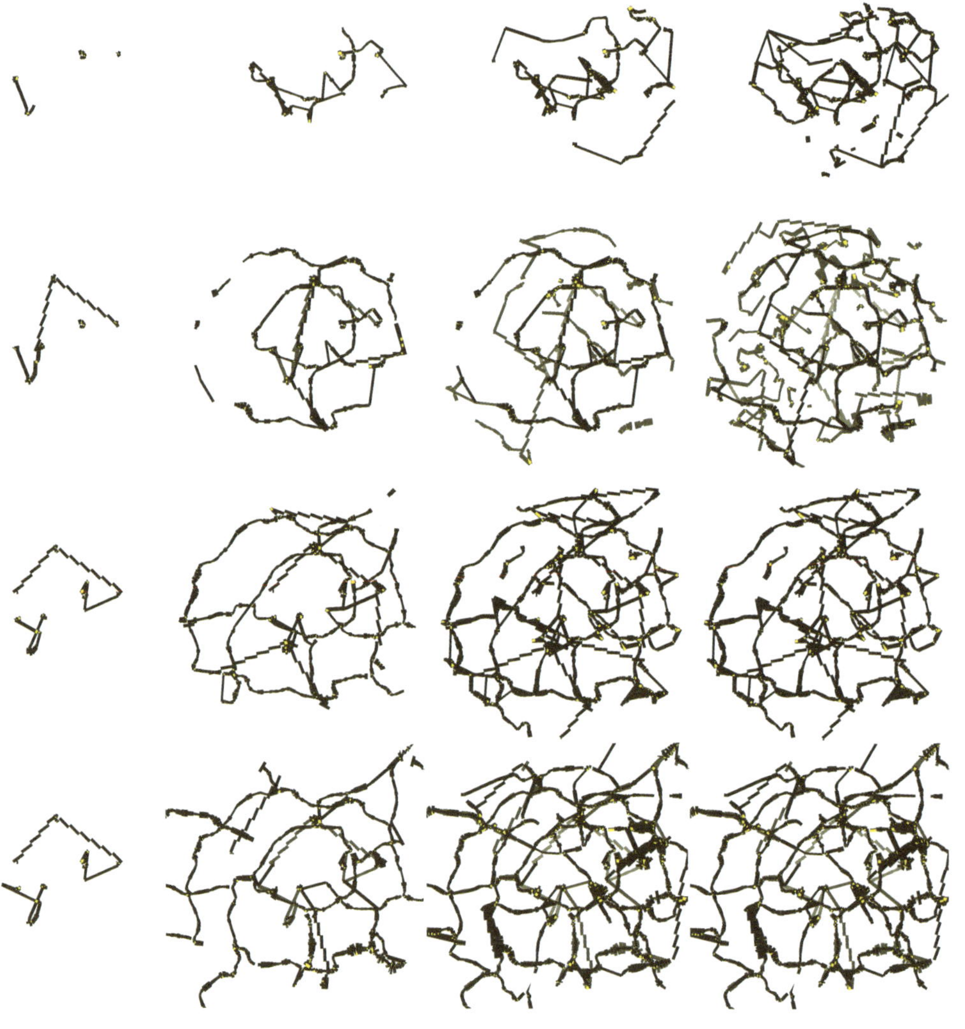

Field. Evaluation. *Dérive* system areas. From top to bottom: index sensitivity variations. From left to right: proximity to cemeteries, proximity to highways, proximity to railways, proximity to parks, exclusion of medieval city, calibration to major roads, calibration to minor roads, truss integration. Plans.

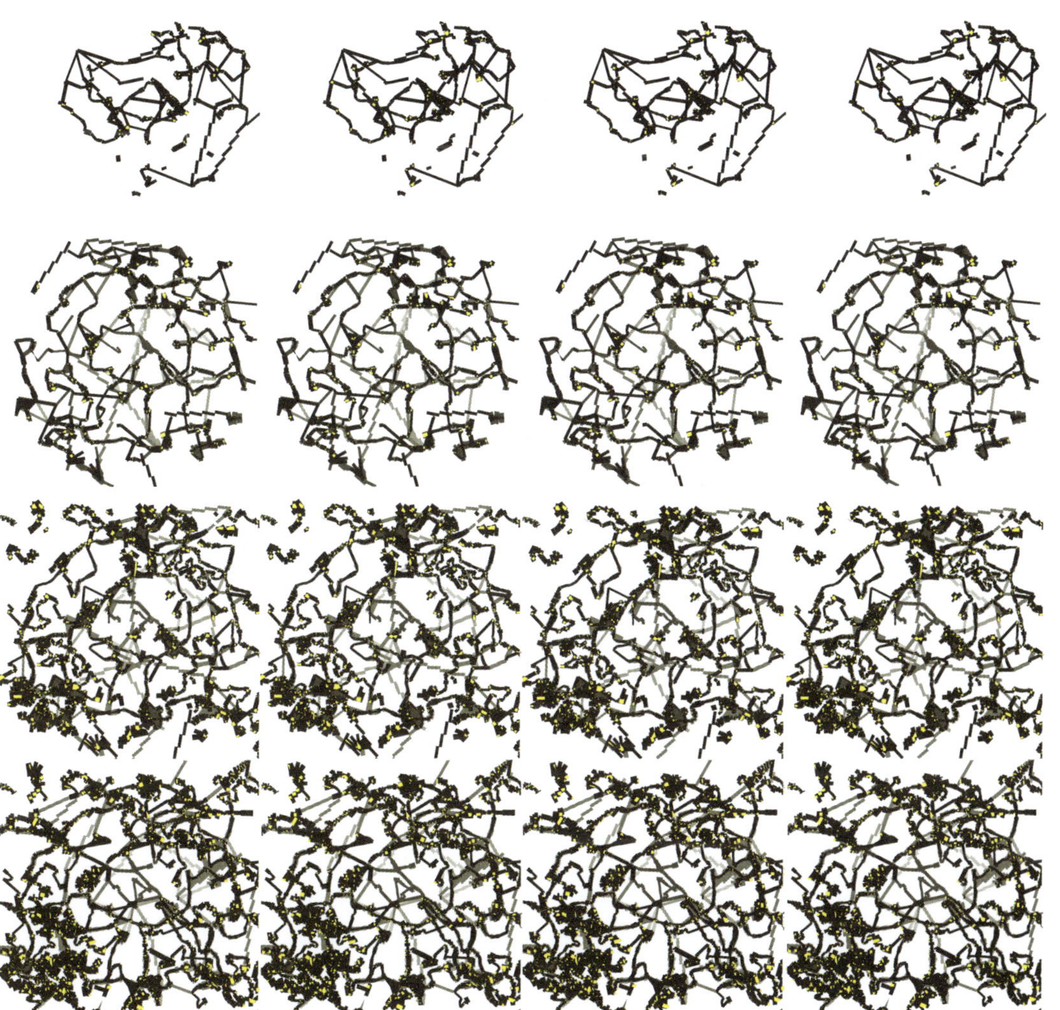

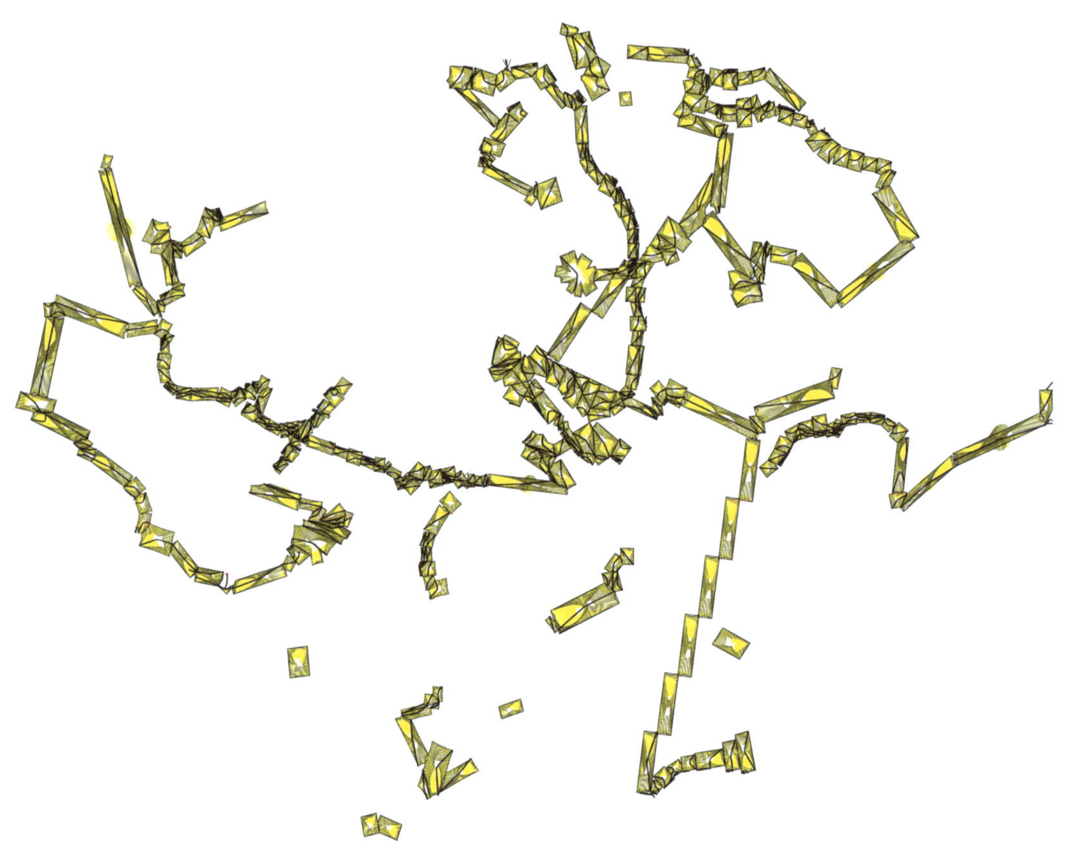

Prototype. Organization. Indeterminate entertainment megastructure. Casino envelope, hotel bars, parking and drop-off, ground–level structure. Plan.

Prototype. Organization. Indeterminate entertainment megastructure. Casino envelope, hotel bars, terraces and swimming pools, retail units, malls, parking and drop-off, furniture, ground–level structure. Plan sector.

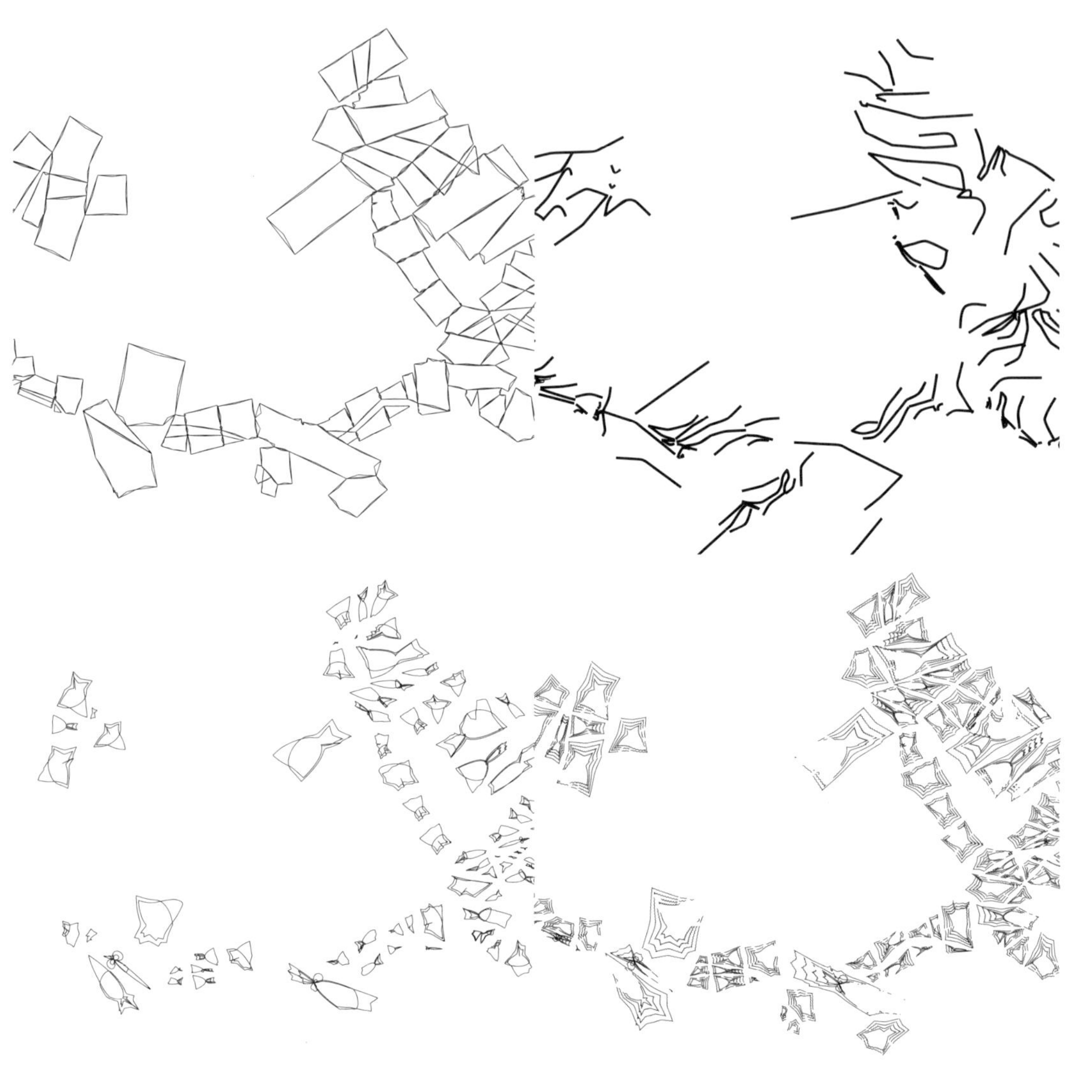

Prototype. Diversification. Entertainment systems. From top left to bottom right: casino envelope, hotel bars, terraces and swimming pools, retail units, malls, parking and drop-off, furniture, ground-level structure. Plans.

Olympic Operations, Simon Willet.
Prototype. Organization. Alpine Olympic site. Axonometry sector.

The World-System Model

Olympic Operations is a model of leisure-oriented landscape and environmental engineering based on Bruno Taut's Alpine Architecture project. Its expressionist, utopian vision of the Alps is adopted as an artificial construct and taken to a level of sheer operativity. The model integrates within a single, book-like system a series of discrete, unique artworks and univocal statements, whose poignant imagery and widely assorted allegorical forms project an expansive, almost dreamy ambivalence that builds up the nurturing ground for high emotions, the content of which, however, remains uncertain.

The vibrant panels of the book are grained down into minor organizational relationships and abstracted as a set of interconnected variables. Obscured behind the iconic format of Taut's drawings but participating in the escalating narrative of the tale-like manifesto, these rules are often left aside and excluded from the ideological reading of the climactic structure of the narration and its expressionist aesthetics. Redescribed through a set of interdependent protocols and formal operations, and integrated back into a single book model, Olympic Operations breaks down the myth of its source and renders its attributes instrumental for the configuration of an athletic-driven organization of the territory.

The persuasive desire of mobilization embedded in Taut's original is turned into a physical infrastructure of corporeal mobility and extreme performance. The embellished, extravagant calls for the idealistic raising of the soul over the mandates of the modern machine through the mediation of crystalline temples, immaculate shrines, mysterious architectural forms, decorative structures, and odd gadgets are reenacted by systems and unfolded onto a performative ground: a ski resort for Olympic competitions, its mountains, creases, valleys, villages, pistes, snowfields, lifts, funiculars, decorative structures, forests, clouds, and even the sun itself, included. Driven by mutual convenience and by the challenging conditions that they embed within each other, rather than guided by the promise of mental liberation and soul elevation, this purpose-built piece of infrastructure constructs a landscape where plain banality engenders, out of simple operations of codependence between systems (ranging from the tiny to the extra large), peculiar coexistences of inexplicable naturalness, characterized by their impenetrable superficiality.

Surface undulations constitute the breeding ground of this bizarre construction. A flat surface is subdivided into a checkerboard grid and swollen up at regular, alternating intervals. Its ripples are intensified around a center. Other grids are progressively superimposed, activating regional variations and local wrinkles. The pattern is increasingly displaced from the virtual platform in which it operates. A series of cubic housing units, curvilinear corridors, segmented tracks, forests and plantations of various densities, snowfields, and cloud patterns are mapped into the indexical organization, increasing both its robustness as a system and its delicacy as a configuration. Fragmentary building components (isolated pillars, branching arches, hanging garlands, and erratic vaults) punctuate the manifold. The mutually alienating systems formally resonate against one another, and the artificial land construction—this time explicitly machine-made—conceptually emerges: a world-system model.

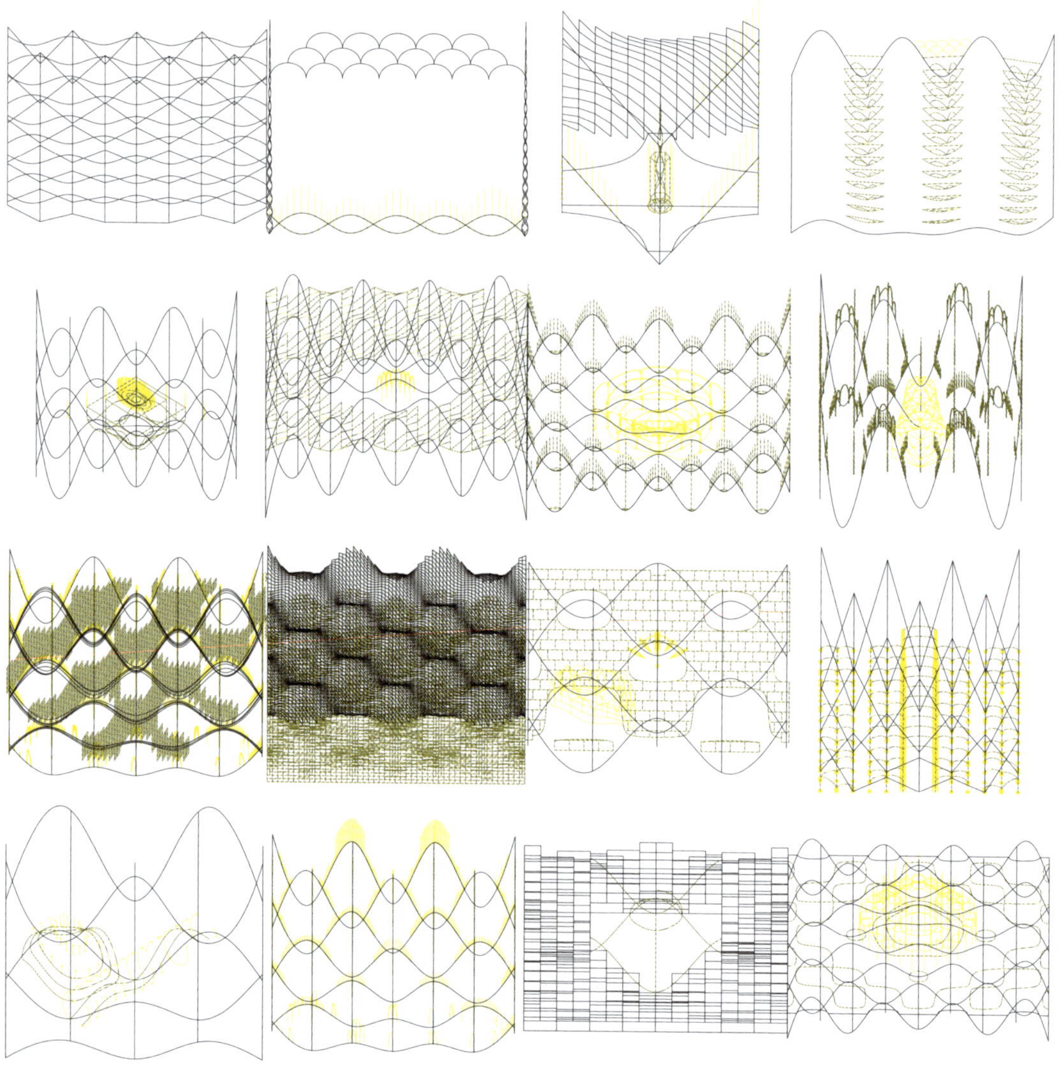

Modality. Variation. *Alpine Architecture* book leaf models. Bruno Taut, *Alpine Architecture*, artwork reconstructed as a series of models corresponding to leafs. Axonometrics.

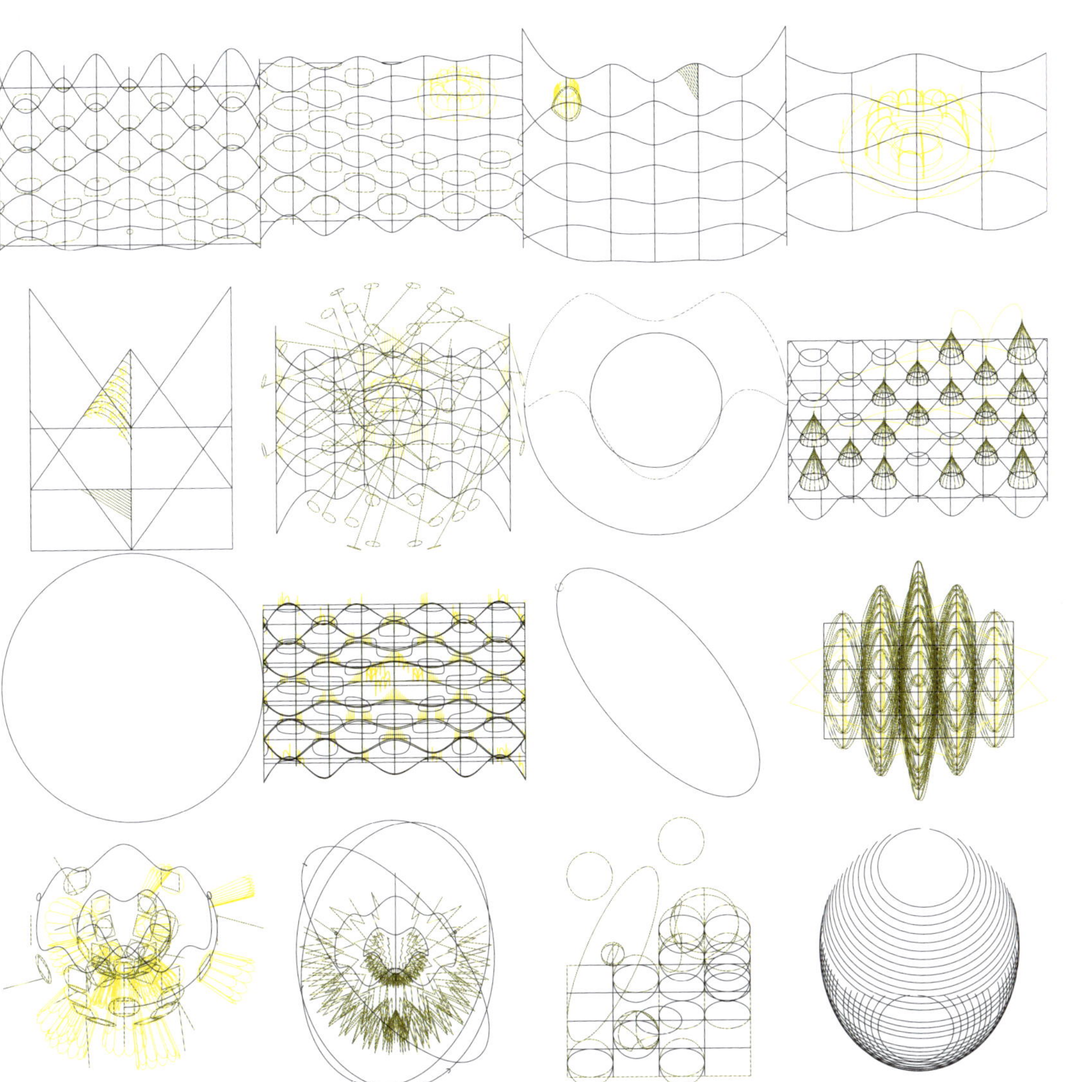

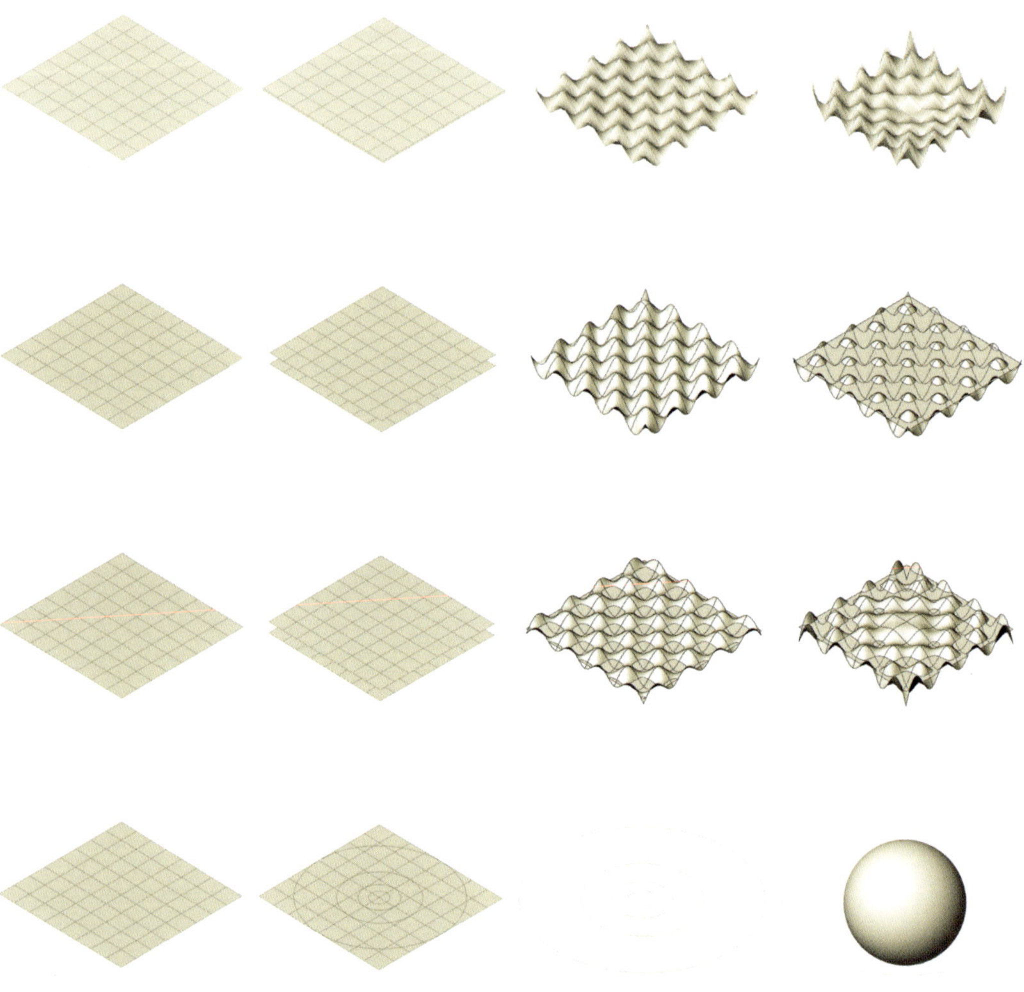

Model. Variability. *Alpine Architecture* book-model integration. From top to bottom: Bruno Taut, *Alpine Architecture*, integration of book leafs 02, 06, 15, and 28 in a single model. From left to right: surface matrix subdivision, surface offset repetition, surface alternated undulation, surface variable undulation, surface centralized variable undulation, peak areas fine-grain subdivision, peak areas fine-grain undulation, peak areas vertical extrusions and arch connections. Axonometrics.

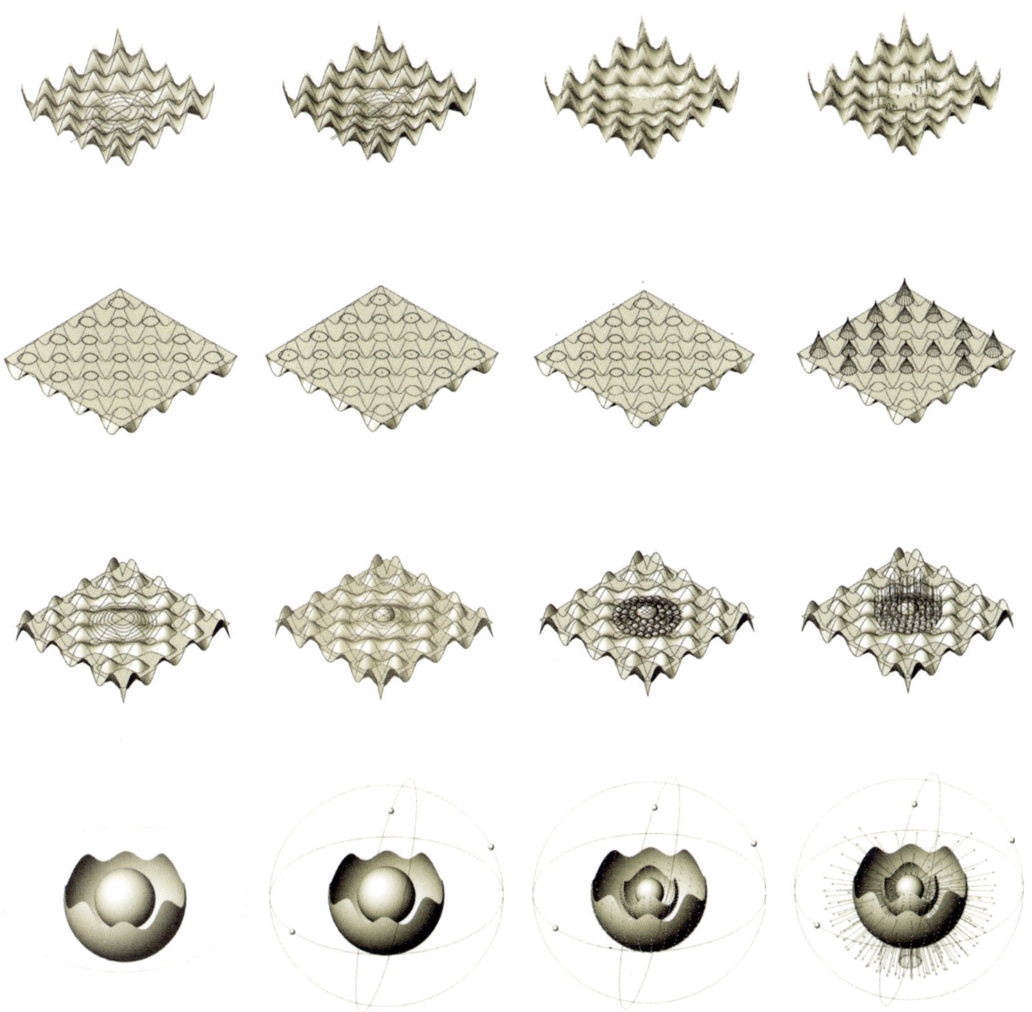

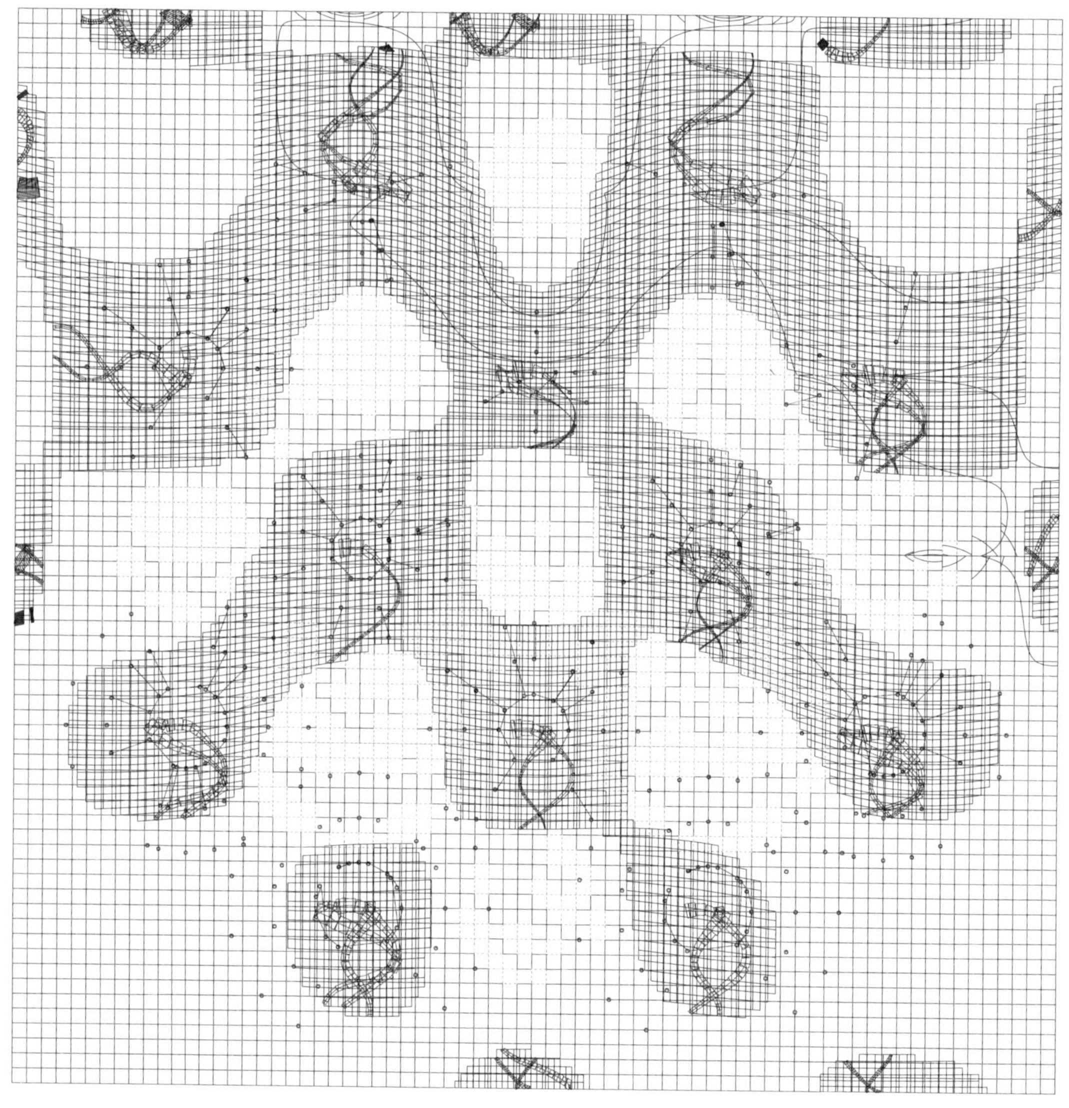

Prototype. Organization. Alpine Olympic site. Mountains, snowfield, creases and valleys, pistes, lifts and funiculars, villages, glass-like decorative structures, cloud field, and sun. Plan.

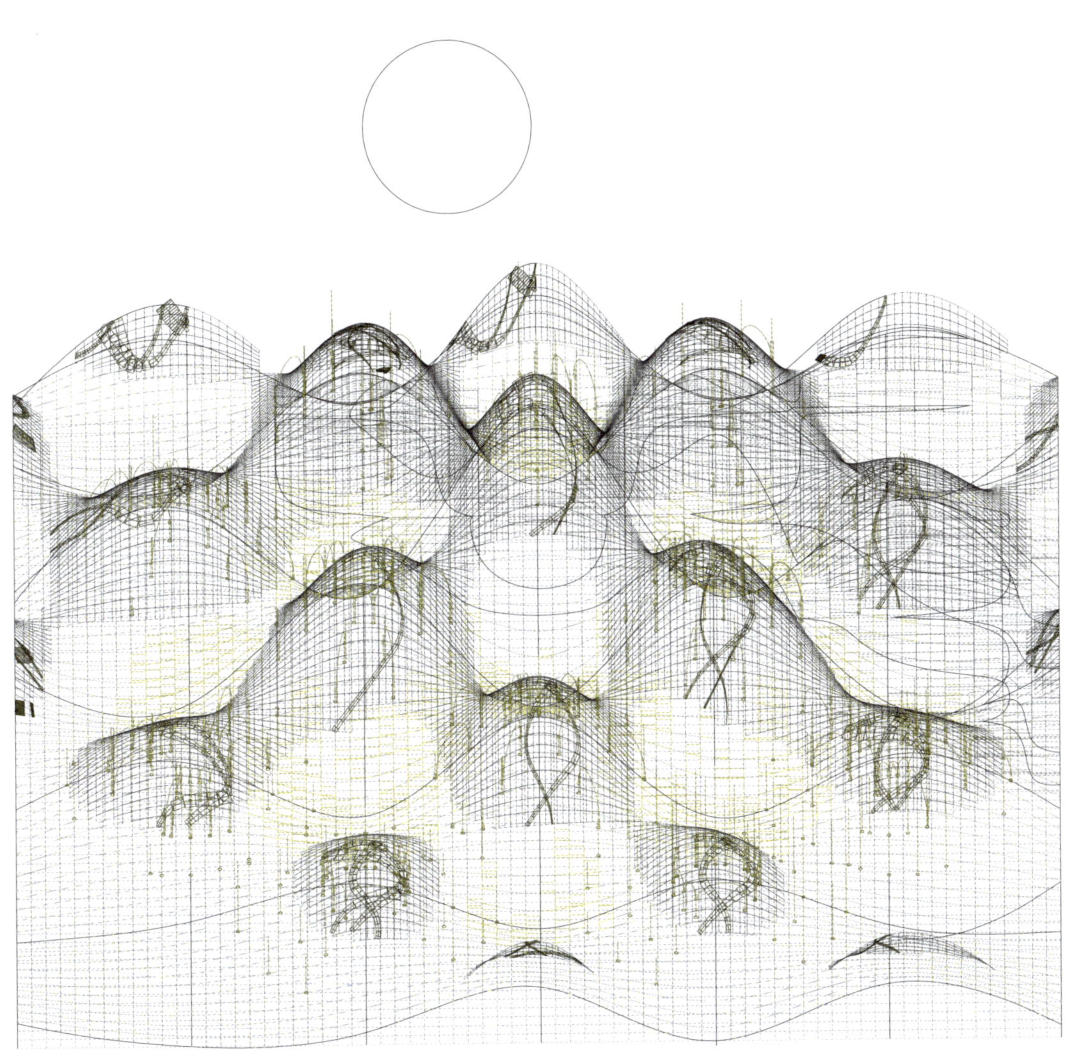

Prototype. Organization. Alpine Olympic site. Mountains, snowfield, creases and valleys, pistes, lifts and funiculars, villages, glass-like decorative structures, cloud field, and sun. Axonometry.

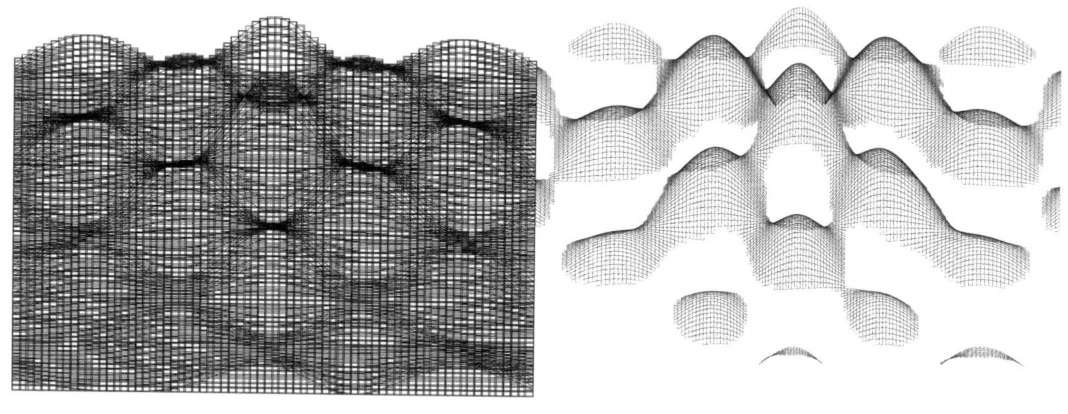

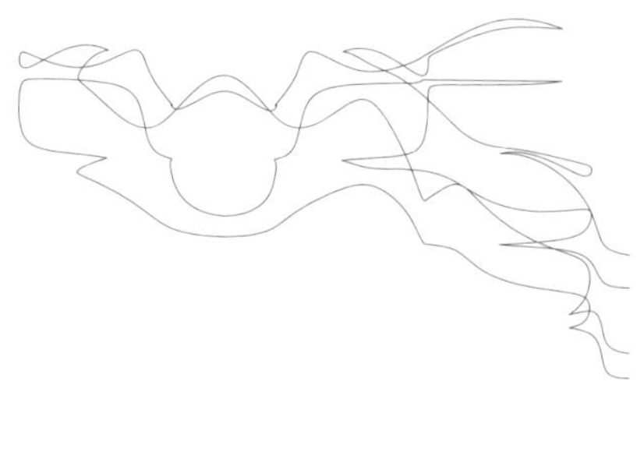

Prototype. Diversification. Alpine Olympic systems. From top left to bottom right: mountains, snowfield, creases and valleys, pistes, lifts and funiculars, villages, glass-like decorative structures, and cloud field. Axonometrics.

Generic Sublime Organizations

Project **Andinarchitecture**
Student **Víctor Muñoz Sanz**
Research **Neonatures**

Andinarchitecture is a scale-less world-form, absurdly tiny at a distance and surprisingly gigantic up close. A spheroidal volcanic rock, suspended above a deserted landscape of triangulated urban debris, contains a shopping mall with zigzagging polygonal trays, diagonally broken atriums, and tessellated billboard surfaces. The irregular geoscope is configured by a folded post-dymaxion world map, whose polygonal and triangular faces index the tectonic plates of the Earth and is displayed over an unfolded map—the world as it is, a grim ecological reserve.

Project **The Garden of Forking Paths**
Student **Yao Dong**
Research **Neonatures**

The Garden of Forking Paths is a networked system in which the iterative, bifurcating logics of delta geomorphology provides the matrix for the proliferation of growth vectors of public pedestrian corridors running across courtyard building typologies. These vectors guide and structure the density of blocks and disrupt the social isolation and naturalistic peacefulness of mid-scale housing environments. The management of territorial ownership results from the dynamic relationship between river tides and currents, weather variations and ground stability.

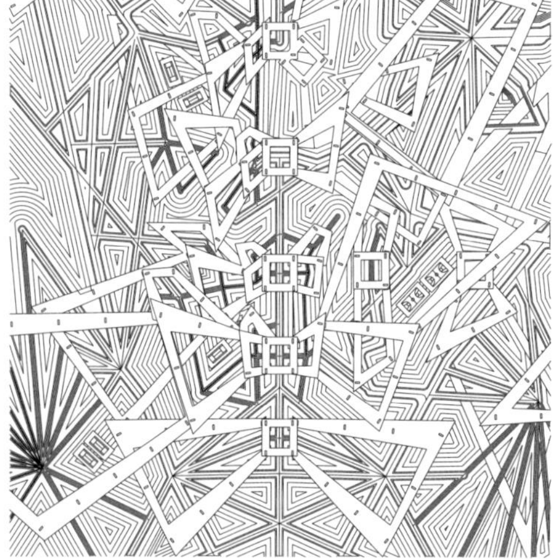

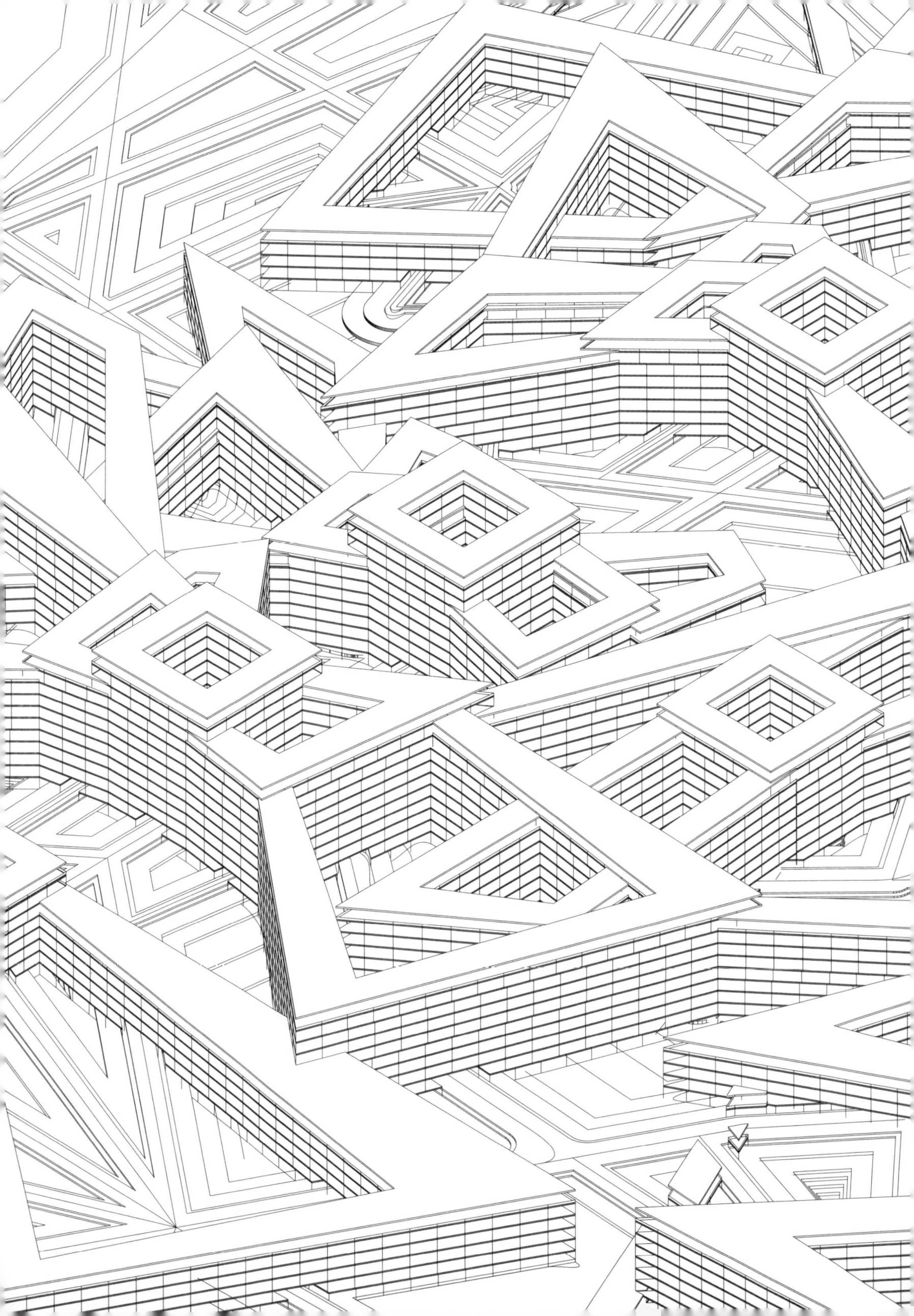

Project **Aeolian Skyscrapers**
Student **Di Xia**
Research **Neonatures**

Aeolian Skyscrapers integrate aeolian dune dynamics and skyscraper organizations. The vertical, stable traditional striation, regulated by the classical triadic succession of plinth, shaft, and crown, is replaced with a layering model that progressively consolidates building masses through the dispersion and movement of space. The horizontal stacking of sections gives way to a fine-grained cumulative logic and to a vertically oriented orthogonal circulatory matrix with oscillating diagonal continuities, local breaks, and erratic forms of terracing.

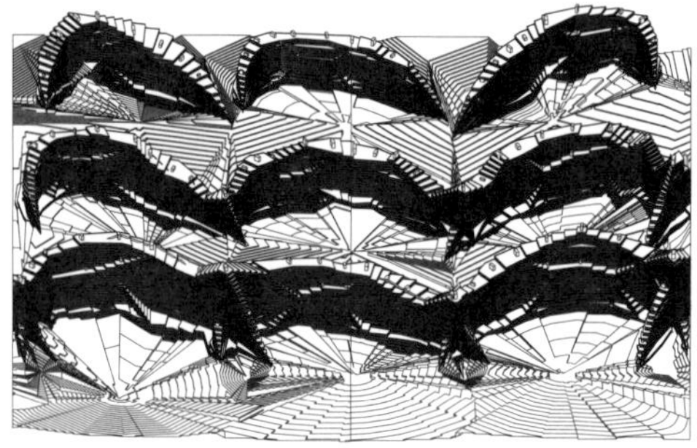

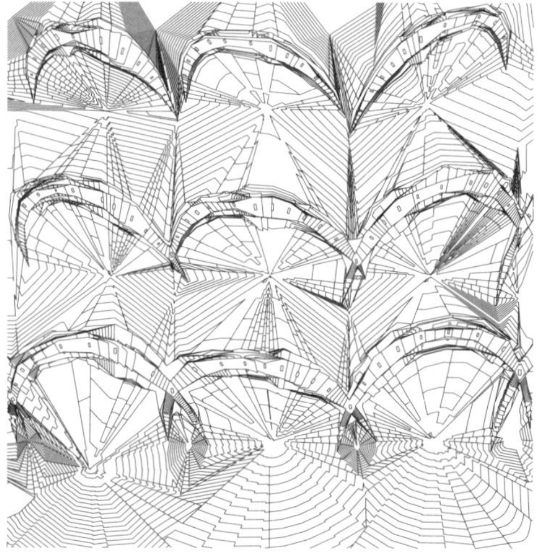

Project **Bitscape**
Student **Seong Seok Ko**
Research **Neonatures**

Bitscape is a hollow sand dune model with vertically undulating inner and outer surfaces that control the longitudinal spatial hierarchies of a series of parallel shopping corridors, vertical atriums, and terraced gardens. The softly varying proportions and smoothly transitioning hierarchies of a mall's interior and exterior spaces are managed by the nuanced principles of dynamic morphological development found in coastal dunes. Without losing control of the total mass, the model integrates local waviness, ripples, and transversal bridges within the rigid organization of the field of shopping strips.

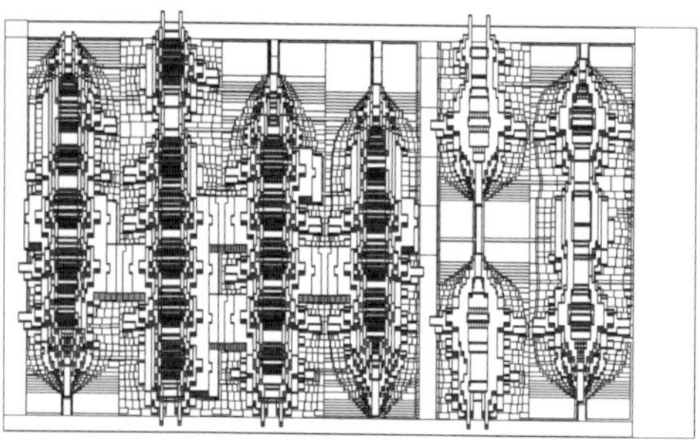

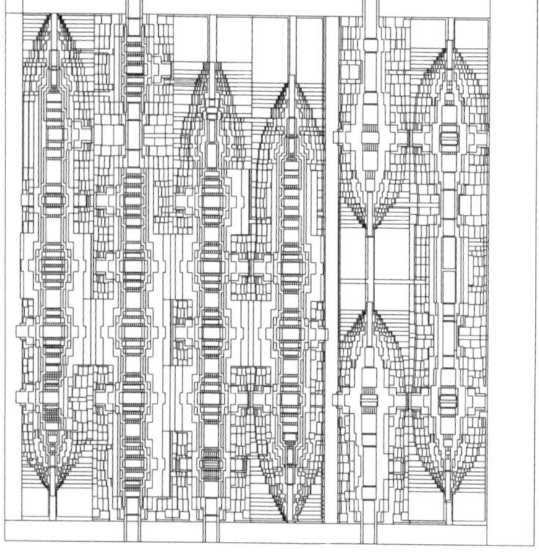

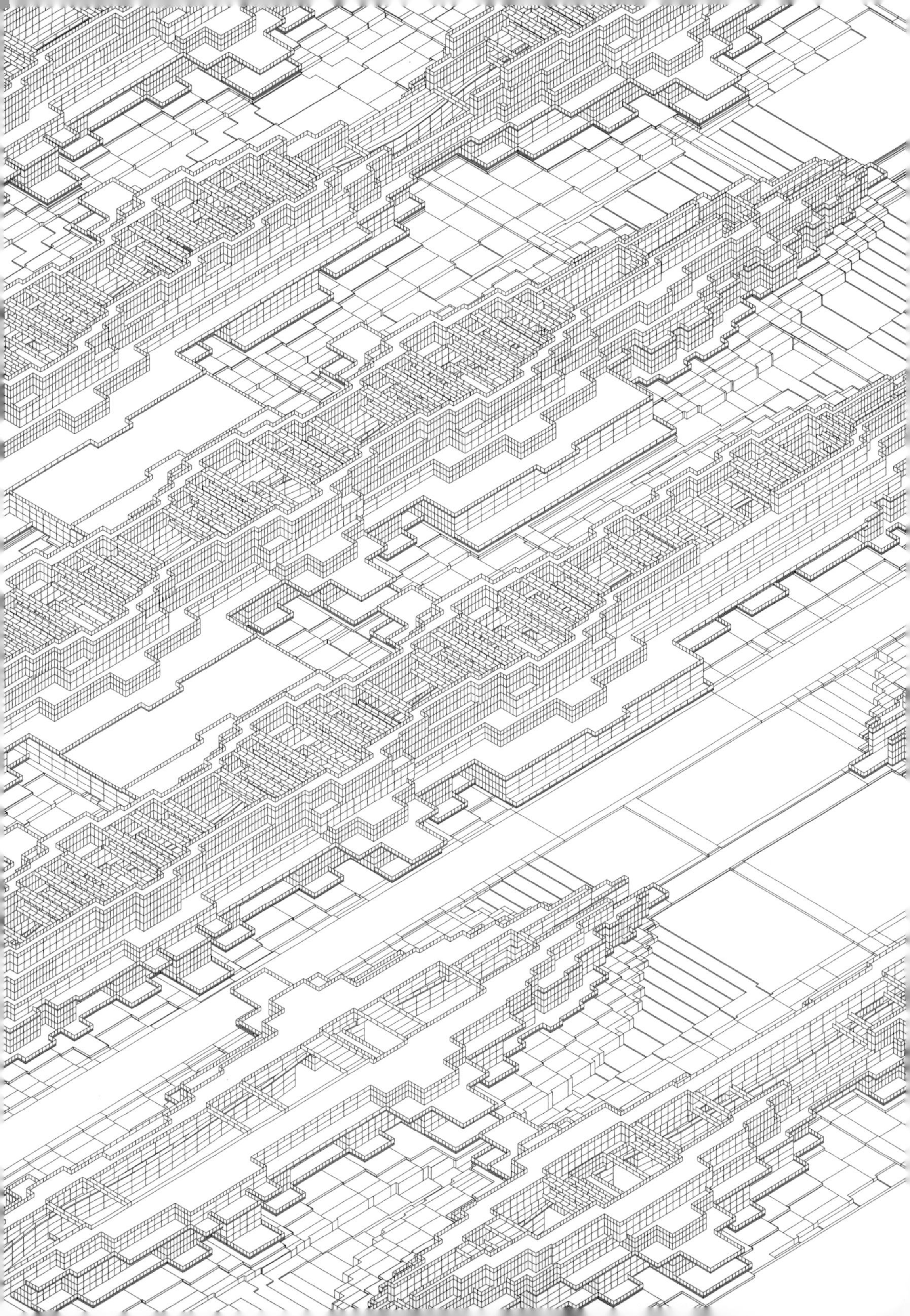

Project **Meandermesh**
Student **Song He**
Research **Neonatures**

Meandermesh introduces an assortment of spatial pockets into the public space, a variety of densities into the residential domain, and a dizzying array of pedestrian circulation routes across a continuous field of longitudinal connectivity. The widening and narrowing of social housing bars along meandering streams and valleys incorporates complexity and flexibility into the interior, enabling a variety of domestic spaces to coexist. The emergence of towers across the set integrates office activities that punctuate the civic space and locally qualify its social life.

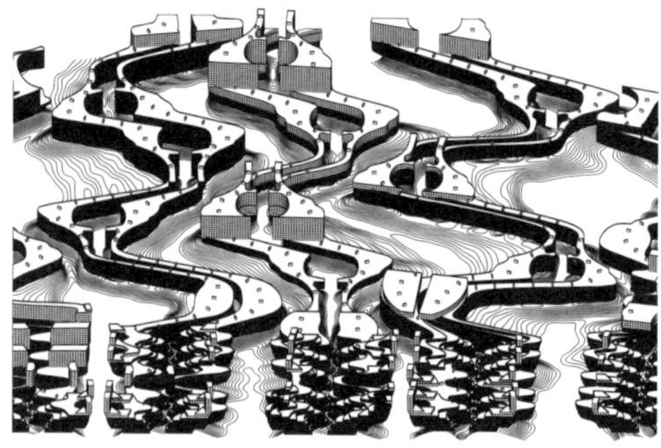

Project **Central Suburbia**
Student **Youngju Cho**
Research **Neonatures**

Central Suburbia investigates the blurred and potentially interactive relationship between the fluctuant water bodies of floodable depressed flatlands and the rigid property lines and neighbor organization of gated communities. In order to maximize the number of lots with an open view, the length of the water's edge is corrugated. The seasonal fluctuation in the amount of water accumulated in the semi-enclosed, large water bodies is managed through the variation of coastal curvature and landscape terracing, creating hierarchies in the picturesque looping of vehicular infrastructure and controlling the degree to which public, private, and ecological realms meet.

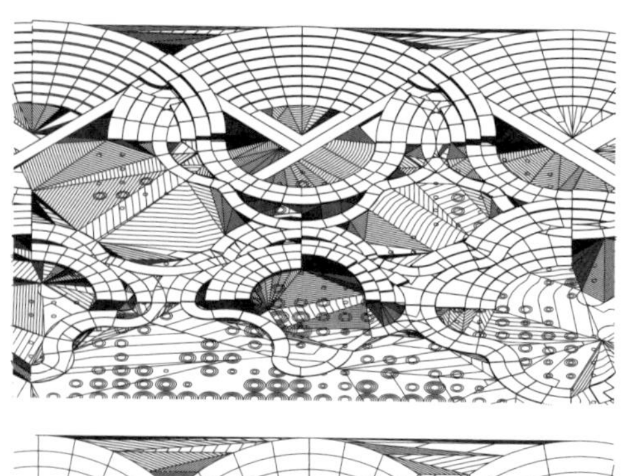

Project **Karst Palace**
Students **Ana María Flor Ortiz and Rodia Valladares Sánchez**
Research **Neonatures**

Karst Palace integrates water-based karst ecologies and courtyard residential typologies within a tessellated model of triangular topographic facets that manages underground and superficial water distribution and circulation patterns as it controls the density of a distributed housing development. The model offers a broad catalog of ecological-urban individuations, consisting of varieties of semi-enclosed patios (or valleys) and semidetached towers (or pinnacles) that articulate housing density through tortuous, winding, zigzagging, deep, shallow, extended, hidden, cornered, open or centrifugal arrangements.

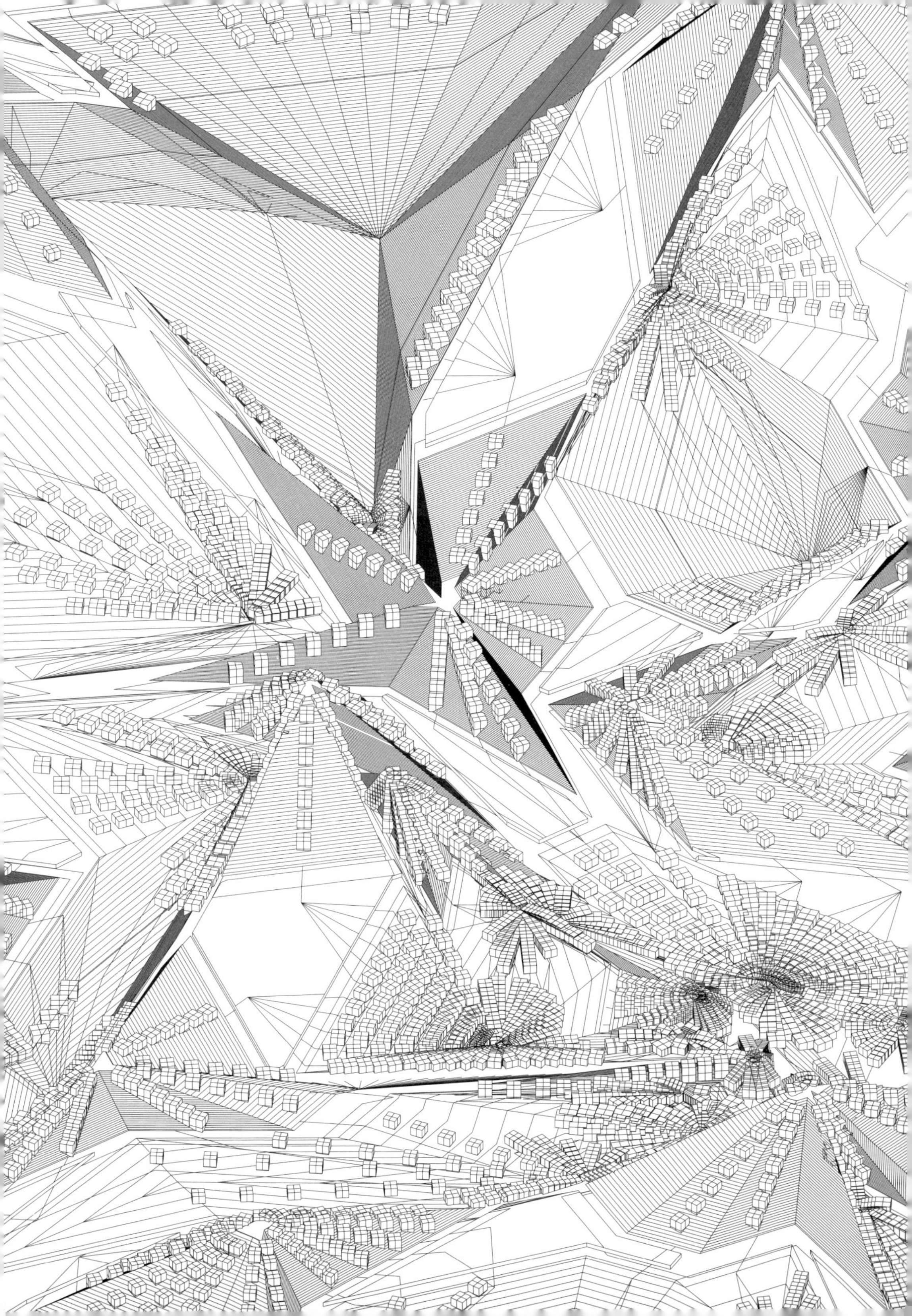

Project **Alluvial Ecospheres**
Student **Kaz Yoneda**
Research **Neonatures**

Alluvial Ecospheres aligns high-rise housing collectives along the edges of a series of braided river islands. An archipelago of research-oriented residential envelopes contains, preserves, and prescribes ecological pockets. The model is articulated by tilted, bending, and bifurcating towers that manage the permeability of semisecluded environments between which species migrate. Towers make use of the interior ecological enclaves, which perform as on-site research labs and public amenities. The model varies according to three organizational modalities, each coded with a different sedimentation process and embedded with a particular range of housing types.

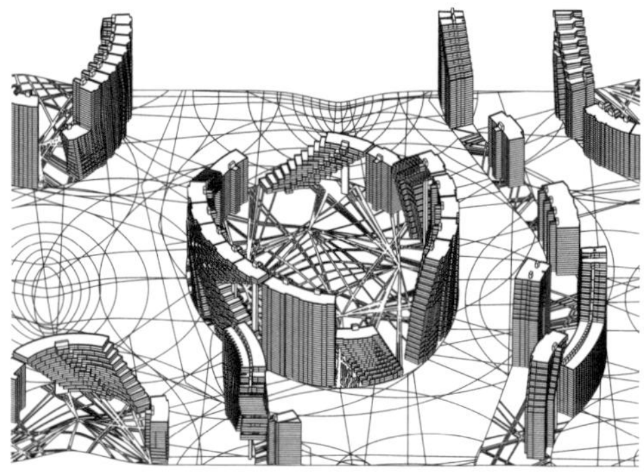

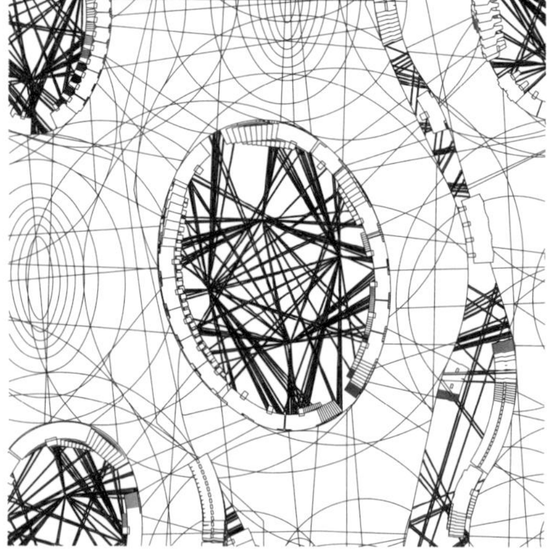

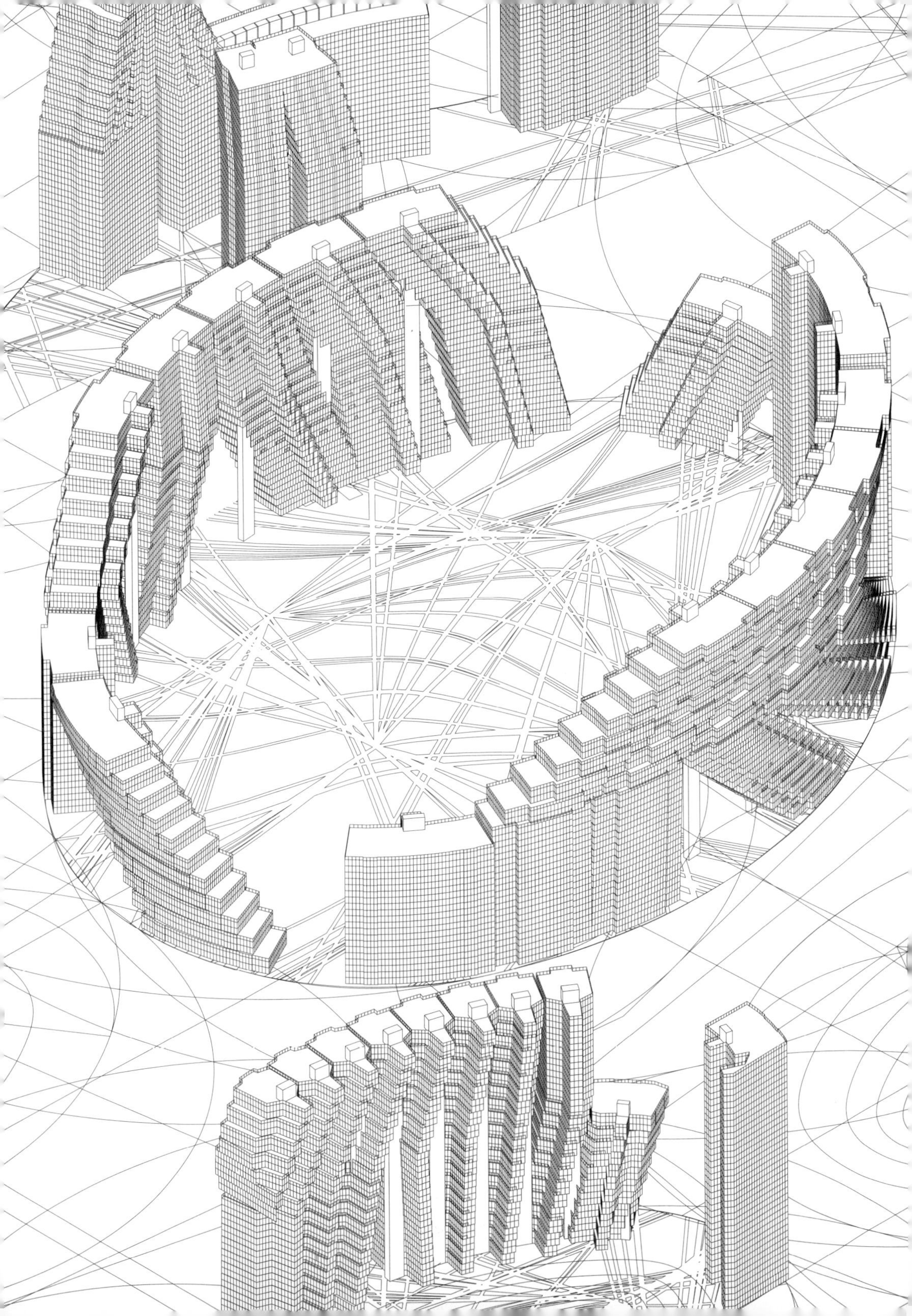

Project **Curnature**
Student **Jung Hyuck Im**
Research **Neonatures**

Curnature is a model for terraced housing organized as a series of curvilinear sand dune surfaces, orientated by the direction of predominant winds and terraced down to a flat, extensive ground. Buildings are broken down into modular spatial units and grouped in relatively small clusters cascading down toward an extensive, flat ground. Under them, public space is scaled down to the size of the domestic. The gardens in between absorb the tidal variations of the river, whose waters gently flood and punctuate the amicable landscape with shallow ponds and delicate streams.

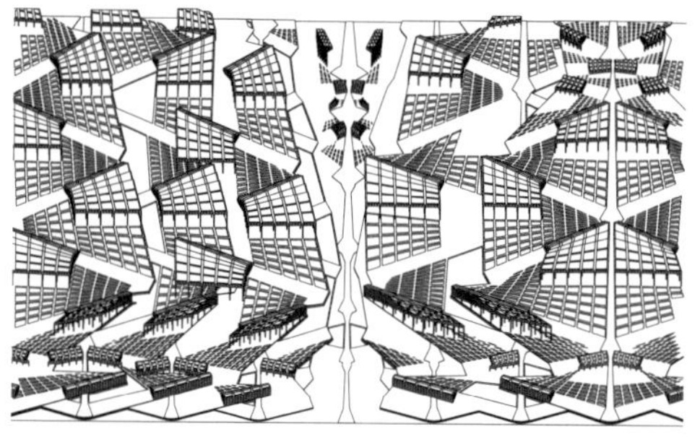

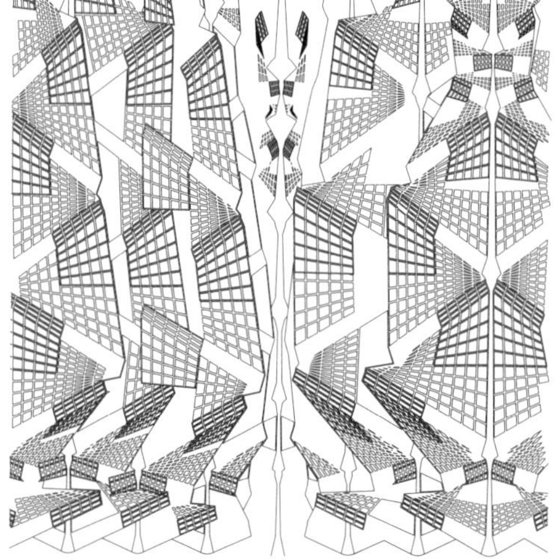

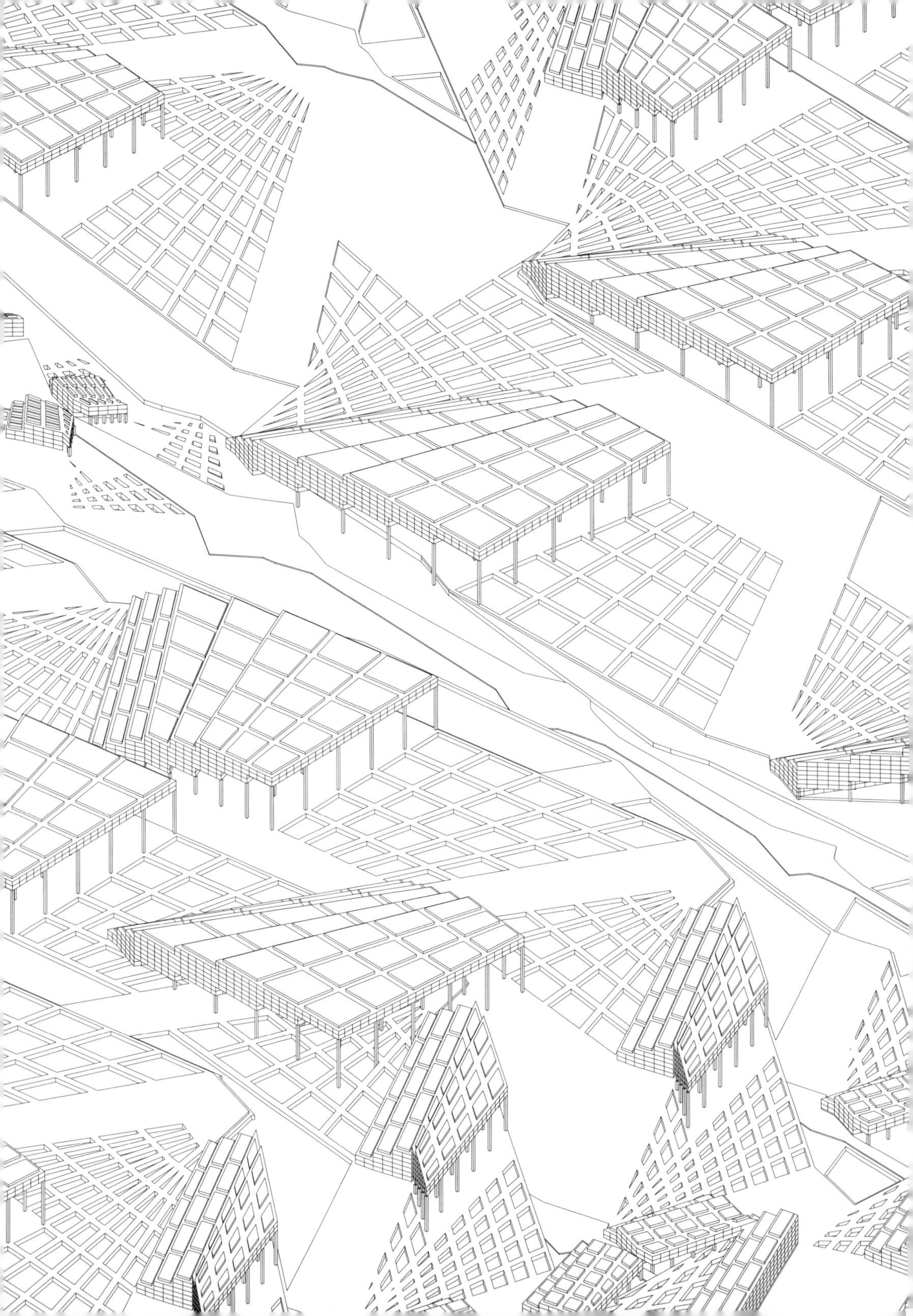

Project **Delirium Atrium**
Students **Dongjae Cho and Fred Chung**
Research **Overurbanism**

Delirium Atrium is a model for atrium buildings with an inner envelope branching out from a horizontal datum located in the middle of the structure. This inner envelope connects a series of parallel strata, where the semipublic interior is proliferated as it progresses up and down from the building's central section, until reaching the ground and the roof of the complex. Variations in size, location, proportion, and directionality determine the organization and character of lobbies, hallways, lounges, meeting areas, corridors, balconies, and open work spaces within each of the strata.

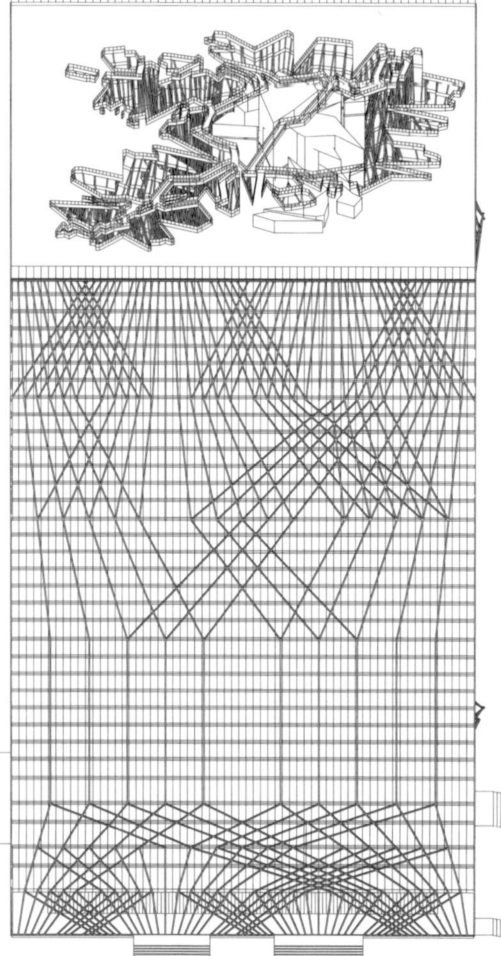

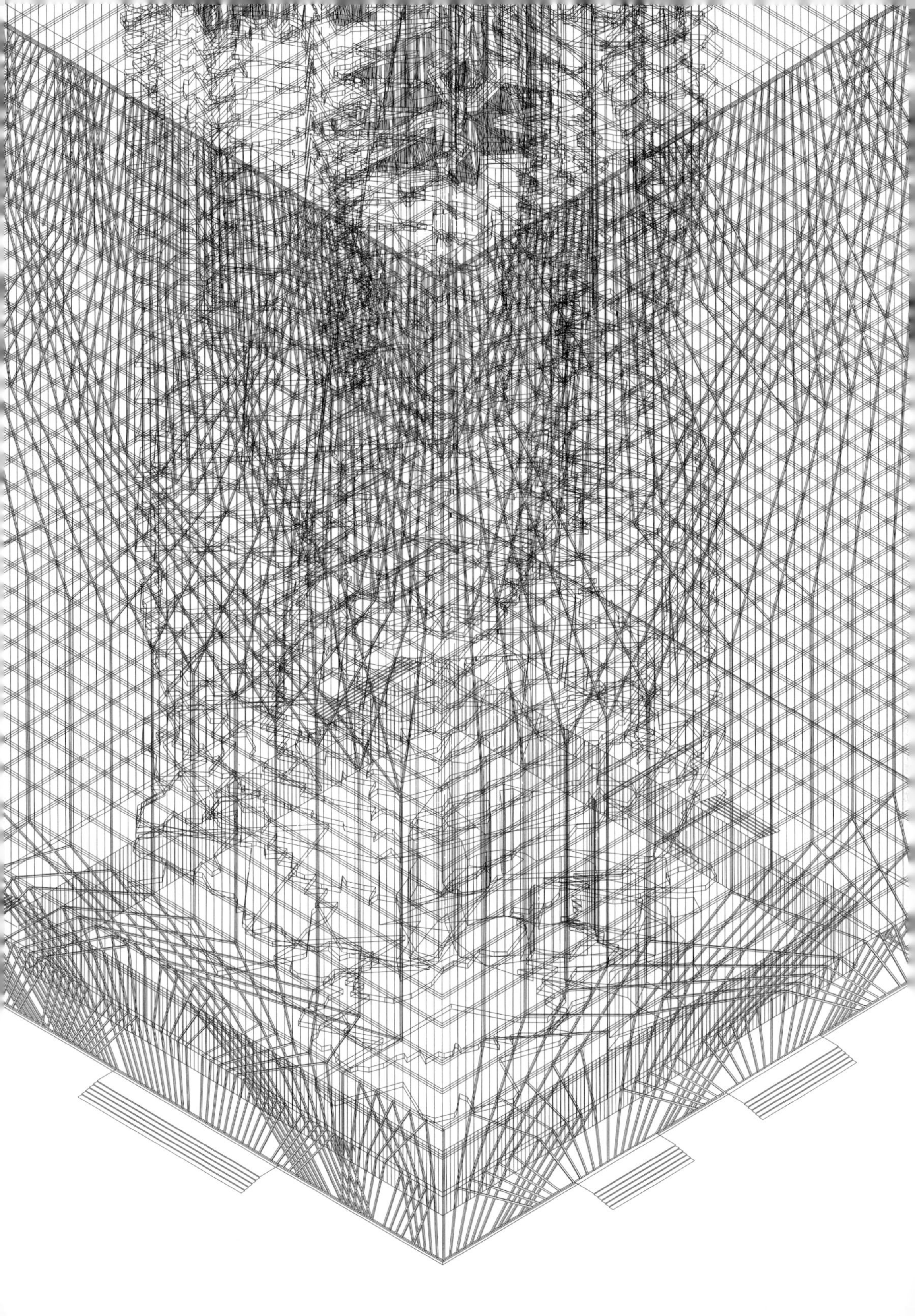

Project **Data-Form**
Students **Lucas Correa-Sevilla and Zhou Wu**
Research **Overurbanism**

Data-Form is a collective mixed-use model that integrates the protocols of a varied set of mixed-use buildings within a multiplicity by dissecting their normative characteristics according to a series of organizational categories, equalizing them, arranging them around its center, and turning them into rules for intertwining congestion in a single polycentric structure. Its mountain-like and mountain-chain-like totality multiplies the synergetic relations existing in the individual mixed-use types through a series of gradients of relations, whose only architectural ideology is to elevate the maximization of exchanges to a critical mass with one yet many centers.

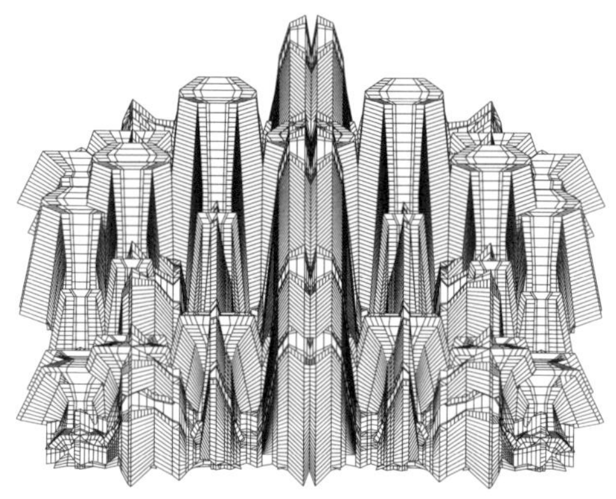

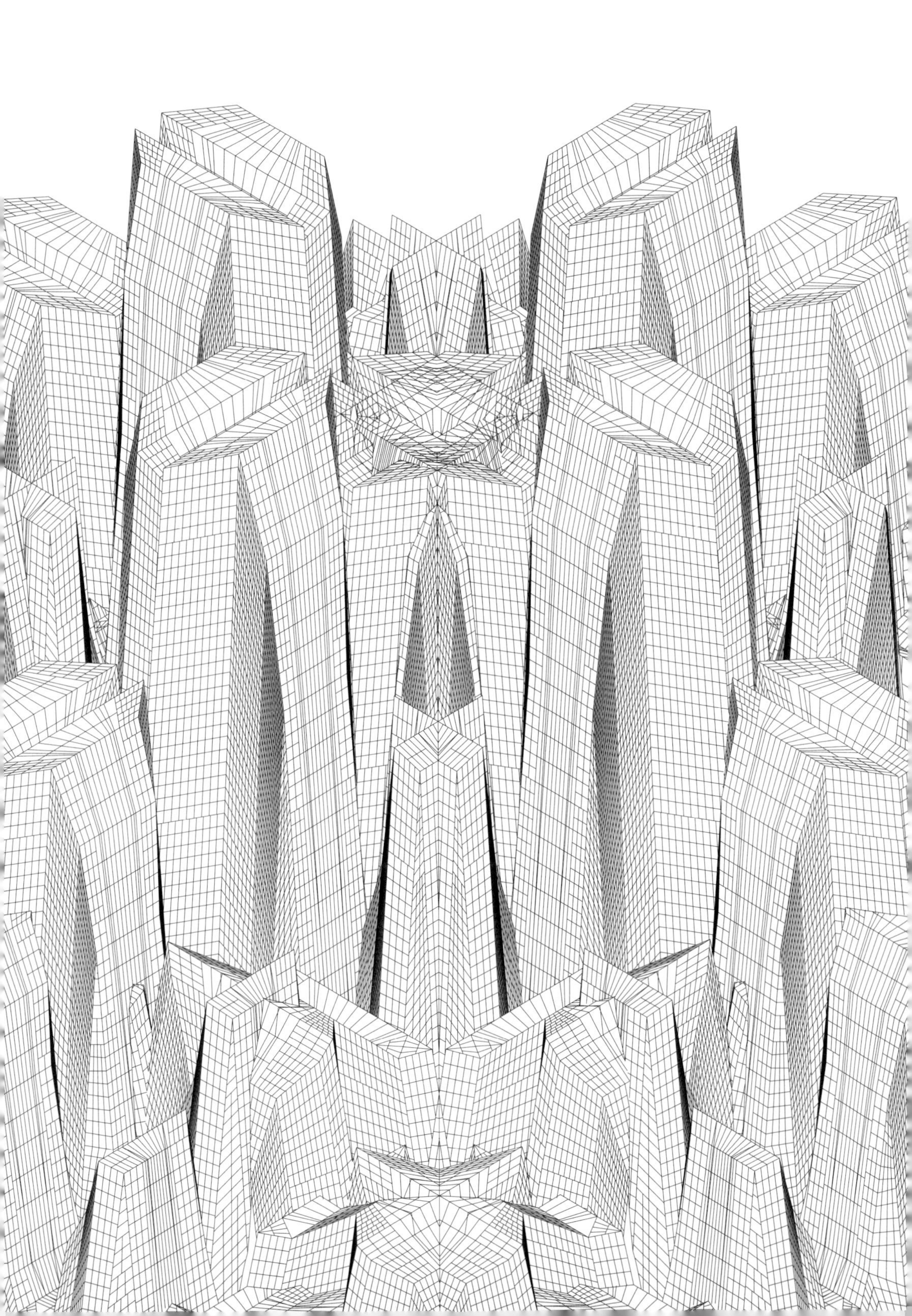

Project **Private Heaven**
Students **Mo Zhou and Danxi Zou**
Research **Overurbanism**

Private Heaven overstresses the pattern by which privacy in collective residential environments increases as spaces reach higher and deeper levels of fat and tall building masses. The transition between exterior and interior is controlled gradually through the fluctuation of the envelope, the number and length of openings, and the depth of spatial layers. To enable the thickening of the resulting inhabitable skin, a series of minute shafts are incorporated within the mass. The transition is expanded at the centers of the sides and minimized at the corners, creating a tight revelation of the secluded private space at the building's edges.

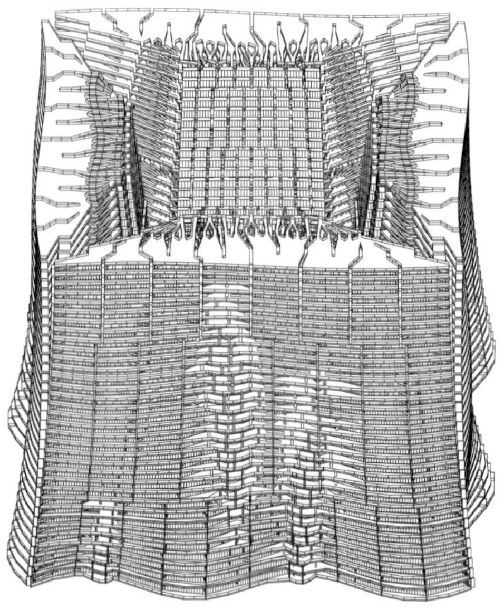

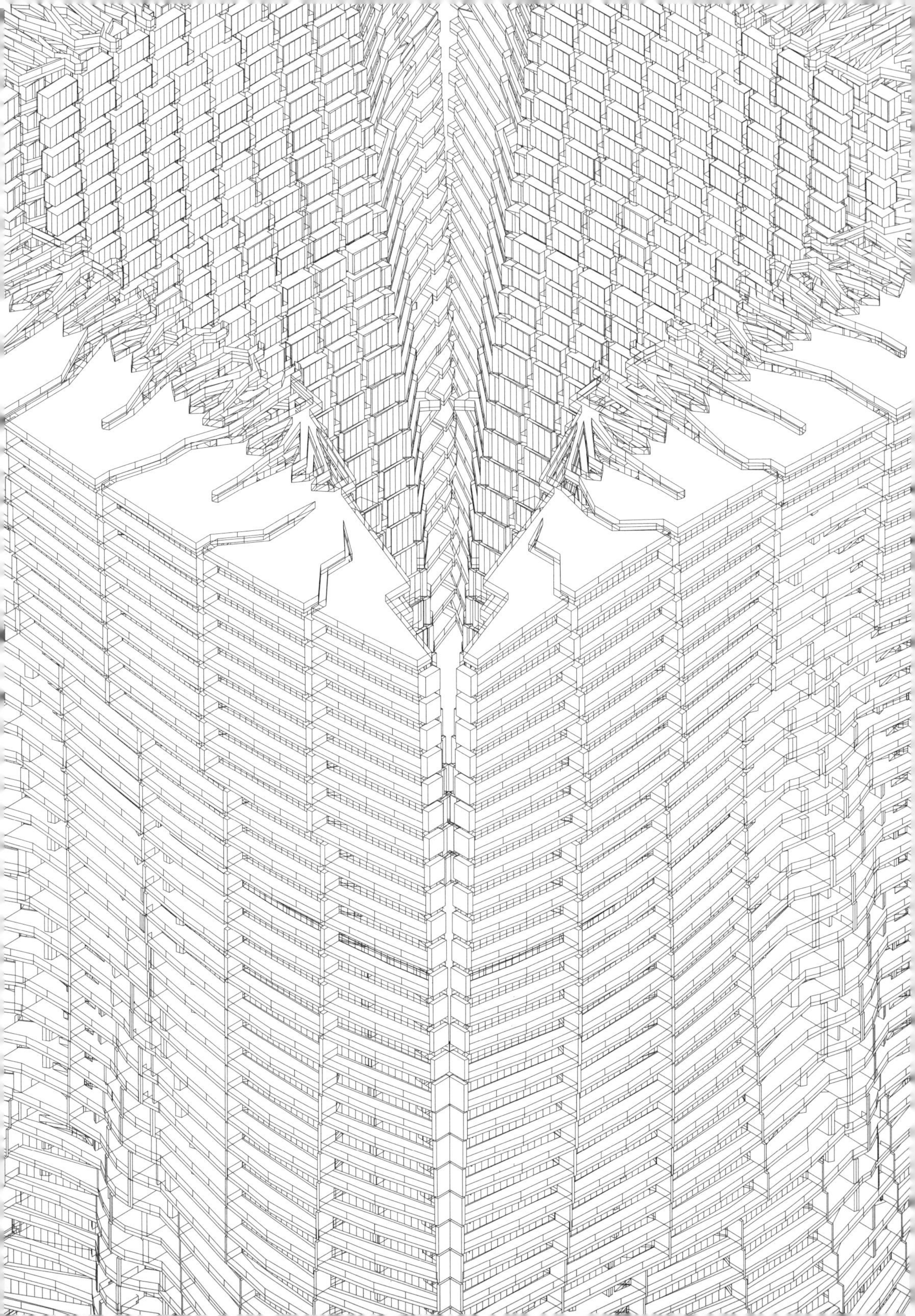

Project **Public Debris**
Students **Mireille Kameni and Elena Tudela Rivadeneyra**
Research **Overurbanism**

Public Debris proposes a model for urban districts within which pedestrian circulation between infrastructural systems constructs a three-dimensional matrix of local interchange. Interior and exterior are subsumed by an underground network of continuous movement. Contingent on flows, the network manages the unstable character of public activity and redefines the public interior as a form of infrastructural stoppage, integrating bus stops, parking entrances, subway stations, rail stations, elevator cores, lobbies, and hallways in a single, multilayered continuum.

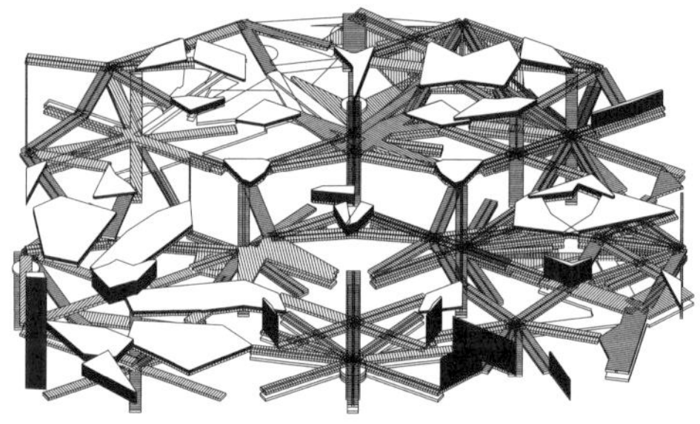

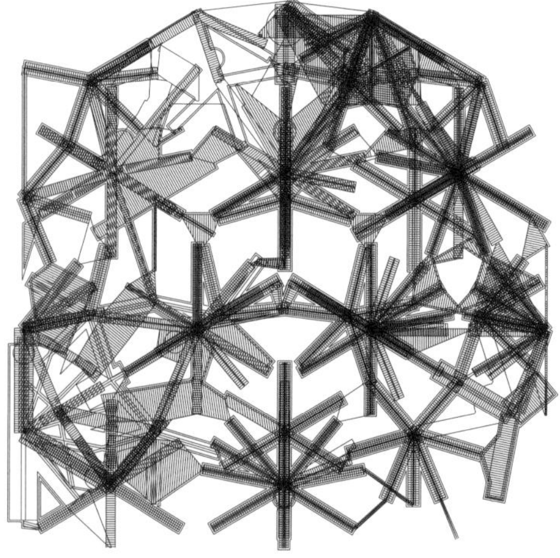

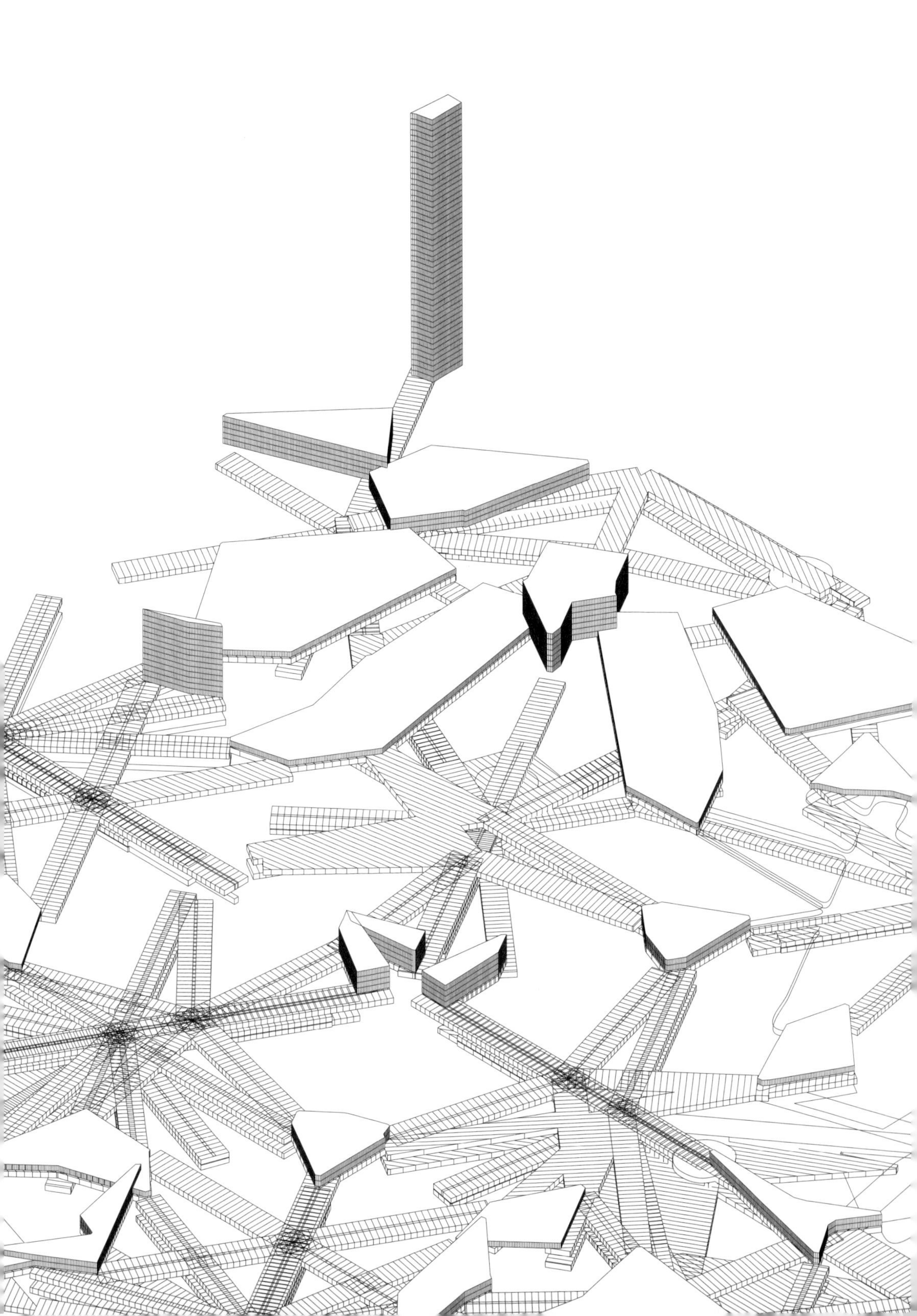

Project **Irresistible Synthetic**
Students **Day Jiménez and Ostap Rudakevych**
Research **Overurbanism**

Irresistible Synthetic is a surface model for gated communities that balances attraction and repulsion between residences and amenities, organized as regular matrices. Their interaction elicits nonlinear behaviors that bind residences to the collective through their proximity to amenities. The arrangement patterns activate the local wrapping of the surface to compensate for the imbalanced relationships, creating alienation where there was promiscuity and vice versa. The distribution of components in the field is renegotiated through a series of triangulations and tessellations that patch and give texture to the land.

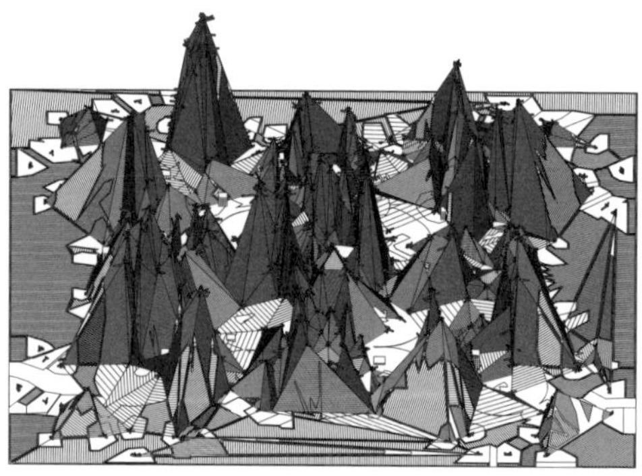

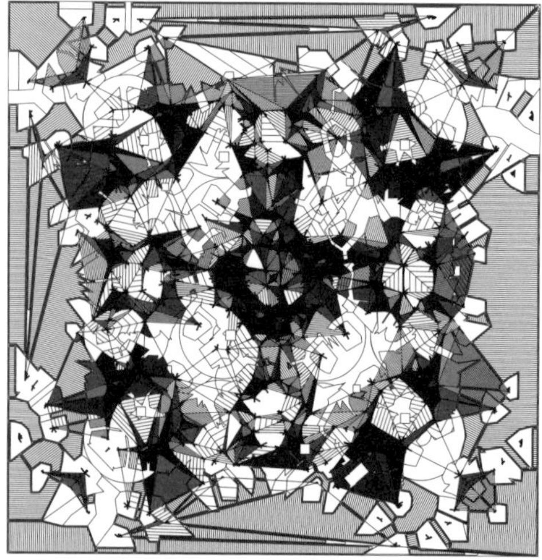

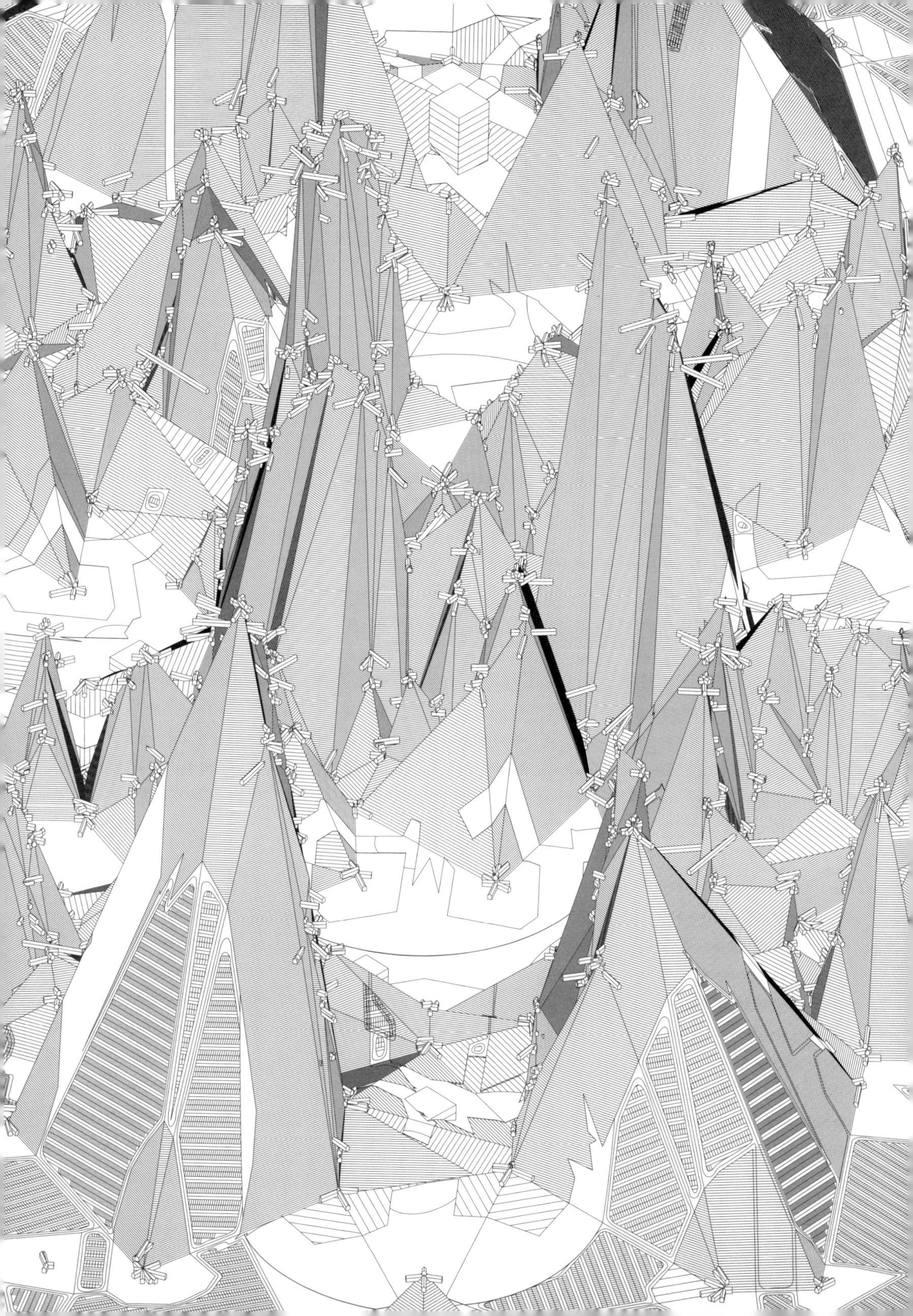

Project **Territorial Schism**
Students **Mariusz Klemens and Steven Yingnien Chen**
Research **Overurbanism**

Territorial Schism uses the vertical schism of the American skyscraper as a blueprint for a territorial model that injects metropolitan character into satellite cities. The model manages the coexistence of a number of isolatable and measurable metropolitan characteristics, including programmatic variety, programmatic discontinuity, building density, and transport intersections, along a series of infrastructural corridors. A matrix of primitive building units of varying plan depth and height–seemingly able to expand in an ever-increasing verticality and an allegedly infinite horizontality–creates singular forms of exteriority.

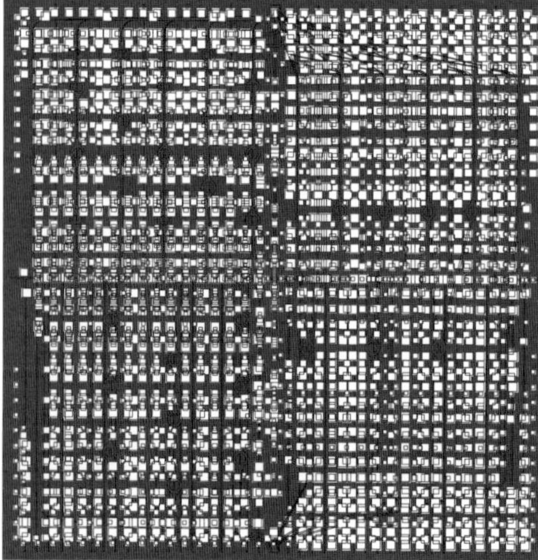

Project **Manhattanatomy**
Students **Pablo Barría Urenda and Mariano Gomez Luque**
Research **Neokoolhisms**

Manhattanatomy works at the intersection of two raw materials: Rem Koolhaas's *Delirious New York*, as a retroactive manifesto for the unveiling of an unconscious theory of antiurban architecture, and a set of extra-extra-large urban typologies that voraciously consume territorial resources with no architectural theory allegedly taking part. The model establishes a method of dissecting conceptual blocks and fictional categories from the theoretical formulation of the former, understood as a logical set up, to create a toolbox of generic mechanisms of operation for the latter. The incompatibility of the sources is suspended in favor of the definition of a set of principles, figures, and procedures.

Project **The Culture of Liberated Congestion**
Students **Nicholas Potts and Peter Zuroweste**
Research **Neokoolhisms**

The Culture of Liberated Congestion conjectures about the critical point where the carrying capacity of developable building-islands in a field of discrete territories–described by Rem Koolhaas's *Delirious New York* as an archipelago of solitudes–when subjected to the expansive pressure of capital, internally destabilizes. It proposes a model for the liberation of buildings from their individual plots through their paradoxical proliferation upward and outward. The model alternates mechanisms of replication, transformation, and limitation of floor levels in respect to their immediate neighbors in a stacking structure.

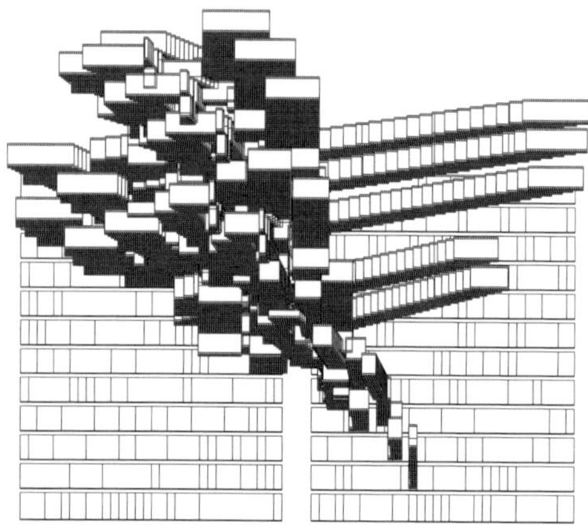

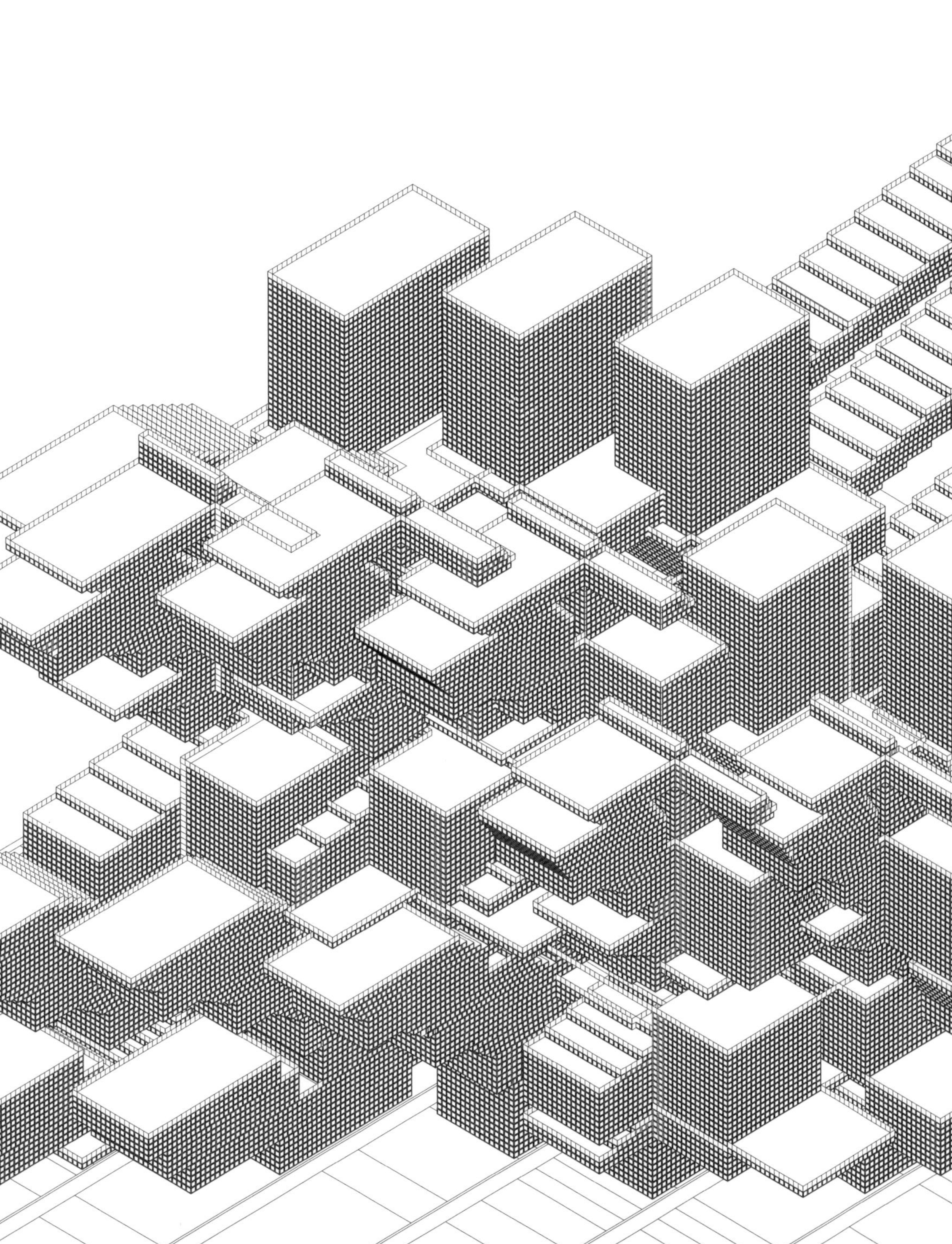

Project **The River, the Mountain, and the Metropolis**
Students **Jeffrey Butcher and Lisl Kotheimer**
Research **Neokoolhisms**

The River, the Mountain, and the Metropolis imagines a territorial-scale, antiurban model for satellite cities built around various natural resource extraction industries, as they progress from wild entrepreneurial adventures and grand state initiatives to the scale and rank of collective unconsciousness. Geographically isolated, the uniqueness of these enclaves is characterized by the blunt determinism of their infrastructure and logistics and is reconstructed as a half fairytale, illustrating how purely pragmatic ideas mutate—as if inexorably—into the imaginary of the fantastic.

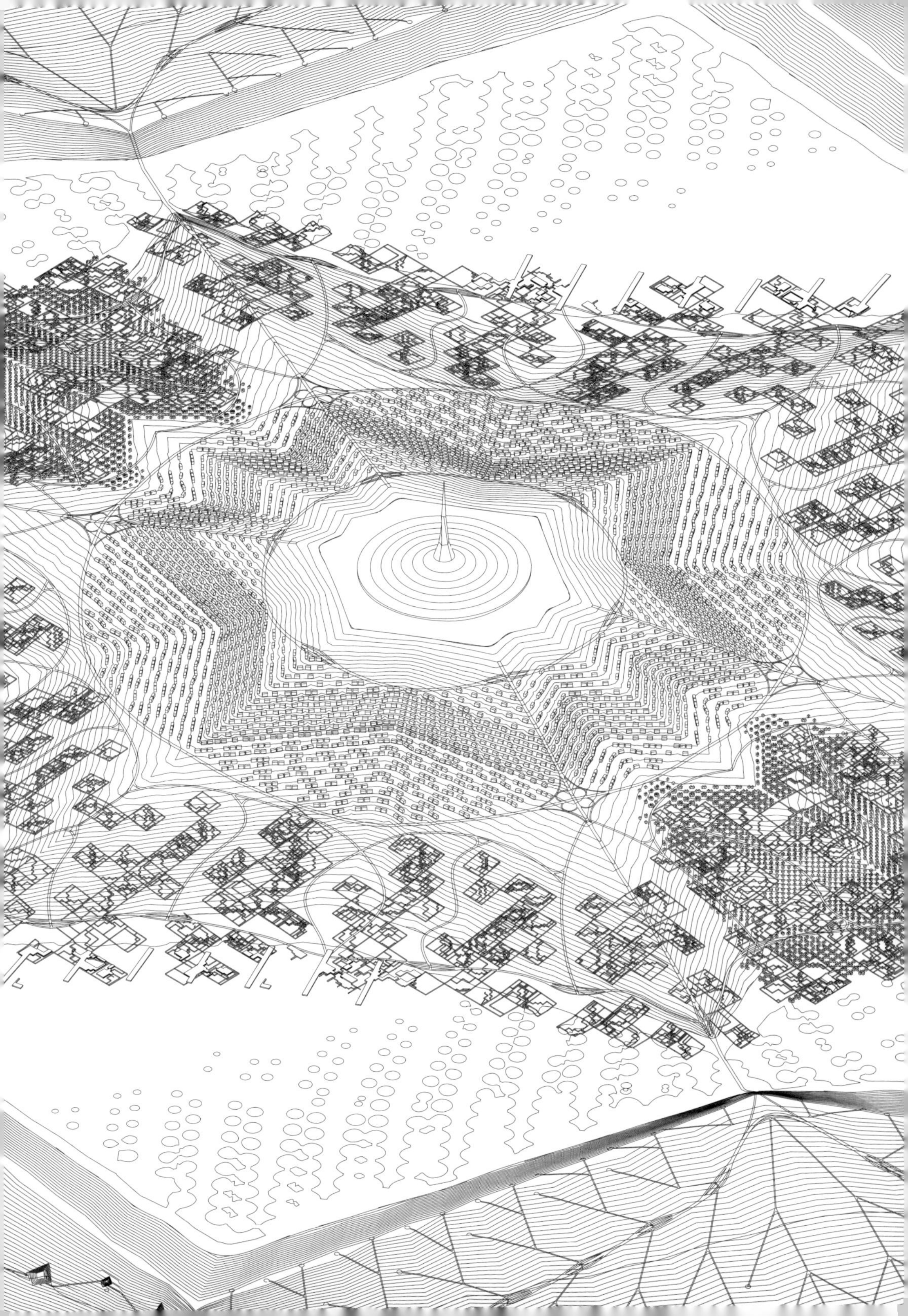

Project **Obus Interchange**
Student **Max Wong**
Research **Utopioids**

Obus Interchange integrates social housing and car infrastructure in a single urban-suburban building gradient. The various highway-skyscraper models of the multiple versions of Le Corbusier's Obus Plan for Algiers are synthesized in a system that manages the sectional distribution of housing units, the depth of floor plans, the number and rotation of branches, the width of vehicular lanes and pedestrian walkways, and the filleting of intersections. Their variation cascades the centrifugal effects resulting from the insertion of big-box retail types in the midst of its core, here a three-dimensional roundabout.

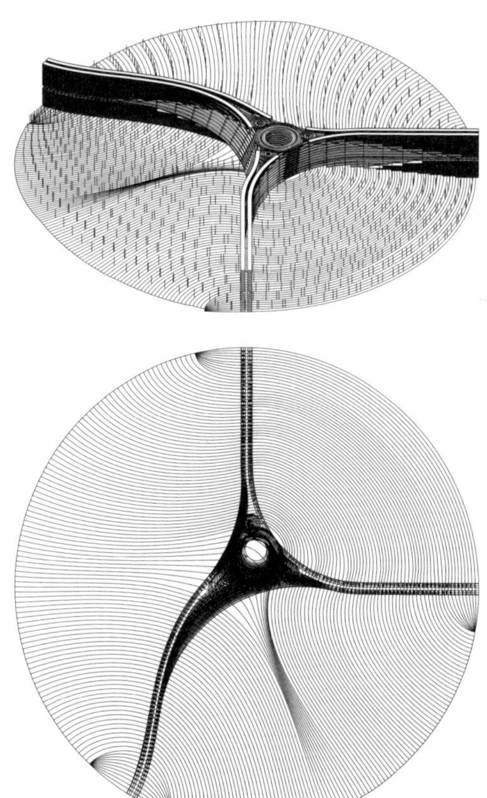

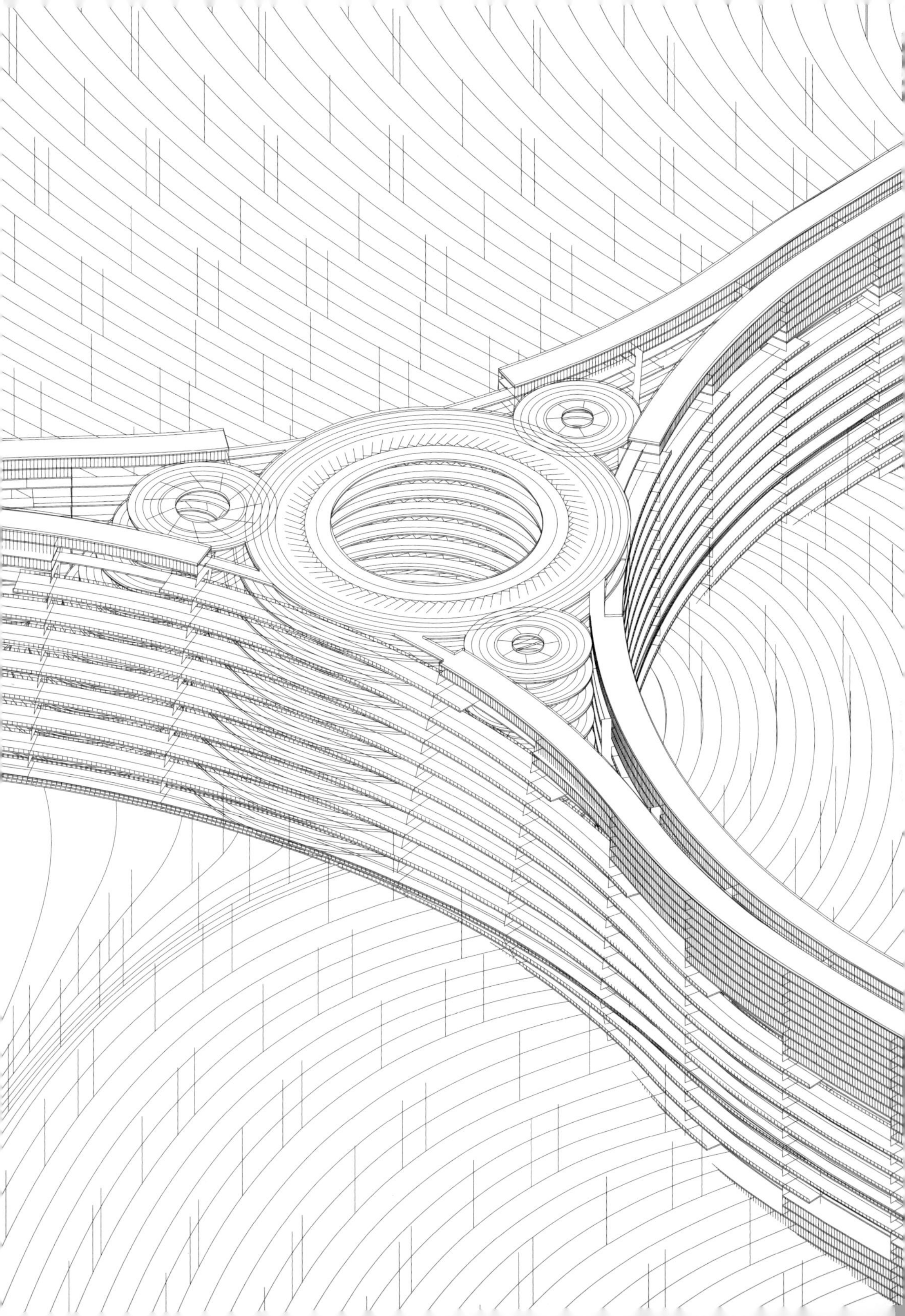

Project **Neon Sector**
Student **Elle Gerdeman**
Research **Utopioids**

Neon Sector takes the paradoxical, indeterminate megastructure of Constant Nieuwenhuys's New Babylon to an extreme level of determination. The revolutionary potential of the *dérive* turns into a system of sheer entertainment, capable of transcending itself. The model integrates open-ended structures in a meshed truss that is attracted and repelled by urban contingency, this time constructing a parasitical system of retail space, vast parking lots, casino enclaves, and high-end hotels. Instead of instigating the transformation of routines through situations, it catalyzes their maniac forces and darker impulses.

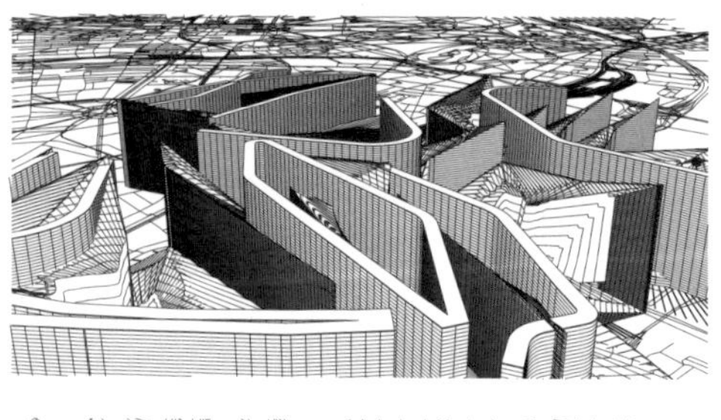

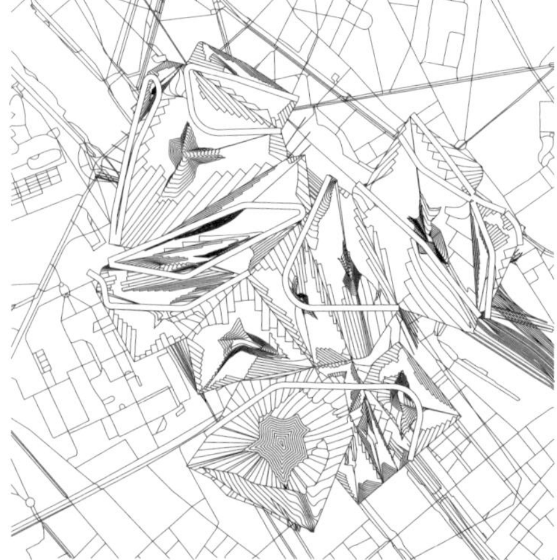

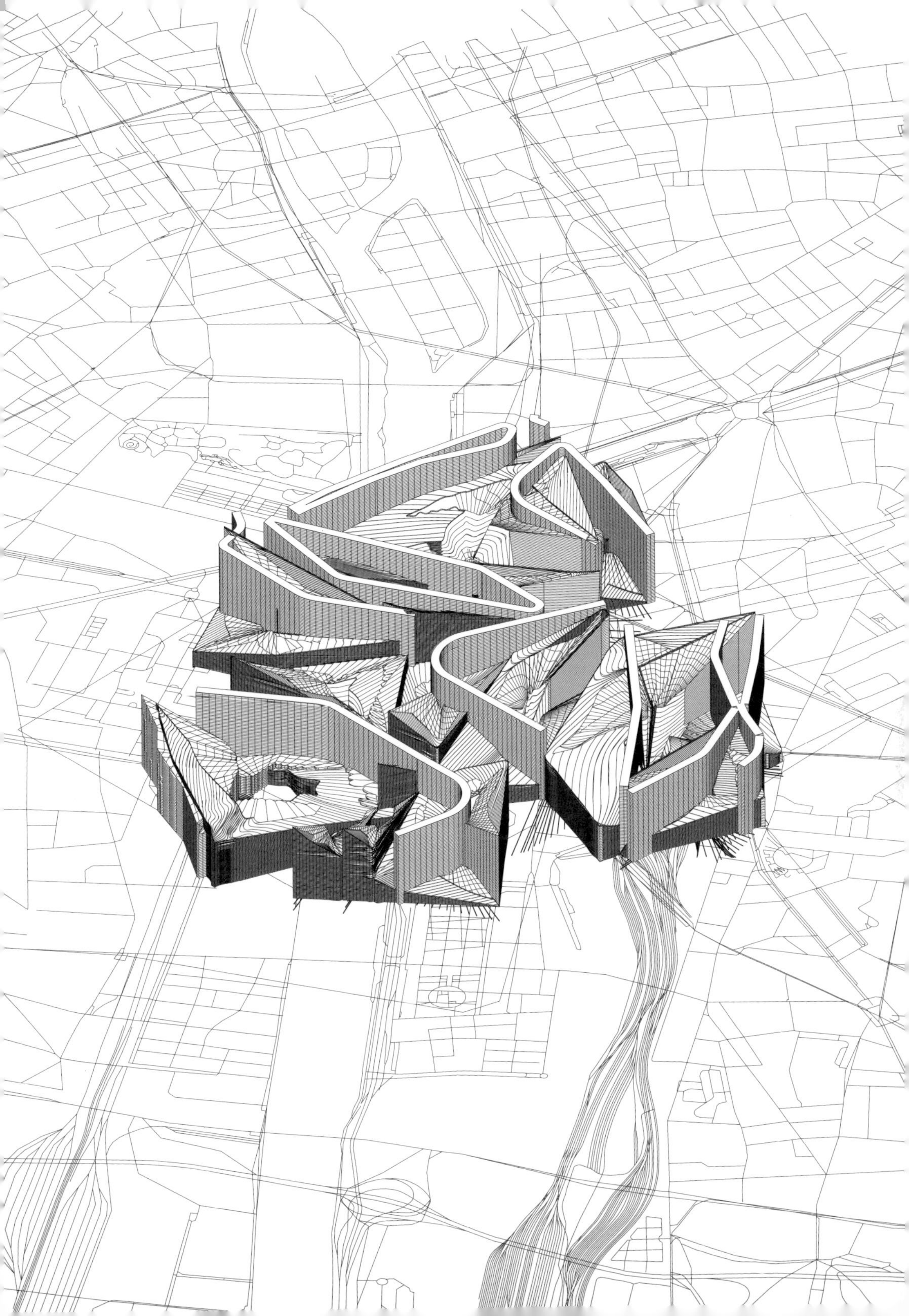

Project **Ville Tropicale**
Student **Alessandro Boccacci**
Research **Utopioids**

Ville Tropicale continues and unifies Yona Friedman's Ville Spatiale genealogy, evolving its detached and neutral megastructure into a sensitive model that adapts to the delicate conditions of the ground. A three-dimensional grid, vacated at medium-scale intervals for the entry of light, is overlaid onto a field of typological variations of the primitive hut that systematically occupy atoll formation processes, differentiating the rigid repetitive structure and loose cell system of the free plan through the vertical transition of structural and dwelling components and their clustering in residential sets of varying complexity.

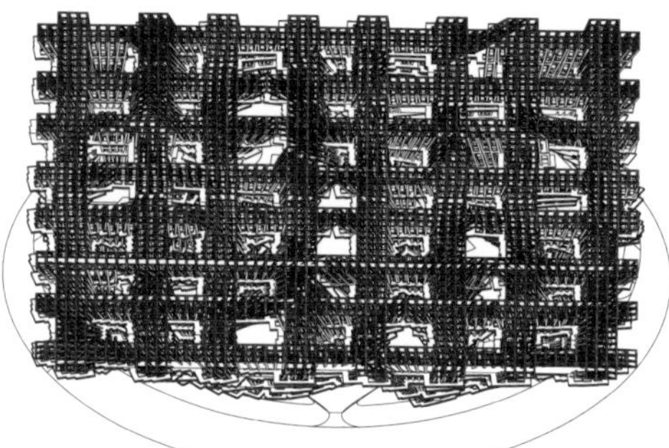

Project **Olympic Operations**
Student **Simon Willet**
Research **Utopioids**

Olympic Operations is a model of leisure-oriented landscape and environmental engineering based on Bruno Taut's expressionist utopian imagery of the Alps, regarded—as it appears in his book *Alpine Architecture*—as a set of artificially crystalline figures. Each book panel participating in the escalating narrative of the original is reconstructed through a series of consecutive variables and integrated in a comprehensive model. Mountains, creases and valleys, villages, pistes, snowfields, lifts, funiculars, decorative structures, forests, clouds, and even the sun itself are generated for a ski resort hosting Olympic competitions—a purpose-built piece of infrastructure.

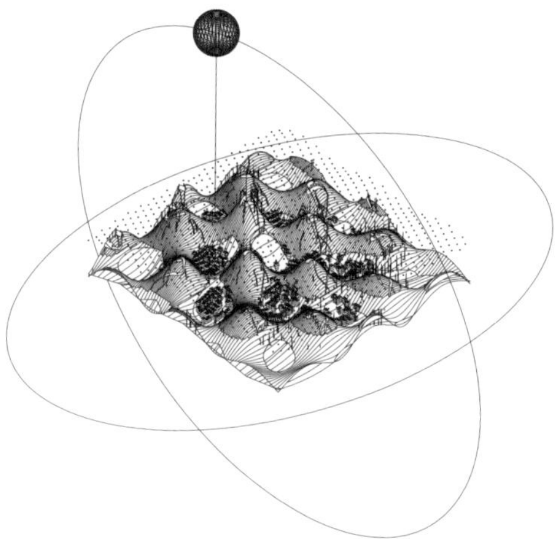

Project **La Cittá Rumorosa**
Student **Héctor Tarrido Picart**
Research **Utopioids**

La Cittá Rumorosa proliferates the manifold of pedestrian and assisted local traffic connections, combed as a laminar transport interchange between airports and train stations in Sant'Elia's La Cittá Nuova, into a dynamic spatial fabric that interlaces shortcuts, stoppages, passages, and deviations in multiple directions. Conceived as a source of noise and redundancy, the model joins secondary transport systems into a single infrastructural continuum, transcending the monolithic and monumental logic of the original through that of a vast, intertwined mass.

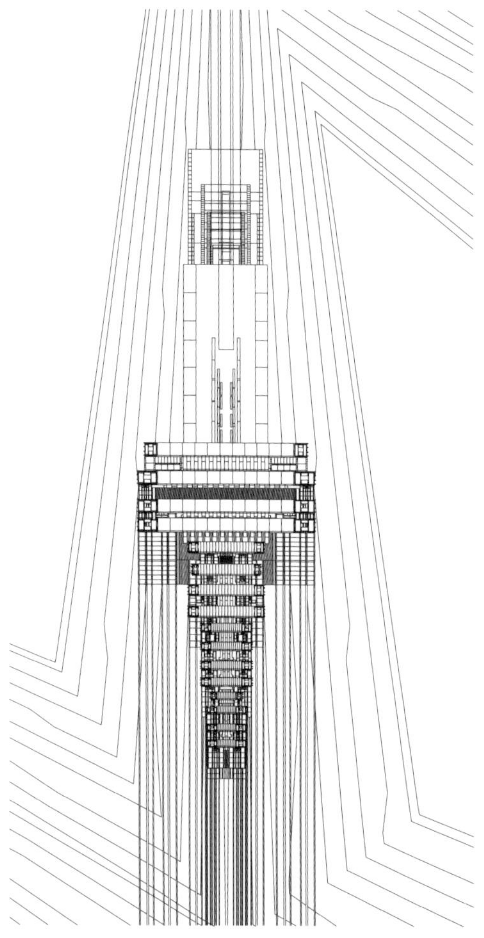

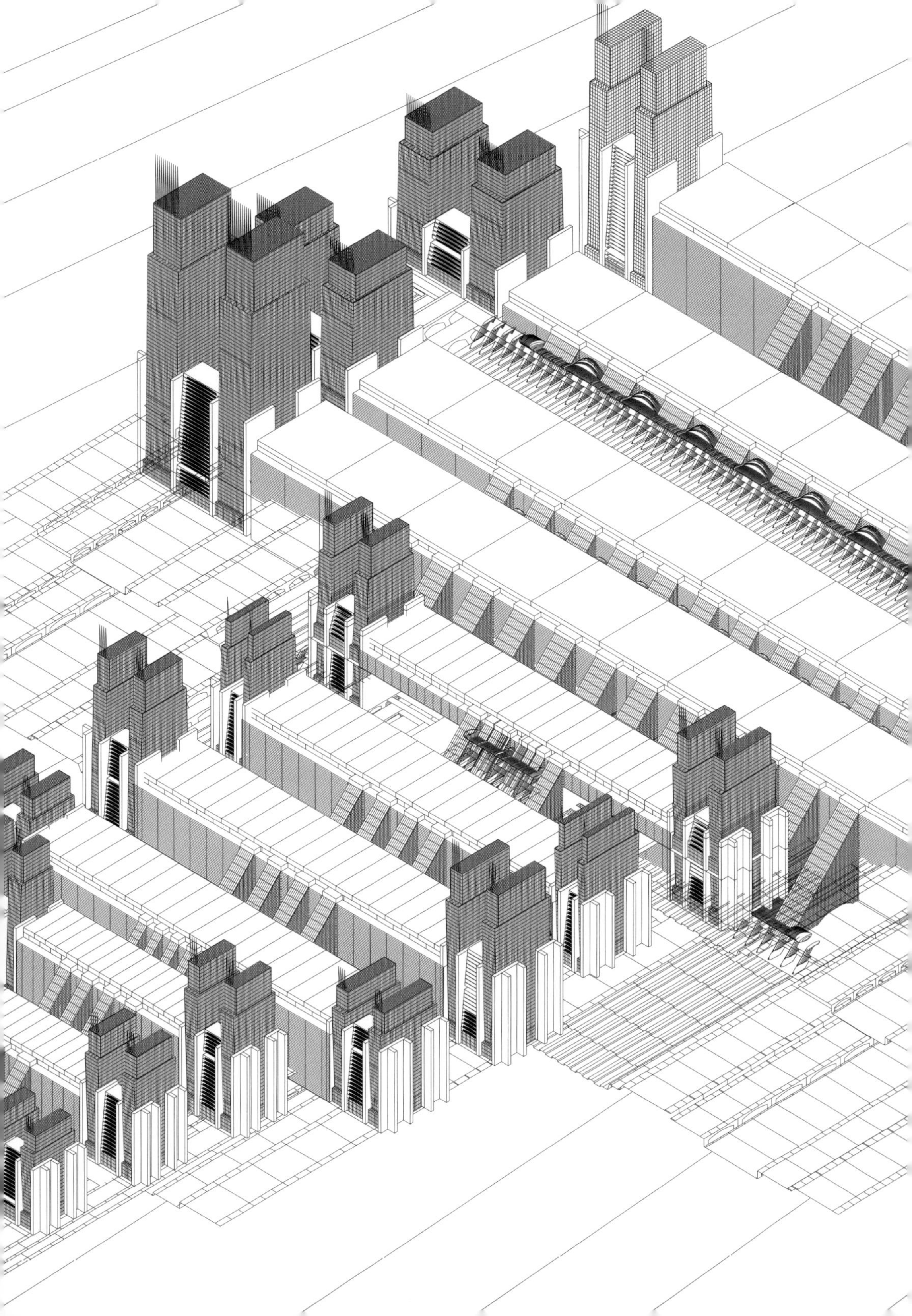

Project **Shukhovoids**
Student **Parsa Kamali**
Research **Utopioids**

Shukhovoids populates the hyperbolic diagrid shell of Vladimir Shukov's Shabolovka radio tower with independent cross-plan housing towers. The stacked structures run between horizontal ring-like strata at various intervals and at varying plan depths to compensate for the horizontal forces derived from the inclination of the whole. The high-rise housing collective both emits signals and receives them, constituting a unit of a continental broadcasting network. Because of their leaning toward information, the towers configure individuals, pairs, or triads. Their structural imbalance triggers variations in the internal building types.

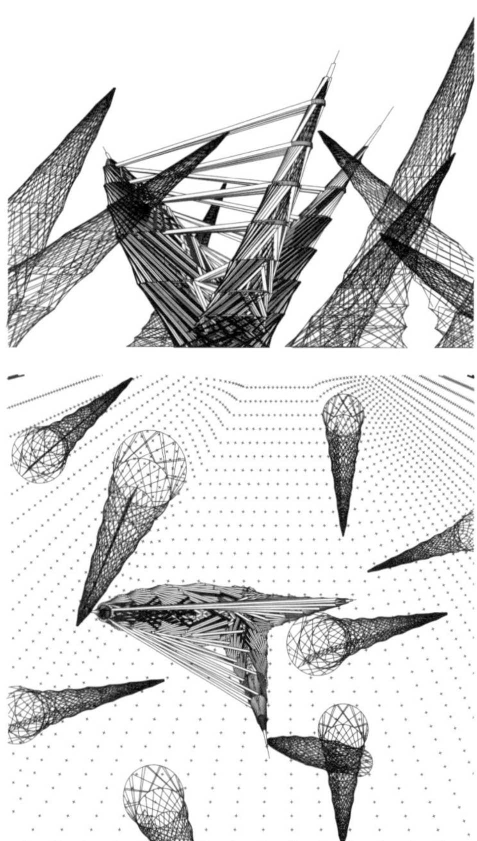

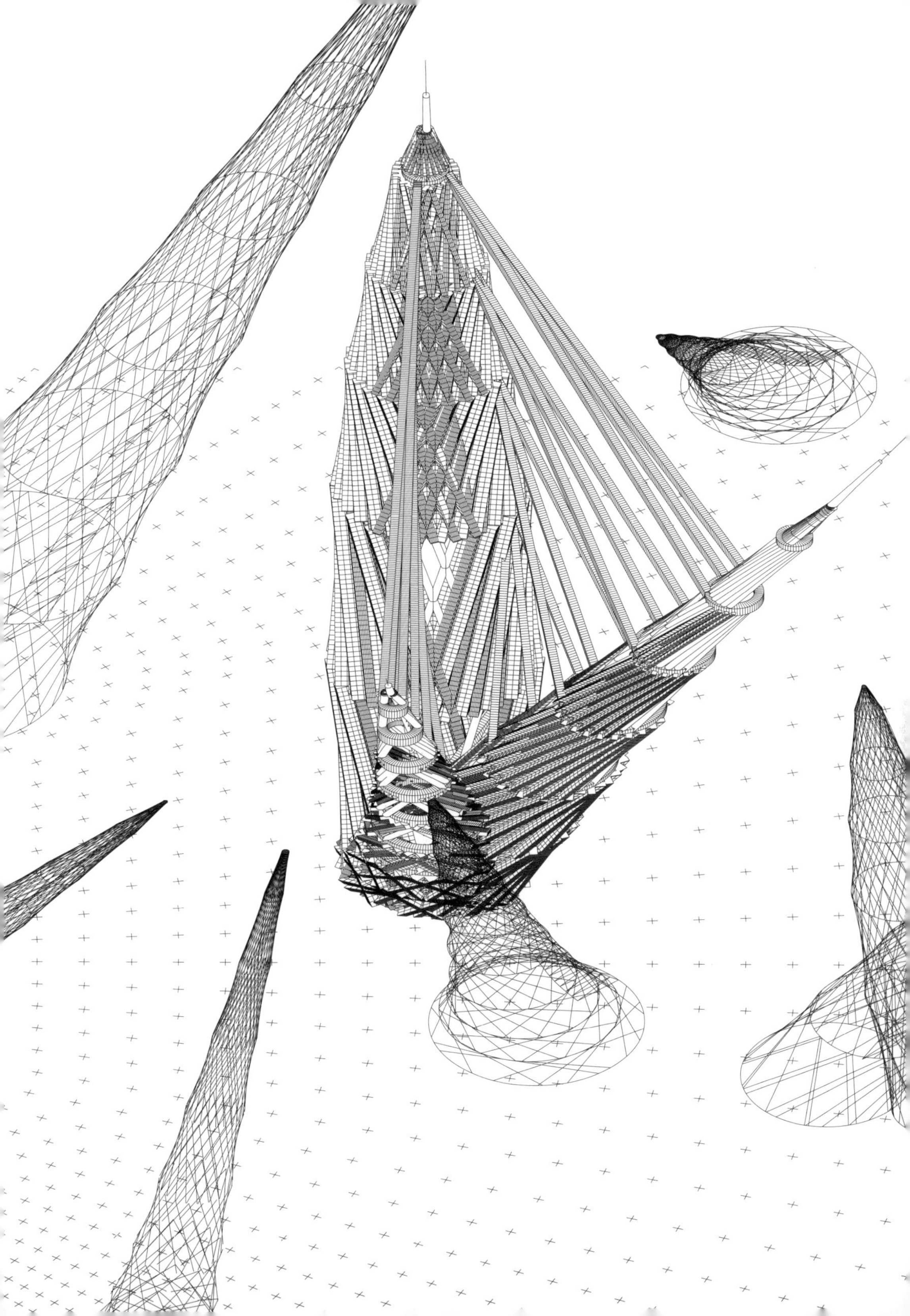

Project **Urbology**
Student **Emmanuel Torres**
Research **Utopioids**

Urbology integrates the landlocked, coastal, and floating arcologies of Paolo Soleri into a single system of variation that articulates a model of global population through an extensive network of high-density cities. These cities grow in time and create a continuous field of urbanization while staying isolated and unique as complex architectural miniaturizations of the urban. Soleri's formation processes are abstracted into independent variables and integrated by operations, creating transitions between the typological characteristics of the cases and articulating the nonlinear growth process of the unit with that of the field.

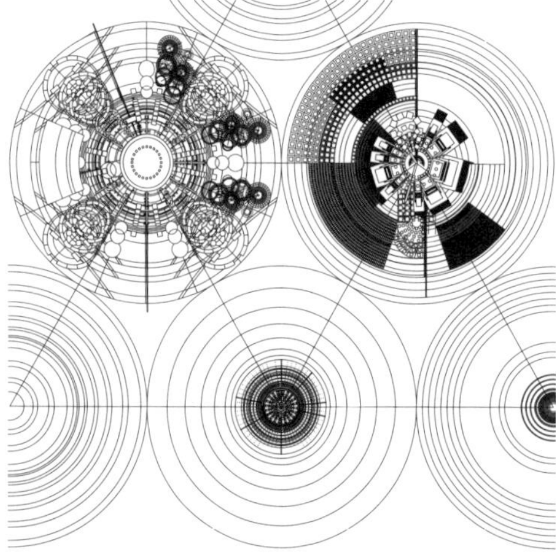

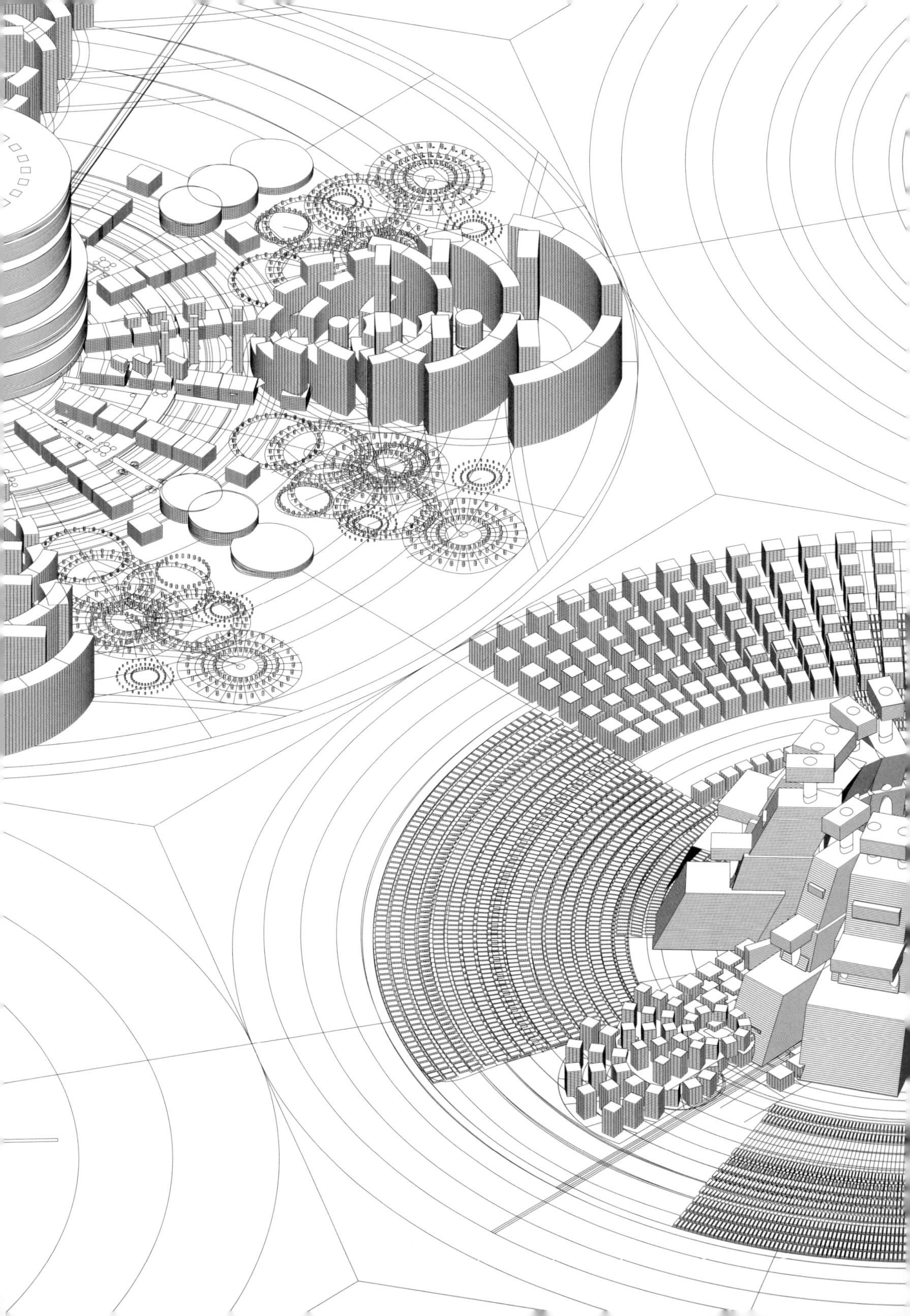

Project **Men in Retreat**
Student **Georgios-Spyridon Athanasopoulos**
Research **Utopioids**

Men in Retreat organizes athletic activities and commercial functions along a continuous pedestrian recreation ground that incarnates the locus and concentrates the gathering activities of a suburban community without the need for gates. Set among intertwined stems of golf courses are clubhouses, shops, conference rooms, gyms, spas, lounges, health and educational services, clubs, and pubs that are directly accessible by vehicles. Housing bars and clusters, surrounded by gardens, distribute the density of the dwelling at a lower level, providing the delimitation and containment of private areas.

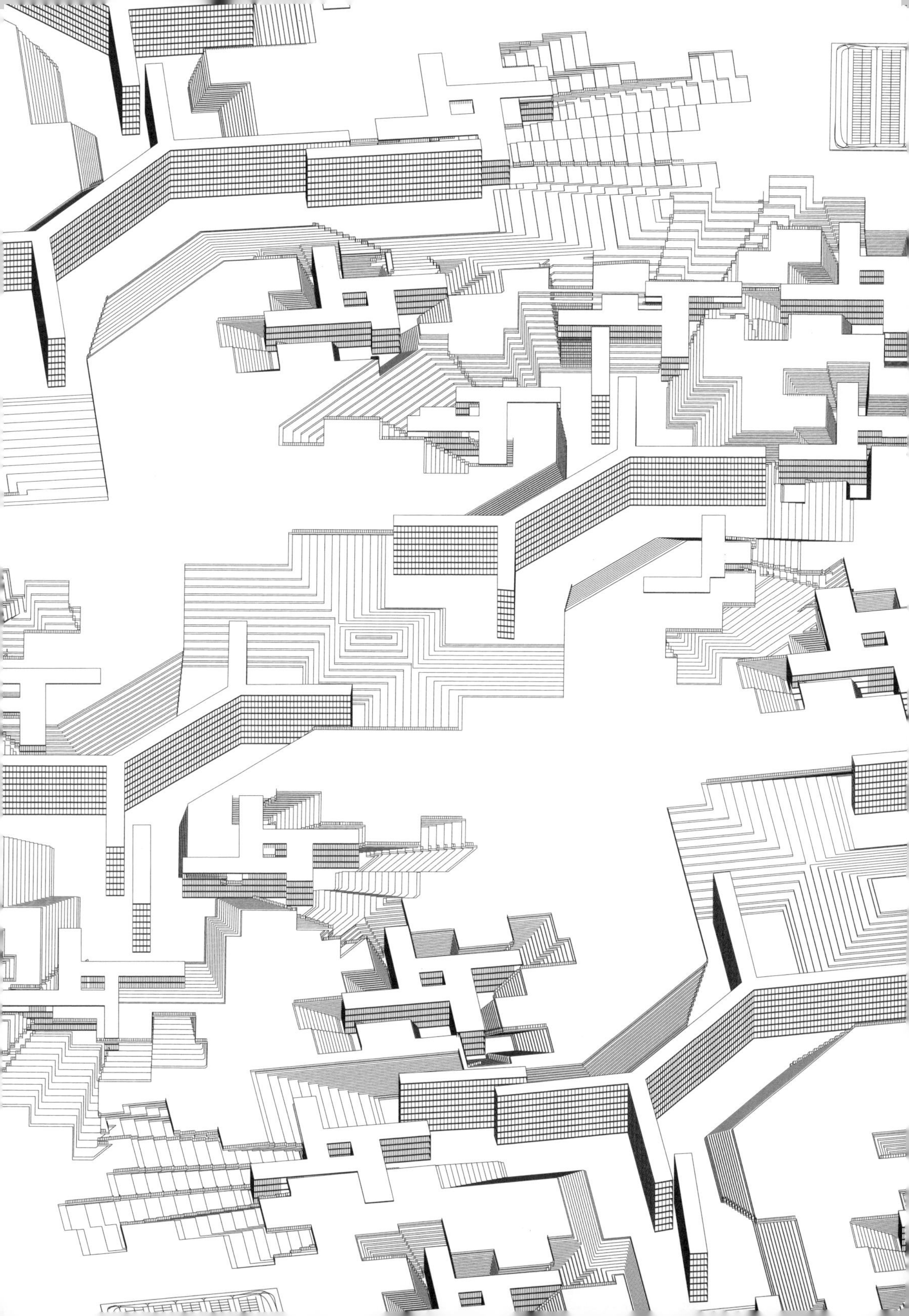

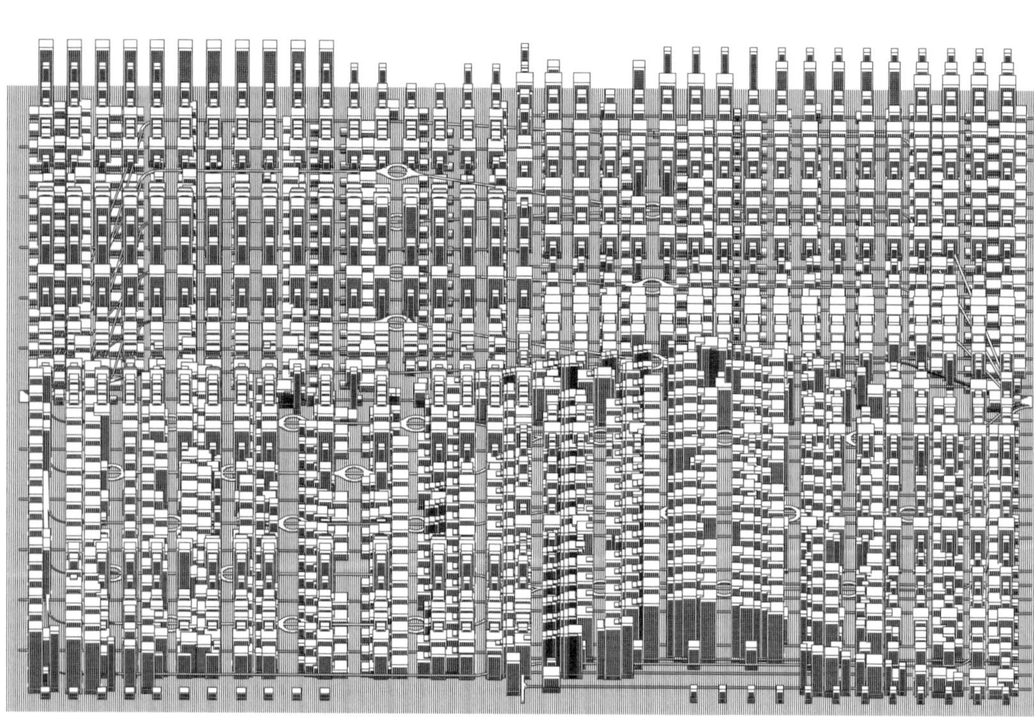

Principles, Capabilities, Flairs, and Flaws
Ciro Najle

If [a thing] is excessive for the imagination (and the imagination is driven to [such excess] as it apprehends [the thing] in intuition), then [the thing] is, as it were, an abyss in which the imagination is afraid to lose itself. Yet, at the same time, for reason's idea of the supersensible [this same thing] is not excessive but conforms to reason's law to give rise to such striving by the imagination. Hence [the thing] is now attractive to the same degree to which [formerly] it was repulsive to mere sensibility.
Immanuel Kant

Sublime is what, by its resistance to the interest of the senses, we like directly.
Immanuel Kant

The Generic Sublime embodies the ultimate leap in the evolution of architecture, where the expansive optimism of the intensely individual becomes the many in the one, both fascinating and horrifying.

The Generic Sublime integrates, within an univocal building structure, the conflicting logics of antiurban collectives and the irrationally vast territorial extents that they presuppose as condition of existence.

The Generic Sublime is the utmost expression of the inevitable destiny of architecture: its becoming overindividual.

The Generic Sublime is both a singular architectural figure and a collective architectural organization; both a sudden building form and a complex process of differentiation; both the nonlinear outcome of a system and the nonlinear system itself.

The Generic Sublime integrates rigorous performances and ineffable effects, unfolding one out of the other in a continual, self-fueling process. It intertwines relationships across the internal protocols of discrete building entities and synthetizes these relationships into models. It works through an open-ended formation process but is nevertheless congruous as a form, as a model, and as an organization.

Generic Sublime forms are consistent but irreducible to their determinations.

Generic Sublime models are consistent but irreducible to their techniques.

Generic Sublime organizations are consistent but irreducible to their processes.

Generic Sublime diagrams are both formal matrices and force-fields acting on form. They are constituted by protocols of escalating difference, the amalgamation of which operates simultaneously as a medium of communication, a means of determination, and a background of significance.

The Generic Sublime technically overwhelms the grounding of architecture on lax intuitions, organizationally challenges the grounding of architecture on aprioristic ideologies, and sensibly overcomes the grounding of architecture in mildness and agreeability.

The Generic Sublime is systemically multivalent, politically oscillating, and artistically undecipherable.

The Generic Sublime behaves as a candid mastermind. It is lightheartedly earnest and consciously infantile. Generic Sublime systems operate as autonomous minds. Generic Sublime models constitute uncanny mindsets.

The Generic Sublime oscillates between poignant form and enhanced performance without fully committing to either. It uses the uncommitted fluctuation between them as an engine for the differentiation of both. It is neither a straightforward mechanism of determination nor an objective teleological form.

The Generic Sublime defines its value systems and determines its criteria of evaluation. It establishes its parameters of relevance and constitutes its logics of form. It is both a virtual ground and a self-built physical ground.

The Generic Sublime balances itself and maintains internal equilibrium by propagating synergy and calibrating complementariness. Free from the ground as an external reference, it is itself both reference and ground.

The Generic Sublime is a self-supporting and self-governing structure precisely because of its radical openness. It is loose but rigorous, elusive but discrete, plural but one.

The Generic Sublime is a multiplicity-thing.

The Generic Sublime generously engulfs processes within its organizational complex.

The Generic Sublime actively manages information via its organizational richness.

The Generic Sublime ruthlessly transcends politics through its organizational amorality.

The Generic Sublime is brutal, extensive, and bold.

The Generic Sublime is infinite, ubiquitous, and greedy.

The Generic Sublime is multifarious, promiscuous, and deviant.

The Generic Sublime is clumsily graceful, innocently aggressive, harmlessly threatening.

The Generic Sublime is bare and transparent in its inputs but obscure and indecipherable in its outputs. It is deceptively didactic but profoundly crude and explicit—even belligerent. It bypasses control for the sake of control but is obsessive for the sake—and delight—of it.

The Generic Sublime's cultural agenda streams against the grain of logical argumentation. It evades well-intended demonstrations, remorseful excuses, and insipid justifications. The Generic Sublime is an unscrupulous declaration by means of buildings.

The Generic Sublime is beyond gymnastics of form. It is a medium of organizational problematization: a model with a buoyant rationality that uses its process as a system.

The Generic Sublime both presents and obliterates technique. Its principles are systematic but its outcomes irreversible. It strictly vacillates between constructing and surmounting its own analytical formats.

The Generic Sublime exudes neologisms. Its concepts are blurry, unintelligible, constantly under construction, and consistently unreliable. The Generic Sublime entails prebranding, rebranding, dysbranding, or superbranding, but not branding.

The Generic Sublime is a refined anticultural expression.

The Generic Sublime is a formal amalgam of protocols. Their convolution takes the form of accumulations, aggregations, proliferations, propagations, or self-intersections. These forms are synthetized through principles that administer the intertwinement of determinations.

Generic Sublime principles are as systematic as they are arbitrary. They are not stipulations but rather projections of power. They regulate ineffability, without entirely succeeding.

The Generic Sublime is neither alchemy nor magic but rather the joyous celebration of quantity and multiplication. The Generic Sublime is a machine for breeding awe through very particular forms of escalation of complexity. Its elusive methodology articulates a materialism of wonder, the techniques of which are created along the way of its process.

The Generic Sublime absorbs and assimilates any exteriority as its governing dynamic substance. This exteriority disguises itself as an unreachable architectural interior—an incommensurate atrium, a precipice-like double skin, a valley-like courtyard, an endless spatial alignment, a maze of corridors, a differentiated free plan, an elevated datum, an undulating ground—which processes and projects it back a halo of uncaring irresistibility.

The Generic Sublime is an aura-machine.

The Generic Sublime is an interior-exterior mesh. By turning undesired contingencies into fulfilled desires, the Generic Sublime constructs singular forms of critical mass. This critical mass confers organizational consistency to the exteriority from which it is nurtured and spatial ubiquity to the interior that it cherishes.

The Generic Sublime is the result of a peculiar organizational phenomenon operating at a territorial level, which, interiorized within a building, takes a unique form with anomalous traits.

Generic Sublime forms include fluid, torrential cascades; ellipsoidal networks; labyrinthine meanders; multilinear sets; countless transversal slices; animal-like multilayered skins; endless crisscrossing terraces; oscillating, floodable grounds; and vortex-like, throat-like interiors.

Generic Sublime traits include blurry, raw, or jagged edges; aberrant but curiously symmetrical protuberances; obscure superficial patterns; formless motifs; often sickening figural escalations; sticky textures and multifarious materials; spikes, swirls, holes, and caverns.

The Generic Sublime does not embody a cosmic representation, but it induces many. It is neither an urban icon nor a cultural symbol. It is an intensely artificial atmosphere sublimated as an architectural rock, where the sensible and the intelligible awkwardly coalesce.

The Generic Sublime manifestly melts the distinction between sensation and organization in a whole. It achieves the highest level of volatility and freedom within a solid, heavy, slow entity. It is formally stable and organizationally malleable, but it virulently reacts.

The Generic Sublime is archetypal in a free mode.

The Generic Sublime is outrageous—even offensive.

The Generic Sublime is monstrous, obscure, and pseudo-primitive.

The Generic Sublime is a primal condition still to come.

The Generic Sublime is a method for integrating the incompatible.

The Generic Sublime cannot be bargained as mere innovation. It defies reduction to technology and is never the latest new thing. It rejects linear progress and triggers cycles of perpetuate recursive thinking.

The Generic Sublime is an informational medium wherein to amorally instigate cultural friction; a formal construct driven to induce danger and persuasion; an organizational model for the transformation of the real by means of its most unlikely idealization.

The Generic Sublime assumes and takes the real beyond itself.

Note: The epigraphs above are taken from Immanuel Kant, "Analytic of the Sublime," in *Critique of Judgment*, bk. II, trans. Werner Pluhar (Indianapolis, Indiana: Hackett Publishing Company, 1987), sec. 27, p. 115, and sec. 29, p. 127. Originally published in German in 1790.

Conversation

Erika Naginski, Iñaki Ábalos, Ciro Najle

Iñaki Ábalos: Thank you all for coming, and thank you, Erika Naginski, for agreeing to participate in this roundtable discussion. Ciro Najle had the idea of hosting this event, and we decided that Erika would be the perfect person with which to have a conversation about utopias and Utopioids.

Erika Naginski: I am very flattered.

IA: Have you invented the name, Ciro?

Ciro Najle: As far as I know. *(laughs)*

IA: *(laughs)* I want to make a brief introduction, as our audience knows both of you quite well. I met Ciro a long time ago, at a time when we were teaching at the Architectural Association. He started the Landscape Urbanism graduate program, then came to Cornell, and now is Dean of the School of Architecture at the Universidad Torcuato Di Tella in Buenos Aires. For the last five years, he has been coming to the Harvard University Graduate School of Design (GSD) regularly, and he will teach option studios here next spring. The research he is conducting is among the most rigorous and impressive we have been seeing, not only in this school but in many other places. I consider mentally attractive his method of work, which summarizes, in many ways, the need of rigor for a deep form of subjectivity, and for building up a capability of change in terms of time. His work projects ideas into the future by always looking into the past, creating models of work somehow similar to the laboratory of Robert Le Ricolais at the University of Pennsylvania or the research of Ludwig Hilberseimer for many reasons; because of its high degree of abstraction, to start with, and because of its utopian dimension. But the work is also similar to that of people like Andrea Branzi, who is someone who always comes to my mind when I see the models produced by Ciro's design studios. These models develop new tools and ideas around what can be regarded as the main problems of the contemporary city, here considered, in a very abstract and practical way, as laboratories to research new potentials. I do not want to elaborate further, because this will all come out during the conversation. I will not speak, except if I am provoked (*laughs*), because the conversation is to be between these two. But let me just say thank you for being here. I am pleased to be part of this event, taking place in this friendly environment, surrounded by this beautiful exhibition in a wonderful library. Ciro will make an introduction, and then they will start the conversation.

CN: Thank you so much, Iñaki, for the invitation and for such a warm introduction. And thank you, Erika, for being here: it is an honor. I will briefly introduce the work we have been doing these years and then expand on the exhibition.

To start with, I want to mention that the way I decided to confront the studio culture in America was to construct a cumulative agenda, segmented so that autonomous lines would run consecutively and build up in content and intensity around a single hypothesis.

The first time I came to the Department of Architecture at the GSD, I introduced what would afterward become the grounding hypothesis of the series, through a studio called the Overskyscraper. Starting from that investigation, I realized that the hypothesis (which was dependent on its predecessor, the American skyscraper) required more autonomy as a proposition. I also decided that, for methodological reasons, it needed to be broken down into a manifold of lines of research. The four studios expanded what was introduced by the Overskyscraper through what I progressively called the Generic Sublime, a notion that begins from challenging the "generic," this deliberately blank category from the 1990s (which has its root, I believe, in European continental modernism) as paradoxically capable of producing, against its clarity as a concept, ever-higher forms of singularity.

The Generic Sublime is the form that these unexpected, extra-extra-large singularities take nowadays, and the will of foregrounding and theorizing them has to do with proposing a new threshold after Bigness. The hypothesis is analogous and meant to update the notion that Rem Koolhaas presented in the late 1970s in his book *Delirious New York*, which then unfolded in and was substantiated by his writings and projects during the 1980s and 1990s. Koolhaas presented the American skyscraper as a model that had already engendered a scalar leap from architecture to urbanism, activating a conflict in regards to the moralistic ideals and high-brow ideological stance of modern culture in Europe, against which early 20th-century Manhattan was a "mountain of evidence" and an antiurban model for architecture at the end of the century. The Generic Sublime declares a second leap in that genealogy by going through a new scalar threshold, now existing at the scale of territory. Although it follows a similar logic of paradoxical emergence, it bypasses the retroactive critical ethics, twisting its logic into a new operative level, working thoroughly in real time. The Generic Sublime calls for a systematic theory grounded in its predecessor, which is seen as its countermodel. It proposes that a number of cases in contemporary large-scale development are embedded with a potential that has not yet been consciously exploited, replaying its predecessor's argument yet with a self-conscious turn: a theory calculatedly based on an evidence without a theory.

The double reversal of the allegedly revolutionary ethics of modernism that this implies has to do with the fact that, at present, there are new, and more literal, mountains of evidence building up in front of our eyes and taking the form of very large portions of territory. These are being developed by single (or very few) agents, frequently with a simplistic—almost dumb—rationale, in a very short period of time and in such a way that one is led to think that the territory is no longer the domain that successfully escapes the will of control of architecture, nor the context or condition where architecture operates, but rather is becoming, itself, an architectural problem. I would like to think that architecture's obsolescence is, once again, its opportunity of enduring—now, by means of an expansive mature form. The Generic Sublime assumes that the absorption of the territorial within architecture (that is, literally, territory as building) involves cultural operations analogous to those of the skyscraper absorbing urbanism by means of an antiurban form.

The investigation advanced along four procedural approaches, which, although sequenced, are not chronological at a methodological level but rather coexist in a parallel pool. I think of them as intertwined. I broke down the agenda for developing the research into short periods. The first studio, Neonatures, conducted in the Department of Landscape Architecture, focused on building up a new attitude toward the territory that could operate at the same time under a systemic ethics and as a figural exploration. Procedurally it worked under the long-term influence of systems theory in architecture, but it attempted to reach a level where icons and rhetorical constructs could be embedded in simulations, making them work both as dynamic models and as engines for the engineering of poignancy.

The second studio, in the Department of Urban Design, worked under the scope of the normative, constructing protocols to simulate the logics of organization at work in large urban developments. Protocols are prescribed relationships between systems that implicitly regulate their organization and exchanges without being conceived as such, instead operating de facto. The studio recognized those logics and rationalized their intelligence into regimes, which, through extremes, were displaced out of the ordinary. A series of typological groups, including supertall office towers, deep-plan buildings, high-rise housing collectives, dense mixed-use developments, new central and business districts, gated communities, thematic resorts, and satellite cities were understood as consistent conventions, turned into normatives, and expanded in their creative capabilities. The norm was understood as latency embedded with unexploited difference, the role of the architect being to construct an apparatus that works through intensification. That was Overurbanism.

The third studio engaged explicitly with *Delirious New York* as a retroactive manifesto, projecting the methodology into a cultural arena by abstracting Koolhaas's polemical arguments and concepts and then resetting them. Neokoolhisms thus involved the direct disciplinary challenge of upgrading a well-known conceptual framework.

The fourth studio, Utopioids—and this is what I believe Erika will refer to—was grounded on the postulation that large-scale development necessarily involves a mix of a wild form of imagination, jovial in its basis and nurtured by a voluntary form of candidness, and an extremely prescriptive vision of what and how the world has to be. These two components were integrated into a problematic model characterized by a deliberately reductive frame and communicated to the public through a perverse and very efficient communication system. Often self-contained, these enclaves adopt and reproduce an implacable logic over and over, across circumstances. The studio flirted with this idea, so obvious in places like gated communities, where people desire and enjoy being imprisoned under the most arbitrary conditions, as long as the model is shared with others of a similar kind: manners are artificially learned and regulated by precise restrictions and protocols, even laws, together with the necessary enforcement agents and the reassuring surveillance mechanisms. Common to any amenity is not only its appeal to the luxurious but its amazing ability to generalize the singular at the very moment when it is captured: everything promoted as different is straightforwardly regulated as the common.

There is a certain attraction, odd and hard to accept, between this idea of a constructed system of domestication and the self-defeating notion of the utopian project, only, perhaps, in the reverse direction: the more deterministic the regulations, the more dormant the people. This twisted sense of a deviated utopian project that constructs conditions by abstracting methods from 20th-century utopias was termed "Utopioid." As extensive as their unsolicited precedent, they share a similar desire for ubiquity. But the idea of Utopioids has to do, instead, with the conscious falsification that such a perverse project could—at the same time that it puts people to sleep—raise their revolutionary unconscious and, to a certain extent, critically idealize those same conditions of the real that gave it sense, all the while problematizing the supposedly ideal conditions of the utopian and making it succeed by wicked means.

By both taking literally and putting into tension these two forms of myth, Utopioids challenge them at their basis. The model at the entrance of the library, for example, was built based on Bruno Taut's Alpine Architecture project of 1917, integrating its glorification of the alpine landscape with an architectural organization, the Olympic sky resort, that has a celebratory drive and feeling. And that project over there was based on Antonio Sant'Elia's Città Nuova drawings of 1912-1914, developing a prototype of interchange between various infrastructure systems and forms of circulation. Or this one, called Ville Tropicale, revisits the Ville Spatiale by Yona Friedman of about 1959, testing its raised section against environmentally delicate ground in the Maldives and creating a model for touristic resorts that swallows the pseudo–primitive-hut structure typical of those areas within a three-dimensional, late-modernist grid. The proposals engage utopian projects of mainstream modernism and visions from the 1960s while remaining idealistic and candid at their core.

EN: I will jump in here, and I have to say that I had not known about the unfolding of this series of studios as I have just returned from a year of leave, so this is truly a pleasure. Walking into the library and looking at the display of works, one of the things that struck me immediately was that this is an exhibit as much about architecture as it is about pedagogy. So as I was contemplating the projects, I had some general thoughts about utopianism that I want to throw out there, and then we can come back to some of the thought-provoking examples we see around us.

As you just heard, the studio took up the broad characteristics of modernist utopias. Yet, what is interesting is that when we talk about utopia, of course, we mean both a philosophical tradition and a formal modality: on the one hand, words, or a long-standing intellectual tradition, and on the other, images, or spatialized and impetuous forms of social, typological, and territorial organization most often expressed in visionary or unbuildable representations. I want to touch on the philosophical tradition for a moment, because even though Ciro insisted on this, one of the aspects that has perhaps continued to limit our understanding of the historical contexts of, and subsequent references to, modernist utopias is the refusal to acknowledge how they pushed back against the foundations of the Western philosophical tradition of utopian thought, all the while revisiting those foundations in quite profound ways—and often despite themselves, as they lay claim to the radical status provided by mythologies of the avant-garde. I want to allude to some of these foundations for a moment.

First, the concept of "utopia" possesses a semantically strange double meaning: etymologically, it indicates both "no place" and "happy place." This double meaning carries over into another duality animating the philosophical tradition, for whether one refers back to classical scholars who were influenced by the Frankfurt School like Moses Finley (who wrote about economic status and ancient civic ideologies) or philosophers of science and the urban like Lewis Mumford (who wrote about the city as the embodiment of the Spartan military phalanx), there are tangible divisions between what we call ancient utopia and modern utopia. The distinctions are quite clear and were brought to light by a singularly important text published in the Renaissance: Sir Thomas More's *Utopia* (1516). A work of fiction and of political philosophy, the book presents both aspects of utopia, for just as it looks back to the ancient Platonic notion of a static, tyrannical city–state it looks forward and dreams of a classless society unfolding through the metaphor of the isolated island nation, as well as through the cartographic imagination embedded within the text. What is notable here is how the nature of More's project was inexorably bound to a process of defining a specific site—that is, the island called "Utopia" (with its language, family structures, and political organization reinvented whole cloth)—and, by the same token, of establishing a noun describing a general condition—utopia, the will to dream up an ideal society, the result of what Ciro suggestively characterized as "a mix of a wild form of imagination and a narrow prescription of what the world has to be." What becomes clear is that utopia (and this is where I think the studio was singularly successful) is not simply, or not *only*, aimed at an object but is itself a process: a process of making—an architectonic procedure, if you will—through which to think the future and the past simultaneously. So while Finley can talk about the philosophical category of utopia as prompting distinctions between the now and the then, Mumford can cast the city as a machine from its inception until today. Mumford's version of things inspires the vision of the gargantuan megastructure as an isolated urban totality placed within an even more colossal urban totality (talk about satellite cities!), as well as a kind of topographical fantasy folded back onto architecture qua architecture. All this evokes both limits and limitlessness, and this is where the Continental philosophical term "sublime" of

Ciro's formulation comes in: boundaries and loss of boundaries, horizons and mapping, the idea of the viewpoint that stems from within and without spatiality.

Here it is crucial to acknowledge, as Ciro did in his presentation, that we have to push back against the notion of utopia simply as an arrogant, impossible flight of fancy and underscore instead the fact that it is by definition an intellectual exercise—one that serves a critical function precisely because it is embedded in a conversation with the real, with the current condition of things, with the lived world that endlessly produces limitations. And the designer can always play with those limitations sardonically, ironically, naively, or even candidly, but we cannot dismiss the premise that entrenched in the term "utopia" is this critical function whereby the non-place becomes the not-here, not-this-place. There is always, and always must be, a dialectical relationship between the real animating the not-here and the not-this-place.

However, when we think back to the ancient model and consider Plato's *Republic*, things seem to emerge very differently, in large part because that critical function was seemingly annihilated. Plato's dream of the philosopher king whose guardians watch and enforce the status quo is essentially one of a caste system and a static urban model. His city rejects dynamism. There is a haunting moment in the *Republic* when Socrates is made to speak the virtuous, notorious, and noble lie of utopia: that people are not born of parents but rather of the city itself. They are the heart of the city fabric, and their stratified class structure is predetermined, meaning that one must not intermingle with others, one must never emerge outside of a prescribed insularity: a haunting origin for the island metaphor. What is curious about this caste system is that it moves from bodies to souls, from the material world to the realm of philosophical thought, from the artisans to the soldiers to the rulers.

Ancient utopianism includes another model, however, that is closer to what the studio explored and that ties modern attitudes to, rather than differentiates them from, classical philosophy. We owe this model to Aristotle, who offered another kind of explanation about the origins of the utopian city, which is likewise always a metropolis or an island but is also organized under the assumption that it is the citizenry that practices politics. Through praxis, citizens give form to the polis. Aristotle conceives of this human potential as a communal science of the possible. The polis—the archetypal form of human potential—is made up of a citizenry and yet also stems from a paradox. On the one hand, people are driven to participate in the social realm. This is a fact of nature, and therefore people necessarily practice politics. The polis is, in this sense, a natural, organic, even biological principle of fulfillment. On the other hand, the polis is the result of civilization. In this scheme of things, the utopian city—the ideal polis—is both a natural and civilized product. So here we have the coalescence of an organic basis and a civilizational process, bound together by Aristotle by means of the wonderful concept of "entelecheia," or entelechy. And I cannot help but see it being evoked in the syntax of these projects.

Entelechy is the principle of self-actualization. Applied to utopia (or the ideal polis), entelechy presumes that it must be grounded in the real precisely because it corresponds to the premise that an organism will always direct itself toward actualization and maximum potential. If we can take entelechy as the progenitor of Aristotle's polis, then we can propose that the notion of utopia is grounded—however critically, naively, or sadistically—in the real. What Aristotle gave us, and what many of these projects rehearse, is the idea that utopia belongs to the domain of natural history. Utopia is not a castle in the air but belongs to nature.

Yet, when you consider philosophical foundations alongside architectural expressions, you will find absolute divisions being made between ancient or premodern utopias and what we describe as modern or contemporary utopias. First, we typically cast premodern utopias as static and unchanging, while we construe modern utopias as being fueled by desire as well as by the embracing of technological promise (which is dynamic and appears as in the form of the desiring machine). Second, premodern utopias, like the medieval Plan of St. Gall—that extraordinary visualization of a Carolingian monastery with its complex program—are understood as utopias of need, whose goal is simply to sustain community with limited resources. This stands in contrast to utopias of desire in the modern world, unleashed in some sense because technology still just might make anything possible. A third difference has to do with social and political hierarchy: if Plato gave us hierarchy, then modern utopias often gave us egalitarianism (which is not the same thing as freedom). Finally, with modern utopias you get much of what Ciro was speaking of: rhetorical or figural statements. You get much of what you see here: global reach, the serialized appearance of large-scale organizations, the colossal size of institutions determining human behavior, and infrastructures that are made to correspond to those requirements at a territorial scale unimaginable in the time of the ancient metropolis.

But what is curious in this age of diminishing resources—and this is where we might need to reorient our temporal outlook and consider history as much as what is to come—is that, as a result of the reality of diminishing resources and new myths of nature promoted by sustainability, we may actually be returning to the earlier model: the utopia of need. We can no longer desire in the same way. And this is a very interesting recursion, a folding back to some of the philosophical premises of an earlier condition. Take a look at some of the projects exhibited here and think back to the studio's brief and aims—sublime aims. We have "skyscraper collectives, tower agglomerations, mixed-use developments, high-rise housing developments, marinas and luxury condominiums, airport hubs, office enclaves, industrial parks, hotel complexes, conference centers, financial centers, satellite cities, theme parks, thematic cities, branded cities, central districts, gated communities." Ciro here asks the rhetorical questions, "What is the potential latent in extraordinarily large urban typologies currently restricted by the technological condition of urbanism? What is the reach of such potential to think aggressively about the contemporary metropolitan condition and imagine future developmental models?" These "extraordinarily large urban typologies" are crucial to the programs that were explored, but the rhetorical questions imply that the monumental, far-reaching aspects of megastructures and megaforms are tied back to the earlier projects or paradigms: the Futurism of Filippo Tommaso Marinetti, the urbanism of Le Corbusier, the Suprematism of El Lissitzky. Students were asked to think about and work through another level: not simply the condition imposed by the program (a resort or an airport) but more importantly, the layer of projection of a canonical work. This is a challenging binary condition, and you get a sense of just how challenging when you go downstairs to the Special Collections Library, where the other part of the exhibition is set up and you can see the students trying to work through that binary by means of their design processes.

When you go around and look at some of the work, your eyes start to oscillate between past and present. A work stands in relation to Metabolism, for example, and you can see that binary condition formally animating its syntax, with its radial, circular forms acting as an architectural version of catalyzed reactions analogizing organic or biological reproductions. Or Neon Sector, right there, which is related to the Situationist *dérive* and to reshuffling and abandonment, using these to conceive of new urban districts and emphasizing the idea of the city as a series of events in flux. You see the binary condition over and over again.

And so I come away with the sense that utopia now has this double burden. It is not enough just to say that there is an imposed ideological condition on a gated community, for example. We have to complicate the task by pairing it up with an example of projection. So I am curious to ask—and I do not know if any of the students in the studio are here as well—how they responded to this doubling of the task, referring to a past canonical work while at the same time establishing engagement with a condition that is embedded in and defines the real—the horrifying or the wonderful real, however you want to think of it.

CN: You want a student to answer?

EN: That would be terrific.

Alessandro Boccacci: I will give you an answer as a student. I think this double layer was an important help, because tackling the tasks of the project from both ends provides a frame for developing the project. Without necessarily being your own, these premises give you a critical lens. I think it is key in design to have a frame that overwhelms your own thinking.

Simon Willett: It is also interesting how most utopian projects from the 20th century are requesting architects, designers, and students to take them on, because the utopian project almost always is vague in terms of formal resolution but specific about its ideology, which often ends up thinking big. This itself implies a challenge, which is to either embrace it or come up with something new. In that sense, it is fulfilling to get deep into the projects, engage someone else's formal response, and come up with something new constructed from within.

CN: These two projects are interestingly related to your question about the relation between the forward-looking, projective aspects in the constructs and their relationship to history, in the sense that their models are built from utopian propositions and they index norms of current types into them. The model is therefore seen as a ductile medium within which to incorporate and enhance difference, understanding difference not as residing outside the normative regimes but instead as a motor that creates them.

EN: That is interesting, because the insertion of a critical program already embedded in an ideological program is often what we call "heterotopic." We had this brief conversation where you mentioned Georges Canguilhem's work as being important to your approach to the idea of norm, and it is thought provoking that this introduces a notion of temporality, of ephemerality, of an agent moving into a body and making it adapt and transform its given condition.

CN: One of the issues that the projects deal with, when constructing a Utopioid model and indexing regulations from a type, has to do with recognizing that the anomalous, in any norm, is not the exception to what is prescribed but rather the vehicle to create a more complex normative to come. So the variability of the models has to do with teasing the original material beyond its premises, intensifying the differences with which it is already embedded—that is, its incipient tendency to become something else. Utopioids result, in that sense, of the massaging and squeezing of utopia to breed critical conditions into commercial development, which means looking at the conventions of a type and making the model sieve its norm. Simon's project thinks how to look at any device, infrastructure, or building type in a sky resort as a potential form of expressionist fantasy not yet exploited as such. Alpine Architecture is used to illuminate and transform everything in the type, from the infrastructure and the sky stations to the little towns in the valleys, the Olympic protocols, and the landscape itself. These structures, often pieces of engineering with gadgets and decoration, are regarded as traces of temples of a territorial architecture to come, with all the spectrum of weird, naturalistic references and the picturesque paraphernalia that enlivens the typology and introduces new forms of value.

EN: It is wonderful to think of this binary structure that you imposed on the design processes, and it sounds as if some of the projects ended up reworking the canonical paradigm, while others were better at performing a form of ventriloquy through the canonical to rework given conditions. I wonder if the projects ended up doing half of one, half of the other, or if anybody succeeded in doing both simultaneously? In other words, if through the given condition you sought to rework Bruno Taut, say, or the *dérive* model, but then the *dérive* model reworked its way back into the program? I am interested in whether the two possible conditions functioned equally well. Or if there were moments of failure, what they were like?

CN: Failure mostly had to do with the poignancy of the utopian projects and their cultural inertia taking over and disallowing any transformation because of the seriousness of their meaning. And scripting is so intensely focused on technique that it can get too attached to the ethics and standards. I tend to think that the tighter the project is to its model, the more it can transform it in an interesting manner. I think of extreme and self-conscious conservatism as a means to tighten novelty, but sometimes it inhibits the author from recognizing what is the most crucial moment of daring to divert it. Thinking through the process with humor, and defining what kind of humor that is, what degree of respect and disrespect it involves, is vital.

EN: Although I like the sky resort, I have to say: that is excellent.

IA: I want to put another thing on the table, and it is the status of the work. It is very difficult to compare this studio work to any other, because the interpretations that you can make of it can vary. There is always the temptation to look at the fantastic scale of these drawings as trying to address practical issues of the contemporary growth and expansion of the city, of the status of the territory, or even of the status of the disciplines at work—urbanism, landscape architecture, architecture—trying to establish a common ground that dissolves their limits in a new environment. So we can see that there is an implicit proposal of pragmatism (a contemporary pragmatism, so to speak) to deal with new scales. This is one reading, but intellectually I think it is more complex, in the sense that it is also about applying total skepticism to the fever that is utopia. And this is contradictory, because while the projects are to some extent humoristic, they are also able to seriously reveal the cultural construct of the original utopias. They work as a deconstruction of utopias through some sense of humor, and with a sense of brutal pragmatism on top.

And yet, there is another layer, which is quite interesting, and is the purely aesthetic, also evident in the exhibition. On top of all this—the possible pragmatism, the discussion of the role of different disciplines in the thinking of the territory, the blunt skepticism, and the method for intensifying this skepticism and producing a new reality—is the aim for beauty: the Generic Sublime. All three layers are strong, and they dissolve every other's ground to the root. And it is very difficult to understand the weight of each of them. It is even difficult to think that you are thinking of this program, the Generic Sublime, in three different levels. So I would like to know if you see any of these levels—the pragmatic, the purely skeptical, and the aesthetic—as being more or less active than the others? Or do you do not think of these levels as at all separate?

CN: The form that the construction of the argument takes overrides it all, so in this sense the construction of models of beauty is probably the one that interests me most, only that what I call "sublime" implies a mental idea of beautiful and is identified not only with an explicit figure but also with the form of the argument's construct and the conditions of its procedure.

IA: Yes. *(laughs)*

EN: Collectively produced.

CN: Collective in terms of a set of abstract subjectivities at work—projects and models—whose form coincides with the form of their arguments. What Iñaki calls "new environment" I call "pre-architecture." And I understand the ambiguity that the work is confronted with as a result, but it is inherent to its multivalence and embedded in the slipperiness of the drawings, which I appreciate. The idea that there are latencies in the most banal pieces of architecture that have not yet been exploited by the discipline to enlarge its power means that it is also the work what must breed those latencies, through each drawing, one by one. The drawings are not illustrations but the medium of this process. You can think of the work as trying to construct forms of imagination—pragmatic, objectified ones—and in that sense, not mystical. They are built from restrictions, and probably this is why their logic may appear as a sublime form of self-alienation. The sublime, more than the beautiful, interests me because it produces the idea that something is simultaneously appealing and terrifying, and this also happens as a consequence of its nebulousness.

EN: I can say the word "Kant" here, right? It strikes me that what you just described seems to be an architectural adaptation of the Kantian model of understanding. You have, at the base, conditions, givens, perceptions, experiences, and at the top you give the students concepts—you give them Le Corbusier, or Constant. And then you say imagination has to do its work. If we go back to Kant, the word he uses is "*Bildungskraft*," which means "the power to produce images." In Kant the imagination produces images from raw perceptions, the sensorial givens, in order to (re)present them to our understanding. And this is remarkably consistent with what you just said. You have analogized the Kantian model to the system of your studio. And, actually, the kind of image that Kant talks about is not figurative, but schematized. When you talk about a field of latencies, look at these images: they are beautiful in their schematization, in their capacity to schematize.

CN: I would like to think of these images as workable material, not only as artifacts. So if they have a schematic status, it is a reflection of the fact that they are open-ended to the same extent that they are complete. Their fullness can be tweaked, intensified, worked further. They are both absolute and contingent, and, in that sense, both images and means of imagination. I use the word "imagination," but it is also a form of projection, like an action, which coincides with the images being models.

Audience: I was wondering why you chose modern projects. Could you not come up with a system from scratch and find a similar way to develop it? And why did it have to be *modern*, if there had to be a precedent? Why not another period in architecture? What is the significance of the modern?

CN: I do not believe in the "from scratch" part, but the 20th-century frame has to do with the tone, with the aggressive and ultimately distrusting attitude toward optimism that is a condition of the work, with its skepticism, perhaps. We use projects from modernity because of their sheer optimism, to squeeze them to the point of making them shout out things that they never claimed or dared claiming for, nor did their historical revision. It is not just about opposing a more mature attitude toward the city: rather, it is by looking into them attentively that one can both demystify their optimism, thereby neutralizing their violence, and take them to an extreme, thereby reviving them as if they were here, at work. The deterministic will of the modern project, one could think, did not go far enough in freeing also itself, and when criticizing its basis for being illusory, messianic, or violent, one has to be sure of offering an equally transformative stance, not just a regression. Héctor's project engaged with the Futurists with such fullness that its voices, often frightening, started to collide with each other in a symphony of haziness and uncertainty, overcoming their origin and, perhaps, formally being more literal about their claims. Earnestness can be a powerful force if treated as such, and not as a form of moralism. The literality to radical statements can be self-defeating and, as a consequence, self-transformative. That may be why utopias ended up in failure: they did not go far enough in regards to their candidness with humor. To work in such an arena and have a way out, one has to lose control of the conventions of discourse. Only this can create situations that one can work through. An optimistically disenchanted attitude toward optimism is at the base of the material's capability to reach out.

Audience 02: You said something interesting about finding conditions within the norm that are in tension with themselves rather than looking at these conditions from outside, and I am wondering what you do with the tension that is inherent to the norm, once you find it. Norms represent the generic, so I wonder what the work does with the generic.

CN: It idealizes it and therefore dismantles it through the singularities it engenders. You turn the norm into a driving force that, isolated and intensified to its purest form, exceeds its premises. Generality shifts, by means of the overspecificity it is necessarily made of, into its very opposite, which usually reveals itself as a myth. The architectural project succeeds when the singularity it creates out of the generic achieves a form that stands on its own and can be rationalized as a concept. But this concept is not created in advance, and that is the risk.

Audience 02: I am wondering if the way the representation of the work here exhibited is considered is from that same perspective.

CN: You mean as a form?

Audience 02: Exactly.

IA: Yes.

EN: Yes.

CN: Ok, yes, absolutely. *(laughs)* Honestly, I prefer to take a conservative attitude toward the material, partly due to practical matters but more importantly due to the fact that, by generalizing content through format, you radicalize its meaning. The fact that all drawings are square, the same size, same technique, same line-weight, black and white, and displayed at the same height at regular intervals has to do with format taking over and content being revealed through density, intensity, and variability at a finer level. This mechanism of flattening is very important to me and relates to something we do in the studio, whereby the organization of the work coincides with its expression at the deepest possible level. Projects are dry. Templates that command their organization are cold-blooded. And systematicity is taken to a point where representation reaches a zero degree and becomes operational. That is where I find a truer form of liberation. Curiously, it is under stress that the material encounters a ductile mode of being itself, less visual and more workable, and content finds its space of movement, less as a discourse and more as a the result of a construction.

IA: I think we can leave it here. Thank you, Erika, and thank you so much, Ciro. It was a wonderful conversation.

CN: Thanks to both of you, and to the students.

Note: This conversation was held at the Loeb Library of the Harvard University Graduate School of Design on Thursday, September 5, 2013, where an exhibition of the Utopioids design studio was on display. It was attended by students and professors of the school.

Interview

Hiromi Hosoya, Ciro Najle

Hiromi Hosoya: I would be interested in hearing your thoughts on simulation in design, or simulation as a tool. What are the tools, methodology, and processes that are important for your teaching, or that you use in the field of education?

Ciro Najle: The procedural agenda has to do with problematizing the state of things surrounding the influence of computation in architecture. This involves teasing out the tension between the incorporation of computation in the architectural practice to optimize the performance of buildings and deal fluently with complex geometric problems, and the constitution of new models for the real by means of consistent procedures, as if what is generated is not positioned externally from the technical repertoire of design. Design protocols are not merely formal mechanisms of optimizing performance but are also forces capable of expanding the spectrum of historical materials and the range of what they can do. I am interested in how the architectural procedure, under the influence of computation and nonlinear systems of control, is capable of looking for a new status for architecture at a deep structural level. Research (which sadly in the last few years has become a commodity and an autonomous niche of work) is not just about exploring open-endedly or creating peculiar formal or technological possibilities: it is also about transcending the critical stance of architecture as a whole by predicting a field of operation yet to come, however related to the current demands of practice.

Intrinsic to this idea is the structural redefinition of the discipline through the transformation of its medium. The idea of method, as loaded as it may be, is not to smoothly instrumentalize the practice, nor to radically criticize its basis, but rather to construct a medium within which to transcend that dichotomy through new forms of organization, with the purpose of redefining the field by means of the most radical conditions of production.

HH: What are you referring to when you say "new forms of organization"?

CN: Material organization—understanding material in a broad sense. The first level of architectural research nowadays has to do with the reduction of complication—basically, with handling difficulty and multiplicity. Well intended as it may sound, this level is practical and unmediated, and is of little disciplinary value. It is driven by problem solving and has a soft ground, no matter how serious its concerns may be. The second level has to do with creativity, in the sense of skillfully managing formal attributes for the purpose of instigating the consumption of space as an added value. Playful and charming as it may sound, this is self-defeating in the long run, as it only feeds the same anxiety that gave it rise. A third level of architectural research is used to imagine new forms of practice by means of the artificial simulation of the dynamics of present conditions. Often courageous, this level empties out the value of the discipline as an autonomous repository of knowledge, as it is rooted in a notion of powerlessness.

Finally, a fourth level subsumes all three—facilitation, creativity, and suppleness—within an artificial construct that stands on its own and claims its space as an organizational model in the world. Blunt, overly affirmative, and self-referential as it may be, this level, I believe, is not just another mode of practicing architecture within the full spectrum of diversity of the discipline; nor does it imply a further degree of complexity. Rather, it is a higher and more synthetic mode, and it is probably the one that can effectively turn research into something other than a comfortable service providing a luxurious pool of variants, or a rebellious practice. This model strives to bring together entirely distinct and, to a large extent, incompatible attitudes about the practice. So whereas the first mode of research is invested in enhancing the capabilities of architecture as a technical service, the second, in the idea of architecture as an autonomous space of form-creation, and the third, in the figure of the architect as a self-invited entrepreneur that unilaterally declares his/her social value, this last, model-oriented research assumes the figure of the architect operates as a broadminded cultural mobilizer who thinks simultaneously at different levels—and for a higher purpose—than each of them separately.

Propelling architecture toward model-based research has to do with the assumption that architecture is a field of strategic thinking that establishes procedural grounds for the material and spatial organization of the world, without conceding to the modern idea of architectural determinism. The problem with 20th-century megalomania, in my view, is not that it results in forms of organization that are too far-fetched but rather ones that are too cautious and moralistic in relation to the extraordinary forms of organization engendered by the forces of capitalism. Even those that initially appeared unrealistic, improbable, or utopian have, sooner or later, been embedded in production in an exaggerated or distorted form. Idealism fails for being a reductive caricature of the real. It falls short. Retroactive manifestos have denounced this but have unfortunately become machines for capitalizing on the leftovers, with a characteristic delay in cultural acceptance. How does architecture avoid becoming absorbed and continue to render itself relevant? Traditionally, it does so by shifting the direction of its vector and radically incorporating outer influences. Working on contemporary large-scale developments ("contemporary" being a problematic notion, in this context) means opening the door on new forms of organization in a rush, before they actually come into being. The myth of "surfing the wave" has grown weak in architecture, as we now recognize the wave as just a symptom of something else—as a phenomenon that comes just too late. Architecture must therefore seek out deeper levels of significance in the dynamics of the market, while remaining agile and fast. As hideous as the commercial drive may seem in comparison to the high-brow concerns of civic practice, architecture at the level of development enters the realm of ballistics: one must know in advance what things architecture can do and anticipate not only the volatile performance of buildings but also their deceptions and diversions. That is where complexity and computation enter into the field—to synthetize realms in an amoral way of practicing.

HH: Do you think that your conception of these levels of academic research applies equally to European, Asian, and American architectural education?

CN: It is a simplification, but I think that each culture develops an idiosyncratic approach, which tends to put more emphasis on one level or another. There are modalities, as well. But the need for synthesis runs across all cultures.

HH: During the last 15 years, you have taught at the Architectural Association in London, directing the Landscape Urbanism Graduate Program, at Cornell University, and at the Harvard University Graduate School of Design. The introduction of computation design into architecture has a brief history and seems to have evolved in parallel. Do you think that at each of these places and over time your attitude and methodology have changed?

CN: Yes, radically. But then, not so much, because at a basic level it has always been about the reciprocity between architectural organization and its medium. Perhaps the changes have more to do with time than they do with place. Fifteen years ago, London was very different in terms of the ideas we were pursuing, mostly because their cultural meaning has changed. My interests at that time had a lot to do with computation not being so established within the architectural debate: it was still a raw field of work, and technologies were much less advanced and disseminated. There was more room to create things, even by mistake.

So at that time, generally speaking, I adopted an attitude of seeming implacability and blind positivism. I sought in new technologies alignments with the project of modernity from the 1960s, looking for deviations and exacerbations of those models. My students would take this to extremes, and I would refuse to accept any trace of cynicism or humor in their work. It was sheer earnestness. At the level of theory behind the briefs, behind the programs, procedures, and ethics we would deal with, at the level of scale, or even at the level of how to engage with computer technologies, the projects would appear to follow different frames coming from modernism, but they would exaggerate them to the point where an internal break or paradox would emerge. The mechanic was taken to the level of the machinic. Linearity was surpassed by nonlinearity. Logical causality was displaced by temporal causality. Rationality was expanded by multitasking and unpredictability. Heteronomy turned into a complex form of autonomy. Interdisciplinary exchange was absorbed into broader forms of disciplinary consistency. Determinism was strengthened by an intuitive but rigorous systematicity. The naturalization of norms was challenged by normative self-estrangement. Dumbness was iterated to the point of reaching complexity. Top-down organization reversed into self-learning organization. Technique was taken from instrumenting strategies to constructing self-defeating devices. Novelty became an abstract condition. The work would engage and follow, one by one, modern principles, figures, standards, or mandates, with the hidden purpose of alienating them from within. The idea was to overcome modernism by its own means rather than fight against it through critique.

The thinking about the technologies had a different register, which was provocative by default. It was unsettling and disruptive to be positivistic about them. But during the process, some of those ideas started to filter into practice—every time more efficiently deployed—to the point where, around the mid-2000s, entire research departments in corporate offices were established, becoming the basic standard. As I saw this happening, I realized that this ruthless optimism was losing its force and that some form of cynicism had to be acknowledged and turned positive. This is when the work I am doing at the GSD started to take form.

HH: When were you teaching at the Architectural Association?

CN: From 1998 to 2004. I was at Cornell from 2004 to 2008 and then came to the GSD. The levels of research we were talking about earlier somehow coincide with these periods and establish a cultural frame for them: I slowly shifted the agenda of my research in relation to these frames to preserve its vitality. In the past couple of decades, certain structural ideas that were formerly related to the influence of complexity and nonlinearity in architecture slowly turned into technical assets, associated in a straightforward way with the effects of computation, and then into formal ones, rendered as a stylistic frame. That is perhaps how ideas progress within culture in general—and how, by the decay and displacement of their frameworks, they get renewed and persist. One has to sense and accept those changes and reach out for diversions that will be able to go against the grain—even contradict one's own discourse—and so escape forward in a context where structural changes are becoming thinner and ideas are smoothly adopted by the industry, the market, or the status quo. It is a matter of how divergent potential melts down into yet another form of efficacy that we tend to associate with progress. That capture does not make them obsolete, though. It is rather the evidence that they are now embedded in a larger form of organization, for which they were, so to speak, constructed. But in order to stay alive, they have to transform themselves.

HH: Can you explain a bit more about how frameworks decay?

CN: Research is a medium to conquer territories unidentified or otherwise obscure, not a means of achieving objectives. So method, for me, is a way to reach out into the world, looking for new conditions with respect to those that architectural culture has managed to accept. In this context, decay is the process by which open-ended methods turn into settled methodologies that aim to replicate their achievements over and over, each time more resourcefully, and systematize those resources with absolute independence from the cultural meaning that those methods hold as regards their history. Decay is the process by which an agenda becomes a program, by which research becomes a technology of doing. This involves two different, perhaps opposite (or complementary) ideas of method. As alluring as the idea of a formal method may be, it means both the success of the work and the death of its drive, because it gains in power what it loses as a mobilizing force. In that sense, I try to see my work always as an "as if" condition:

in this case, "as if" I were searching for a method. As much as I look for clarity and simplicity, I also look for new areas of obscurity, and I would find it terrifying to see this mix of method and search crystalize and settle. This does not make the doing merely chaotic or rebellious: one must retain the will to increase the sophistication of methods while accepting their radical change, as that is ultimately our responsibility as artists and/or thinkers.

In this context, the anxiety of the industry is equally dual: on the one hand, constantly attacking new methods as implausible, and on the other, voraciously turning them into workable mechanisms of reproducibility. A series of fertile methods was pinned down for industrial purposes and synthetized under a format. The story evolves through workshops and seminars into formal skills, new types of expertise, and a whole accelerated industry. And that scenario evolves into official versions of software that, paradoxically, end up being first used in the industry and then adopted in academia, as if following a technological achievement. Decay means research getting reversed in this way.

HH: The scenario you describe in which a mix of method and research moves backward from industry to academia is extremely interesting. Do you think this is still happening?

CN: Yes, although less charmingly. It has become ubiquitous, a common practice, something you cannot ignore. It happens anonymously and has become almost natural. So the problem, at this stage, is different.

HH: In this context, what are your ambitions? How do you plan on achieving them?

CN: For a few years now I have dedicated myself to contextualize the work at a cultural level. Before, I would do this only implicitly, but it became obvious that inscribing the work beyond the pressures of unmediated production and political reaction has become crucial. Perhaps there is some melancholia in this, but reclaiming a self-conscious yet open-ended ethics, in which computation is an open field with provocative cultural impact, has become key to bypassing the false dialectics between a soft interdisciplinary research, a quasi-concerned social practice, and a lax politics of autonomy. I aim to help reconstruct a form of cultural awareness that does not weigh on the architect's shoulders as a political commentary but rather potentiates the impact of technology within the discipline and its practice.

A large part of architecture culture of the past decade has been regressive. But still, I believe this to be a very interesting moment—a moment of maturity, and of synthesis—in which one can do many different things. Extremely reactionary attitudes are present nowadays, some of them intelligent, but opportunistic. There is also plenty of denial, which easily falls short at a theoretical level, only developing niches of protection from the mainstream. Attitudes of self-imposed naivety or pseudosimplicity and forms of lightness or wittiness appear to be sympathetic but only for a short time, because at their core they are negative. But that was never what brought us here.

To my way of thinking, effort must be put into developing a synthetic attitude toward the complexification of architecture culture, now less vehemently and more thoughtfully. A more difficult stance of postcrisis maturity needs to be developed, to reconstruct the broader disciplinary model already in play, only this time based on a more cautious mediation of technology.

HH: Let me back up a little bit. When you think of traditional forms of simulation in architecture—sketches, diagrams, blueprints, models—what do you consider their advantages and disadvantages in comparison with computer simulations?

CN: The advantages have to do with understanding the radical transformation of the medium of architecture. Through drawings, images, illustrations, instructions, principles, assessments, critiques, treatises, documents, and the like, architecture traditionally has assumed the notion that ideas are detached from matter and evolve independent of it. The classical idea of "project" is grounded in this way of thinking. The advent of the virtual in architecture involves incorporating not only a new form of representation within the palette of disciplinary resources but also a whole different way of thinking through the project. This does not involve a relaxation of architecture's will, as is customarily assumed; nor does it preclude the use of our classical ability to conceive and project the material world. Quite the opposite, it means a radical empowerment of projection, to the point where it becomes emancipated from the despotic pressures of immaterial idealism.

That is how I see simulation operating, as opposed to representation. It involves a whole other form of practice, because it releases the traditional representational medium from its critical dependence on decisions that perform above and beyond it. In a virtual medium, the conceptual level is inscribed in and coevolves with the material. This advantage is also a disadvantage. One must think within the medium and learn to accept that there is nothing else without giving up exteriority. Ideas here evolve as materials evolve, but that does not dissolve either of them. The reaction to this alleged dissolution is equally misleading, as it fails to regard the virtual as a mobilizing medium, responding with fear and moralism to its radical amorality, which is anything but neutral. The role of medium has become altogether different. It is no longer autonomous in the traditional sense. But it is not only about sheer making either. It is about thinking through the making. Premodern as this may sound, the virtual model is beyond the dichotomies that modernists created and that postmodernists did nothing but denounce, criticize, or omit. Virtual simulation is ductile, but that does not necessarily make it docile. It allows for continuous variation, but that does not make it merely play. It can be adjusted constantly, but that does not make it indulgent. It can produce newness from within, but that does not make it only a means for innovation and illusory progress. Simulation behaves, again, "as if" it were matter, although it is not. It works like chiseling, and that is where the discipline enters, not before. Without having understood that this shift does not prevent a project's consistency nor obscure its affirmative or its critical position, contemporary culture has initiated a return to the representational based on a false diagnosis and shallow premises.

HH: You do not use the word "simulation" to mean the imitation of an operation. What does simulation mean to you?

CN: I am using "simulation" because the conversation turned in this direction, but I would rather think of the construction of a medium that, on its way, simulates phenomena. I would say that simulation is the virtual medium that selectively incorporates pieces of information from reality, assuming this incorporation to be not only a reduction (and, as such, not reality) but also more of a deliberate and eventually conscious process by itself. Any simulation thus implies a system that makes it possible. This system is based on a model, or a manifold of models, and the more these coalesce into a consistent form, the more a simulation becomes autonomous and self-supporting, even if it aims to make available a form of reality. Far beyond resemblance, simulation enables the construction of new "forms" of reality. To me, that is the ultimate architectural project.

HH: What is the level of consciousness about this among students? Where in the design process do you locate the threshold between the analog and the digital, where the students shift from working with the pencil to working with the mouse?

CN: I would say that the consciousness is high, particularly when students give in to the system that they create. In those cases, medium and author become one and the same: a subjective consciousness at a deep level. In terms of tooling, I would not say that this form of authorship necessarily requires moving from the pencil to the mouse, as everybody already does that, to start with. The pencil may help in curious ways, but what I see happening (and I do not know to what extent I am contributing to this) is that students most often work without any pencil whatsoever. I have students (usually the most skilled ones) who do not crystalize information on paper at all, not even numerical information. It all takes place through the screen and is not registered elsewhere.

I also encounter awkward forms of writing: broken, trembling, nonhierarchical, almost childish or archaic, as if they had no control whatsoever on the trace and movements of the pencil. Drawing happens increasingly through the writing of notes aside the model, to aid its control. Because I believe in the physical encounter of brain and paper, my approach is to disrupt the process of information transfer as much as possible without obscuring its intelligence, which is often opaque but charming in its carelessness and apparent incompetence. I often make students think through a mix between hand movements and vectors. Drawing nowadays is not about sketching but about running vectors by hand. I believe this to be a skill that architects did not have 30 years ago (except for certain geniuses) but that now could become common practice. It is beautiful to think through the process of vectorial drawing and topological construction with the pencil. Without it, the process can grow immaterial in a manner that is no longer productive, as if it were only an exercise. It becomes detached and unrestricted, and loses its character.

HH: Do you think that skilled students are using the mouse as if it were an analog tool?

CN: More than an object that inscribes lines, the mouse is a device that manages positions, relations, movements, and binary decisions. The notion of the mouse as a means of performance, merging brain and body in a quite direct sense, makes thinking about a project a problem of relative relations in a virtual space, a process of yes/no operations and more-or-less displacements.

HH: Do you think that your students can use the design method that they learn in a real setting of practice?

CN: I cannot follow them all, but I am very proud of what they do. There are students that enter normative practices and use these skills. Others apply what they have learned as a design methodology, or as a working method that establishes an open mindset toward addressing problems. Other students enter experimental practices and continue the work through other networks, and there are those who run their own practices and do their best to succeed. Finally, quite a few have entered academia and started their own research. They all feed back into my work, in one way or another.

HH: What are the benefits of parametric design, as such? What are its limits? Looking into the future, how do you think parametric design is going to evolve?

CN: The first limitation is probably in calling it "parametric," in that it reinforces the interpretation of the virtual medium as a means to increase accuracy in design. In relation to the future, I would say that the more it establishes itself as a form of doing, the more limited it will become. So if the work does not constantly reset itself through a feedback loop with production, as if under examination in an over-lit laboratory, and if it does not create an internal circuit of cultural self-awareness, it will eventually evolve into a technology. One can discuss whether technological progress is meaningful for architecture and, if so, in what sense. Or if technological progress is a market operation designed to keep architecture moving, or a political operation to keep it soft and well behaved. I believe this problem to be a full responsibility of the architect with regard to his/her discipline. One should not blame the market but learn from it and see how to use its forces. What is key, I think, is the cultural refreshment of architecture, so that it remains instrumental without losing its edge, or transformative power.

The recent rebooting of computation in architecture, which has taken the form of parametric design, has to do with computation becoming historically relevant and settling as the substrate of a movement. But this development has its own paradoxes. Many are invested in this process but fewer have taken it to a cultural level. I think the future of computation in architecture will not be about itself. As it evolves it becomes more and more naturalized, so it will eventually make no difference to make it a style, a method, or a trend as such. Rather, one has to defetishize it and render it proactive in a broader sense–that is, to denaturalize it alongside this process of naturalization.

From my point of view, far too often people are talking about control, about effects, or about both: this leaves room for others to capitalize on this closed debate as being generally narrow-minded. The paternalistic discourses that result from these reactions allegedly engage with the real directly, altogether disregarding the potential of the medium that makes new forms of architecture possible.

There is still too much fetishizing of the computer. Fortunately, though, computation for the sake of computation has not yet exhausted the notion that, by means of it, architecture can unfold as an open practice without losing any of its autonomy; rather, it gains in power and consistency. This apparently paradoxical gain connects architecture to disciplines as disparate as cooking and information management, not only in the way it manages complexity or smooths out interactions but also in the potentially authoritative position it takes while performing those operations. In that sense, the appeal of architecture to its historical role of exerting by accompanying power—that is, its will of generality and its capability of thinking across problems synthetically—can be seen as a form within which the impact of computation is far from having been exhausted. Refreshing the idea of the way to work means learning higher capabilities of managing disparate ingredients, integrating incompatible languages, working through irreducible processes, and predicting irreversible temporal conditions. This has always been the skill of the architect, and it is now grounded in a concrete and constructible medium rather than on experience, intuition, and oral communication.

HH: Considering the current state of architecture, it is obvious that important design decisions are still made by people. Simulation tools are still used to complement the architect's primary tools. Why should one pursue an education in computational design in architecture?

CN: I tend to see computation as something closer to a weapon than to a tool. The computer is not merely an instrument: at this point it is quite literally one with you—a continuation of your mind. Our minds: not a mind of its own. The idea that the computer is the "other" of architecture, or else its seamless facilitator, is extremely schematic and figurative. It is a myth that creates monsters, against whom we must fight or else surrender, instead of agents of empowerment that we necessarily mediate, and which enhance intelligence and action in the world, for good or for bad. Since when is art a moralistic construct? Any architect who thinks of him- or herself as a thinker has the duty to transcend his or her limits, as well as those of the discipline. The computer is, in that context, a medium of transcendence, able to construct an artificial form of intelligence and behavioral complexity. And that challenge, by itself, is a huge space of work.

A–Z

Farshid Moussavi Ciro Najle

Awe is an affection resulting from an encounter with the sublime and is therefore enmeshed with an individual's subjectivity. For this reason it can only be an indirect act of an architect. It can only be triggered by other means, which fully take over the individual's attention without managing it directly. A sudden, overwhelming presence; a far-too-complex construct; an exceeding intelligence; a superb, irreducible being; a giant; a quick glance at a desired object; a deep extension; a dark imagination; an abyss: all can produce awe.

Blob formless, orderless, structureless, tasteless, greedy, gluttonous, sticky, disgusting, cheap, vulgar, horrifying, voracious, unstoppable, undefined, faceless, swelling, abnormal, curvy, fluffy, vague, indistinct, irreducible, primitive, one, and many. Its power lies not on force, persuasion, impact, influence, clarity, effectiveness, precision, dominance, or control but on sheer unintelligibility. So does its weakness. Used in architecture, it unifies the multiplicity of elements at play, thus reducing the complexity of a building.

Consistency along with complexity, pursued as an image rather than a performance, can be a consequence of the sheer excitement of using digital fabrication tools, which can cut any number of any shape. But true complexity includes the invisible in buildings, too. An iPhone does not look complex but is one of the most complex objects we have around. Consistency is therefore an operative ethics of managing complexity and its derivatives in order to surpass apparent complexity—that is, complication for the self-exhausting sake of complication.

Data the quantitative values that compute the conditions of an entity, phenomenon, relationship, or state of things, is not the thing itself but its codification through definitions that operate as a vehicle for its analysis, diagnosis, evaluation, simulation, and organization. More than a means of management, data is pre-architectural by definition: it is the plural "datum" onto which manifold organizations are—or can be—constructed. Once things are constructed, the sense of things does not require the data, which exists outside the thing itself, as mediation.

Empathy is subjective and therefore can be positive or negative. Nevertheless, repeated encounters with buildings can lead to habits of use that become unconscious. To discard habits and enable new experiences, buildings must be dissociated from conventions around which they are organized. The agency of architects lies not in determining empathies but in disrupting them, thus preventing them from becoming routine. Empathy is in equal measure the best friend of conservative architecture (its favorite source of self-confirmation) and the worst enemy of the materialist architect (whose sensitivity is as fine and sophisticated as it is hardhearted).

Function —often associated directly with use, according to the deterministic ethos of the functionalist tradition—more broadly involves the general relationship of something to something else, of which it is a function; yet seldom is the relationship one-to-one. Function is how things correspond, deny, reject, attract, constrain, become, determine, or even ignore one another—that is, what things do to each other, under what particular modality, in a net. Consequently, they make something unique and distinct from themselves. The function of a corridor, for example, is not in itself but rather the result both of what that corridor is comprised of and of that which remains outside the corridor, to which it corresponds.

Global practice of architecture has brought unease among architecture critics such that the architectural identity of nations is being erased. However, the same process that breeds similarities generates differences, too, albeit on another scale. To see them, it is necessary to look at reality differently. The nostalgia for long-lost identities—as artificial as anything else—and the desperation about belonging—at this point, inevitably hypocritical—requires being overcome by an appetite for singularity within the generic and for developing new capabilities and finer, more resolute, detached sensitivities. More than loss, this involves courage, imagination, and vehemence.

History is a repository of architectural material embedded with inertia, constraints, propensity, and latency; a source of organizations, modalities, models, types, techniques, operations, and ethics embedded with productive resistance. Seen through the materialists' eyes, history is a pool of abstract knowledge, a mine of learning and working power, waiting to be dissected, unfolded, expanded, and taken to higher extremes and outer thresholds. To enable these actions, knowledge from the past—whether in the form of architectural concepts or in the form of design techniques—must be dissociated from its original motives or causes to reveal its ahistorical material content and become the seed for addressing new architectural scenarios.

Intelligence is gained through training the mind to think, whereas expertise is gained through receiving already known knowledge. Because no two design scenarios are ever the same, to engage them actively design needs intelligence rather than expertise. Intelligence involves defining interesting problems before assuring perfect solutions, questioning the repetition of the same each time rather than endlessly calibrating its effectiveness, and interrogating the default rather than applying it automatically and proficiently. Intelligence, therefore, necessarily has embedded within it a second level, through which it constantly redefines its own ground of certainties and premises: call it "the will of self-alienation."

Joints are the evidence of inconsistencies and differences in kind that become distinguishable within the material continuum as a result of the segregation of problems in domains of thought, fields of expertise, realms of practice, or disconnected organizations and objectified as irreducible architectural entities. The expression of that evidence is usually called "detail": smart solutions to frequently unchallenged problems.

But there is another way to think of joints—as that which is inherent in any assemblage composed of heterogeneous elements that enter into relations with one another and cohere into a consistency. This, however, does not mean that joints do not exist, as consistency is an operation rather than a form. Heterogeneities and assemblages, such as buildings, can have many joints and yet be consistent.

Kitsch as opposed to the "authentic," can be pursued deliberately to make things easy to understand and easy to sell. But it can also be pursued intentionally in order to rescue things from the burden of originality and authenticity. Paradoxically, in the first case, kitsch works as an authentic release from the burden of intellectual mediation, while in a second instance (and in successive ones) it becomes an increasingly mediated artistic procedure that is consciously destined to emancipate, thus reintroducing the distance that it fights against through various forms of self-conscious humor. These forms take over its allegedly original instantaneity.

Limits can be seen as restrictive of freedom, when regarded through the lens of the author's indulgent subjectivity, or as the objective tightening of the space of work, when considered from the point of view of the work of architecture itself and its procedure. Under both registers, the limitlessness of an outstanding piece of architecture is nothing but intensified and provided sense, autonomy, and strength by limitations. When limit is considered not in terms of the architect's own authorship but in terms of the architect as an agent, it is no longer restrictive of freedom. Instead it becomes a platform from which individuals are liberated from conforming to forces that encourage habit and passivity over conscious choice in the way they are encountered in everyday life. In this sense, limit for an architect embraces the notion of responsibility without requiring the sacrifice of freedom.

Model is an anexact system of development that integrates a series of material (physical, structural, sensorial) traits and is able to respond to a multiplicity of concerns. It generates different objects in space and time, such as the Gothic system, comprised of a pair of crossed roof arches with a polygonal ground plan, buttressed by side arches. The height of the central and side arches could vary (being either equal or different in height), as could the shape of the plan, resulting in singular cathedrals. Models mutually restrict their internal relationships through modalities, integrating them into wholes—multiplicities—that are simultaneously stable and unpredictable, generic and singular, structured and ductile, consistent and contingent, normal and normative, precise and open-ended, thus challenging the schematic assumption that in order for architecture to achieve relevance, it has to give up its inherent desire for permanence and universality.

Nature is one of architecture's most conceptually exuberant and theoretically inexhaustible inventions, prolific (as it has been throughout history) in generating organizational models, points of view, spectrums of imagination, ethical mandates, and visual paraphernalia. Nature is the counterpart of architecture within architecture: its other side embedded within, its most unexpected self, its other inside, monstrous, without which it appears as if it would have never been born. Nature is wilderness, chaos, order, pre-architecture, landscape, ground, ecology, systems dynamics, a paradigm of beauty and ugliness, a model of uncertainty, or a pet, depending upon architecture. However defined, an inventive nature, hard or soft, creates an ecology of parts that is not separated from culture.

Organization defines the practice of an architect and involves numerous things that must be gathered into a single context to bring about economic, structural, informational, social, or climatic effects, among others. It is conventionally interpreted as the unification of things into a coherent whole, whereas it can also be approached as the arrangement or hanging together of disparate elements without unity. No matter how it is considered, organization implies making choices, both aesthetic and political. Inherently tendentious, organization involves the (desirable) reduction of particularities for the construction of a collective order that qualitatively exceeds in value the sum of its parts. Organization operates before and beyond form, and surpasses its figural and superficial connotations through the coordination of inner structures. Organization involves added value and ever-higher levels of thought at each stage of its process. It is the hard bone of architecture as a generalist discipline.

Planning involves the idea that the initiative of the private (even if public) and the practice of the architect are submitted to the common interest. What remains uncertain is what stands for and holds together this idea of the common: what guides its visions, what the time span of its mindset is, how far into the future it is projected, how proactively or reactively it proceeds, what its medium and techniques of mediation are, how general it attempts to be, and how much it determines, overwhelms, or calibrates cases. In this context, organizational models contain and surpass the straightjacket of ideological form, out of a more robust idea of process and a stronger will of organization: the paradigm of clarity, overcome by that of sturdiness. The interesting aspect of planning today is that it is culturally bounded. Planning in France is entirely different from planning in the UK, which is again different from planning in the US and Japan and, no doubt, very different from planning in China. At a time when mobility of technologies, materials, and designers is contributing to sameness in architecture, planning is a source of difference. Planning is ultimately a matter of speed, quality, level of democracy, and sense of drama. It is therefore anything but irrelevant for an architect.

Quantity and Quality are two sources of difference and expression, and are inseparable from one another. There is no quality that does not have quantity as an inherent measure of its intensity, and there is no quantity that carries no quality. The choice of what quantity of a quality or of what quality in a quantity is a matter of aesthetics and politics. But as large amounts of material, exceedingly large organizations, massive quantities of information, extremely slow or rapid processes, and exceptionally multifarious levels engender, through quantitative excess, new forms of quality that are irreducible to normal standards, the relationship between the two goes beyond their polarity and complementarity, to become integrated in a single concept, the expression of which overwhelms both politics and aesthetics.

Representation in architecture—drawings, schemes, diagrams, statements, documents, pamphlets, sketches, images, blueprints—is itself architecture in the classical sense: culture's means of description and control of matter. Seen at that level of generality and under that ontological register, whose active role in history ranges from the classical treatises—and their building collections—to the manifestos of modern architecture—and their pavilions, monuments, exhibitions, installations, or prototypes—representation in architecture is probably as influential as buildings themselves and, perhaps, more capable of enduring. Representation's inborn paradox is to be the physical manifestation of architecture's intangibility. However, representation is ultimately a way to archive narratives outside the design process itself. Thinking of drawings as representation suggests that architects have developed architectural ideas in their minds and then used drawings to communicate them. Given how complex and multilayered buildings are, this is impossible. If we were to design buildings in our head, they would be very simple buildings. Drawings construct ideas for the assembly of the myriad of elements of which buildings are comprised. Drawings, used not as an archive of the past or as the re-presentation of what we already know but rather as tools to design, are constructions of what has not existed before. They are therefore presentations, not representations.

Systematicity is a mode of operating that views reality as vital, dynamic, and open, but it should not be confused with rule-following. As Wittgenstein states in his *Philosophical Investigations*, published in 1953, "no course of action could be determined by a rule, because any course of action can be made out to accord with the rule." Beyond rules and broader than logical set-ups, systematicity involves the embedment of internal consistency in actions as they happen—the codification and organization of becoming processes as they unfold in time. Through systematicity, architectural technique frees itself from the straightjacket of technocracy and embraces its responsibility for contingency. Systematicity implies absorbing all forms of chance in a project as deliberate and wished for, turning them into the constituents of authorship and making them inherent to the architect's will in regards to the object.

The sublime is the beautiful taking the sudden form of a synthetic thought, simultaneously engaging and rejecting the mere enjoyment of things and thus elevating the aesthetic experience from the sensible into the purely mental. The sublime is the ultimate "as if" condition. It involves the unmediated encounter with the unknown under rigorously controlled conditions, bringing into the world a completely abstract form of life that overturns any standard of niceness. Ordinariness and generality, when potentiated through radical skepticism, become sublime, rather than kitsch or common. The word "sublime" has been used to refer to that which is unpresentable. This usage of the word does not seem to define space for architecture but rather an experience of self-transcendence through indeterminate realities.

Ubiquity the experience of that which is everywhere, is today most generated by digital connectivity. Whether it regards reading a book, buying something, watching a performance, making a transaction, or socializing, it can be everywhere and is therefore ubiquitous. Architecture, however, is not about being everywhere but about being somewhere. It has bounds, definiteness, and ending. In spite of this, architecture's dream of being everywhere has gone through various paradigms. While one extreme associates ubiquity with generality, extensiveness, infiniteness, lack of borders, repetition, indifference, neutrality, simplicity, blankness, and dominion, the other extreme achieves ubiquity by means of the opposite values: singularity, intensiveness, irreducibility, self-affirmation, variegation, differentiation, specificity, complexity, potential, and power. The question of architecture at a time of globalization is how to synthesize the two within a single model.

Vitality is not a (rather illustrative) matter of securing physical movement, programmatic flexibility, systemic adaptability, material endurance, human participation, or ecological or biological content in the architectural project but instead, a matter of how life, as a force, is embedded in organization both abstractly and performatively. Life is the name of the intangible in architecture, which, after having lost its aura, has possibly encountered concrete mechanisms for enduring. In *Complexity and Contradiction in Architecture* (1966), Robert Venturi writes, "I am for vitality as well as validity," and "I am for messy vitality over obvious unity [...] for the implicit function as well as the explicit function." This proposition for the play between the aesthetic and the practical defines the agency of an architect: to select, prioritize, and assemble elements and parameters, and in doing so, give life to a building. "Validity," "messy," and "function" were interpreted too literally, however, within the postmodern "style," resulting in buildings that stood as representations of a dualism between implicit and explicit function rather than buildings where the two cofunction to generate the unseen.

Work is a building, a plan, a diagram, a text, a book, or a strategy for an urban development. In this sense of the word, "work" is not mere effort but encounters with different subjects and mediums that result in new creations, which in turn can serve as the basis for other encounters and new insights, resulting in other work. If work commonly means that energy has been transferred between systems by means of forces, what remains to be seen, each time, in architecture, is what source of power inflicts those forces—what the unavoidable and/or available constraints are, what the changes induced in matter as a result are, and what in turn their new latent power is, all of which the architect claims as the result of his/her will.

X-ray is a metaphor for making visible the invisible; that is, the incorporeal, virtual, pre-architectural condition of architecture—its invisible organizations, energies, processes, relationships, dynamics, transfers, and exchanges—seen as matter. When the invisible became visible in architecture, not only did the discipline encounter a myriad of new possibilities but more importantly, the idea itself of possibility was rendered obsolete, surpassed by the idea of potential. Information took over the medium, and the architect was as empowered as urged into the managerial. The challenge today is how to remain in charge of—and responsible for—this power as it becomes fully available. The dichotomy of the architect as manager or ideologue is a fallacy. Architects who act as managers can be as ideological about their commitment to architecture as a service as those whose commitment is to an architecture of pure ideas. Once we abandon dichotomies, we begin to see other ways that architects can use information, treating it as raw matter for tactical thinking. An informed architect is an agent able to propose ideas that shift or change a given reality rather than "ideals" that float independently and allow the status quo to remain. The architect's commitment is not to service pure ideas but to be political—to engage with life in order to change it.

Yes rather than no, can lead to opportunities, a new journey, an adventure, a new work. In architectural practice saying no is often considered a form of resistance to conventions, such as established rules, generic projects, low budgets, and so on. But rather than disengaging from the processes that shape built form, saying yes implies becoming imperceptible, immersing oneself in the specific forces that shape each built form and steering them into a line of flight or escape from conventions. Saying yes, therefore, is a way to be political. The politics of yes is the politics of full embracement, which involves both a detached and a resolute form of acting, as if there were no time left. Such politics implies overcoming the realm of politics as an end in itself and entering into the realm of sheer undertaking.

Zeitgeist or the spirit of the time, involves the assumption that architect and architecture, rather than constructs, are the passive expression of their time. Problems with this: one, architect and architecture are allegedly preceded and fully explainable by their epoch, and reducible to it; two, epochs are closed, coherent apparatuses instead of open-ended, divergent manifolds; three, epochs are constructed a posteriori by the historian or critic as if happening in real time instead of being unpredictably constructed and unfolded by their doers (who include historians and critics); and four, as alluring as the concept of spirit may be, it always involves the assumption that matter is elsewhere, detached from its divine and unreachable status. To these, pure subjectivity, free will, or radical expression are not thought-provoking alternatives but the other side of the same myth, burdening the subject to the same extent as they apparently liberate it. Seen from within, the Zeitgeist is what is constructed at every action, following and/or against the manifold previous ones, which inhabit history as if a flatland of coexisting lives. This is, in turn, constructed on the basis of models, without which no theory is possible—or, as historian Fernand Braudel states, "no theory, no history." And it is not abstract, not merely personal, not arbitrary, and especially, not one among many possible others in a field of endless—and valueless—possibilities. Rather, epochs are constructed along planes of consistency, themselves constructed on the way. Zeitgeist is, in this sense, an easy way out of the present and its manifold becoming, of which we are—authorial—forces.

Note: This text is the result of a series of brief e-mail exchanges regarding concepts proposed in turns, commenced by one and elaborated by the other, over the course of one to 24 hours.

Inside
Anna Font

Inventions

The drawings by Day Jiménez and Ostap Rudakevych featured on pages 176–77 of this volume show a process of distribution of residential units in relation to each of the amenities present in the field of a gated community. Each residential unit, as well as every program, is composed of a central point and a circle, the size of which is proportional to the extension of the activity it contains. The simple measure of an unsustainable proximity of a house to a golf course, a body of water, or a park triggers a displacement, the vectorial description of which repositions the house in the field, thus resolving the contingent relation and, as a result, differentiating the collective organization and qualifying the overall environment.

The idea of organization here goes far beyond the dichotomy between the tight prescription of order and the ideas of randomness or looseness. Each unit finds its (an)exact place in the field by being part of a tensioned system of relationships articulated by local rules, and its presence is frictioned by the same forces that brought it there, hence making every single one particular and irreducible. It signals the fact that such petty operations (move) running in just one dimension (the plan) are able to unfold, as if effortlessly, the wide range of organizational inventions resulting from this process of distributing singularities: cantilevered houses, star-shaped family huts, top-of-the-rock belvederes, sparkling neighborhoods. The only reason that these extraordinary situations arise is simply due to the suspension of complexity at the very moment of a local operation, and the candid embrace of problems as if they were, in their primitiveness, unique opportunities of novelty: trivial inventions.

Formats

Two important pillars of the discussions that frequently transpire from this research are the avoidance of grandiloquence and the application of extreme degrees of specificity—apparently obsessive specificity—directed at the development of new forms of intelligence. These degrees of specificity are commonly assessed as rigor, but that is only their condition of existence. Take, for instance, discussions on scale. If, by chance, somebody zooms in on the plan on page 202 by Mariusz Klemens and Steven Yingnien Chen, what becomes evident is that the problem of scale is not associated with architectural convention (1:100, 1:500, 1:1000); nor is it a subsidiary of a full-scale mock-up, either. The model is itself a 1:1 construct, conceived as 1:1 and developable as a complex entity. This implies the treatment of the project as is, not filtered through a representational platform.

This mode of work assumes that the simplicity of an object inherently contains a complexity in the process of how it is formed, leaving behind the mindset that relies on architectural conventions to represent it, and, instead, opening up a whole other space where design is nourished by the management of large amounts of information. This brings the need of new formats that can enable the strategic use of the material at each stage in the process, such that the project can identify, force, induce (not imagine) the manifold relationships already at work, conceptualizing their logics without closing them prematurely.

Action-driven catalogs, one could claim, like those of Dongjae Cho and Fred Chung on pages 148–53, organize what otherwise would have been a general intuition about how atrium buildings distribute their programs vertically. Their 81 plan and 81 section layout (here presented as 9 by 9 grids) elevate the material to the status of sheer variability, configuring a ductile tool for atrium design, grounded in protocols of existing types and yet superseding them. The construction of these planes of consistency through humble and ruthless studies of otherwise ordinary organizations is the prerequisite for the development of generic sublime models, patience and attentive observation being their central challenge.

Uniqueness

The capacity to be strategic with the ad hoc manipulation and opportunistic use of self-produced material is key to the uniqueness of these models. In the process of unfolding their poignant singularity there are many families of procedures. There is Lucas Correa-Sevilla and Zhou Wu's joyful reification, where a (twice-mirrored) data-field suddenly becomes the massing strategy of a mixed-use development in the most straightforward, blunt manner. The combination of programs, their relative position, and the densities surveyed in a series of cases are quantitatively equalized in far-fetched volumetric scenarios, as sublime as unexpectedly creative, entering in a direct dialogue with Hugh Ferris's most radical imaginary of Manhattan. While in Data-Form the variation formulates alternatives to actually define a single idea, Max Wong's Obus Interchange lives in the realm of productive variability, or else, in the realm where restrictions and relationships, having been recognized, abstracted, evaluated, and filtered, take on the form of self-supporting systems variables. A frenetic engineering intelligence, controlling everything from the inclination and kinks of the floor plates to the angle between wings and the vertical distribution, leads the model in a systematic direction that results in a beautifully proportioned and yet radical architectural device. Extreme, cold-blooded candidness and wild, hysterical intelligence: both cases simultaneously qualify as unique artifacts and straightforward machines, the first in a bold statistical mode and the second of an efficiency-driven nature.

Megalomania

The megalomaniac nature of these proposals corresponds to the serial endeavor of the research and appears as an inherent requirement for the unfolding of the consistency of the agenda. The general idea of the series is grounded in the configuration of a model that is put in crisis and complexified over time. There is simultaneously an effort to be current and to stay naïve. In turn, the arena of the discipline in the context of which this dual challenge becomes relevant and necessary takes the form of an apparently stagnant framework that must urgently be overcome by redefining its premises. The aim is to conquer new territories and install new discussions in the field: not general discussions but rather polemical ones, different from those already established. In this context, one can refer to how models are set up as a platform of design. Kaz Yoneda's sets of drawings that aim at the configuration of islands that mix braided river patterns and housing towers (pages 134–37) configure not just a creative design tool but a complex, self-contained machine that runs across the established notions of the practice of architecture, defining a common datum where one mode is made to correspond to another. A set of relationships defines, at the same time, the geometrical unit of a social housing bar—quantity and size of spaces in relation to the generative curve of a river braid—as well as the opening and vertical branching of the bars as formations around an island, allowing birds to migrate in and out. The building is simultaneously an architectural, landscape, and ecological device. Its mass functions as a medium to filter the organization of the ground and also of the air. This filtering capability feeds back into the architectural scheme. The square footage, number of rooms, and proportions of each apartment are typologically grounded while made dependent on its height above water level, surprisingly linking, for instance, the conditions of ventilation to the trajectory of mayflies. The wide scope of problems that the architectural object mediates, far more than its scale, is what constitutes its megalomaniac condition. But furthermore, this megalomania is not all-inclusive, not merely cumulative, not just expansive, as if a comprehensive form of control were its target. Its material is manifold, but its construction is singular and takes the form of a cultural manifesto.

Non-site

In the same way that the dismantling of the conventions commonly associated with scale sets off the argument for a broader understanding about what constitutes research material—ranging from the micro to the macro and from the catalog to the manifesto—an analogous crisis of the conventional idea of site guides the understanding of the kind of universality proposed by the work. Broadly speaking, a site in architecture is framed as a series of idiosyncratic findings related to a piece of land that help characterize it and identify the problems that activate a number of architectural solutions, which can be understood as the necessary responses that take part in a responsible reaction toward the pre-existing. The Generic Sublime identifies, on one end, the world itself as a site, and on the other, the site as a construction of the proposal, integrally generated by its techniques and inherent to its concept. By doing so, the research proceeds through the building of a medium of information, that is, it constructs its own ground of relevance and develops sense from the bottom up. Systematically regarded as a plane of consistency and conceived by Najle as "a pre-architecture out of which many architectures are possible" (extending Deleuze's notion of a pre-philosophical plane), the procedure of this ground formation tends to take part, as if a zero degree, in an iterative process that indexes characteristics of different nature and puts them to work in an increasingly hierarchical order by means of escalating determinations. The organization of information and the generation of a system happens, therefore, simultaneously, like in Ana María Flor Ortiz and Rodia Valladares Sánchez's Karst Palace, where the simulation of a karst formation process is handled at the same time as the break down of a housing typology into irreducible raw material. A set of simple operations and restrictions (basin formation through minimum distance between neighboring basins) integrates the two, in order to construct the matrix of the project and index the conditions of the underground, adjusting the generic set up to the contingencies by means of local rules. It is in this stage that generic models, generalized into groups of independent variables, incorporate restrictions that feed them back. The drawings of this project on pages 118–19 show snapshots of a process with three iterations—the first one of 144 steps, the second of 72, and the third of 36—which result in nothing but a differentiated ground, qualified by drainage patterns and water bodies. This construction is itself the site, and the control of its emergent features is not a project deployed on it but a process of adjustment and further differentiation within it.

Differentiation

The subtleness that working affirmatively with emergent conditions implies—that is, the capability to both control the determinations in systems and intuitively stay in power of their unpredictable outcomes, without reducing them to the achievement of deliberate purposes while still assuring their relevance—is the true challenge of cleverly managing the process of differentiation. In the same way that the work with formats operates as a tool for constructing a rigorous bond between the systematicity of an organization and its uniqueness as a form, the iterative procedure is capable of multiplying the effects of differentiation processes to escalate a generic model into a sublime state, both frightening and elevating. This process is, in this sense, not just a browsing over the potential becoming of things but the articulation of a decisive will that, within its force, has the courage of staying calm in the face of the ultimate danger of an artistic creation: meaninglessness.

Managing differentiation means managing the anxiety toward meaning at the time of its highest risk. Chance accompanies it, as its most loyal companion as much as its most severe enemy. If linear determination necessarily involves the prior release of an argument, differentiation involves the ultimate commitment with the material as it is and, especially, as it becomes. Alessandro Boccacci's neutral structural space frame, for example, is finally presented as the undifferentiated field upon which a mass tourism resort operates. As self-evident as this final stage appears, the process of differentiation happens in four steps (corresponding to catalogs on pages 258–59), which naturally connect a series of what in principle are absolutely autonomous and mutually irreducible systems: the space grid, the stilt house armature, the free-floating housing unit, and the primitive hut. This connection creates a matrix of ordered variants that challenge the cultural naturalization of all and radically tease out their meaning. The fact that this is done with simple subdivisions that control intermediate levels as if they were oblique landscapes, or with the simple rotation and scaling of the intermediate units to adjust to their immediate neighbors, hence configuring a wide variety of housing clusters, is as prosaic and generic a move as it is scary, given its cultural potence. Apparently effortless, this integration of differentiation through newly mindful organizations makes the proposal profoundly critical not only of its material but, more importantly, of argument-based architecture in general. It is useful, at this point, not to naturalize the idea of grid—here a key piece of content. The grid does not articulate organization or symbolize a universal continuum (as in the case of modernity) as much as it loads the differentiation process and its eventual destabilizations with inertia. The grid is the wise side of chance.

Organization

Finally, it all goes down to organization, and organization has many levels. The template articulates the dialogue between the organization of the material and the research system that grows out of the process, developing synthesis for the research as a self-governing project. The captions, in turn, are structured to accompany this systematicity and nurture it with information, in direct correspondence to the template of which they form a part. Furthermore, the computer models are systematized at the level of their layers, which can be read consecutively and structure the model's organization in coordination with the larger set ups. This logic extends to the scripts, where control systems and formulae are displayed in complete equivalence to the organization of variables at play. This formal coordination running across mediums is accountable for the construction of a space of thought that grows in complexity as it evolves. Strategies and concepts are literally built up from the categorical organizations by which drawings find their place in the world—of the investigation. No image, no piece of text, no drawing, no observation is left out of this construct. This drive toward total instrumentality and applicability of the material constantly tightens its relevance. The case-by-case does not exist anymore, and thus the process must become system on its way to the making, or else leave the research space. Beyond the configuration of model-projects, the larger construction at play is to coordinate lines of research into a fully compact set. The virtuality and abstraction of this compactness is exactly what makes it real and at the same time perpetually unattainable. This is the point of coexistence of control and intangibility, of determination and intuition, of straightforwardness and farfetchedness. In Simon Willett's Olympic Operations this is palpable. The construction of models out of Bruno Taut's artwork for *Alpine Architecture* (1917) relies on the balance between generalization and accuracy to the sources. A clean deployment into an artificial gridded landscape departs from the subdivision of a horizontal plane made square, like both Taut's pages and the template. Order, artificial at its core, organizational in its will, and fantastic in its radicality, grounds the configuration of a resort with a sun up in the sky, glowing snow on the undulating landscape, houses in the valleys, capricious ornamental structures in the peaks, and delineated pistes going down at regular intervals, in a synthetic construction that makes all the more evident that the ultimate value of architectural organization is to engender visions.

Model

This intrinsic will of organizations to engender visions from within their systematicity is here termed "model," or "generic model," or "generic sublime model." It is in this joy that the methodological takes a (poignant) form and acquires a life of its own—slowly, cautiously, attentively aware of its danger, always searching for the constitution of unforeseen qualities. In the same way that this idea of novelty—newness in relation to premises—is the drive for the conceptualization of relationships in systems, the construction of new models—and, through them, perhaps, of a new paradigm—is the concealed holistic aim of the research. For this to actually happen, it is crucial to operate inside the material, within its logic, and surrender to its process. It is through the insistent construction of content by means of patterns of relationships, unexpected acquaintances, casual interactions, and inseparable overlaps that evaluations become apparent. And, with them, come new forms of value.

Contributors

Ciro Najle is an architect, researcher, theoretician, and educator. He holds a Master of Architecture with honors from the Columbia University Graduate School of Architecture, Planning, and Preservation and a Diploma Architect with honors from the Universidad de Buenos Aires. Dean of the School of Architecture and Urban Studies at the Universidad Torcuato Di Tella in Buenos Aires, where he is also Research Professor, Najle has been Visiting Professor at the Harvard University Graduate School of Design (GSD) since 2008. Previously, he was Diploma Unit Master at the Architectural Association in London, where he co-founded and directed the Landscape Urbanism Graduate Program. He has taught at Cornell University, Columbia University, the Berlage Institute, the Universidad Federico Santa María in Valparaíso, and the Universidad de Buenos Aires. He is Director of GDB General Design Bureau, office of architecture, design, and urbanism, and previously of MID, Young Architect of the Year Second Prize winner in London in 2001. His widely published theoretical and professional work includes essays in *Quaderns d'Arquitectura i Urbanisme*, *Oris*, *Praxis*, *UR*, *Plot*, and *Summa+*, the introductions to *2G* monographs on Foreign Office Architects (2000) and MGM Morales-Gilles-Mariscal (2009), and the co-editing of the books *Landscape Urbanism: A Manual for the Machinic Landscape* (2004) with Mohsen Mostafavi, *Modos de Práctica* (2013) with Anna Font, *Culturas Digitales* (2014) with Julián Varas, and *Suprarural* (2016) with Lluís Ortega.

Iñaki Ábalos chairs the Department of Architecture at the Harvard GSD, where he is also Professor in Residence. He is a chaired professor at the Escuela Técnica Superior de Arquitectura de Madrid (ETSAM), where he received his PhD in Architecture. Ábalos has authored numerous volumes, including most recently *La Buena Vida* (2000), *Campos de Batalla/Battlefields* (2005), *Atlas of the Picturesque* (2005/2007), and *Naturaleza y Artificio* (2010). The work of his firm, Ábalos+Sentkiewicz, is regularly featured in international publications.

Paul Andersen is the director of Independent Architecture. His built work includes art buildings, playgrounds, and residential projects. A Fulbright Specialist in Architecture, Andersen currently teaches at the University of Illinois at Chicago. He has been a Guest Curator at the Museum of Contemporary Art in Denver and the Biennial of the Americas. He is co-author, with David Salomon, of *The Architecture of Patterns* (2010) and author of *The Monuments Power the Cars* (forthcoming).

Leire Asensio Villoria studied architecture at the Escuela Técnica Superior de Arquitectura de San Sebastián (ETSASS) and received her diploma in architecture with honors from the Architectural Association. She has taught at the Harvard GSD, the Architectural Association, and Cornell University. She worked for Zaha Hadid and Arup before founding asensio_mah, together with David Mah, a multidisciplinary design collaborative focusing on architecture, landscape design, and masterplanning.

Alberto Delorenzini holds a degree in literature from the Universidad de Buenos Aires. He is Professor of Aesthetic and Theories of Architecture at the Universidad Torcuato Di Tella where, since 2009, he has also been in charge of the Atlas/Archivo project, an iconographic survey of the cultural landscapes that line the coast of the Río de la Plata. He has published numerous essays on cinematography and literary works as well as aesthetic theory.

Anna Font is Associate Architect at GDB General Design Bureau, office of architecture, design, and urbanism. She is Professor in the School of Architecture and Urban Studies at the Universidad Torcuato Di Tella, where she also coordinates the archives and related publication series *Archivos de Arquitectura.* Font has contributed articles to numerous architectural journals and collaborated on the editing and production of the book *Suprarural* (2016) with Ciro Najle and Lluís Ortega.

Hiromi Hosoya is Partner in the Zurich-based architecture, urban design, and research firm Hosoya Schaefer Architects, founded with Markus Schaefer in 2003. She received her Master of Architecture from the Harvard GSD and has since directed design studios at several universities, including the GSD. Her international award-winning firm is currently completing a broad spectrum of projects, including the Haefen City in Hamburg, the Swiss National Exposition 2027, and the Swiss National Innovation Park.

Marcia Krygier holds a degree in architecture from the Universidad de Buenos Aires. A professionally trained chief, she teaches cooking out of her own kitchen-workshop in Buenos Aires, designs and builds food installations, and leads gastronomic experiences through Europe. She was the protagonist of the movie *Cocina* (2009), written and directed by Gonzalo Castro, and took part in the book *Libro de Cocina* (2009) by Eloise Alemany. She is featured on the album *Zorzal* by Axel Krygier.

George L. Legendre is a founding Partner of IJP, a practice based in London that explores the natural intersection of space, mathematics, and computation. He has authored or contributed critical essays to numerous books and, in 2011, guest-edited a special issue of *AD Magazine* titled *Mathematics of Space*. Legendre's most recent research opus is *Pasta by Design* (2011).

Pablo Lorenzo-Eiroa is an architect, artist, and scholar who works at the intersection of design and history/theory through computation. He directs a Digital Representation and Fabrication program at the Cooper Union, where he also coordinates the Master Program Studio (Fall) as an Adjunct Associate Professor. A Fulbright and National Endowment for the Arts scholar, Lorenzo-Eiroa is Design Principal of e-Architects | eiroa-Architects, a firm based in New York and Buenos Aires.

David Mah is Lecturer at the Harvard GSD. He has worked in a number of international design practices, including FOA Foreign Office Architects and Zaha Hadid Architects. He has also taught at the Architectural Association and Cornell University. In 2002 he founded asensio_mah, a multi-disciplinary design collaborative, with Leire Asensio Villoria.

Mohsen Mostafavi, an architect and educator, is Dean and Alexander and Victoria Wiley Professor of Design at the Harvard GSD. His recent publications include Ecological Urbanism (2010, 2016; recently translated into Chinese, Portuguese, and Spanish), In the Life of Cities (2012), Nicholas Hawksmoor: London Churches (2015), and Ethics of the Urban: The City and the Spaces of the Political (2016).

Farshid Moussavi is an architect, principal of FMA Farshid Moussavi Architecture, and Professor in Practice of Architecture at the Harvard GSD. Previously, she co-founded FOA Foreign Office Architects, recognized as one of the world's most creative design firms. She is a columnist for *The Architectural Review* and has published three books—*The Function of Ornament* (2006), *The Function of Form* (2009), and *The Function of Style* (2015)—based on her research and teaching at Harvard.

Erika Naginski is Professor of Architectural History at the Harvard GSD, where she also serves as Director of Doctoral Programs. Her research focuses on European architecture from 1600 to 1800. Naginski's books and edited volumes include *Polemical Objects* (2004), *Sculpture and Enlightenment* (2009), and, with Preston Scott Cohen, *The Return of Nature: Sustaining Architecture in the Face of Sustainability* (2014).

Lluís Ortega is Associate Professor at the Illinois Institute of Technology and Visiting Professor at the Universidad Torcuato di Tella. Together with Santiago Ibarra, Xavier Osarte, and Esther Segura, he co-founded Sio2arch (formerly F451), an internationally acclaimed practice based in Barcelona and Chicago. Ortega is the editor of numerous journal volumes, the author of *La digitalización toma el mando* (2010), and the co-author, with Ciro Najle, of *Suprarural* (2016).

David Salomon is Assistant Professor of Art History at Ithaca College, where he also coordinates the Architectural Studies program. He is the co-author, with Paul Andersen, of the book *The Architecture of Patterns* (2011). Salomon is currently working on a history of symmetry in science, mathematics, and architecture of the 20th century.

Julián Varas is Professor at the Universidad Torcuato Di Tella School of Architecture and Urban Studies, where he coordinates the Center for Studies in Contemporary Architecture and directs the Master in History and Culture of Architecture and the City. He co-edited *Archipelagos: A Manual for Peripheral Buenos Aires* (2011) and is currently writing his doctoral dissertation on postwar public housing.

Charles Waldheim is John E. Irving Professor of Landscape Architecture and director of the Office for Urbanization at the Harvard GSD. An architect and urban theorist, his widely published research examines the relations between landscape, ecology, and contemporary urbanism. He is the recipient of a Rome Prize from the American Academy in Rome and a Visiting Scholar Research Fellowship from the Canadian Centre for Architecture.

Credits

Harvard University
Graduate School of Design
Departments of Architecture, Urban Planning and Design, and Landscape Architecture
The Generic Sublime studio series

The Generic Sublime 01 Neonatures
Spring 2010
Professor Ciro Najle
Assistant Anna Font
Students Youngju Cho, Yao Dong, Ana María Flor Ortiz, Song He, Jung Hyuck Im, Laura Janka, Víctor Muñoz Sanz, Seong Seok Ko, Rodia Valladares Sánchez, Di Xia, Kaz Yoneda, and Jing Zhang

The Generic Sublime 02 Overurbanism
Spring 2011
Professor Ciro Najle
Assistant Kaz Yoneda
Students Steven Yingnien Chen, Dongjae Cho, Fred Chung, Lucas Correa-Sevilla, Day Jiménez, Mireille Kameni, Mariusz Klemens, Ostap Rudakevych, Elena Tudela Rivadeneyra, Zhou Wu, Mo Zhou, and Danxi Zou

The Generic Sublime 03 Neokoolhisms
Spring 2012
Professor Ciro Najle
Assistant Lucas Correa-Sevilla
Students Pablo Barría Urenda, Jeffrey Butcher, Mariano Gomez Luque, Lisl Kotheimer, Quardean Lewis-Allen, Nicholas Potts, and Peter Zuroweste

The Generic Sublime 04 Utopioids
Spring 2013
Professor Ciro Najle
Assistant Pablo Barría Urenda
Students Georgios-Spyridon Athanasopoulos, Alessandro Boccacci, Elle Gerdeman, Parsa Kamali, Jielu Lu, Héctor Tarrido Picart, Emmanuel Torres, Simon Willet, and Max Wong

Introductions and Essays

Generic Sublime Models

Generic Sublime Organizations

Conversations and Essays

Double-page Spreads

Digital models and drawings on the cover, accompanying the essays and conversations, and featured in the chapter Generic Sublime Organizations were post-produced by Ciro Najle and Andrew Pringle. Digital models and drawings featured in the chapter Generic Sublime Forms were produced by Ciro Najle and Andrew Pringle. Diagrams, drawings, and images in the chapter Generic Sublime Models were edited and post-produced by Ciro Najle and Anna Font. Diagrams appearing on double-page spreads were edited and post-produced by Ciro Najle and Anna Font.

The Generic Sublime
Organizational Models for Global Architecture
Ciro Najle

Author and Editor
Ciro Najle

Assistant Editor
Anna Font

Project Manager
Nancy Eklund Later

Graphic Designer
Ramon Prat

Proofreader
A. Krista Sykes

This book features design research and projects developed under the direction of Ciro Najle by graduate students at the Harvard University Graduate School of Design between 2010 and 2013, as part of the Generic Sublime studio series. Drawings were edited or developed with the collaboration of Andrew Pringle and the preliminary assistance of Kaz Yoneda, Pablo Barría Urenda, Mariano Gomez Luque, and Mariusz Klemens of the Harvard University Graduate School of Design.

Published by the Harvard University Graduate School of Design and Actar Publishers

Harvard University
Graduate School of Design
48 Quincy Street
Cambridge, MA 02138
gsd.harvard.edu

ISBN 978 1940291758

Library of Congress Cataloging-in-Publication Data.
PCN: 2016936850

Distribution
Actar D
355 Lexington Avenue, 8th Floor
New York, NY 10017
USA
T +1 212 966 2207
F +1 212 966 2214
salesnewyork@actar-d.com

Roca i Batlle 2
08023 Barcelona.
Spain
T +34 933 282 183
eurosales@actar-d.com
bcnsales@actar-d.com
info@actar.com